《金融研究》

Journal of Financial Research

精编版

2021年（下卷）

《金融研究》编辑部 ◎ 编

中国金融出版社

责任编辑：马海敏　张翠华
责任校对：刘　明
责任印制：张也男

图书在版编目（CIP）数据

金融研究：精编版.2021年.下卷/《金融研究》编辑部编.—北京：中国金融出版社，2022.9

ISBN 978-7-5220-1675-7

Ⅰ.①金… Ⅱ.①金… Ⅲ.①金融学—文集 Ⅳ.①F830-53

中国版本图书馆CIP数据核字（2022）第112003号

《金融研究》（精编版）2021年（下卷）
《JINRONG YANJIU》（JINGBIANBAN）2021 NIAN（XIAJUAN）

出版
发行　中国金融出版社
社址　北京市丰台区益泽路2号
市场开发部　（010）66024766、63805472、63439533（传真）
网上书店　www.cfph.cn
　　　　　（010）66024766、63372837（传真）
读者服务部　（010）66070833、62568380
邮编　100071
经销　新华书店
印刷　保利达印务有限公司
尺寸　169毫米×239毫米
印张　28.5
字数　427千
版次　2022年9月第1版
印次　2022年9月第1次印刷
定价　75.00元
ISBN 978-7-5220-1675-7
如出现印装错误本社负责调换　联系电话（010）63263947

《金融研究》
（精编版）
编写人员

本 卷 主 编：周诚君　卜永祥
编辑部主任：王　鹏
统　　　稿：林梦瑶　李文华

前　言

《金融研究》是中国人民银行主管、中国金融学会主办，对国内外公开发行的正式出版物。创刊40余年来，《金融研究》已成为引领国内学术前沿的理论性、政策性、实践性兼备的权威学术期刊。2005年荣获第三届国家期刊奖。2012年入选国家社科基金资助期刊。《金融研究》编辑部设在中国人民银行金融研究所，负责期刊的组稿、审稿、编辑和出版发行等工作。

为面向国内外读者更广泛、充分地推广《金融研究》所刊载的研究成果，进一步提升期刊的学术和政策影响力，同时促进学术成果转化，更好地服务于中央决策和宏观管理部门的履职需要，《金融研究》编辑部自2019年起对已刊载论文编写精编版，每年分上、下两卷结集出版。

本书是《金融研究》2021年第7~12期共66篇论文的精编版，并结合当前经济金融热点研究领域分类编排。精编版论文为中英文对照，每篇中文内容约2500字，充分考虑了国内外读者的阅读习惯和知识背景，对论文研究背景与意义、研究主题与思路、研究方法与理论依据、数据及来源、主要结论与政策建议、创新与贡献以及未来研究扩展方向等进行了概括和提炼，以期更完整、准确地介绍论文的精华与贡献。精编版同时兼顾现实性、政策性、学术性和可读性，注重提炼思想，阐述观点，力求用简洁生动的语言讲好中国故事，立足文章结论提出有针对性的政策建议，以供参阅。

如需论文完整版，请查阅正刊或登录《金融研究》网站（www.jryj.org.cn）下载论文 pdf 版。

欢迎扫描二维码关注《金融研究》

微信公众号（ChinaJFR）

目录 CONTENTS

01 宏观经济与货币政策

中国的利率体系与利率市场化改革
………………………………………………………… 易 纲（002）

新时代全面建成小康社会的辉煌成就及新征程展望
——基于"中国平衡发展指数"的综合分析
………………………… 许宪春 刘婉琪 彭 慧 张钟文（014）

预测中国宏观经济变量：专家与模型的组合预测
………………………………… 梁 方 沈诗涵 黄 卓（018）

美国货币政策溢出效应、中国资产价格波动与资本账户管理
………………………… 吴立元 赵扶扬 王 忏 龚六堂（021）

中国季度 GDP 的即时预测与混频分析
………………………………… 王 霞 司 诺 宋 涛（025）

人力资本偏向金融部门如何影响实体经济增长？
………………………………… 刘贯春 司登奎 刘 芳（029）

流动性覆盖率监管会影响货币政策传导效率吗?
——来自中国银行业的证据
………………………………………… 庄毓敏 张 祎（032）

收入差距、信贷约束与房价波动
………………………………………… 陈金至 温兴春 宋 鹭（036）

借贷便利创新工具能有效影响商业银行贷款利率吗?
………………………………………… 邓 伟 宋 敏 刘 敏（039）

全球金融周期与跨境资本流动
………………………………………… 谭小芬 虞梦微（042）

利差、美元指数与跨境资本流动
………………………………………… 缪延亮 郝 阳 费 璇（045）

经济开放与货币需求：国际金融风险及持币成本的测度
…… 秦 朵 卢 珊 王惠文 Sophie van Huellen 王庆超（049）

中国制造业与房地产业协调发展的测度与判断
………………………………………… 皮建才 宋大强（052）

02　金融稳定与风险防范

对金融风险传染机制的定量研究
——基于中国上市银行数据的模拟
………………………………………… 马 骏 何晓贝（056）

流动性幻觉与高杠杆率之谜
………………………………………… 张成思 刘泽豪 何 平（060）

地方政府隐性债务与城投债定价
………………………… 刘晓蕾　吕元稹　余　凡（064）

政策连续性、非金融企业影子银行化与社会责任承担
………………………………………… 韩　珣　李建军（067）

隐性杠杆约束、流动性风险和投资者情绪
………………………………………… 祝小全　陈　卓（070）

控股股东股权质押与高杠杆公司杠杆操纵
——基于我国 A 股上市公司的经验证据
………………………… 许晓芳　汤泰劼　陆正飞（073）

企业金融化与劳动收入份额变动
………………………………………… 罗明津　铁　瑛（076）

03　绿色金融

环境税率、双重红利与经济增长
………………………………………… 牛　欢　严成樑（082）

环境规制、融资约束与企业污染减排
………………………… 陈诗一　张建鹏　刘朝良（085）

环境信息公开的绿色创新效应研究
——基于《环境空气质量标准》的准自然实验
………………………………………… 王　馨　王　营（088）

金融政策与经济低碳转型：基于增长视角的研究
………………………… 潘冬阳　陈川祺　Michael Grubb（092）

我们为什么需要绿色金融？
——从全球经验事实到基于经济增长框架的理论解释
....文书洋　张　琳　刘锡良（095）

环境灾害冲击对银行违约率的影响效应研究：理论与实证分析
....王　遥　王文蔚（099）

碳定价、双重金融摩擦与"双支柱"调控
....王　博　徐飘洋（102）

中国绿色金融政策、融资成本与企业绿色转型
——基于央行担保品政策视角
........................陈国进　丁赛杰　赵向琴　蒋晓宇（105）

气候变化冲击下的涉农信用风险
——基于2010—2019年256家农村金融机构的实证研究
....刘　波　王修华　李明贤（108）

"多言寡行"的环境责任表现能否影响银行信贷获取
——基于"言"和"行"双维度的文本分析
....李　哲　王文翰（111）

生态法治对债券融资成本的影响
——基于我国中级环保法庭设立的准自然实验
....高昊宇　温慧愉（115）

04 银行经营与企业融资

中国银行业结构性全要素生产率增长研究
.... 朱 宁 刘伟其 于之倩 王 兵（120）

金融政策竞争中性原则与民营企业融资纾困
——来自突发公共卫生事件的准自然实验
.... 吕怀立 王文明 鄢姿俏 侯 亮（124）

高铁时空压缩效应与公司权益资本成本
——来自 A 股上市公司的经验证据
.... 郭照蕊 黄 俊（127）

半强制股利政策与股权融资成本
.... 王春飞 郭云南（130）

改进的效率测算模型、影子银行与中国商业银行效率
.... 李丽芳 谭政勋 叶礼贤（134）

高管薪酬延付与银行利润效率
——基于银行微观视角的研究
.... 王艳艳 王成龙 于李胜 蓝一阳（138）

税率"锚定效应"与企业投资决策
.... 郑登津 孟庆玉 袁 淳（141）

05 金融市场

中债估值识别了债券信用风险？
　　——基于跳跃视角的实证分析
　　　　.. 史永东　郑世杰　袁绍锋（146）

杠杆投资者融资交易行为模式研究
　　——来自A股市场的经验证据
　　　　.. 康文津　顾　明（149）

市场摩擦对特质风险溢价的影响效应
　　——基于A股主板市场的实证分析
　　　　.. 李少育　张　滕　尚玉皇　周　宇（152）

市场操纵降低了中国股票市场的信息效率吗
　　——来自沪市A股高频交易数据的经验证据
　　　　.. 孙广宇　李志辉　杜　阳　王　近（155）

宏观经济信息与金融市场关联性
　　——来自混频动态条件相关系数模型的证据
　　　　.. 周开国　邢子煜　杨海生（158）

限购政策是否降低了上市房地产企业价值？
　　——基于强度双重差分法的经验研究
　　　　.. 梁若冰　张东荣　方　心　林细细（161）

06 国际经济与贸易

反倾销如何影响跨国并购
.... 杨连星（166）

关税冲击与中国进口行为
.... 张国峰　陆　毅　蒋灵多（169）

劳动力成本对中国加工贸易规模及转型升级的影响
.... 毛其淋　盛　斌（172）

服务贸易开放、市场化改革与中国制造业企业生产率
.... 彭水军　舒中桥（175）

提高出口退税能够"稳就业"和"稳外贸"吗？
.... 王君斌　刘河北（178）

07 普惠金融与社会发展

企业履行社会责任的共赢效应：基于精准扶贫的视角
.... 潘健平　翁若宇　潘　越（182）

"活在当下"还是"未雨绸缪"？
——地震对中国城镇家庭储蓄和消费习惯的长期影响
.... 章　元　刘茜楠（185）

金融素养与家庭储蓄率
——基于理财规划与借贷约束的解释
.... 吴卫星　张旭阳　吴　锟（188）

新型农村社会养老保险参与决策中的同群效应
……………………………………张川川　朱涵宇（191）

学区房溢价的影响因素：教育质量的视角
……………………张　勋　寇晶涵　张　欣　吕光明（195）

风险分散与中国混合型基本养老保险制度改革研究
……………………………………彭浩然　程春丽（198）

城市服务多样性与劳动力流动
——基于"美团网"大数据和流动人口微观调查的分析
……………………………………张文武　余泳泽（201）

网红直播打赏收入影响因素的实证研究
……………………廖　理　王新程　王正位　张晋研（204）

08 公司治理与公司金融

董事会断裂带与企业薪酬差距
……………………………徐灿宇　李烜博　梁上坤（208）

失业保险与公司财务杠杆
……………………彭　章　施新政　陆　瑶　王　浩（211）

上市企业员工满意度与创新
——来自"中国年度最佳雇主100强"的经验证据
……………………………许红梅　倪骁然　刘亚楠（214）

管理者能力与资本市场稳定
…………………… 张　路　李金彩　袁振超　岳　衡（217）

卖空机制、双重治理与公司违规
——基于市场化治理视角的实证检验
………………………… 徐细雄　占　恒　李万利（220）

金字塔式控股结构与上市公司资本运作的机会主义倾向
………………………… 郑志刚　郇　珍　黄继承　赵锡军（223）

控股股东股权质押与员工持股计划"工具化"
——基于A股上市公司的实证研究
………………………………………… 邱杨茜　黄娟娟（226）

放松卖空管制能够抑制并购商誉泡沫吗？
………………… 孙诗璐　张斐燕　郑建明　刘艳霞（230）

中小股东积极主义对债券持有人财富的溢出影响
——基于网络投票数据的实证研究
………………………… 曾爱民　吴　伟　吴育辉（232）

01 Macroeconomics & Monetary Policy

China's Interest Rate System and Market - Based Reform of Interest Rate
.... YI Gang (237)

Great Achievements in Building a Moderately Prosperous Society in All Respects in the New Era and Prospects for the Country's New Journey: Statistical Monitoring and Analysis Based on the China Balanced Development Index
... XU Xianchun　LIU Wanqi　PENG Hui　ZHANG Zhongwen (240)

Forecasts of Macroeconomic Variables in China:Combination Forecasts of Surveys and Models
.... LIANG Fang　SHEN Shihan　HUANG Zhuo (243)

Spillover Effects of U. S. Monetary Policy, China's Asset Price Fluctuations and Capital Account Control
... WU Liyuan　ZHAO Fuyang　WANG Chan　GONG Liutang (246)

Nowcasting China's Quarterly GDP Using Mixed - Frequency Data
.... WANG Xia　SI Nuo　SONG Tao (249)

Does Human Capital in the Financial Sector Affect Real Economic Growth in China?
.... LIU Guanchun　SI Dengkui　LIU Fang (252)

Does the Liquidity Coverage Ratio Regulatory Requirement Affect the Efficiency of Monetary Policy Transmission? Evidence from China's Banking Industry
.... ZHUANG Yumin　ZHANG Yi (255)

Income Gaps, Credit Constraints, and House Price Fluctuations

.... CHEN Jinzhi　WEN Xingchun　SONG Lu (258)

Do Innovative Lending Facilities Affect Bank Loan Interest Rates?

.... DENG Wei　SONG Min　LIU Min (261)

The Global Financial Cycle and Cross - border Capital Flows

.... TAN Xiaofen　YU Mengwei (264)

Interest Rate Differential, the Dollar Index, and China's Capital Flows

.... MIAO Yanliang　HAO Yang　FEI Xuan (267)

Openness and Money Demand: Measuring the Opportunity Cost Effects of International Financial Markets

.... QIN Duo　LU Shan　WANG Huiwen　Sophie van Huellen

WANG Qingchao (270)

Measuring and Analyzing Coordinated Development between the Manufacturing Industry and the Real Estate Industry in China

.... PI Jiancai　SONG Daqiang (273)

02　Financial Stability & Risk Management

A Study on Financial Contagion: A Simulation Based on the Chinese Banking Sector Data

.... MA Jun　HE Xiaobei (276)

Liquidity Illusion and High Leverage Ratio Dilemma

.... ZHANG Chengsi　LIU Zehao　HE Ping (279)

Local Government Implicit Debt and the Pricing of Chengtou Bonds
.... LIU Xiaolei　LYU Yuanzhen　YU Fan (282)

Policy Continuity, Non - financial Enterprises' Shadow Banking Activities, and Social Responsibility Activities
.... HAN Xun　LI Jianjun (285)

Implicit Leverage Constraints, Liquidity Risk, and Investor Sentiment
.... ZHU Xiaoquan　CHEN Zhuo (287)

Controlling Shareholders' Share Pledging and Leverage Manipulation in High - Leverage Companies: Evidence from China
.... XU Xiaofang　TANG Taijie　LU Zhengfei (290)

Financialization and Labor Share: Firm - level Evidence from China
.... LUO Mingjin　TIE Ying (293)

03　Green Finance

Environmental Tax, Double Dividend and Economic Growth
.... NIU Huan　YAN Chengliang (296)

Environmental Regulation, Financing Constraints, and Enterprise Emission Reduction: Evidence from Pollution Levy Standards Adjustment
.... CHEN Shiyi　ZHANG Jianpeng　LIU Chaoliang (299)

The Impact of Environmental Governance Policy on Green Innovation: Evidence from China's Quasi - Natural Experiment
.... WANG Xin　WANG Ying (302)

Financial Policy and Low - Carbon Transition of the Economy: A Growth Perspective

…………… PAN Dongyang　CHEN Chuanqi　Michael Grubb (305)

Why Do We Need Green Finance? Global Empirical Facts and Theoretical Explanations in an Economic Growth Framework

………………… WEN Shuyang　ZHANG Lin　LIU Xiliang (308)

The Impact of Environmental Disasters on the Bank Default Rate: Theoretical and Empirical Analysis

……………………………………… WANG Yao　WANG Wenwei (311)

Carbon Pricing, Dual Financial Friction and Dual Pillar Regulation

………………………………… WANG Bo　XU Piaoyang (314)

China's Green Finance Policy, Financing Costs and Firms' Green Transition: A Central Bank Collateral Framework Perspective

CHEN Guojin　DING Saijie　ZHAO Xiangqin　JIANG Xiaoyu (317)

Climate Change and the Credit Risk of Rural Financial Institutions

………………… LIU Bo　WANG Xiuhua　LI Mingxian (319)

Corporate Environmental Responsibility and Bank Credit: Text Analysis of Words and Deeds

………………………………………… LI Zhe　WANG Wenhan (322)

The Impact of Environmental Rule of Law on Bond Financing Cost: Evidence from Environmental Courts in China

………………………………… GAO Haoyu　WEN Huiyu (325)

04 Banking Operation & Financing

Structural Total Factor Productivity Growth in China's Banking Sector
.... ZHU Ning　LIU Weiqi　YU Zhiqian　WANG Bing (328)

Competitive Neutrality and Non-State-Owned Enterprises' Access to Debt Financing: A Quasi-Natural Experiment during the COVID-19 Pandemic
...... LYU Huaili　WANG Wenming　YAN Ziqiao　HOU Liang (331)

The Spatiotemporal Constraint Effect of High-speed Railway and Corporate Equity Capital Cost: Empirical Evidence from China's A-share Listed Companies
.... GUO Zhaorui　HUANG Jun (334)

Semi-Mandatory Dividend Policy and Cost of Equity
.... WANG Chunfei　GUO Yunnan (337)

Improved Efficiency Measurement Model, Shadow Banking, and the Efficiency of Chinese Commercial Banks
.... LI Lifang　TAN Zhengxun　YE Lixian (340)

Effects of China's Compensation Deferral Policy on Bank Profit Efficiency: Evidence from the Bank Level
　　WANG Yanyan　WANG Chenglong　YU Lisheng　LAN Yiyang (343)

The Tax Rate Anchoring Effect and Enterprise Investment Decisions
.... ZHENG Dengjin　MENG Qingyu　YUAN Chun (346)

05 Financial Market

Does China Bond Valuation Identify the Credit Risk of a Bond? An Empirical Analysis Based on a Yield - Jump Perspective

　　　……………　SHI Yongdong　ZHENG Shijie　YUAN Shaofeng (349)

The Trading Behavior of Margin - Leveraged Investors: Evidence from Chinese Stock Markets

　　　………………………………………　KANG Wenjin　GU Ming (352)

The Effects of Market Frictions on Idiosyncratic Risk Premium: An Empirical Study of the Main Board of China's A Stocks

　　　……　LI Shaoyu　ZHANG Teng　SHANG Yuhuang　ZHOU Yu (355)

Does Market Manipulation Reduce the Information Efficiency of China's Stock Market? Empirical Evidence from the Shanghai A - share Market's High - Frequency Trading Data

　　　……………　SUN Guangyu　LI Zhihui　DU Yang　WANG Jin (358)

Macroeconomic Information and Financial Market Connectedness: Evidence from A DCC - MIDAS Model

　　　…………………　ZHOU Kaiguo　XING Ziyu　YANG Haisheng (361)

Do Purchase Restriction Policies Reduce the Corporate Value of Listed Real Estate Companies?

　　　……　LIANG Ruobing　ZHANG Dongrong　FANG Xin　LIN Xixi (364)

06 International Economy & Trade

How Anti - dumping Affects Cross - border Mergers and Acquisitions
....YANG Lianxing (367)

Import Tariff Shocks and Chinese Import Behavior
.... ZHANG Guofeng　LU Yi　JIANG Lingduo (370)

The Effects of Labor Costs on the Scale and Scale and Upgrading of China's Processing Trade
....MAO Qilin　SHENG Bin (373)

Service Trade Liberalization, Marketization, and the Productivity of China's Manufacturing Firms
....PENG Shuijun　SHU Zhongqiao (376)

Can Increasing the Export Tax Rebate Stabilize Employment and Foreign Trade?
.... WANG Junbin　LIU Hebei (379)

07 Inclusive Finance & Social Development

The Win - Win Effect of Corporate Social Responsibility: Evidence from Targeted Poverty Alleviation Programs
.... PAN Jianping　WENG Ruoyu　PAN Yue (382)

" Living in the Moment" or " Saving for the Futuren? Long - Term Effects of Earthquake Experiences on Chinese Urban Household Savings Rates and Consumption Habits
.... ZHANG Yuan　LIU Qiannan (385)

Financial Literacy and the Household Savings Rate: The Role of Financial Planning and Borrowing Constraints
.... WU Weixing　ZHANG Xuyang　WU Kun (388)

The Influence of the Peer Effect on Participation in China's New Rural Pension Scheme
.... ZHANG Chuanchuan　ZHU Hanyu (391)

The Determinants of School District Housing Price Premiums from the Perspective of School Quality
... ZHANG Xun　KOU Jinghan　ZHANG Xin　LYU Guangming (394)

Risk Diversification and the Reform of China's Mixed Basic Pension System
.... PENG Haoran　CHENG Chunli (397)

Urban Service Diversity and Labor Mobility: An Analysis Based on Big Data of Meituan and a Micro Survey of a Floating Population
.... ZHANG Wenwu　YU Yongze (400)

Factors Affecting Online Celebrities' Tips
　　LIAO Li　WANG Xincheng　WANG Zhengwei　ZHANG Jinyan (403)

08　Corporate Governance & Corporate Finance

Board Faultlines and the Firm Pay Gap
.... XU Canyu　LI Xuanbo　LIANG Shangkun (406)

Unemployment Insurance and Financial Leverage of Firms
.... PENG Zhang　SHI Xinzheng　LU Yao　WANG Hao (409)

Job Satisfaction and Firm Innovation: Evidence from "China's Best
Employer Award 100" Winners
················· XU Hongmei　NI Xiaoran　LIU Yanan (412)

The Effect of Managerial Ability on Capital Market Stability
········ ZHANG Lu　LI Jincai　YUAN Zhenchao　YUE Heng (415)

Short Selling, Dual Governance, and Corporate Fraud:
An Empirical Test Based on Market-oriented Governance
················· XU Xixiong　ZHAN Heng　LI Wanli (418)

Opportunistic Tendency of Capital Operation in Listed
Companies with Pyramidal Ownership Structure
ZHENG Zhigang　HUAN Zhen　HUANG Jicheng　ZHAO Xijun (421)

Controlling Shareholder Equity Pledge and Employee Stock Ownership Plan
"Instrumentalization": Evidence from the A-Share Market in China
················· QIU Yangqian　HUANG Juanjuan (424)

Can Relaxing Short Selling Constraints Inhibit M&A Goodwill Bubbles?
SUN Shilu　ZHANG Feiyan　ZHENG Jianming　LIU Yanxia (427)

Spillover Effects of Minority Shareholders' Activism on Bondholders'
Wealth: An Empirical Study Based on Network Voting Data
················· ZENG Aimin　WU Wei　WU Yuhui (430)

01 宏观经济与货币政策

中国的利率体系与利率市场化改革*

易 纲

利率是重要的宏观经济变量，利率市场化是经济金融领域最核心的改革之一。改革开放以来我国一直在稳步推进利率市场化，建立健全由市场供求决定的利率形成机制，中央银行通过运用货币政策工具引导市场利率。经过30多年的持续推进，我国的利率市场化改革取得显著成效，已形成比较完整的市场化利率体系，收益率曲线也趋于成熟，为发挥好利率对宏观经济运行的重要调节功能创造了有利条件。

一、利率是宏观经济中的重要变量

利率是资金的价格，对宏观经济均衡和资源配置有重要导向意义。作为反映资金稀缺程度的信号，利率与劳动力工资、土地地租一样，是重要的生产要素价格，同时，利率也是对延期消费的报酬。考察利率对行为和配置资源的作用，主要以真实利率（也称实际利率，即名义利率减去通胀率）为尺度。理论上，自然利率是宏观经济总供求达到均衡时的实际利率水平。实践中，利率的高低直接影响老百姓的储蓄和消费、企业的投融资决策、进出口和国际收支，进而对整个经济活动产生广泛影响。因此，利率是宏观经济中的重要变量。

利率对宏观经济运行发挥重要的调节作用，主要通过影响消费需求和投资需求实现。从消费看，利率上升会鼓励储蓄，抑制消费。从投资看，

---

* 原文刊载于《金融研究》2021年第9期。
作者简介：易纲，经济学博士，中国人民银行。

利率提高将减少可盈利的投资总量，抑制投资需求，即筛选掉回报率低的项目。利率对进出口和国际收支也会产生影响，国内利率下降，刺激投资和消费，提升社会总需求，会增加进口，导致净出口减少，同时本外币利差缩窄，可能导致跨境资本流出，影响国际收支平衡。当然，真实世界中利率传导机制及宏观经济变量之间的关系要比上面的简化说法复杂得多。

均衡利率由市场供求关系决定，是企业、居民和金融机构等市场主体的储蓄行为、投资行为、融资行为在金融市场中共同作用的结果（主要通过银行存贷款、债券市场、股票市场、保险市场等进行投融资活动，并将金融资源配置到实体经济和各类资产上）。市场在配置资源中发挥决定性作用，配置过程是在产权清晰的基础上，通过市场交易形成的价格来导向的。在这个过程中，利率作为资金的价格决定资金流向，从而决定金融资源配置的流向。改革开放以来中国经济发展的奇迹证明，社会主义市场经济主要由金融市场来配置资源的效率要比计划经济高得多，广大人民群众的福利要好得多。中长期看，宏观意义上的利率水平应与自然利率基本匹配。由于自然利率是一个理论上抽象出来的概念，具体水平较难估算，实践中一般采用"黄金法则"（Golden Rule）来衡量合理的利率水平，即经济处于人均消费量最大化的稳态增长轨道时，经通胀调整后的真实利率 R 应与实际经济增长率 G 相等。若 R 持续高于 G，会导致社会融资成本高企，企业经营困难，不利于经济发展。R 低于 G 时往往名义利率也低于名义 GDP 增速，这有利于债务可持续，即债务杠杆率保持稳定或下降，从而给政府一些额外的政策空间，但也有研究表明，至少在新兴市场 R 低于 G 不足以避免债务危机。总体上 R 略低于 G 是较为合理的，从经验数据看，我国大部分时间真实利率都是低于实际经济增速的，这一实践可以称为留有余地的最优策略。但 R 也不能持续明显低于 G，若利率长期过低，会扭曲金融资源配置，带来过度投资、产能过剩、通货膨胀、资产价格泡沫、资金空转等问题，超低利率政策难以长期持续。

由于利率不仅影响微观主体投资收益、融资成本，更是平衡宏观经济总供求的关键，成熟市场经济体都将利率作为重要的宏观经济调控工具。央行确定政策利率要符合经济规律、宏观调控和跨周期设计需要。我国货币政策的最终目标是"保持货币币值的稳定，并以此促进经济增长"，利率是实现货币政策目标的关键。

按照党中央、国务院战略部署，我国持续推进利率市场化改革，既适应中国国情，又与国际基本接轨，在有序放松利率管制的同时，高度重视建立健全由市场供求决定利率、中央银行通过运用货币政策工具引导市场化利率体系，发挥好利率对宏观经济运行的重要调节功能。

二、我国已形成较为完整的市场化利率体系

经过近30年来持续推进利率市场化改革，目前我国已基本形成了市场化的利率形成和传导机制，以及较为完整的市场化利率体系（见图1），主要通过货币政策工具调节银行体系流动性，释放政策利率调控信号，在利率走廊的辅助下，引导市场基准利率以政策利率为中枢运行，并通过银行体系传导至贷款利率，形成市场化的利率形成和传导机制，调节资金供求和资源配置，实现货币政策目标。

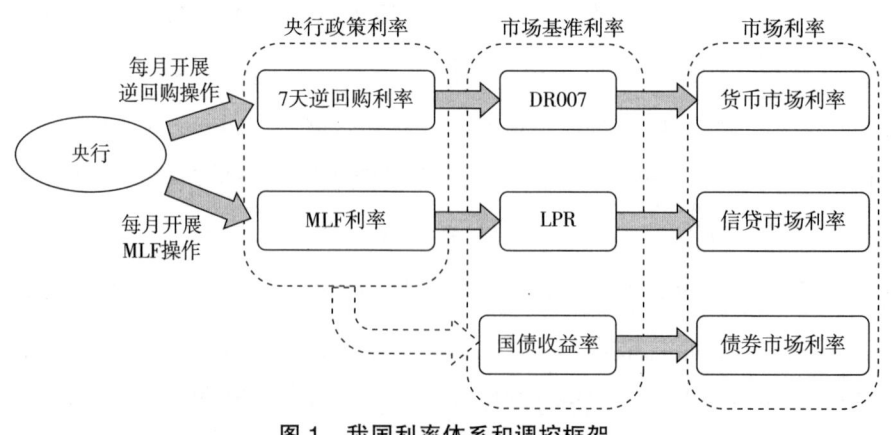

图1 我国利率体系和调控框架

我国主要利率品种见表1。

表 1 我国主要利率品种

利率品种	目前利率水平	简介
公开市场操作（OMO）利率	7天 2.2%	短期限逆回购操作利率
中期借贷便利（MLF）利率	1年期 2.95%	央行投放中期资金的利率
常备借贷便利（SLF）利率	7天 3.2%（=7天逆回购利率+100BP）	央行在利率走廊上限向金融机构按需提供短期资金的利率
贷款市场报价利率（LPR）	1年期 3.85%，5年期以上 4.65%	报价行按自身对最优质客户执行的贷款利率报价的算术平均数
存款基准利率	活期 0.35%，1年期 1.5%	人民银行公布的商业银行对客户存款指导性利率
超额准备金利率	0.35%	央行对金融机构超额准备金支付的利率，是利率走廊的下限
法定准备金利率	1.62%	央行对金融机构法定准备金支付的利率
上海银行间同业拆借利率（Shibor）	目前隔夜在2%、3个月期在2.35%附近	由信用等级较高的银行自主报出的同业拆借利率的算术平均数
国债收益率	目前10年期国债收益率在2.85%附近	通过市场交易形成的债券市场利率参考指标

我国市场化利率体系中，最为重要的利率品种包括：

（一）公开市场操作（OMO）利率与利率走廊。公开市场操作7天期逆回购利率是央行短期政策利率，目前利率水平为2.2%。央行通过每日开展公开市场操作，保持银行体系流动性合理充裕，持续释放短期政策利率信号，使存款类金融机构质押式回购利率（DR）等短期市场利率围绕政策利率为中枢波动，并向其他市场利率传导。同时，通过以常备借贷便利（SLF）利率为上限、超额准备金利率为下限的利率走廊的辅助，将短期利率的波动限制在合理范围。其中,SLF是央行按需向金融机构提供短期资金的工具,由于金融机构可按SLF利率从央行获得资金,就不必以高于SLF利率的价格从市场融入资金,因此SLF利率可视为利率走廊的上限。目前7天期SLF利率为3.2%,也就是7天期公开市场逆回购利率加100个基点。近期,人民银行推动SLF电子化操作方式改革,有序实现全流程电子化,有利于提高操作效率,稳定市场预期,增强银行体系流动性的稳定性,维护货币市场利率平稳运行,有效防范流动性风险。超额准备金利率是央行对金融机构存放在央行的超额准备金付息的利率,由于金融机构总是可以将剩余资金放入超额准备金账户,并获得超额准备金利率,就不会有机构愿意以低于超额准备金利率的价格向市场融出资金,因此超额准备金利率可视为利率走廊的下限。目前超额准备金利率为0.35%。

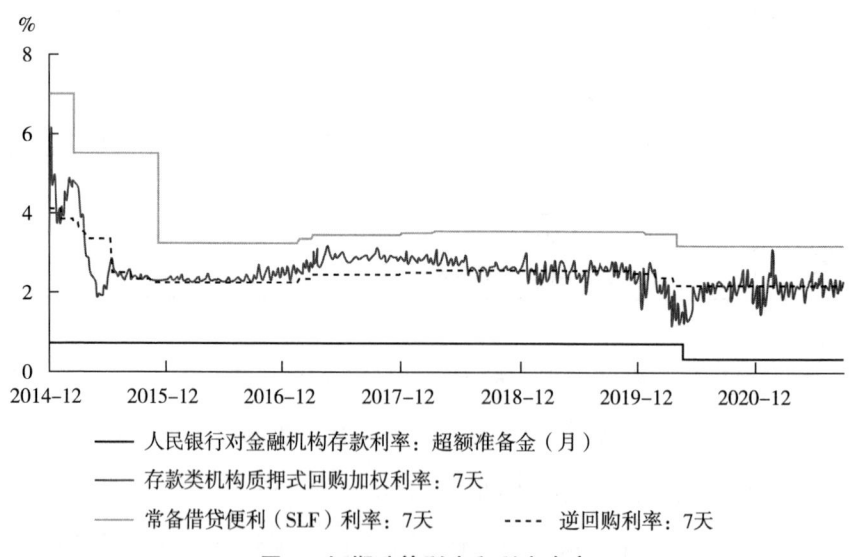

图2 短期政策利率和利率走廊

(二)中期借贷便利(MLF)利率。MLF利率是央行中期政策利率,与公开市场操作7天期逆回购利率共同构成了央行政策利率体系。目前

1年期MLF利率为2.95%，代表了银行体系从中央银行获取中期基础货币的边际资金成本。2019年以来，人民银行逐步建立MLF常态化操作机制，每月月中开展一次MLF操作，通过以相对固定的时间和频率开展操作，提高操作的透明度、规则性和可预期性，向市场连续释放中期政策利率信号，引导中期市场利率。以一年期同业存单（AAA+）到期收益率为例，近两年除2020年第一季度受新冠肺炎疫情冲击影响，与MLF利率出现临时性偏离以外，其他时间基本围绕MLF利率为中枢波动（见图3）。

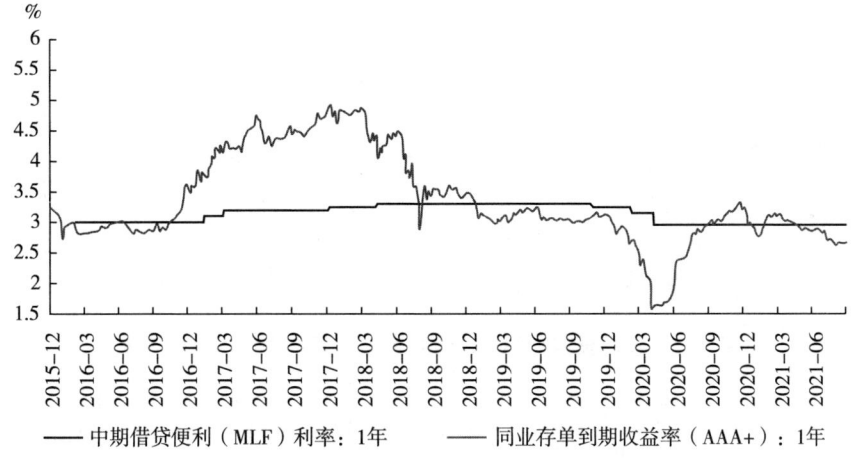

图3　中期政策利率和同业存单利率

（三）贷款市场报价利率（LPR）。2019年8月，人民银行推进LPR改革，报价行在MLF利率的基础上，综合考虑资金成本、风险溢价等因素报出LPR，充分反映市场供求状况。经过两年来的持续演进，金融机构新发放贷款已基本参考LPR定价，存量贷款也已完成定价基准转换，LPR已代替贷款基准利率，成为金融机构贷款利率定价的主要参考基准，贷款利率的市场化程度明显提升。改革后，贷款利率隐性下限被打破，LPR及时反映了市场利率略有下降的趋势性变化，有效发挥方向性和指导性作用，引导贷款实际利率有所下行，并且形成了"MLF利率→LPR→贷款利率"的利率传导机制，货币政策传导渠道有效疏通，贷款利率和债券利率之间的相互参考作用也有所增强（见图4）。

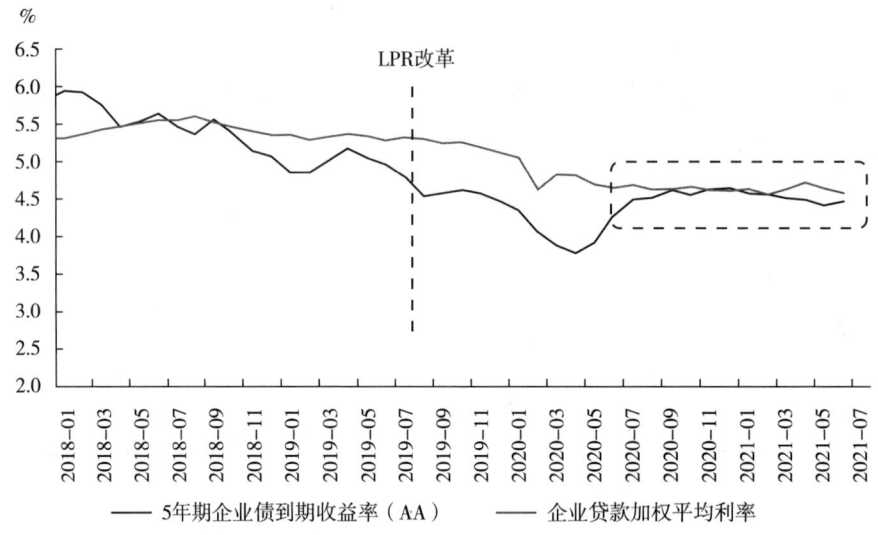

图4 改革后贷款利率和债券利率的相互参考作用有所增强

（四）存款准备金利率。存款准备金利率是央行对金融机构存在央行的准备金支付的利率，分为法定准备金利率和超额准备金利率。目前，我国的法定准备金利率为1.62%，有利于平衡各方面利益，支持金融机构可持续发展。2020年超额准备金利率由0.72%降至0.35%，与活期存款基准利率一致，统一了居民在商业银行的活期存款利率与商业银行在央行的超额准备金利率水平，比较公平。同时，降低了商业银行超额准备金的收益，提高了其闲置资金的机会成本，有利于促使银行提高资金使用效率，鼓励其用好自身资金，增加信贷投放支持实体经济。

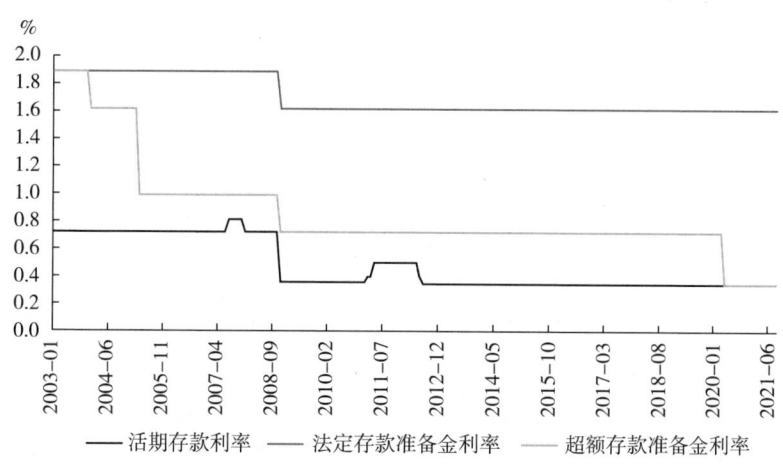

图5 存款准备金利率

（五）上海银行间同业拆放利率（Shibor）。2007年人民银行推出了Shibor。Shibor是由信用等级较高的银行组成报价团自主报出的人民币同业拆出利率计算确定的算术平均利率，是单利、无担保、批发性利率，包括隔夜到1年期的8个期限品种，形成了完整的期限结构，可为不同期限金融产品定价提供有益参考。目前Shibor已被应用于货币市场及债券、衍生品等市场各个层次的金融产品定价。自Shibor建立以来，人民银行持续对Shibor进行监督管理，有效地保证了Shibor的报价质量。同时，按照借鉴国际共识与最佳实践的总体思路，人民银行积极参与国际基准利率改革，指导利率自律机制和中国银行间市场交易商协会分别发布了境内伦敦银行间同业拆借利率（Libor）转换系列参考文本，为境内金融机构应对Libor退出提供了有利条件。

此外，存款基准利率过去发挥了重要作用。随着利率市场化改革的推进，当前金融机构可自主确定存款实际执行利率。几乎每个家庭都有存款，存款是最重要的金融公共服务产品，涉及广大人民群众切身利益。存款利率是在一定规则下由市场决定的。央行公布的存款基准利率作为指导性利率，为金融机构存款利率定价提供了重要参考。从国际经验看，存款利率一般比其他市场利率更加稳定。当前我国1年期存款基准利率为1.5%，以此为基础既可以上浮也可以下浮，可以说处于"黄金水平"，符合跨周期设计的需要（见图6）。2013年9月人民银行指导成立了市场利率定价自律机制，对金融机构利率定价行为进行自律管理。利率自律机制参考存款基准利率形成了存款利率自律约定，对维护存款市场公平合理的竞争秩序发挥重要作用。2021年6月利率自律机制将存款利率自律约定上限，由存款基准利率上浮一定比例改为加点确定，有利于进一步规范存款利率竞争秩序，优化存款利率期限结构，为推进利率市场化改革营造了良好环境。将来如有下浮需要，市场主体也可自主决定。

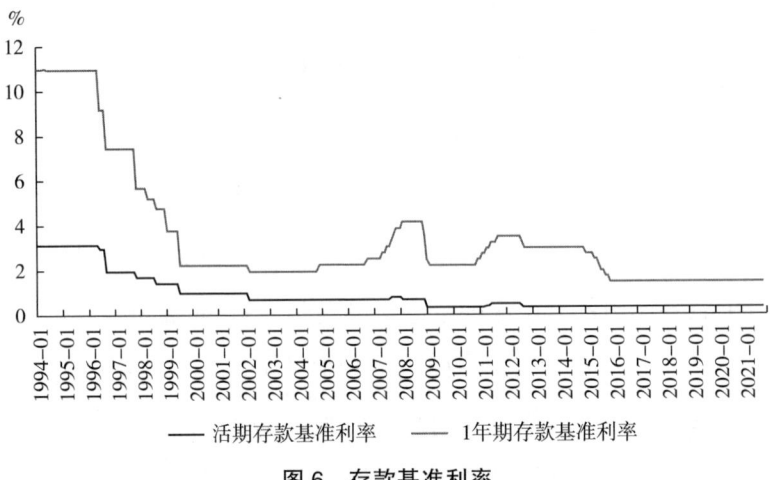

图6 存款基准利率

三、我国的收益率曲线已趋于成熟

在市场化的利率体系中，基准性的收益率曲线非常重要，可为各类金融产品和市场主体提供定价参考。收益率曲线反映利率由短及长的期限结构，是由各期限金融产品的主要参考基准利率共同组成的一个体系。收益率曲线的短端为隔夜和7天回购利率DR，长端为国债收益率。国际上看，即便是债券市场较为发达的美国，其国债收益率曲线也主要在中长端发挥作用,货币市场等短端利率仍主要参考联邦基金利率和 Libor(改革后将转为 SOFR)。对收益率曲线的不同部分,央行与市场发挥的作用有所差异。对于收益率曲线的短端,央行控制着基础货币的供给,通过公开市场操作和中期借贷便利等投放短期和中期基础货币,直接影响短期和中期的市场基准利率。对于收益率曲线的中长端,则主要基于市场对未来宏观经济走势、货币政策取向等的预期,由市场交易形成,投资者和政策制定者可以从中观察重要的市场信息。

中国国债收益率曲线的编制发布日趋成熟。自 1999 年发布第一条人民币国债收益率曲线以来,中国国债收益率曲线的编制发布工作日趋稳定成熟。包括中央结算公司、外汇交易中心等基础设施及彭博等国际信息商均编制国债收益率曲线,财政部、人民银行、银保监会均在官方网站发布中央结算公司编制的收益率曲线(见图 7)。美国有影响力的国债收益率曲线则主要是美国财政部和彭博编制的曲线。中国国债收益率曲线中最受市场关注的是 10 年期国债收益率走势,该期限附近市场价格点丰富,日均成交近 500 笔、成交量超过 200 亿元。

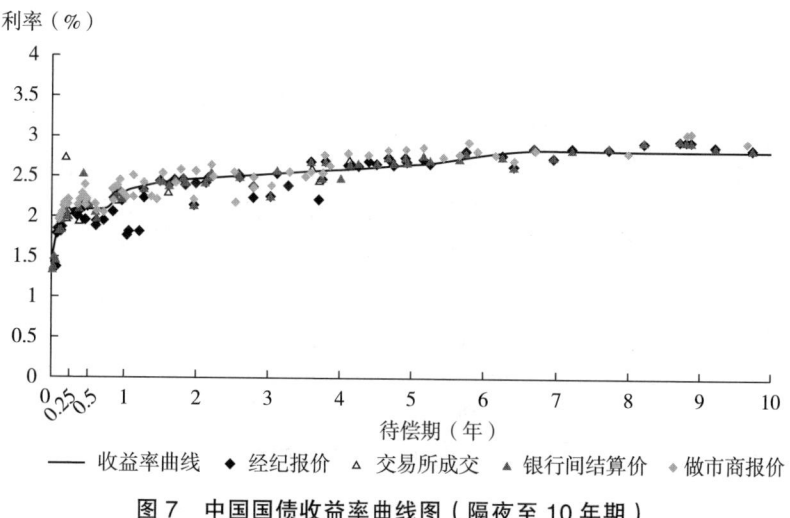

图 7 中国国债收益率曲线图(隔夜至 10 年期)

中国国债收益率曲线的应用日益广泛。目前,国债收益率曲线被市场机构广泛用于风险管理、公允价值计量和交易定价参考，在债券市场上发挥重要作用。将国债收益率作为发行及重定价参考利率的永续债、浮息债等规模近3.7万亿元。地方政府债券、超长期限国债在招标发行时采用中债国债收益率曲线作为发行定价的基准，迄今累计应用于超30万亿元债券发行。国际方面，2016年中国3个月期国债收益率纳入特别提款权（SDR）利率篮子，为境外央行类及商业机构投资中国债券市场提供定价参考。

中国国债收益率曲线的市场基础与发达市场相比仍有差距。成熟的收益率曲线能够较好反映宏观经济增长和通货膨胀的变化。从规模上看，我国国债市场存量为21万亿元人民币，而美国国债市场规模超过28万亿美元。从换手率看，我国国债尤其是长期限国债换手率相对较低，10年期以上国债换手率不足1倍，远低于美国的5.3倍。从报价价差看，我国做市报价平均价差明显高于美国。近年来中美两国国债收益率的相关性有所上升。以10年期国债收益率为例，2010—2015年两者相关系数为0.3，2016年以来相关系数为0.67（见图8）。中美国债收益率利差是各种因素的综合反映。

图8 中美10年期国债收益率

关于常规货币政策和非传统货币政策。资产购买工具不属于常规货币政策工具，而是央行在市场出现问题时的被迫选择。央行长期实施资产购买操作会产生危害市场功能、财政赤字货币化、损害央行声誉、模糊央行解决市场失灵和货币政策立场之间的界限、引发道德风险等诸多问题。应当尽可能避免实施资产购买操作，如果必须实施，应当坚持三个原则：一是央行干预的目的应当是帮助市场恢复正常运转，而非替代市场。二是央行的干预措施应尽可能走在市场前面，从而快速稳定市场情绪，避免市场失灵进一步恶化。三是应尽可能减少资产购买规模，缩短持续时间，力求资产购买实施力度与市场失灵的程度保持一致。当前全球主要发达经济体的利率长期趋于下降，一些经济体的政策利率已接近于零利率甚至负利率。中国的经济潜在增速仍有望维持在5%~6%的区间，有条件实施正常货币政策，收益率曲线也可保持正常的、向上倾斜的形态。中国将尽可能地延长实施正常货币政策的时间，目前不需要实施资产购买操作。

人民银行将按照党中央、国务院战略部署，继续深入推进利率市场化改革，着力健全市场化利率形成和传导机制。一方面，继续完善中央银行政策利率体系。继续巩固以公开市场操作利率为短期政策利率和以MLF利率为中期政策利率的中央银行政策利率体系，理想状态为市场利率围绕政策利率为中枢波动。着力完善利率走廊机制，有序实现SLF操作全流程电子化。另一方面，持续强化市场基准利率培育。优化LPR报价形成机制，督促报价行提高报价质量，对报价行进行考核并实行优胜劣汰，适时公布LPR历史报价。拓展回购利率DR在金融产品中的运用，进一步巩固DR的基准性。按市场化原则培育国债收益率曲线。

与此同时，利率市场化既要"放得开"也要"形得成"。当前深化利率市场化改革的一个重要矛盾在于市场化利率在"形得成"和传导方面存在障碍，其原因包括监管套利、金融市场不成熟等造成的市场分割，以及融资平台预算软约束、存款无序竞争等财政金融体制问题。下一阶段，要继续加强监管、优化营商环境、硬化预算约束、化解金融风险，为进一步深化利率市场化改革提供更有利条件。

新时代全面建成小康社会的
辉煌成就及新征程展望*

——基于"中国平衡发展指数"的综合分析

许宪春 刘婉琪 彭 慧 张钟文

中国共产党建党 100 周年之际,全面建成惠及十几亿人口的更高水平的小康社会,是我们党向人民、向历史作出的庄严承诺,也是实现中华民族伟大复兴中国梦的关键一步。本文紧扣新时代我国社会主要矛盾和全面建成小康社会的时代内涵,深入学习理解"十三五"和"十四五"规划纲要,结合发展不平衡、不充分问题的一些新情况、新变化,基于清华大学中国平衡发展指数,重点对党的十八大以来我国全面建成小康社会期间经济发展、社会治理、文化建设、脱贫攻坚、人民生活和生态环境等核心内容进行统计监测与分析,综合反映了我国全面建成小康社会所取得的辉煌成就。进一步结合监测结果展望新征程,深入剖析了全面建设社会主义现代化国家面临的问题与挑战,并提出了相应的对策建议,为助力解决新时代我国社会主要矛盾,为开启全面建设社会主义现

---

* 原文刊载于《金融研究》2021 年第 10 期。

作者简介:许宪春,经济学博士,教授,西南财经大学统计学院,清华大学中国经济社会数据研究中心,清华大学经济管理学院,上海财经大学统计与管理学院;刘婉琪,博士研究生,西南财经大学统计学院,清华大学中国经济社会数据研究中心;彭慧,博士研究生,上海财经大学统计与管理学院,清华大学中国经济社会数据研究中心;张钟文,经济学博士,清华大学中国经济社会数据研究中心,清华大学经济管理学院。

代化国家新征程提供决策参考。

中国平衡发展指数的构建立足于新时代我国社会主要矛盾，将"人民美好生活需要"同"发展不平衡不充分"联系起来，充分满足全面建成小康社会监测体系的要求。第一，"内容全"的体现。中国平衡发展指数的指标体系涵盖了"人民美好生活需要"的内容，并将"人民美好生活需要"具体化为经济发展、社会进步、生态环境、民生福祉四个维度，其中，"人民美好生活需要"同"全面建成小康社会"联系密切，都是人民对美好生活向往的集成体现。第二，"人口全"的体现。基于"小康路上不落一人，惠及全体人民"的思想，中国平衡发展指数的指标体系选取了"贫困发生率"指标来反映各地区脱贫攻坚进展，考察生活在贫困标准以下的人口占全部人口的比重，以从"人口全"的角度进行监测。第三，"区域全"的体现。中国平衡发展指数的构建充分考虑了地区间、城乡间的发展不平衡问题，以期重点监测全国整体层面、区域间及城乡一体化协调发展中存在的挑战和问题。

结果表明：新时代以来，全面建成小康社会取得了历史性成就。（1）经济发展持续向好。2019年，经济平衡发展指数为53.46，比2012年的43.61增加9.85，经济发展总体趋势稳步向前。由于人口老龄化程度加深，我国劳动年龄人口占比持续降低，人力资本平衡发展指数稳中趋降，从2012年的70.78下降到2019年的68.04。（2）社会治理水平不断提升。2019年，每十万人社会组织数量平衡发展指数为45.31，较2012年的28.02增加了17.29，社会组织的管理模式不断规范化、制度化。2019年每十万人拥有律师数平衡发展指数为20.26，较2012年的9.96增加了10.30。（3）文化软实力日益凸显。2019年社会文明平衡发展指数为34.17，较2012年的16.10增加了18.07，文化建设步伐加快。（4）脱贫攻坚取得全面胜利。党的十八大以来，我国脱贫攻坚战取得了举世瞩目的全面胜利，贫困发生率平衡发展指数从2012年的49上升到

2020年的100。（5）人民生活水平显著提高。2019年居民人均可支配收入平衡发展指数为34.58，较2012年的17.18增加了17.40。2019年居民人均消费支出平衡发展指数为38.78，较2012年的18.49增加了20.29。（6）生态环境明显改善。2019年空气质量平衡发展指数为62.30，较2012年的47.55增加了14.75。2019年水质量平衡发展指数为55.84，较2012年的49.79增加了6.05。

乘势而上开启全面建设社会主义现代化国家新征程，需要紧紧围绕人民美好生活需要，牢牢聚焦解决发展不平衡、不充分问题。基于中国平衡发展指数的测算结果，针对不平衡、不充分问题中较为突出的领域进行深入剖析，发现全面建设社会主义现代化国家仍面临以下突出问题和挑战：区域差异有待进一步缩小，城乡发展不平衡问题仍然突出，创新能力不适应高质量发展要求，居民可支配收入不平衡不充分现象还较为突出，基本公共服务均等化程度有待进一步完善，生态环境治理现代化水平有待进一步提升。

为了解决好发展不平衡、不充分的问题，更好地满足人民美好生活需要，从中国平衡发展指数出发，聚焦前文剖析的全面建设社会主义现代化国家面临的突出问题与挑战，提出以下建议：（1）坚持推进重大区域发展战略，构建区域协调发展新格局。要结合各地区的区位特征，精准施策，发挥地区比较优势的同时，努力补上发展短板。推动市场一体化建设，促进区域间合作发展，畅通东中西和南北之间的经济循环。（2）有力实施乡村振兴战略，推进我国城乡融合发展。依靠技术进步发展农业产业，与发达国家相比，我国农业科技创新还有很大提升空间。推进以人为核心的新型城镇化，大力推进"乡村建设"行动。推动实现城乡要素自由流动。（3）加强技术创新体系和扩散体系建设，不断提升国家创新能力。加强基础研究和行业共性技术的研究，完善技术创新体系建设。建立覆盖面广的科技成果转移专业机构，构建治理良好、有效运转的技术扩散体系。（4）完善收入分配政策，进一步缩小收入分配差距。提高劳动者报酬在初次分配中的比重，进一步完善劳动保护制度和多渠道就业保障制度。强化税收的再分配功能，逐步提高直接税比重，进一步降低增值税税率。进一步完善社会保障体系，强化政府社会管理和公共服务的职能，尽可能地提高社会保障水平、扩大社会保障覆盖面。（5）深化养老、医疗和教育等领域改革，促进基本公共服务均等化。建立财务可持续、促进公平的养老保障体系。全面推进健康中国建设，建立稳定的公共卫生事业投入机制。着力解决教育资源均等化问题，推进城乡义务教育一体化发展和优质均衡发展。（6）促进生态环境治理现代化，实现可持续发展。完善能源消费总量和强度的"双控"制度，重点控制化石能源消费，同时要推动清洁能源的低碳、安全、高效利用，提升生态系统的碳汇能力。数字化赋能生态环境治理，优化布设大气、地表水、海洋、土壤等监测网点和设施，打造全面感知、实时监控、天地海一体化的生态环境智慧监测和预警系统。

预测中国宏观经济变量：
专家与模型的组合预测*

梁 方 沈诗涵 黄 卓

随着中国经济的高速发展，预测中国宏观经济发展趋势也越来越重要。然而，准确预测中国宏观经济面临诸多困难。比如，受限于数据的可得性和缺少具有信息含量的经济指标增加了准确预测中国宏观经济的困难。此外，经济预测普遍面临着未来无法预知事件带来的不可避免的不确定性及由预测模型和方法导致的可控的不确定性。

计量模型的发展为预测经济变量提供了很多有利工具，模型预测已经成为预测中国宏观经济变量的重要方法。另外，专家预测可以及时对政策发布和可预期的变化进行调整，成为第二类重要的预测方法。专家预测综合考虑不同机构的预测，比模型预测包含了更多信息，而模型预测的优势在于具有便于复制的预测过程。将专家预测和模型预测组合，可以结合二者的优势，提升预测精度。自从 Bates 和 Granger（1969）提出组合预测（Forecast Combination）的思想，组合预测逐渐发展成为提升预测精度的主要方法，因其简单、有效而被广泛应用于预测宏观经济变量的研究中。

本文将组合预测方法应用于中国国内生产总值（GDP）增长率和居

---

* 原文刊载于《金融研究》2021 年第 7 期。
    作者简介：梁方，经济学博士，助理教授，中山大学国际金融学院；沈诗涵，博士研究生，加州大学洛杉矶分校；黄卓，经济学博士，副教授，北京大学国家发展研究院。

民消费价格指数（CPI）增长率的预测，比较专家预测和模型预测的效果，并探究组合预测能否提升预测精度。对 CPI 增长率和 GDP 增长率两个宏观经济指标，比较模型、专家及组合预测的效果，并通过进一步分析预测误差来比较模型和专家预测在不同经济时期的表现。

本文从多角度选取预测模型。使用区制转移类模型，反映高风险状态和低风险状态之间转换的动态性，描述经济平稳运行时期和下行时期 GDP 和 CPI 增长率不同的变化趋势。混频数据预测模型能够利用月度数据的信息含量，提升对季度宏观变量的预测精度。在使用混频数据的基础上，通过采用混频误差修正模型考虑具有协整关系的月度宏观经济变量对季度 GDP 和 CPI 增长率的预测作用。通过使用混频向量自回归模型，实现了采用多维高频宏观经济数据预测 GDP 增长率和 CPI 增长率。另外，由于 GDP 和 CPI 的增长率均为一阶单整的时间序列，本文也使用差分自回归移动平均模型进行模型预测。

专家预测以"朗润预测"中各机构对宏观经济变量的专家预测为基础。本文选择"朗润预测"主要有两点原因，一是包含多个机构对中国宏观经济变量的预测，并且样本时间长；二是"朗润预测"中包含的对中国宏观经济变量的预测均由国内著名的学术机构或领先的商业组织提供，一定程度上可以保证数据的可靠性和连续性。

在模型预测与专家预测的基础上，本文通过多种方法进行组合预测。组合预测方法包括简单平均、基于预测误差设定组合权重的组合预测方法、以贝叶斯信息准则为基础的贝叶斯模型平均法。本文通过多种方法对模型和专家预测进行组合，探究组合预测是否有助于提升预测精度。

本文构建了包含国内生产总值、居民消费价格指数、固定资产投资额、社会消费品零售总额、出口总值、进口总值、工业增加值、M_2 供应量、上证综指波动率、全国银行间同业拆借市场利率、金融机构人民币各项贷款余额、商品房新开工面积、发电量、消费者预期指数和国房景气指数共 15 个变量的宏观经济系统，通过混频向量自回归模型实现使用多维高频宏观经济数据预测 GDP 增长率和 CPI 增长率。

实证结果表明，专家对 CPI 和 GDP 增长率预测的效果总体上优于模型预测。专家预测几乎包含了模型预测的所有信息，说明专家在进行预测时已经考虑了计量模型预测的结果。进一步，我们发现专家预测的精度在 2008 年至 2010 年间明显高于模型预测。在经济波动时期，专家通过对实际经济运行环境和政策方向的把握，及时调整预期，得出更准确地预测。另外，组合预测有助于提升预测精度，对专家预测进行加权组合得到的专家平均预测效果优于大多数的单一专家预测；"模型—专家"组合预测的效果超过了所有的模型组合预测和大多数专家预测。本文从样本外基准预测的选取和滚动预测方法两个角度检验了实证结果的稳健性，结果表明，组合预测对于预测精度的提升不依赖于基准预测的选取，参数估计窗口的时间宽度变化没有影响文章的主要发现。

本文贡献主要体现在以下几个方面。首先，国内将组合预测方法应用于预测中国宏观经济变量的研究主要集中于构建组合预测模型，在组合预测中考虑专家预测信息的研究较少。与模型预测相比，专家预测能够根据宏观经济运行状况和宏观政策发布及时调整，不断吸纳新信息，有助于提升预测精度。本文通过使用组合预测方法对专家预测和模型预测进行组合，研究同时考虑专家预测信息与模型预测结果是否有助于提升预测精度，对已有文献作出补充。其次，本文比较了不同经济时期专家预测和模型预测的效果，发现在经济波动时期专家预测明显优于模型预测，并解释了造成专家和模型预测效果差异的原因。

美国货币政策溢出效应、中国资产价格波动与资本账户管理*

吴立元　赵扶扬　王　忏　龚六堂

大量实证研究证实，美联储货币政策会对中国等新兴市场国家产生重要的溢出效应。2008年国际金融危机后，美国实施了极度宽松的货币政策。2008年12月，美联储将基准利率降至零，并且维持零利率达7年之久，直到2015年12月开始进入加息周期并持续到2019年。除了大幅降息之外，美联储还实施了大规模的量化宽松政策，资产负债表大幅扩张。与此相伴随，世界范围内流动性宽裕，各国资产价格也显著上涨。随着美国经济的复苏，美联储开始加息，全球流动性随之收紧，中国的汇率、资本账户、资产价格也会出现波动。在新冠肺炎疫情的冲击下，全球经济受到巨大影响，美联储再次将联邦基金利率降至零利率水平，并重启量化宽松政策，美联储资产负债表急剧大幅扩张。当前随着疫情的缓解，美国经济逐步复苏，通胀快速上升，再次出现美联储紧缩货币政策甚至加息缩表的强烈预期。包括中国在内的新兴市场国家将再次面临美联储在极度宽松货币政策之后的货币紧缩冲击。回顾历史，20世纪80年代初拉美债务危机，20世纪80年代末日本经济泡沫破裂，1997年东南亚金

---

* 原文刊载于《金融研究》2021年第7期。

作者简介：吴立元，经济学博士，助理研究员，中国社会科学院世界经济与政治研究所；赵扶扬，经济学博士，讲师，中央财经大学经济学院；王忏，经济学博士，副教授，中央财经大学金融学院；龚六堂，数学博士，教授，北京工商大学国际经管学院、北京大学数量经济与数理金融教育部重点实验室。

融危机，都与美国货币政策有着千丝万缕的联系。当前，我国经济进入新发展阶段，深刻认识新发展阶段的内涵和特点，需要准确把握我国所面临的机遇和挑战。当今，世界正经历百年未有之大变局，不稳定的外部环境将是我国新发展阶段的主要特征之一。美联储极度宽松货币政策之后的紧缩产生的溢出效应是我国面临的重要外部风险挑战之一。因此，进一步厘清美国货币政策对我国资产价格和宏观经济的传导机制，完善资本账户管理和开放，应对美联储加息可能带来的流动性紧缩局面，是一系列需要回应的问题。总的来看，本文以2016年美国加息事件为背景，研究了上述问题。

本文基于引入金融摩擦与房地产的小国开放动态随机一般均衡模型，复制了2016年前后中国宏观经济一系列特征事实。本文进一步分析了美国货币政策溢出效应的具体传导渠道：发现国外利率升高后，资本的流动具有外部性，导致国内资产价格加速下跌，其通过金融加速器使国内投资下降、资产价格进一步下跌，从而国内资产的预期回报进一步下降，加剧了资本外流，构成了两个正反馈机制。我们在符合中国经济结构特征的参数组合下对模型进行了反事实模拟，证实了上述反馈循环显著放大了美国加息冲击对中国经济波动的溢出效应，从而证实了资产价格渠道是美国货币政策紧缩影响中国经济波动的重要渠道。最后，本文用严格的福利分析方法，研究了是否存在最优资本账户管理强度及资本账户管理对货币政策独立性的影响。研究发现，存在最优的资本账户管理强度，并且随着央行对经济波动的重视程度增强，最优资本账户管理强度也随之增大，同时资本账户管理会显著提高货币政策的独立性。其背后的经济直觉非常清晰，即资本账户管理存在两种效应：一方面，资本账户管理可以有效缓解国外利率冲击对经济波动的影响，降低跨期选择的扭曲；另一方面，其也会影响国民财富的最优配置。因此，最优的资本账户管理应同时兼顾宏观审慎和提高效率两个方面。适当的资本账户管理政策也有利于分担央行的宏观审慎管理压力，从而提升货币政策的独立性。根据以上逻辑，中国应保持适度的资本账户管理。本文认为，中国放开资本账户存在一些重要条件，一方面，中国经济金融系统抗风险能力足够强，此时美国货币政策冲击对我国资产价格波动影响较小，因而对经济波动影响也较小，对扭曲的放大效应也就大幅度减小；另一方面，中国的资产回报率逐渐与发达国家收敛，中国金融机构的国际化经营能力大幅增强，中国居民有非常强烈的在全球范围内配置资产的需求，此时放开资本账户带来的资本有效配置效应将大幅增强。

与现有文献相比，本文主要贡献如下：在一个统一的框架下同时复制了2016年美国加息后中国宏观经济出现的一系列特征事实，并提出了资本流动外部性与金融加速器相互作用的双反馈机制，将美国货币政策的溢出效应与资产价格波动联系起来，证明中国房地产市场是美国利率影响中国经济的重要途径，同时，分析了最优资本账户管理强度问题。

在上述讨论基础上，本文提出以下政策建议。第一，逐步建立健全常态化管理机制。国际上通常将资本账户管制分为"墙式管制"和"门式管制"，前者是指对资本账户的长期管制，后者是指总体上开放而对异常情况进行管制。2020年IMF首次公布的全球资本管制措施分类显示，即使是发达国家，也常常进行资本管制。中国可逐步建立对异常资本流动的常态化管理机制，尤其是严重影响资产价格的异常资本流动，实际上我国这一方面已经有相应的政策实践。第二，探索更加市场化的动态管理措施，例如征收风险准备金、托宾税、宏观审慎税等。冰岛曾在2016年针对资本流入短期激增的紧急情况对部分流入外资收取高达75%的无息准备金，储蓄一年后降至40%。巴西曾在20世纪90年代与2008年国际金融危机后实施了托宾税政策管控资本流动。韩国在2011年开始对银行非存款外汇负债收取"宏观审慎税"，时间越长，税率越低，从而以市场化手段抑制短期热钱流动。在借鉴国际经验的基础上，我国可以在相关方式上多方面创新。第三，渐进稳妥推进资本账户开放。比如，可以先完善人民币汇率形成机制市场化与金融市场开放，着力提高国内金融机构竞争力及金融市场的抗风险能力，在此基础上推进资本账户开放；按照风险从低到高的顺序逐渐开放，例如有学者建议先开放应收账款的流转等经常项目与资本项目交界地带的项目；坚持先试点再推广的渐进改革方法，可在临港新片区等金融开放的前沿阵地先行先试。

中国季度 GDP 的即时预测与混频分析*

王 霞 司 诺 宋 涛

国内生产总值（GDP）作为一个国家和地区经济状况的综合反映，其预测问题得到了世界各国统计机构和研究单位的广泛关注。无论是宏观调控政策的制定，还是企业发展战略的调整，都依赖于对 GDP 的准确预测。然而，由于各国仅对季度 GDP 进行核算，并且发布日期存在 3 周左右的时滞，传统预测方法缺乏时效性，无法对当前经济形势给予准确判断。实际上，与 GDP 密切相关的部分指标，如工业增加值、进出口、社会消费品零售总额等，不仅存在月度核算资料，而且发布时滞更短。若在 GDP 预测中引入这些数据信息，则可以提高 GDP 预测的时效性，及时修正对当前经济形势的判断，进而更迅速地制订宏观调控方案。

在 GDP 的混频预测方面，国外学者进行了许多探讨。综合来看，用于预测宏观经济变量的混频模型主要分为两类。一类是混频抽样模型（MIDAS）及其派生模型。MIDAS 模型借助权重函数将不同频率变量纳入同一回归模型中，避免了传统模型需要将高频数据低频化的缺陷，在宏观预测中得到了大量的应用；另一类是基于混频因子模型构建的一系列预测模型。相对于 MIDAS 依赖于权重函数的设定及 MFVAR（混频

---

* 原文刊载于《金融研究》2021 年第 8 期。
作者简介：王霞，经济学博士，副教授，中国人民大学经济学院；司诺，经济学硕士，中山大学岭南学院；宋涛，环境科学博士，副教授，厦门大学经济学院。

VAR）存在过多待估参数等问题，混频因子模型能够通过共同因子实现降维的目的，在充分利用多个月度指标提供数据信息的同时，避免了待估参数过多引起的自由度下降问题。近年来，国内学者在GDP的混频预测方面展开了一些有益的尝试。部分文献选择不同的预测变量，采用MIDAS模型对我国GDP进行了短期预测，很大程度上提高了我国GDP的预测精度和预测时效性，为我国经济运行态势的测度和宏观经济政策制定提供了重要的理论依据和经验证据。

然而，正如现有文献所述，国内现有文献普遍采用的MIDAS模型不仅受到分布滞后多项式设定形式的约束，而且无法囊括过多解释变量。此外，受数据发布日期差异、统计规则、春节效应等因素的影响，我国月度数据存在碎尾现象和数据缺失问题。由于MIDAS和MFVAR模型无法处理碎尾数据和缺失数据，研究者需要对数据进行插值补齐，基于完整的数据进行预测。这不仅引入了数据度量误差，而且缺乏时效性。为了提高时效性，货币当局和资本市场十分关注统计局的数据发布情况，一旦有新数据发布，他们就会更新对当前经济形势的判断和对重要经济变量的预测。然而，基于MIDAS或MFVAR进行分析时，为了保持尾部数据齐整，需要舍弃最新发布的数据，损失了能够代表近期经济态势的最新数据信息。

为了解决数据缺失、碎尾数据等问题，本文借助郑挺国和王霞（2012、2013）构建的同比混频动态因子模型对我国GDP进行即时预测。与MIDAS和MFVAR模型相比，本文采用的混频因子模型不仅可以处理碎尾数据，而且允许数据中存在缺失值，最大限度保证了数据的时效性和真实性。通过收集实时碎尾数据，本文在2001年1月至2020年12月期间确定了782个数据发布日，将季度GDP预测的时效性由"季度"提高到"日度"，即在每个数据发布日，均利用最新发布的数据更新GDP的预测结果。另外，除了用于GDP即时预测外，本文还得到其他一系列有意义的结果：第一，估计实际 GDP 季度同比增速序列。GDP 数据仅在每年 4 月、7 月、10 月和次年 1 月公布上一季度的同比增速。该模型可以估计得到 GDP 同比增速序列的月度实现值，例如，在每年 5 月，可以估计得到当年 2—4 月相对于上一年 2—4 月的季度同比增速。这为决策者判断当前经济形势提供了一定的数据基础；第二，构建实际 GDP 月度同比增长率序列。除了可以得到共同因子的平滑估计外，本文还可以得到特定因子的平滑估计，二者加总，即可构造实际 GDP 月度同比增长率的平滑估计序列；第三，估计月度指标中的缺失数据。如前文所述，受统计规则限制、春节效应等因素的影响，部分月度指标存在数据缺失问题。本文模型可以基于其他指标实现值对月度指标中的缺失数据予以估计，形成不存在缺失值的完整序列。

根据实证分析，本文的研究结论可大致概括如下：第一，混频因子模型能够有效解决实时预测中需要面临的数据问题，包括混频指标、碎尾特征、数据的周期性缺失等。第二，本文将 GDP 预测的频率由传统 AR 模型的"季度"提高到日度。这不仅提高了 GDP 预测的时效性，而且可以充分利用最新发布的数据信息。即只要有新的数据发布，在每个数据发布日，即可更新 GDP 的预测结果，可以将最新的经济活动信息迅速地体现到 GDP 预测中。第三，随着可利用信息的增加，混频因子模型的预测效果进一步提高，从而能够为宏观经济政策的制定和企业发展战略的实施等提供更可靠的经济预判。特别是在扩张和下行等经济状况变化较大的时期，混频预测结果具有趋近于 GDP 真实值的明显趋势。这说明混频因子模型中更新的月度数据信息在 GDP 预测中发挥着重要作用。第四，基于混频因子模型的估计结果，本文估算了拟 GDP 季度同比增长率和 GDP 月度同比增长率序列两个月度序列，为我国宏观经济与政策分析提供了重要的数据支持。

本文探讨的 GDP 即时预测，特别是以"日度"为频率，对季度 GDP

的预测结果进行实时更新，能够将最新的经济活动信息迅速地体现到GDP预测中，从而可以为宏观经济政策的制定及企业发展战略的实施等提供更及时、可靠的经济预判。从宏观经济调控角度而言，相关部门可以基于最新数据实时更新对当前经济状况以及未来经济形势的判断，进而制定出更具有时效性、更合理的宏观调控政策；从企业微观决策角度而言，企业能够更加明晰地认识当前经济形势，从而调整投资方案和发展战略等。这无论是对国家层面的宏观调控还是市场层面的微观决策都具有重要意义。另外，业界对于宏观数据的发布十分关注，并会基于发布的数据调整对宏观经济的预期。行业研究报告等也会基于最新发布的数据信息更新宏观经济的预测；彭博社发布的经济学家预测数据，允许经济学家在数据发布之前一小时对数据进行实时更新，因此，"即时预测"也是业界关注的热点之一。

人力资本偏向金融部门如何影响实体经济增长？*

刘贯春　司登奎　刘　芳

服务实体经济是金融业的重要使命。然而，一段时间以来，实体经济"冷"与虚拟经济"热"是我国经济发展的典型特征。关于两者的脱节现象，一种主流观点认为，有限的人力资本过度配置到了金融部门，抑制实体部门的研发创新活动并导致经济增长率下滑。然而，由于借贷双方的信息不对称普遍存在于金融部门的信贷配置过程，人力资本偏向金融部门有助于消除信贷合约摩擦，而信贷规模扩张有利于促进实体经济增长。那么，是否存在一个最优的人力资本配置比例使得金融部门和实体经济实现协同发展？利用理论模型和实证检验，本文试图回答这一问题。

理论上讲，人力资本配置到金融部门对实体经济发展同时存在正向和负向双重作用。一方面，人力资本聚集到金融部门会损害实体经济增长，影响渠道包括：第一，人力资本配置到金融部门会挤出劳动力和资本等要素在生产部门的分配；第二，金融部门会将财富从生产部门转移走，企业家精神被弱化并降低生产活动的内在激励；第三，聪明人成为金融从业者意味着企业家才能整体处于较低水平，创新能力相对不足。尤其

---

* 原文刊载于《金融研究》2021 年第 10 期。
作者简介：刘贯春，经济学博士，副教授，中山大学岭南学院；司登奎，经济学博士，副教授，青岛大学经济学院；刘芳，经济学博士，助理研究员，上海社会科学院世界经济研究所。

是现阶段我国的产权保护力度还在不断完善中，吸引聪明人成为企业家的激励还相对不够。另一方面，人力资本配置到金融部门促进实体经济增长，作用路径包括：第一，通过金融产品创新和加剧金融部门竞争来强化吸收社会存款的能力，可供使用的贷款规模增加；第二，缓解借贷双方存在的信息不对称，并精确识别企业还贷能力以强化合同执行力；第三，改善信贷资源在不同融资约束企业之间的配置，提高全社会的资本配置效率。

鉴于此，本文首先构建一个包含银行业和企业的两部门经济增长模型，强调人力资本偏向金融部门对实体经济增长存在资本"挤入"效应和创新"挤出"效应，两者呈现倒"U"形关系。同时，由于研发创新活动主要依赖于人力资本，资本"挤入"效应较弱而创新"挤出"效应较强，人力资本配置比例的最优阈值要低于实体经济增长率情形。类似地，由于上述两种效应在不同要素依赖型城市的相对重要性存在显著差异，从而导致人力资本配置比例的最优阈值理应存在显著差异。具体地，在研发创新型城市和外部融资依赖度低的城市时，由于经济增长更加依赖于技术进步，人力资本偏向金融部门的最优比例相对较小。

随后，基于2008年我国经济普查数据和2003—2015年271个地级市数据的计量回归结果证实了上述理论推断。依据实体经济增长率和研发创新活动的人力资本配置比例最优阈值，城市可以被划分为三种类型：一是同时促进实体经济增长和研发创新活动，即资本"挤入"效应占据主导地位；二是同时抑制实体经济增长和研发创新活动，即创新"挤出"效应占据主导地位；三是抑制研发创新活动但促进实体经济增长，即人力资本配置比例介于实体经济增长率和研发创新活动的最优阈值之间。反事实估计结果显示，一旦人力资本实现完全有效配置，将带来实体经济增长率约0.45%的提升，且贡献率随经济发展呈现放大效应。特别地，2011—2013年中国工业企业数据为人力资本偏向金融部门与实体经济增长的倒"U"形关系提供了微观证据，证实了人力资本配置到金融部门会显著提升企业获得银行信贷的规模，且有助于改善信贷资源在不同企业间的配置扭曲。

  本文研究发现，人力资本在金融部门与实体部门之间的最优配置阈值是客观存在的。整体来看，绝大多数城市存在人力资本过度配置到金融部门的现象，进而抑制研发创新活动并降低实体经济增长。需要注意的是，限于数据可得性，本文采用的是2008年人力资本配置存量数据，而社会人才被吸引到金融部门的现象在近几年更明显。结合理论分析和实证结论，本文提出如下政策建议：第一，合理监管金融部门的盲目扩张，强化其对实体经济的金融服务功能，尤其是对研发创新活动的资金扶持。事实上，面对新冠肺炎疫情冲击，国家出台的一系列金融支持政策，不仅切实降低了企业融资成本，还在一定程度上有助于优化人力资本配置。第二，由于人力资本偏向金融部门的根本原因在于高薪酬，可以考虑调整薪酬分配结构以期提升工业企业对社会人才的吸引力。第三，不同城市对各类生产要素的依赖度呈现异质性，因地制宜地调整人力资本配置十分必要。

流动性覆盖率监管会影响货币政策传导效率吗？*

——来自中国银行业的证据

庄毓敏　张祎

2008年国际金融危机后，巴塞尔委员会在夯实"三大支柱"的基础上构建了全球统一的流动性监管框架，并将其纳入《巴塞尔协议Ⅲ》，以弥补传统资本监管主导的银行监管框架的不足。其中包含的两个核心指标流动性覆盖率（Liquidity Coverage Ratio，LCR）和净稳定资金比例（Net Stable Funding Ratio，NSFR），分别从短期和长期视角对银行流动性水平提出了最低监管要求，旨在降低极端压力情景下的资产抛售和银行挤兑风险。

尽管国外学者的前期理论研究为流动性监管规则的设计提供了逻辑基础，但现有研究尚未完整揭示流动性监管对货币政策传导过程的潜在影响路径。在此背景下，政策界和学术界仍然对流动性监管的潜在影响存在疑虑，这也在一定程度上影响了流动性监管的全球实施进程。那么，流动性监管是否真的会阻碍货币政策的传导过程？流动性监管，尤其是LCR监管要求对货币政策传导效率的影响机制是什么？如果流动性监管

---

* 原文刊载于《金融研究》2021年第11期。

作者简介：庄毓敏，经济学博士，教授，中国人民大学财政金融学院、中国财政金融政策研究中心；张祎，经济学博士，中国银行总行。

与货币政策传导过程确实存在潜在冲突,应如何实现两者之间的协调关系?鉴于此,本文从 LCR 监管要求出发,探究流动性监管对货币政策传导效率的潜在影响,这也是宏观审慎框架下流动性监管与货币政策相互协调的重点问题。

理论方面,本文将 LCR 监管约束纳入传统的 Monti-Klein 模型,并基于 LCR 监管要求重新定义了流动性短缺成本,从而刻画出 LCR 监管约束对货币政策传导效率的潜在影响及其作用机制。理论模型表明,商业银行流动性短缺成本的存在是货币政策得以有效传导的重要前提,LCR 监管要求改变了商业银行面临的边际流动性短缺成本,因而会对货币政策传导效率产生一定影响,但这种影响取决于商业银行流动性管理行为选择:商业银行囤积流动性资产不利于货币政策的有效传导,而降低对短期融资渠道依赖、提高负债质量的行为则有助于提升货币政策传导效率。

在此基础上,本文借助我国流动性监管过渡期的时间窗口,采用手工收集的我国 65 家商业银行 2015—2019 年的 LCR 监管披露数据样本对相关假设进行了实证检验,为流动性监管的影响评估与机制分析提供了中国经验。实证研究结果表明:第一,LCR 监管要求会对货币政策传导效率产生显著影响,且这种影响与商业银行流动性管理行为选择有关。第二,LCR 水平较低的部分城市商业银行或农村商业银行往往采取囤积流动性资产的方式快速提升短期流动性水平,这一行为对货币政策传导效率产生了阻碍作用,而大型银行和股份制银行依托于融资渠道优势,更多地进行融资渠道的管理和转换,在实现 LCR 提升的同时,也保障了货币政策的传导效果。第三,LCR 监管要求在区分宏观经济环境与银行微观特征后对货币政策传导效率具有异质性影响,且与 NSFR 监管要求和资本监管要求存在显著的交互作用。这也在一定程度上表明,流动性监管要求对货币政策传导效率的影响与商业银行的自身状况及其行为选择有关。

本文研究具有以下政策参考意义。第一，客观评估流动性监管对货币政策传导效率的潜在影响，并结合不同经济时期、针对不同类型银行实施灵活的流动性监管制度安排。第二，金融管理部门应关注并引导商业银行在应对 LCR 监管要求时的流动性管理行为，以保障货币政策的传导效果。还应考虑流动性监管与资本监管的交互作用，结合商业银行的微观特征与管理行为，优化与完善银行监管指标体系，提高监管协调性。第三，商业银行应积极调整资产负债结构以应对 LCR 监管所带来的潜在冲击。在资产端，应重视合格优质流动性资产（High Quality Liquidity Asset，HQLA）的结构优化，而非单纯追求规模增加；在负债端，应降低短期批发融资依赖度、提高负债质量，从而有效应对商业银行短期流动性风险，提高银行经营的稳健性与安全性。

本文的学术贡献有以下几方面。第一，创新地将流动性覆盖率监管要求纳入 Monti-Klein 模型，通过理论推导揭示出 LCR 监管对货币政策传导效率的影响机理，不仅拓展了传统银行经济学模型的应用范围，还从银行层面揭示了准备金政策在银行体系的利率传导机制。第二，运用手工收集的我国 65 家商业银行 LCR 监管披露数据，实证检验了 LCR 监管对货币政策传导效率的潜在影响及其作用机制，为商业银行流动性监管理论研究提供了新的证据，弥补了现有流动性监管文献中 LCR 监管研究的缺失。第三，基于理论和实证研究，梳理了流动性监管与货币政策传导之间的逻辑关系，并客观地评价了流动性监管对货币政策传导效率的影响，为流动性监管的全球实施提供了中国经验，并为宏观审慎监管框架下流动性监管与货币政策的协调机制设计提供了有益参考。

限于 LCR 数据的可获得性及样本长度，本文对 LCR 监管要求的影响研究还有待进一步深入，对商业银行的流动性管理行为的描述还不够精确。LCR 监管要求如何影响银行间市场？LCR 监管要求是否会对货币政策的其他传导渠道产生影响？这些都是目前亟须解决的重要问题。未来希望能够通过《巴塞尔协议Ⅲ》流动性监管实践的观察视角，更精确地刻画现实监管环境下商业银行的流动性管理行为。

收入差距、信贷约束与房价波动*

陈金至　温兴春　宋　鹭

　　收入差距、信贷约束与房价一直以来都是社会各界关注的热点话题。国际货币基金组织（IMF）于2020年9月发布的报告指出，全球实际房价指数再创新高，达到了167.26（以2000年第一季度为基期），在被统计的63个样本中，有47个的国家和地区房价都呈现出了上涨态势。一方面，在美国次贷危机后，收入差距与信贷之间关系受到学者广泛关注，普遍发现在国际金融危机爆发前夕，中低收入家庭存在负债率迅速拉升的现象；另一方面，大量研究表明，信贷约束的放松对房价上涨具有显著的助推作用。一个自然的问题是，是否存在收入差距变动通过信贷渠道进而影响房价的传导渠道呢？遗憾的是，该问题在现有文献中鲜有提及。

　　事实上，由于不同收入人群的购房需求是不同的，通过金融杠杆的放大效应，理论上收入分配的变化应该会显著地影响房价波动。因此，本文在Liu等（2019）的基础上，试图建立一个一般性的异质性代理人框架，从收入差距影响信贷约束的渠道解读房价变动。研究表明，收入差距、信贷约束和房价三者之间是紧密相关的。具体而言，收入差距的减少会使低收入者的相对收入水平提升，这放松了低收入者购房的信贷

---

* 原文刊载于《金融研究》2021年第11期。
　　作者简介：陈金至，经济学博士，讲师，南京审计大学政府审计学院；温兴春，经济学博士，讲师，对外经济贸易大学金融学院；宋鹭，经济学博士，研究员，中国人民大学国家发展与战略研究院。

约束。一方面，信贷约束的放松使（加总的）住房流动性溢价下降，该效应抑制了房价上涨；另一方面，由于低收入者的住房边际效用更高，且收入上升后的低收入者通过撬动更多资金加大了其对住房市场的影响权重，由此抬高了全社会的住房边际效用，从而抵消了流动性溢价下降的负向影响，并最终促使房价上涨。进一步地，通过对44个国家和地区1970—2017年的跨国面板数据的实证分析表明，低收入者收入占比上升对于信贷约束放松和房价提升的作用显著强于高收入者收入占比下降的作用。综上所述，本文认为，收入差距的缩小通过放松低收入者的信贷约束，提升了整个社会的住房需求，并最终抬升了房价水平。

本文的创新之处有以下三点：一是前人关于收入差距对房价的解释更多停留在静态分析层面，本文通过引入信贷约束渠道使得模型呈现出更多动态特征。二是既有研究往往利用代表性代理人模型来讨论信贷约束与房价之间的关系，本文将异质性代理人纳入模型进行分析，丰富了研究维度。三是已有文献更多从实证层面直接研究收入差距与房价之间的关系，较少对其中的传导机制进行深入分析，本文通过构建理论模型清晰刻画了收入差距、信贷约束与房价三者间的传导机制，为理解房价上涨的背后因素提供了新的视角，为之后相关政策的制定提供了新的启示。

本文研究具有较强的现实意义。当前的中国房地产市场出现了一二线城市与三四线城市分化的态势。根据CREIS中指数据的统计，与一二线城市在土地供应量和成交量增长约10%的情况相比，2020年，三四线城市的土地供应量和成交量分别下降49%和48%。中国房地产市场与银行信贷、政府收入和社会投资关系密切，如果其遭遇断崖式下跌，可能会引发系统性金融风险。中央提出"六稳六保"方针，体现了对民生就业、金融稳定和投资预期的深度关切，收入差距缩小本身就是保障基本民生的重要手段。本文研究也表明，收入差距的缩小对于扩大社会的融资需求、防止房价崩盘从而稳定投资预期有重要作用。

　　结合当前经济形势，本文提出了如下政策建议：（1）着力缩小收入差距。大量文献表明，提升城市化率能有效降低农业和非农部门间的劳动生产率差异，从而显著缩小收入差距。中国国家统计局公布的数据显示，2008—2019年，常住人口城镇化率从46.99%上升至60.6%，城乡居民可支配收入之比也从3.11下降至2.64。上述事实表明，城市化进程的加速是当前收入差距缩小的重要动力。当然，人口的城市化并非简单的"居民化"，而是城市居民的"市民化"，只有真正提高人口质量和完善公共服务的均等化，才能在未来较高的城市化阶段进一步缩小收入差距。（2）依据本文结论，因城市化所引起的居民和城乡收入差距缩小与大城市的高房价问题看似难以平衡。但本文认为，收入差距缩小带来的房价上涨实质上是低收入者住房条件改善所致，其与"投机行为推高房价"逻辑有着本质不同，在政策制定过程中需加以区分。实践中，为了抑制大城市房价过快上涨并进一步缩小收入差距，可考虑通过继续推动"保障性安居工程"和发展房屋租赁市场（特别是完善租售同权制度）以增加低收入人群的住房供给，以缓解城市化率提升与房价高涨之间的内在冲突。（3）对于存在房价崩盘风险的地区，要在有效防范风险的基础上，引导信贷资源向低收入群体倾斜，大力发展普惠金融。由于低收入者往往面临较强的信贷约束，导致其对于信贷环境的变化更加敏感。因此在制定政策时，应更多考虑弱势群体，充分发掘其有效信贷需求，此举一方面能满足低收入群体对于住房的刚性需求，对房地产行业需求形成有效支撑；另一方面能抑制高收入群体的投机行为、打击房价泡沫，以此促进房地产和金融市场的平稳健康发展，真正将"房住不炒"理念落至实处。

借贷便利创新工具能有效影响商业银行贷款利率吗？*

邓 伟 宋 敏 刘 敏

为更好地引导商业银行降低社会融资成本、促进经济高质量发展，我国央行创设了以中期借贷便利（MLF）为代表的借贷便利工具。与美联储等中央银行在危机期间推出的借贷便利工具相比，我国创设的借贷便利工具并不是临时性的救助工具，已发展成为我国货币政策工具箱中的常态化工具，承担着向商业银行提供基础货币并支持信贷合理增长，发挥有效影响商业银行贷款利率等重要作用。更为重要的是，在我国利率体系与利率市场化改革进程中，中期借贷便利利率被赋予中期政策利率的地位，并以此引导银行贷款利率（易纲，2021）。特别是2019年8月人民银行改革完善贷款市场报价利率（LPR）形成机制，在MLF利率基础上，综合资金成本、风险溢价等因素报出LPR，LPR逐步取代贷款基准利率。由此而提出的问题是：借贷便利创新工具能有效影响商业银行贷款利率吗？本文针对这一现实问题进行研究，对我国利率体系与利率市场化改革具有理论和现实意义。

事实上，自20世纪八九十年代以来，尤其是美国次贷危机和国际金融危机爆发以后，借贷便利工具被许多国家的中央银行所运用，但借贷

---

* 原文刊载于《金融研究》2021年第11期。

作者简介：邓伟，经济学博士，副教授，中南财经政法大学会计学院；宋敏，经济学博士，教授，武汉大学经济与管理学院；刘敏，金融学博士，讲师，中南财经政法大学会计学院。

便利工具能否对商业银行贷款利率产生有效影响仍存在较大争议。同时，国外的借贷便利工具在实施背景、政策定位等方面与我国存在较大差异，国外相关研究结论缺乏借鉴作用。特别是在我国多种货币政策工具并存并用的环境中，多种货币政策工具的组合操作使得不同货币政策工具的效果相互影响、相互重叠，形成观测到的综合调控效果，这给研究借贷便利创新工具的政策效果带来了困难。由于缺乏较好的因果关系识别策略，目前国内还没有学者对借贷便利工具对银行贷款利率的影响开展实证研究。本文基于我国的制度背景分析认为，借贷便利工具在制度设计上提高了商业银行主动申请借贷便利的积极性，商业银行通过质押合格担保品的方式，借助借贷便利工具可以获得大规模、低成本的资金，从而起到促进降低银行贷款利率的作用。

本文基于我国央行创设借贷便利工具这一准自然实验，以借贷便利工具的运用需要商业银行提供合格担保品这一要求为切入点，手工搜集2009—2017年我国银行业100家商业银行的年报等数据，对我国借贷便利工具能否对商业银行贷款利率产生有效影响这一问题进行实证研究。本文的主要结论如下：第一，借贷便利工具可以显著影响商业银行贷款利率，央行的借贷便利操作规模越大，其对商业银行贷款利率的降低作用越强。第二，借贷便利工具可以通过商业银行合格担保品渠道发挥作用。本文研究发现，商业银行持有的合格担保品规模越大，其从央行获取的借贷便利规模越大，对其贷款利率的降低作用越强。

本文的主要贡献在于：第一，利用手工搜集的商业银行合格担保品数据，更直接地论证了借贷便利工具的作用机制。已有关于我国借贷便利工具传导机制的实证研究均没有考虑商业银行层面的合格担保品信息，未能论证借贷便利工具如何通过商业银行担保品渠道发挥政策效应。本文基于我国借贷便利工具需要商业银行提供合格担保品这一要求，手工搜集了100家商业银行的合格担保品数据，通过实证研究为借贷便利工具可以通过商业银行担保品渠道发挥作用提供了直接的微观证据。第二，本文从商业银行贷款利率的视角，研究了借贷便利这一货币政策创新工具的政策效应，证实了借贷便利工具的有效性，丰富了现有文献。本文研究发现，央行利用借贷便利工具向商业银行提供大规模、低成本的资金可以有效降低商业银行贷款利率，且这一作用随着时间的推移逐渐增强，证实了我国借贷便利工具对商业银行贷款利率调控的有效性。

本文的研究发现对我国货币政策担保品管理框架建设及借贷便利类货币政策的实施具有借鉴意义。第一，央行可以利用借贷便利工具进行货币政策调控，通过调整借贷便利操作规模、操作利率、合格担保品范围的方式发挥调控商业银行贷款利率的作用，这对完善LPR形成机制及促进降低社会融资成本具有积极作用。第二，关注借贷便利操作利率的调控效果。借贷便利工具是一种数量型和价格型兼具的混合型货币政策工具，既包含操作规模，也包含操作利率。本文的研究发现，央行实施的借贷便利规模越大，其对商业银行贷款利率的降低作用越强，表明央行通过调整借贷便利操作规模可以有效影响商业银行贷款利率。从我国借贷便利操作的实际情况来看，央行主要通过调整借贷便利操作规模的方式进行借贷便利类货币政策调控，而借贷便利操作利率变化较小且总体呈现下降趋势，其能对商业银行贷款利率产生多大的影响尚缺乏实证研究。因此，进一步探索借贷便利操作规模和操作利率在作用机制、政策效果等方面的差异，对改进我国借贷便利类货币政策的调控效果，完善利率体系和利率市场化改革具有启示意义。

全球金融周期与跨境资本流动*

谭小芬 虞梦微

随着全球金融一体化程度的加深,各个国家金融状况的联动性不断上升,造成不同国家的金融周期存在协同变动,"全球金融周期"的概念由此诞生并被广泛讨论(Rey,2013)。全球金融周期可以看做是一组推动因素的合集,包括美国货币政策、全球风险偏好等(Cerutti 等,2019)。如果一国的资本流动受全球金融周期的影响过大,那么该国就很可能频繁地经历与国内基本面无关的资本流入激增和突然中断。全球金融周期除了会放大一国资本流动和金融周期的波动,也可能放大一国经济周期的波动幅度,从而造成经济的不稳定。比如,当一国处于经济繁荣阶段,同时叠加宽松的全球金融状况,这可能会导致过多的资本涌入,导致该国的信贷过度扩张和资产泡沫,而过度的信贷扩张和资产泡沫易触发金融危机(Gourinchas 和 Obstfeld,2012)。

在当前复杂的国际经济金融形势背景下,研究全球金融周期对跨境资本流动的影响尤其具有现实意义。已有文献发现,在经济面临压力的时期,资本流动主要受全球因素的驱动(Fratzscher,2012)。IMF(2020)发现,在新兴市场的经济基本面并无明显恶化的背景下,新冠肺炎疫情冲击导致了新兴市场经历了前所未有的资本外流,而这主要是由全球风险规避和不确定性上升所导致。面对新冠肺炎疫情冲击,很多新兴市场

---

* 原文刊载于《金融研究》2021 年第 10 期。
作者简介:谭小芬,经济学博士,教授,中央财经大学金融学院;虞梦微,中央财经大学金融学院博士生。

经济体都经历了大量的资本外流，但有一些国家受到的冲击相对较小。面对相同的全球金融冲击，为何各国的跨境资本流动受到的影响存在明显的异质性？各国宏观经济基本面和经济结构性因素能否解释这种差异？由于全球金融周期对一国来说是不可控的外生冲击，但是本国的经济基本面和结构性因素则可通过政策进行调整和干预。因此，研究上述问题，可为应对全球金融冲击带来的跨境资本流动风险提供政策建议。有鉴于此，本文使用主成分分析从全球42个主要的股票市场指数中提取全球因子，作为全球金融周期的代理变量，研究了1997—2017年全球金融周期对跨境资本总流入的影响，并在以下三方面对已有文献形成补充和扩展：一是采用全球股票市场因子而非VIX等指标，更广泛地考虑到除美国之外的其他大型经济体金融状况的影响；二是在推动—拉动因素分析框架中，发现全球金融周期这一推动因素对跨境资本流动具有显著的影响，同时考察如何调整拉动因素才有利于缓解外部推动因素对跨境资本流动的冲击，降低金融体系的脆弱性。虽然大部分文献强调国内特定因素在资本流动中的拉动作用，但对于国内特定因素是否会加强或削弱全球金融周期对资本流入的影响的研究则相对较少，本文对此有所贡献；三是在全球金融周期影响日益增强的背景下，本文为汇率制度调整及其市场化改革提供了新的实证支持。

本文发现：（1）全球金融周期对跨境资本流入的影响十分显著，并且该影响对于跨境资本流入的细分项（FDI、股票类证券投资、债券类证券投资和跨境银行信贷）都成立；（2）在危机期间，新兴经济体的证券投资流入（包括股票和债券）对全球金融周期的敏感性会上升，而由于避险资产的"避风港效应"，发达国家的证券投资流入对全球金融周期的敏感性在危机期间会减弱；无论是发达经济体还是新兴市场经济体，跨境银行资本流入在危机期间受全球金融周期的影响最大，这证实了跨境银行在全球金融市场波动中的重要性；（3）与危机前相比，危机后债券类证券投资流入对全球金融周期的反应更加敏感。

此外,本文着重回答了为什么全球金融周期对各国资本流动的影响存在异质性这一问题。本文发现:(1)拥有良好的宏观经济基本面(经济增速和利率处于相对较高水平)的国家对全球金融周期的敏感性较低;(2)资本账户开放程度或金融发展程度越高的国家对全球金融周期的敏感性越高;(3)更富有弹性的汇率制度(浮动汇率和中间汇率)尽管并不能完全隔绝全球金融周期的影响,但是相比于固定汇率制度,可提高一国抵御全球金融周期冲击的能力。最后,本文通过中介效应模型表明,美国货币政策冲击是全球金融周期的重要来源,它会通过全球金融周期影响跨境资本流动。

面对全球金融周期,政策制定者可从以下几方面来应对:

第一,进一步建立和完善跨境资本流动监测、预警和响应机制,采用宏观审慎政策来降低金融体系、跨境资本流动和外汇市场的顺周期性。除应关注资本流入规模,还应关注资本流入结构,尤其是跨境银行信贷流入和债券类流入,这对金融稳定至关重要。跨境银行信贷流入在风险较高的时期,对全球金融周期的敏感性会进一步增加,这可能会使一国面临资本流入的骤停和逆转,增加国内金融风险。危机后债券类证券投资流入规模上升,且对全球金融周期的敏感性增加,因此,也需要密切关注这种形式的资本流动对于全球金融周期变化的反应。

第二,良好的宏观经济基本面和合理的经济政策制度有助于一国缓解外部冲击。(1)各国应采取可持续的稳定化宏观经济政策,夯实经济基本面,增强经济和市场韧性;(2)在渐进开放资本项目的同时,采取适度的资本管控;(3)提高汇率的灵活性,但并非一定要采取完全浮动的汇率制度。

利差、美元指数与跨境资本流动*

缪延亮　郝　阳　费　璇

随着金融双向开放稳步推进，我国跨境资本流动可能出现中长期的结构性调整。一方面，疫情后全球化减速或逆转，或导致直接投资等长期稳定性资本流动减少；另一方面，发达国家大规模宽松，可能推升短期投机性资本流动风险。在外部经济金融形势日趋严峻复杂的背景下，理解我国跨境资本流动的驱动因素，并在此基础上提高人民币汇率的灵活性，对于构筑新发展格局下更有效的金融安全网具有重要意义。

跨境资本流动受到推动（Push）和吸引（Pull）因素共同驱动，利差是推动和吸引因素的综合体现。发达经济体通常利率较低，推动资本流向新兴经济体。政策制定者高度关注利差变动对跨境资本流动的影响。尽管如此，获取利差的套息行为并非中国跨境资本流动的唯一动机，相关实证研究提出套汇（获取汇率变化带来的汇差）也驱动跨境资本流动。考虑中国的实际情况，除了利差和汇率外，是否还存在其他决定中国跨境资本流动的关键因素呢？

为了探究这一重要问题，本文聚焦于美元指数（DXY）的重要性。通过时变参数向量自回归的方法，在实证研究引入美元指数后发现，美元指数是决定中国跨境资本流动最为关键的因素。这一结果在样本区间的各个时间段均成立，且美元指数比利差、人民币汇率对资本流动更有

---

* 原文刊载于《金融研究》2021年第8期。
作者简介：缪延亮，经济学博士，中央外汇业务中心首席经济学家；郝阳，经济学博士，中央外汇业务中心；费璇，经济学博士，中央外汇业务中心。

解释力。为何在中国跨境资本流动问题上，汇率比利率更重要，而且多边美元汇率又比人民币兑美元双边汇率更重要？我们把这一问题称为"中国的跨境资本流动之谜"。为解开这一谜题，我们深入研究美元指数影响资本流动的影响渠道，并提出中国跨境资本流动的分析框架。

本文发现美元指数主要通过两个渠道影响资本流动，导致美元指数的解释力更强。一是通过汇率预期渠道。由于历史上人民币弹性较低，当非中国经济基本面的因素导致美元升值（美元指数上升）时，人民币出现贬值预期，套汇资本因而流出（如2014—2016年）。同样，当美元贬值（美元指数下降）时，人民币出现升值预期，套汇资本持续流入（如2008—2012年）。因而在人民币兑美元汇率不够灵活调整的情况下，美元指数通过影响人民币汇率预期，从而驱动资本流动。二是通过风险情绪渠道。已有文献表明美元周期和全球风险情绪高度相关，美元指数已成为最显著的全球投资者风险情绪指标。美元作为全球最主要的融资货币，其币值变化通过资产负债表效应影响全球主要金融机构提供流动性的意愿和能力。

美元指数又是由什么因素解释？尽管实证上中美利差对资本流动的影响力不及美元指数，但本文研究表明中美利差仍能在统计意义上解释并领先于美元指数。中美利差首先是反映了两个经济体之间的经济基本面分化。但是，随着中国经济日益变强的外溢效应，中美经济基本面的分化也在很大程度上驱动并反映了欧洲、日本和美国经济基本面的分化。这样看来，尽管DXY不包含人民币，中美利差仍可以解释并领先于美元指数。从这个意义上讲，政策制定者仍要关注利差，因为我们发现利差和美元指数都是中美分化的表现，是一枚硬币的两面，而且利差在实证意义上具有一定领先性。

图1总结了本文的主要逻辑。中美利差是中美基本面分化的同步指标，利差与资本流动因而具有较强相关性。利差虽然可以通过套息交易

引起资本流动变化,但仅是次要渠道。中美基本面分化决定了美元指数,美元指数是决定资本流动的重要决定因素。美元指数主要通过两个渠道影响资本流动变化,一是通过影响汇率预期,二是通过影响风险情绪驱动资本流动。

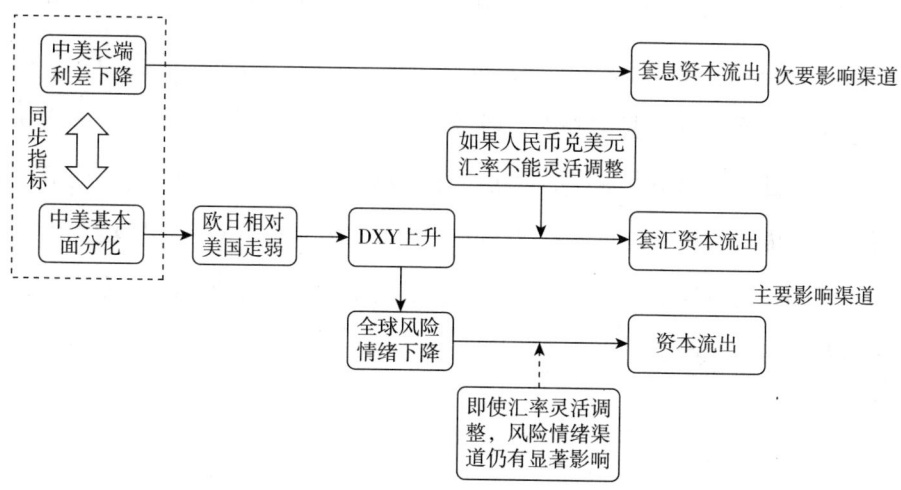

图 1　本文的逻辑框架

本文最重要的贡献在于揭示了一个新的比利差更重要的决定资本流动的关键因素——美元指数。本文通过实证研究发现利差对跨境资本流动的解释力不如美元指数,同时也发现中美利差能够在统计意义上解释 DXY 美元指数。我们从人民币汇率形成机制的根源上将这两个看上去相互矛盾的发现统一起来。历史上,人民币兑美元双边汇率并未充分实现清洁浮动,因而人民币兑美元双边汇率并不完全和立即体现中美经济基本面的变化。这种滞后和不足反应会通过两种渠道的力量被纠正过来。一种是利差变化导致的套息资本流动,这是传统渠道,也是文献和政策制定者讨论较多的渠道。本文强调的是一个新的和更重要的渠道,即中美基本面分化会通过中国经济显著的溢出效应影响 DXY 指数走势,而后者不仅影响人民币兑美元双边汇率预期,还通过改变风险情绪来影响中国乃至全球的跨境资本流动。我们从实证上证实后一渠道完全主导前一渠道，表现为在汇率价格变动滞后和不足时，资本流动会受套汇交易和风险情绪影响而大幅波动。提高汇率的灵活性不仅能提高货币政策的独立性，还将显著减少资本流动的数量超调。

因此，应当继续坚持人民币汇率形成机制市场化改革，保持汇率弹性，更好地发挥汇率在宏观经济稳定和国际收支平衡中的"自动稳定器"作用。同时，不断推进我国外汇市场建设，在外汇市场的交易主体、交易产品和监管等方面不断完善，促进汇率市场的价格发现功能。我们相信，随着人民币汇率灵活性的提高，利差和DXY美元指数对中国跨境资本流动的影响都会减弱，汇率预期更多受到中国国内因素的影响，美元指数和利差的舒适区间会越来越宽。

经济开放与货币需求：国际金融风险及持币成本的测度*

秦　朵　卢　珊　王惠文　Sophie van Huellen　王庆超

改革开放以来，中国经济逐步融入世界。毋庸置疑，开放对中国的宏观经济带来了诸多积极影响，但不容忽视的是，在经济开放大环境下，国际金融市场风险可以在世界范围内迅速转移和传播。那么，经济开放所致的持有国际金融资产的机会成本因素如何影响中国货币需求？目前鲜有文献系统讨论这一问题。在宏观经济的实证研究中，货币需求模型的成熟性是有广泛共识的，其主征在于相对长期的时不变性。近年来，随着经济开放进程，货币需求模型中所考虑的持币成本变量不仅来自本国经济，还扩展到国际经济。在开放经济下，单一的美元利率或日元利率不足以代表国外机会成本变量。因此，本文将货币需求模型中代表国际机会成本的理论变量设为潜变量，该潜变量的测度可以从大量国际金融指数综合加总生成。如何构造出能测度该潜变量的综合指标，从而估算由经济开放引起的国际金融对我国货币需求的影响，是本文要解答的问题。具体地，该问题包含两个方面：在中国这样一个有着持续稳健的金融政策且以国内经济需求为主导的经济大国，国际金融市场对中国的

---

* 原文刊载于《金融研究》2021年第9期。

　　作者简介：秦朵，经济学博士，荣誉教授，伦敦大学亚非学院；卢珊，经济学博士，讲师，中央财经大学统计与数学学院；王惠文，工学博士，教授，北京航空航天大学经济管理学院；Sophie van Huellen，经济学博士，讲师，伦敦大学亚非学院；王庆超，经济学博士，数据科学家，Expedia Group。

货币需求是否存在某种规律性的总体影响？如果存在，其影响程度、形式及金融市场的构成和地理区域来源又如何？

自2008年国际金融危机以来，不少学者认识到在传统的宏观经济学框架中，尚缺乏既能充分代表金融市场，又能匹配实体经济宏观变量的总量指标。如何利用模型构造金融市场的总指数，从而提高宏观模型的精度，成为研究热点。目前计量经济学中利用模型构造金融总量指标最常用的方法是主成分分析法，或与其类同的因子分析法。用该类方法生成的指标，其主要弱点是缺乏指数构成的时不变性。Qin等（2018）从方法论的角度反思，指出金融总量指标的构造属于综合指数构造的范畴，按照测度理论中的因果关系应被划为复合型测度一类。而主成分或因子分析法却仅适用于构造反映型测度类的指标。从变量降维的角度看，构造复合型测度类综合指数要求的条件比构造反映型测度指标更复杂，而且构造后者所通用的共方差最大要求并不适用于构造金融总量指标。

本文研究是对Qin等（2018）的进一步扩展。首先，从底层金融指标的选取上，本文把范围扩展到国际金融市场。其次，本文探讨了分步骤的变量降维方法，即依次通过无监督和有监督两个步骤实现降维，生成综合指数。与基于实体宏观经济的变量相比，本文选取的M_1不仅受国际金融市场的冲击更为直接，且与应对金融市场冲击的宏观政策研究需求关系更为密切。最后，将生成的综合指数称为CIFI（Composite International Financial Indices）。本文根据货币模型的动态特征构造了长期和短期两种CIFI，并将这两种指数引入M_1需求模型，作为国际机会成本的理论潜变量的可观测替代变量。模型使用月度数据，样本期为1993年9月至2015年6月。

本文发现，在M_1需求模型中，本文构造的CIFI指数在过去的20多年中一直是统计显著的。其中，短期CIFI指数的回归系数一直保持较强的时不变性，即使是在2008年国际金融危机的冲击下也是如此。长期

CIFI 回归系数的时不变性相对较弱，体现在金融危机前和危机过后两个时间段。这意味着，央行针对金融危机实施一揽子计划的应急措施，主要阻断了来自国际金融市场的长期非均衡风险。总的来看，只要经济开放，国际金融市场总体对中国 M_1 需求具有规律性的影响。从两种 CIFI 指数的构成结构看，短期 CIFI 中金融风险的主要来源是货币市场、银行业、期货市场及股票市场，对长期债券市场的作用甚微。而在长期 CIFI 中，长期债券市场的作用则显著得多。从金融风险前导性的角度看，期货市场和货币市场的指标往往比其他市场的指标更具前导性。从地理区域的角度看，虽然美国、西欧、日本等地的权数较大，但其他地区的指标也不容忽视。这充分表明，任何一两个国家的利率远不足以代表国际持币成本。此外，不少指标的权数及其构成结构都具有一定的时不变性，这为国际金融风险的监控提供了有效信息，也有望为货币政策的制定提供新的统计分析与预测工具。

  本文构造的 CIFI 的算法框架为决策者提供了实用的数据分析工具，通过利用分步骤的指标降维所构造的综合指数来扩展现有的宏观模型，建模者就可考察和评价国际金融市场不同指标对不同宏观目标的直接关联度，用其监控来自不同地区和市场的外部金融冲击，并实时评估其总体风险。本研究为利用模型监测国际金融市场影响宏观经济提供了新的思路，且算法框架能拓展到更多领域，比如在国际经济学中存在大量的国际宏观潜变量，这些潜变量的构造也可以借鉴分步骤的指标降维思路。

中国制造业与房地产业协调发展的测度与判断*

皮建才 宋大强

  目前，我国制造业的高端化发展已成为必然，而制造业的发展需要生产性服务业和生活性服务业的高效配合。总体而言，生产性服务业与制造业的总体耦合协调度发展趋势良好，房地产业作为生活性服务业的重要组成部分，其与制造业的耦合协调度将直接影响着我国制造业转型升级的进程。数据显示，2004—2016年，我国35个大中城市的商品房平均销售价格均实现了大幅度增长，其中，20个大中城市房价的年均增长率超过10%[①]。然而，房地产市场的快速发展却给制造业企业的生存带来了巨大的成本压力。比如，有的企业难以承受高企的用地成本，为了生存而不得不向外寻求大规模、成本低廉的工业用地。值得强调的是，房地产业的发展常常是以制造业的高度发展为前提，一旦经济体内的制造业企业长期缺失，房地产业的发展将会变得不可持续。既然制造业的发展离不开房地产业的支撑，房地产业的发展也需要制造业的带动，那么两产业是否实现了良性协调发展？本文尝试对制造业与房地产业的协调发展情况进行测度与判断，从而为制定出两产业良性互动的政策提供参考。

---

* 原文载于《金融研究》2021年第9期。
  作者简介：皮建才，经济学博士，教授，南京大学经济学院；宋大强，经济学博士研究生，南京大学经济学院。
① 相应数值由作者计算得出，原始数据来自《中国房地产统计年鉴》。

本文手动搜集了2004—2016年我国各省（区、市）29个细分制造业与房地产业方面的数据，基于耦合协调度模型对样本年份中制造业与房地产业的耦合协调度进行测算。同时，本文借助投入产出表分别测算了制造业对房地产业的总带动效应和房地产业对制造业的总带动效应，通过比较制造业与房地产业对彼此的总带动效应来判断制造业（房地产业）是否为房地产业（制造业）的主要关联行业，进而尝试从内在机制上找出两产业的最佳耦合度，并运用面板门槛回归方法推算出制造业与房地产业最佳耦合协调度的取值范围。进一步地，本文还通过实证检验的方法考察了制造业与房地产业的协调发展对全要素生产率和经济增长率的影响。此外，考虑到在中国房地产业发展过程中，我国相继出台了一系列房地产调控政策，本文进一步将调控政策作为外部冲击，使用渐进式双重差分法分析了外部冲击对制造业与房地产业耦合度的影响。

结果表明，两产业的互动程度不断增强，由2004年的失调发展上升到2016年的良好协调发展；分区域研究发现，中西部地区制造业与房地产业的耦合协调度略高于东部地区；东中西部地区房地产业的总体发展水平均于2012年前后超过制造业。此外，在投入产出表的42个行业中，制造业是房地产业的主要关联行业，但房地产业却不是制造业的主要关联行业。换言之，当制造业对房地产业的关联程度与房地产业对制造业的关联程度相接近时，两产业的相互依赖程度才有可能达到理想状态，即两产业的耦合度达到最佳。计量结果表明，东部地区制造业与房地产业协调发展的过程中会产生一些负面的经济影响。面板门槛模型的实证结果表明，当制造业与房地产业的耦合协调度处于0.64至0.71之间时，两产业耦合协调度的上升既有助于全要素生产率的提升，也有利于经济增长率的上升。此外，对于房地产过度发展地区而言，限购政策改善了地区内制造业与房地产业的耦合度。

基于以上结论，本文得出以下三点政策启示：第一，制定产业政策时，需要充分考虑制造业和房地产业对彼此的带动效应。第二，加强市场监管，为制造业与房地产业的健康发展营造有利环境。作为服务业的重要组成部分，房地产业的健康、稳定发展能为制造业的发展提供有效的物质保障，同时也有利于提升其与制造业的互动效率，促使两产业的耦合协调度保持在一个较高的水平。第三，限购政策的推行不宜采取"一刀切"的方式，否则会损害制造业与房地产业良性协调发展所带来的积极经济效应。对于经济发展水平高的东部地区城市而言，限购政策的重点可放在"限制各种名目的炒房和投机性购房"之上；对于经济发展水平低的中西部地区城市而言，可因地制宜地实施限购政策，引导房地产业发挥出积极作用，实现制造业与房地产业的良性协调发展。

本文的创新点主要有四个方面。其一，已有研究往往围绕着房地产市场价格对制造业的影响展开，很少关注制造业与房地产业的协调发展情况，而本文在这一方面进行了突破。其二，廓清了制造业与房地产业的互动机制。其三，尝试从内在机制上找出两产业的最佳耦合度。其四，探讨了房地产限购政策这一外部冲击对两产业耦合度的影响。

未来研究的一个拓展方向是，如果能够获取发达国家的制造业与房地产业数据，可对发达国家制造业与房地产业的耦合协调度进行测度。通过对比国内外制造业与房地产业协调发展情况，进一步论证产业间的良性互动对经济高质量发展的重要性。

02　金融稳定与风险防范

对金融风险传染机制的定量研究[*]

——基于中国上市银行数据的模拟

马 骏 何晓贝

后疫情时代，全球债务占GDP比重大幅攀升，防范系统性金融风险将是各国监管机构的长期任务。研究显示，金融风险传染是一个小的冲击演化成系统性金融风险的关键。然而在实践中，银行压力测试是静态的，并不考虑金融风险在金融机构之间的传染，因而很可能低估一个小的冲击造成的后果。2008年国际金融危机后许多国家的央行投入大量资源开展金融风险传染机制方面的研究，尤其是构建涵盖金融风险传染的宏观审慎压力测试模型。但针对我国金融机构之间风险传染的研究非常有限，现有文献大多集中在对金融市场交易和价格数据的实证分析，而对金融机构之间的金融风险传染机制的研究少且过于简化。如果缺乏对机构间风险传染机制的模拟和压力测试，决策机构就难以预判潜在的风险点及风险传染路径，也就难以制定有效的审慎监管政策来防范危机或在危机中及时进行政策干预。

为填补这个研究空白，本文基于31家中国上市银行的资产负债表数据，对银行系统资产抛售传染的过程进行沙盘推演，考察价格渠道形成

---

[*] 原文刊载于《金融研究》2021年第9期。
作者简介：马骏，经济学博士，兼职教授，北京大学国家发展研究院；何晓贝，经济学博士，北京大学国家发展研究院。

的金融风险传染机制。与现有文献相比，本文的贡献主要体现在三个方面。首先，根据我国银行间交易的特征纳入了多种可能被抛售的债券资产，基于中国债券市场的微观数据测算各资产的需求曲线，为解释银行的抛售行为提供了基础。其次，在资产分类的基础上，建立了银行的最优行为方程，分析银行的资产负债表结构和金融资产特性对银行抛售行为的影响，弥补了现有文献中微观基础不足的问题。最后，探讨银行面临资本充足率不足条件下的金融风险传染机制，有助于决策机构在风险发生初期识别风险的性质和可能的后果。

本文将银行由于偿付能力降低而去杠杆的过程抽象为资本充足率监管指标的硬约束引发的资产负债表收缩。模型概况如下：在资本充足率不达标的情况下，银行需要抛售资本占用的资产来满足监管规则要求。银行根据多个因素选择抛售哪些资产及各类资产的抛售量。资产抛售引发资产价格下跌，不同资产的价格变化由抛售量和资产市场深度决定。对于按公允价值计价的资产项目，持有同类资产的其他银行也会面临资产价格下降、资本减计的影响。由于公允价值变动的损失，初始期以后也可能有银行因为资本充足率不足而开始资产抛售，导致资产价格进一步下跌。如此循环，直到达到新的价格均衡点。

本文的重点是刻画银行在约束条件下的最优抛售行为。银行的目标函数是选择各类资产的抛售量来最小化抛售造成的损失。资产抛售的损失由公允价值变化损失和投资损失两部分构成。约束条件是资本充足率，即保证在抛售之后的预期资本金规模达到监管要求。本文将银行持有的资产按照风险权重和流动性的角度分为利率债、同业存单、票据及信用债四类，分别估算它们的市场深度和价格弹性。

银行在选择抛售资产的类型和抛售量时主要受以下几个因素的影响：首先，资产的风险权重。在其他条件不变的情况下，出售风险权重越高的资产越有助于提升资本充足率。其次，资产需求曲线。在其他条件不变的情况下，资产价格弹性越大，投资收益损失和公允价值计价损失越大。最后，银行的资产负债表结构。在其他条件不变的情况下，银行在公允价值计价的会计项目中持有某类资产的余额越大，抛售该资产形成的损失也就越大。以上三种因素的共同作用构成银行的最优抛售行为。

为了便于各年数据之间的横向比较，本文假设银行的资本充足率"监管要求"从原有的基础上提升一个百分点。从模拟的结果可以得到以下几个结果：第一，可以看出金融风险传染的路径。传统的银行压力测试是静态的，只能显示冲击后的直接效应。本文考虑了金融风险传染，可以动态展示随后几期的效应，即金融演化的过程。第二，可以看出银行选择抛售资产的逻辑。在面临资本充足率约束时各银行选择抛售的资产中票据的抛售量最大，其次是信用债，最后是同业存单，而利率债没有遭到抛售。银行不抛售利率债的原因是利率债的风险权重为零，抛售利率债对于提升资本充足率没有帮助。信用债和票据的风险权重一样，但票据的流动性显著高于信用债，因此银行抛售票据的规模显著高于信用债。第三，可以看出银行最优行为加剧风险传染的机制。尽管各个银行均预期票据市场深度较高、抛售不会造成明显折价，但事实上所有银行的最优行为加总造成了票据抛售量最高，票据价格跌幅更甚于信用债。

为了对我国银行业的稳健性有更全面的观察，本文基于2017—2019年的数据分别进行模拟，得到以下几个结论：第一，在同样的资本充足率冲击下，2017年银行资本充足率在初始期不达标的个数最高，其次是2018年，最后是2019年。这表明整体而言银行的资本充足率水平在逐年上升。第二，除了冲击在初始期造成的直接效应强度不同，各年风险传染的强度也是递减的。从各类资产市场深度的变化趋势来看，2017—2019年资产的市场深度逐渐增大的情况显著改善了金融风险传染效应。第三，金融风险的传染呈非线性。例如，2017年的模拟结果显示，在第4期、第5期时抛售已有收敛趋势，但第6期又有所扩大。

综合上述模拟结果，本文得出以下结论和政策含义。第一，债券市场深度是影响金融风险传染效应的重要因素。2017—2019年，随着我国金融市场深度的提升，金融风险传染的效应有所降低，即在这三年里银行系统的稳健性有所提高。第二，由于信息不对称，单个银行的最优行为加总后可能成为放大风险传染的因素。这体现在银行均选择抛售流动性好的资产，反而造成该资产的价格下跌幅度更大，对持有同类资产的银行造成公允价值计价损失。第三，金融风险的演化呈非线性。金融风险的演化过程取决于多种因素，包括银行的资产结构分布。实践中很难判断金融风险什么时候开始、什么时候结束，这对于选择宏观审慎政策的实施和退出的时机带来了很大挑战。因此，对于监管当局而言，探索有效的工具以识别风险发生的信号和判断危机的阶段都至关重要。第四，建立动态的、模拟金融风险传染的宏观审慎压力测试至关重要。从模拟结果可以看出，静态的银行压力测试模型只能看到冲击发生期的直接效应，无法预判随后几期的金融风险传染效应，这会大大低估对风险的评估。

流动性幻觉与高杠杆率之谜*

张成思 刘泽豪 何 平

党的十九届五中全会对建立现代财税金融体制提出了明确要求，特别是对不断健全防范化解重大风险的体制机制做出了重大部署，凸显了党中央对于切实维护金融稳定、坚决守住不发生系统性风险底线的高度重视。经济运行过程中杠杆率过高是触发系统性风险的潜在因素，厘清我国高杠杆率问题的根本性成因，并找到这一问题的有效解决方案，对于落实在金融体系中"堵漏洞、强弱项，下好先手棋、打好主动仗"的要求，切实提高经济发展质量和资源配置效率，具有重要现实意义。

在信用货币体系下，中央银行行使货币发行职能。从表面上看，信用货币体系下经济运行所需的流动性似乎完全归结于中央银行。一种普遍的看法是，流动性不足问题（即在需要购买商品和服务时没有足够的货币）可以通过中央银行发行名义货币得到解决。按此逻辑，信用货币体系下似乎不应存在明显的流动性不足和高杠杆率问题。然而从实际情况看，信用货币体系下债务（贷款）占比居高不下形成经济体的高杠杆率现象普遍存在，传统货币理论对此难以给出合理且令人信服的解释。

针对中国近年来的杠杆率上升问题，已有研究尝试从宽松的宏观政策、政府隐性担保、市场竞争环境下银行对国有企业的软预算约束等角

---

* 原文刊载于《金融研究》2021年第7期。
作者简介：张成思，经济学博士，教授，中国人民大学财政金融学院、中国财政金融政策研究中心；刘泽豪，经济学博士，副教授，中国人民大学财政金融学院；何平，经济学博士，教授，清华大学经济管理学院。

度寻找答案。然而，基于类似视角的研究却并未得到一致结论。这意味着有必要深入理论层面对杠杆率形成的本质原因进行阐释。

为此，本文从经典货币理论出发，研究信用货币体系下流动性不足问题的本质及其影响，阐释流动性不足与经济中的高杠杆率相伴而生并非巧合，而是因为流动性不足驱动了高杠杆率（过度投资带来的借贷冲动）。流动性不足指的是经济主体在需要购买商品或服务时没有足够的购买力。而在信用货币体系下，经济主体的购买力取决于所持有货币的真实价值，即真实购买力，因为商品和服务的卖方关心的是货币的真实价值而非名义数量。与此对应，流动性背后的价值支撑，也即名义货币发行的背后所对应的真实购买力，而非流动性的名义数量，是决定社会流动性充裕程度的关键。

从国家层面看，央行发行的货币是央行代表国家持有的负债，其价值由债务人未来的现金流及债务人为这项负债提供的担保决定。国家的财政收入就是债务人未来的现金流，而央行持有的储备资产就是债务人为负债提供的抵押品。因此，流动性的价值支撑由央行储备资产和政府财政收入共同决定。可以证明，流动性不足的问题主要来自流动性背后的价值支撑不足，而非仅是流动性的名义数量短缺。宽泛意义上的流动性泛滥本质上是流动性名义数量的泛滥所致，对应的投资过度和杠杆率过高看似是流动性的泛滥所致，本质上反而是流动性的价值支撑不足造成的。传统意义上的流动性不足经常被误解为名义货币量的短缺，从而希望能够通过扩张名义货币量来解决流动性不足问题。但这无法增加货币的真实购买力，因而难以解决因流动性不足而导致的高杠杆率困境。基于传统货币理论理解流动性供给问题时通常关注流动性的名义数量，因此可能会产生一种幻觉，即央行投放了大量流动性，而流动性不足及其带来的高杠杆率问题还是没有得到解决（消费者需要购买商品和服务时仍然没有足够的货币）。

流动性的价值支撑不足会导致杠杆率攀升,进而带来经济异常波动,增加风险隐患。随着经济增长和经济规模的扩大,社会所需要的流动性总量不断提高(交易规模不断扩大)。如果仅关注流动性的名义数量而忽略其背后的价值支撑,就可能会依靠扩张流动性的名义数量来满足社会日益增长的流动性需求。然而,由于流动性名义数量的增加并不能增加货币的真实购买力,因此流动性的价值支撑无法增加。相反,相对于流动性需求的提高,流动性背后的价值支撑反而下降,流动性缺口相应增加。这就是为何在信用货币体系下经济周期的扩张阶段也会出现流动性不足而触发风险。也就是说,经济快速增长伴随着流动性需求快速增加。如果流动性背后的价值支撑部分没有对应补充,流动性短缺问题可能进一步加重,从而造成杠杆率居高不下,甚至会引发流动性危机。

鉴于此,本文构建了信用货币体系下的偏好冲击和流动性冲击模型,从而推演出流动性的价值支撑与杠杆率形成机制之间的联系。与Diamond和Dybvig(1983)的经典理论相比,本文的贡献是将信用货币引入到消费者、银行及企业互动的三期模型中,从而进一步刻画流动性的价值支撑与经济杠杆率之间的逻辑联系。在本文的理论模型中,期限错配问题导致希望提前消费的消费者(即没有耐心的消费者)可能会受到流动性约束。在遭遇流动性冲击时,没有耐心消费者的购买力取决于货币供给所对应的流动性背后的价值支撑。当全社会流动性的价值支撑水平充足时,消费者拥有足够的真实购买力,社会最优资源配置可以实现。然而,当全社会流动性的价值支撑不足时,没有耐心消费者所持有的真实购买力受限,受到流动性约束,这限制了短期商品价格,提高了长期名义投资的相对收益率,激发了更多的长期投资。过度投资带来了借贷冲动,从而驱动了杠杆率升高。宽泛意义上的流动性充盈本质上是流动性的名义数量很多,对应的投资过度和杠杆率过高看似是流动性泛滥所致,本质上反而是流动性的价值支撑不足的反映。

本文对理解当前中国经济的杠杆率问题具有一定启示。特别是近年来，社会各界针对中国经济的杠杆率问题展开了热烈讨论，决策部门也实施了去杠杆、降杠杆和稳杠杆等对应的多种行政措施，但与此同时也面临着去杠杆带来了经济下行压力，一部分强制性去杠杆措施还可能会带来资源配置扭曲。因此，亟须深入机制层面更科学地探索高杠杆率的形成原因，对症下药，因情施策。基于本文研究结论，当流动性的价值支撑不足时，仅仅增加名义货币的数量无法解决流动性的价值支撑短缺而导致的高杠杆问题，反而可能引发通胀。只有增加发行货币所对应的储备资产的数量以增加流动性背后的价值支撑，才能解决流动性短缺困境，以更好地实现"十四五"期间加快构建新发展格局的战略目标。

地方政府隐性债务与城投债定价*

刘晓蕾　吕元稹　余　凡

随着地方政府债务规模的扩大，地方政府债务风险近年来成为监管者和投资者关注的焦点。根据2013年审计署所发布的《全国政府性债务审计结果》，截至2013年6月底，地方全部政府性债务（包含负有担保责任的债务和可能承担一定救助责任的债务）达到了17.89万亿元。但地方政府债务负担缺少系统性的衡量方法，这尤其体现在隐性债务为主的市级政府层面。与此同时，城投债这一混合企业债和市政债特征的债务工具品种具有较为特殊的性质。1994年《预算法》限制了地方政府凭借自身信用发行政府债券的能力，地方政府通过设立融资平台的方式发行了大量城投债。虽然城投债被普遍认为是含有政府隐性担保的，但隐性担保主体认定尚未有共识。

本文研究了地方政府隐性债务如何影响城投债定价，并进一步探讨市场认定的隐性担保主体的变化。首先，本文构建了地方政府隐性债务指标。地方政府融资平台的债务占市级政府隐性债务比重较大，但官方审计公布的债务数据尚未全面覆盖到地级市层面，于是本文根据发债企业公开披露的数据，通过加总地级市政府下属地方政府融资平台的全部有息债务来测度地方政府隐性债务总量。其次，本文通过将加总后的

---

* 原文刊载于《金融研究》2021年第12期。
  作者简介：刘晓蕾，金融学博士，教授，北京大学光华管理学院；吕元稹，会计学博士研究生，加州大学洛杉矶分校安德森商学院；余凡，金融学博士，教授，克莱蒙特麦肯纳学院。

地方政府下属融资平台有息债务总额分别除以地方政府预算收入、地方 GDP 和地方固定资产投资总额获得了衡量地方政府隐性债务负担率的三个指标。市级政府总隐性债务规模平均为年度地方政府一般预算收入的 3.02 倍，地方 GDP 的 32.91% 和地方社会固定资产投入的 56.23%。

在实证检验中，本文预测如果市场认为城投债价格中包含地方政府的隐性担保，城投债的利差应该与地方政府隐性债务负担率相关。与这一假说一致，实证结果显示，地方政府隐性债务负担率越高，当地城投债利差越高。这一结果在 2008 年 5 月至 2018 年 4 月城投债二级交易市场和一级发行市场样本中，以及加入、不加入发行主体固定效应的面板回归分析中均成立。

进一步地，本文通过时间维度的分析，探讨了市场中违约事件及政府政策变化是否带来投资者所认定的城投债隐性担保主体的变化。本文的结果显示，市场及投资者认定的市属城投债的隐性担保责任主体在时间维度上是从中央政府到市级政府，再到市级加省级政府变化的。

2011 年 4 月，云南省省级城投平台滇公路向债权银行发函表示本金无法兑付。虽然这一事件并非直接的城投债违约，并且事件最终在政府的协调下得以解决，但事件带来的投资人对城投债风险认知的潜在影响可能是巨大的。实证结果显示，地级市层面政府隐性债务负担率与当地城投债利差之间的关系在滇公路违约事件之前并不显著，而在事件之后则变得显著了。这一结果意味着在违约事件前，财政软预算约束使得市场较少考虑地方政府隐性债务风险的差异性，投资人理解的城投债隐性担保主体很可能是中央政府，因此并不关注发债主体所属地方政府的债务状况。而在违约事件后，投资者在城投债定价中开始普遍关注地方政府隐性债务负担率的信息，这时候市场所认为的城投债隐性担保的主体开始逐渐转变为城投债所属的市级地方政府。

2014 年 10 月，《国务院关于加强地方政府性债务管理的意见》（以下简称 43 号文）对外公布，明确了建立"借、用、还"相统一的地方政府债务管理机制，要求剥离融资平台的融资职能，建立规范的地方政府融资机制。43 号文意图厘清城投公司和地方政府的关系，同时明确了市级政府可以通过省级政府代为发行地方债用于置换其政府性债务。因此，我们预期该政策会把融资平台的部分债务转移至省级地方政府资产负债表内，省级政府的隐性债务负担率开始成为城投债定价的重要影响因素。实证结果与假说一致，省级政府隐性债务负担率对该省内市级城投债利差的影响在 43 号文之后变得显著。

2021 年 8 月，六部门发布的《关于推动公司信用类债券市场改革开放高质量发展的指导意见》特别提到了"健全定价机制，促进形成充分反映信用分层的风险定价体系"，地方债务融资从隐性化到显性化的规范是其中的重要改革内容。本文的研究显示这一改革方向有助于建立合理的风险定价体系。因隐性担保没有确定的法律约束力，其本身来自投资者对未来地方政府兜底的预期，市场预期的频繁改变会加剧市场价格的波动，不利于市场合理定价。而以地方政府为借债主体的地方债，化隐性担保为政府主体信用，将有助于建立合理分层的风险定价体系，从而提高市场的有效性，促进债券市场高质量发展。

政策连续性、非金融企业影子银行化与社会责任承担*

韩 珣 李建军

随着我国多元化影子信贷市场的发展，非金融企业部门也开始充当实质性信用中介，成为影子银行中介的参与主体。影子银行高杠杆、高风险和信息不对称较高等特点，使得参与影子银行活动的经济主体面临更高的现金流不确定性，加剧了虚拟经济与实体经济的风险联动性。基于此背景，探究非金融企业影子银行化的经济后果，对于抑制经济"脱实向虚"和防范系统性金融风险具有重要的理论和现实意义。

对非金融企业影子银行化的研究，已有文献从企业从事影子银行业务的业务机制、驱动因素和经济后果等角度展开（韩珣等，2017；王永钦等，2015）。从非金融企业影子银行化的经济效果来看，企业之间的金融漏损行为会进一步加剧金融资本配置不合理的现状，降低整个社会信贷资源的配置效率，从而导致社会生产效率和社会福利水平的双重损失（刘珺等，2014）。

然而，已有文献忽略了另一种可能性，即企业基于利润动机从事影子银行业务也会对企业社会责任承担产生影响。随着类金融资产与实体投资的回报率差距变大，企业履行社会责任承担的机会成本可能会提高。

---

* 原文刊载于《金融研究》2021年第9期。
作者简介：韩珣，经济学博士，讲师，北京第二外国语学院经济学院；李建军，经济学博士，教授，中央财经大学金融学院。

具体来看，如果能通过类金融投资业务获得较高回报，则企业通过履行社会责任提升业绩的动力将会减弱。因此，企业参与影子银行业务可能会弱化企业履行社会责任的意愿，影响其社会责任承担水平。已有研究表明，政策的调整会对微观企业行为和宏观经济运行等方面产生影响。然而，已有研究并未关注到政策连续性对非金融企业影子银行化与社会责任承担之间关系的影响。本文拟从这一方向作出探索性研究。

基于 2006—2017 年沪深两市 A 股非金融上市公司数据，本文剖析了非金融企业影子银行化对社会责任承担的影响，并进一步研究了两者之间的关系在市场套利动机、公司治理情况及外部融资能力不同企业中的表现。最后，本文进一步考察了政策连续性对非金融企业影子银行化与其社会责任承担之间关系的影响。

本文的贡献主要在于：其一，扩展了非金融企业影子银行化的研究范畴。与以往研究着重讨论企业影子银行业务的内在机制、识别方法、驱动因素及其对社会福利的影响等不同，本文探讨了非金融企业影子银行化对社会责任承担的影响。其二，丰富了政策连续性对微观企业行为的研究，试图验证政策连续性对非金融企业影子银行化与社会责任承担之间关系的影响机制。其三，本文进一步从金融与实体的相对风险和信号传递两条渠道，阐释了政策连续性程度的提高对企业影子银行业务与社会责任承担之间关系的影响。

本文研究发现，企业从事高风险、高收益的影子银行业务会抑制其社会责任承担，且这种负向关系在市场套利动机较强、公司治理水平较差及外部融资能力较弱的企业中更为显著。政策连续性程度的上升会减弱非金融企业影子银行化与社会责任承担之间的负向关系。其机制在于政策连续性程度的上升会通过金融投资与实体投资的相对风险和信号传递渠道，减弱非金融企业影子银行化对社会责任承担的负向影响。

本文研究不仅丰富了已有关于影子银行、非金融企业金融化等领域研究，对于提高政策连续性和平稳性、抑制经济"脱实向虚"及防范系统性金融风险集聚等也具有参考意义。有鉴于此，本文提出以下政策建议：第一，进一步加强非金融企业持有类金融资产的信息披露，增强公司财务报表透明度。第二，进一步完善公司治理结构，强化企业社会责任承担意识。第三，进一步增强政策的稳定性连续性，引导形成合理预期。第四，不断推进金融供给侧结构性改革，优化融资结构，加强对影子银行体系的功能性监管，引导金融更好地服务实体经济发展。

隐性杠杆约束、流动性风险和投资者情绪*

祝小全　陈　卓

2014年8月开始施行的《公开募集证券投资基金运作管理办法》针对固定收益类基金设定了140%的杠杆上限，对股票型基金的杠杆比例未有明确的限制。但是在投资实践中，股票型基金并未选择通过融资进行投资，甚至预留较高比例的现金（Boguth和Simutin，2018），以此应对赎回和预期外的投资机会。这种自主施加的零杠杆约束其实是一种"隐性"杠杆约束，使基金有动机在流动性收紧时，通过持有高市场风险头寸的股票而间接实现"隐性杠杆"。基于这一背景，我们利用2003—2019年以股票投资为主导的主动管理型开放式基金，探究其持仓的总市场风险暴露的经济含义。

具体而言，我们将所有股票型基金和偏股型基金看成一只假想的巨型基金，以持仓占比为权重，估算该基金投资组合中A股总市场风险头寸的时间序列。基于Brunnermeier和Pedersen（2009）的理论，流动性恶化时，额外一单位资金的获取成本上升，"合意杠杆"可能超过"可得杠杆"的上限，杠杆约束收紧而影响定价核，由此可以预期，这一序列背后隐藏着既定的流动性风险因子。整个基金行业持股的风险偏好反

---

*原文刊载于《金融研究》2021年第10期。
作者简介：祝小全，经济学博士，讲师，对外经济贸易大学金融学院；陈卓，金融学博士，副教授，清华大学五道口金融学院。

映了机构投资者所面临的隐性杠杆约束的松紧程度，也从侧面反映了整个资本市场的流动性强弱。

本文尝试检验不同资产对这一基于基金总市场暴露的流动性指标变动的敏感程度是否能够预测其收益。结果表明，隐性杠杆约束所隐含的流动性风险在股票和基金截面上的无条件定价失效，但是基于情绪和流动性区制的条件定价有效。具体而言，市场氛围较理性时，或流动性收紧时，对隐性杠杆约束敏感度较低（较高）的股票或基金，因在边际效用最大时产生较少（较多）支付而具有较高（较低）的流动性风险，由此投资者对其要求较高（较低）的期望收益作为风险补偿。对比之下，在高情绪期的区制内，这种风险与收益的权衡关系因卖空限制而失效。

结合自 2010 年 3 月开始的融资融券的分阶段试点，本文比较了隐性杠杆约束在融资融券标的与非融资融券标的两类股票中的定价效率。我们发现，对于非融资融券标的，其隐性杠杆约束的敏感度与其期望收益的负向关系表现出更大程度的扭曲。这一结果验证了我们前述关于条件定价的前提假设，即在高情绪的市场区制内，卖空限制形成隐性杠杆的紧约束，进而影响定价核。此外，考虑到相较于大盘基金，中小盘基金因在流动性收紧时具有更强的流动性偏好，我们将基金持仓的隐性杠杆约束进一步分解，发现小盘基金持股加权的总贝塔序列更能及时捕捉市场流动性收紧的风险。

稳健性分析主要从四个方面展开。其一，考虑到基金持仓占比可能被动变化，个股贝塔可能发生"漂移"，构造隐性杠杆约束的测度时引入滞后期来区分基金的主动决策和被动应对。其二，2006 年股权分置改革涉及限售股解禁，可能急剧改变股票流动性，而 2008 年金融危机和 2015 年股市剧烈波动前后，流动性螺旋形流失。为排除结果仅由极端期驱动的可能，剔除相应区间重复检验。其三，替换使用基于股吧发帖文本的看涨情绪指数或纳入市盈率的情绪指数，重新定义投资者情绪的高区制和低区制。其四，依据换手率定义流动性强、弱区制，主要结果均一致。最后，划分牛、熊市作为安慰剂检验。结果表明，流动性风险的定价不完全依赖于市场周期。

本文从两个方面拓展了文献。第一，利用基金持股明细构造了隐性杠杆约束的测度，验证其刻画市场流动性的合理性，为其赋予了丰富的经济意义。随着个人投资者市场参与度的提高及高频交易的引入，传统的换手率等指标在刻画流动性时的代表性可能有所减弱（Baker 和 Wurgler，2007）。从这个角度看，基金持股的总风险敞口通过捕捉机构投资者受杠杆约束的程度，释放了流动性是否充裕的信号。第二，探讨了非融资融券标的等显性约束与隐性杠杆约束之间的交互，为流动性风险的条件定价提供了直接证据。

须阐明的一点是，基金半年度的持仓披露可能导致估算持股风险敞口时存在信息损失，我们通过剔除橱窗粉饰动机较强的基金来缓解这一偏误，但是依然留下诸多值得探究的问题。比如，基金经理的择时能力及投资者的申购赎回是否系统性地影响基金持仓，再比如，基金的持股偏好是否会在高情绪的市场氛围中表现出羊群效应等，进而影响到定价效率。

本文的发现具有如下政策启示：一方面，在稳定市场的政策制定中，应将投资者情绪纳入考虑范畴。尤其是新冠肺炎疫情之后，资本市场进入相对宽松的流动性环境，关于机构资金持股"抱团"或"瓦解"的讨论未休。当市场分歧加剧，投资者更应谨防过度杠杆化的风险。另一方面，融资融券制度在一定程度上可缓解传统机构投资者面临的杠杆约束，改善定价效率。资本市场应致力于推进金融创新，壮大专业机构投资者的力量。

控股股东股权质押与高杠杆公司杠杆操纵 *

——基于我国 A 股上市公司的经验证据

许晓芳　汤泰劼　陆正飞

股权质押已成为中国资本市场一种普遍的融资方式，股东进行股权质押的上市公司及被质押的股权数量均不断增长。而股权质押尤其是高杠杆率公司的股权质押往往存在着较大的风险，一旦因股权质押公司的股价暴跌而触及平仓线，出质人不仅会面临巨大的偿债压力，而且很可能导致控股股东失去上市公司的控制权。因此，为避免股价暴跌导致触及平仓线，质押股权的控股股东往往具有强烈的动机驱使上市公司进行市值管理，并且他们也常常具备这种能力。而改变会计政策选择和调整公司信息披露行为，是上市公司进行市值管理的常用手段。

然而，已有研究主要聚焦于影响公司利润表信息质量（尤其是盈余信息质量）的市值管理行为，鲜有研究关注影响资产负债表信息质量的市值管理行为。实质上，控股股东出于自身利益，也可能使公司在股权质押后通过杠杆操纵掩盖坏消息，以降低债务违约风险和质押股份被强制平仓的风险。所谓杠杆操纵，是指利用表外负债和名股实债等财务活

---

* 原文刊载于《金融研究》2021年第10期。
　　作者简介：许晓芳，管理学博士，教授，北京工商大学商学院；汤泰劼，会计学博士生，北京大学光华管理学院；陆正飞，经济学博士，教授，北京大学光华管理学院。

动安排及其他会计手段,降低资产负债表呈现的杠杆水平的行为(许晓芳和陆正飞,2020),它是资产负债信息质量的一个较好的代理变量,杠杆操纵程度越高,则资产负债信息质量越差。许晓芳等(2020)提出"杠杆操纵"测度模型,研究发现公司会利用杠杆操纵降低公司所呈现的账面杠杆率以掩盖债务风险,特别地,那些高杠杆率公司更可能更大程度地进行杠杆操纵以降低账面披露的杠杆率水平。此外,2012年深交所与上交所公布的新退市制度方案,增加了公司净资产为负数(一年年末净资产为负数应提出退市风险警示,连续两年年末净资产为负数股票应暂停上市,连续三年年末净资产为负数股票应终止上市)等退市条件,从而使上市公司难以通过仅仅操纵利润就达到避免退市的目的。因此,为降低债务违约风险、避免因杠杆率指标被暂停上市或终止上市等原因而遭受控制权转移,那些进行了股权质押的高杠杆公司的控股股东往往具有强烈的动机驱使上市公司进行杠杆操纵。

那么,杠杆操纵究竟是否是那些控股股东股权质押的高杠杆公司进行市值管理的重要手段呢?鉴于此,本文聚焦于资产负债表信息,考察了高杠杆公司控股股东股权质押对杠杆操纵的影响,并在以下两方面对已有文献形成补充和扩展:一是丰富和拓展了杠杆操纵影响因素方面的文献。已有关于杠杆操纵影响因素的文献极少,且主要是从杠杆率、融资约束等公司特征角度进行研究,而本文从控股股东股权质押视角,实证检验了其对公司杠杆操纵的影响。二是拓展和深化了股权质押经济后果方面的文献。已有文献极少从资产负债表信息角度研究股权质押经济后果,而本文聚焦于资产负债表信息,从杠杆操纵这一视角研究了公司控股股东股权质押带来的影响,研究结果表明资产负债表信息操纵也是其导致的重要经济后果之一。相关分析得出了以下研究结论:其一是与未有控股股东股权质押的高杠杆率公司相比,控股股东股权质押的高杠杆率公司进行杠杆操纵的可能性更大,且控股股东股权质押比例越高的高杠杆率公司，杠杆操纵程度越大；其二是控股股东股权质押正向影响公司杠杆操纵的效应在成长性更差、短期偿债压力更大、媒体关注程度更高、股价崩盘风险更大的高杠杆率公司中更为显著。

根据上述分析结论，得到以下四方面政策启示：（1）应当防范控股股东股权质押后的杠杆操纵行为，特别是应重点关注成长性更差、短期偿债压力更大、媒体关注程度更高以及股价崩盘风险更大的高杠杆率公司；（2）应当进一步规范控股股东股权质押行为，特别是高杠杆率公司的控股股东股权质押行为，当这些控股股东股权质押比例越大时，他们越可能进行更多的杠杆操纵，因而监管部门应当重点关注质押比例高的控股股东质押行为；（3）应当关注股权质押融资中的杠杆操纵行为所带来的金融风险，警惕那些控股股东股权质押比例高的高杠杆率公司所隐瞒的债务风险，防范微观企业杠杆风险的不断累积而对宏观经济产生的不良影响，防范和化解系统性金融风险；（4）应当重视杠杆操纵等资产负债表信息操纵行为，加强对资产负债表信息质量的监管力度，而不能仅仅关注基于利润表信息的盈余操纵行为，从而防止社会有限的信贷资金流向隐瞒了高负债风险的出质人，有效提高信贷资源配置效率。

企业金融化与劳动收入份额变动*

罗明津　铁瑛

党的十九大报告指出，坚持在经济增长的同时实现居民收入同步增长、在劳动生产率提高的同时实现劳动报酬同步提高。既有研究普遍发现，劳动收入份额下降在20世纪80年代后已成为全球趋势，但基于2008年国际金融危机后的上市公司数据却显示，我国劳动收入份额在国际金融危机后并未显著下降，甚至表现出震荡上升的趋势。与此同时，伴随着危机后虚拟经济的持续膨胀及实体经济收益的下行，中国经济表现出经济金融化特征，在微观层面主要体现为实体企业金融化快速加深。同一观察期内，我们既发现上市公司劳动收入份额波动上升，又观察到企业金融化快速扩张。那么，一个直觉性的猜测是，中国新近出现并快速发展的企业金融化是否可能是2010年后劳动收入份额增长的重要原因？如果是，其发生机制是什么？是否具有可持续性？

既有研究也已经注意到了经济金融化与劳动收入份额之间的关系，有研究基于传统的宏观层面上直接探讨经济金融化对劳动收入份额的影响，也有研究基于微观企业层面进行了探讨，但一方面，既有基于微观企业层面研究全部基于发达国家样本，中国作为世界最大的发展中国家，仅基于发达国家样本的研究结论可能在中国不具有直接的适用性；另一

---

* 原文刊载于《金融研究》2021年第8期。

作者简介：罗明津，经济学博士，助理研究员，上海对外经贸大学国际发展合作研究院，上海交通大学上海高级金融学院；铁瑛，经济学博士，副研究员，上海对外经贸大学国际经贸研究所。

方面,完全基于发达国家样本也限制了既有研究的视线,他们均在"委托—代理"框架下基于自利的管理者为迎合股东利益或追求短期高额收益所做的经营决策调整来尝试解释企业金融化对劳动收入份额的影响。但显然,仅仅基于"委托—代理"框架不足以解释中国企业金融化与劳动收入份额之间的关系,更无法区分出中国企业金融化对劳动收入份额潜在的"盈利溢出"与"技术抑制"效应,因此,也就无法对企业金融化的潜在影响做出合理判断。

鉴于此,本文基于微观层面探讨了中国企业金融化对劳动收入份额的影响及作用机制,尝试在如下三个方面对既有文献做出边际贡献:第一,本文将经济金融化与劳动收入份额之间关系的研究拓展至微观层面。相比于其他基于发达国家微观企业样本的研究,本文立足于中国,提出并识别了企业金融化影响劳动收入份额的"盈利溢出"效应与"技术抑制"效应。本文结论有助于补充经济金融化与劳动收入份额关系的微观机制和经验证据。第二,既有研究往往缺乏对于企业金融化行为内生性的充分讨论,研究结论往往停留在相关关系层面,少数研究也尝试引入工具变量来克服上述内生性问题,但对于工具变量的合理性缺乏充分的讨论。本文尝试基于前沿的合成工具变量法克服企业层面的工具变量难题,基于管理层特征为企业金融化行为构造了合成工具变量,并对其合理性进行了一系列严格的检验,这不仅有助于进一步提升本文参数估计的精度和可信度,同时也证明了企业金融化与劳动收入份额之间的因果关系。此外,我们同时构造了金融化峰值事件,借助事件分析法进一步证实了它与劳动收入份额之间的因果关系。第三,本文跳出经典的"委托—代理"框架,从金融领域超额收益的角度识别了"中国式"企业金融化,这不仅有助于增进对于企业金融化行为的理解,同时结合本文所发现的两大机制,更具有现实价值。即企业金融化对我国劳动收入份额的拉动效应基于特定的超额收益背景,因此不仅是不可持续的,而且还可能会有长期损害，企业金融化所带来的经济"脱实向虚"更需要我们时刻警惕和防范。

　　本文基于国际金融危机后的2007—2017年A股上市公司样本，从微观层面探讨了企业金融化对劳动收入份额的影响及作用机制，相关分析得出了三个基本结论：一是我国企业金融化对劳动收入份额具有显著的正向作用。企业金融化一方面通过提升企业盈利对劳动收入份额增加产生贡献，即"盈利溢出"渠道，另一方面也通过对技术进步的抑制对劳动收入份额起到了显著的提升作用，即"技术抑制"渠道。二是企业高管的劳动收入份额获益显著小于普通员工，说明经典的"委托—代理"框架并不能有效地解释中国企业的金融化行为。三是企业金融化的影响和金融市场收益率具有强相关性，表明企业金融化的动力来自金融市场的收益激励。这意味着企业金融化看似是金融市场超额收益背景下的"理性选择"，但它对于劳动收入份额的拉动作用并不具有可持续性。

　　根据上述分析结论，得到以下政策启示：（1）应当客观、全面地认识企业金融化对劳动收入份额的作用。一方面，我们应当承认企业金融化确实为危机后劳动收入份额的提升产生了积极作用；另一方面，我们更需要清醒地认识到企业金融化拉动劳动收入份额并不是可持续和无条件的。企业金融化对劳动收入份额的正向影响依赖于金融市场的高收益率。（2）更加值得重视和警惕的是过度金融化和经济"脱实向虚"所带来的远期损害。金融市场收益率不会长期维持高位，而企业金融化对劳动生产率的负面抑制却实实在在地发生着。劳动收入份额提升的根本动力在于技术进步与合理分配，这就意味着，盲目依赖金融化拉动劳动收入份额提升只是饮鸩止渴，即便能在短期获得一定的纸面收益，从长期来看则是对经济增长潜力的挥霍。（3）因势利导，引导企业回归实体。一方面要在金融市场上加强金融监管，进一步规范金融主体行为，加大打击各种金融乱象，审慎监管金融衍生产品的过度创新；另一方面，在房地产市场上，继续坚持"房住不炒"的基本原则，促进房地产市场健康有序发展。此外，还需要引导并激发金融服务与实体投资的高度协同，继续推行鼓励创新的相关政策，落实实体投资的金融支持和保障，不断增强企业的投资信心。

03　绿色金融

环境税率、双重红利与经济增长*

牛 欢 严成樑

改革开放以来，我国经济高速增长也伴随着环境污染，"未富先污"的现象制约经济的可持续和高质量发展。污染导致环境疾病医疗负担和健康人力资本损失，"未富先污"叠加"未富先老"进一步加重了医疗负担，并可能面临着陷入"环境贫困陷阱"的风险。当前，中国经济已从高速增长阶段转向高质量发展阶段，更加强调经济增长与环境保护的相互协调，绿色发展成为高质量发展的内在要求。党的十九大报告指出，必须树立和践行绿水青山就是金山银山的理念，坚持节约资源和保护环境的基本国策，像对待生命一样对待生态环境。生态环境保护和经济发展是内在一致的，生态环境保护可以转化为现实生产力。环境污染已成为制约中国经济高质量发展的重要因素。如何兼顾经济发展不突破生态红线和环保治理不突破经济安全运行底线，实现"绿水青山就是金山银山"可持续发展模式，已是当务之急。

近年来，我国出台了一些重要举措。一方面，推动环保费改税。《中华人民共和国环境保护税法》自2018年1月1日起实施，环保部门对大气污染物、水污染物、固体废物和噪声等污染物征收环保税，有利于从源头上减少污染。另一方面，加大对环境污染治理的投入力度。根据国家统计局提供的数据，我国环境污染治理投资总额从2000年的1 060.7

---

* 原文刊载于《金融研究》2021年第7期。
作者简介：牛欢，经济学博士，中央财经大学经济学院；严成樑，经济学博士，教授，中央财经大学经济学院。

亿元增加到 2020 年的 10 638.9 亿元。环境经济政策并不单纯只有保护环境这单一目标，而应该包含实现经济增长的任务，因此，实现环境红利与经济发展红利的双重目标是环境税的价值所在。即要从环境和经济发展两方面来全面理解环境税收政策实施的效果。环境税对经济增长的影响仍存在争议，存在两个问题值得探讨：第一，面临经济增速变低和环境保护双重压力，探讨环境税是否能实现"双重红利"具有理论和现实意义。第二，面对"未富先污"叠加"未富先老"社会问题，环境税能否帮助摆脱"环境贫困陷阱"是值得研究的问题。

在此背景下，本文构建了一个包含环境税、污染存量和预期寿命的世代交替模型，研究环境税对环境红利和经济发展红利的影响。基于新古典增长模型的研究表明，环境税能够实现双重红利（环境红利和经济发展红利），这契合"绿水青山就是金山银山"的绿色发展理念。从传导机制看，环境税通过负收入效应使得资本积累下降，同时，环境税通过健康效应使得预期寿命延长，这又使得资本积累增加。环境税通过影响资本积累，进而影响环境质量和经济发展。此外，环境税率上升使得用于环境治理的政府支出增加，这使得经济更容易产生环境红利。基于内生增长框架的分析表明，环境税有助于摆脱"环境贫困陷阱"，这为解释国家之间的收入差距提供了一个参考机制。数值模拟结果显示，在新古典增长框架和内生增长框架下，均存在最优的环境税率可以极大化人均产出和经济增长率。

根据上述结论，本文政策建议主要包含以下几点：第一，经济中存在最优环境税率，过低的环境税率会使得环境污染恶化，而过高的环境税率又会抑制经济增长。2019 年我国环境税仅占总税收收入的 0.14%，现行环境税是污染费平移而定，低于当前国民经济在环境保护上所支付的成本水平。OECD 数据显示，2019 年 OECD 国家中欧洲与环境相关的税收收入占 GDP 的比重为 2.245%；2019 年中国与环境相关的税收收入占

GDP 的比重为 0.59%。结合我国经济发展现实，我们认为可适度提高我国的环境税率。具体地，制定设计差别化税率时应统筹考虑当地的环境承载能力、污染现状和经济社会发展，重点提高高污染和高碳排放行业的环境税率，以实现减污降碳协同治理目标。第二，根据污染积累方程设定，污染取决于治理投入、清洁生产技术和环境治理技术的进步，涉及如何激励技术革新与应用及调整产业结构降低产出排污系数。一方面，推进产业优化升级。利用财税、投资和金融政策来遏制"两高一低"项目盲目发展，推动传统产业优化升级，加快工业领域绿色转型。同时，推动新兴技术与绿色低碳产业融合，不断提高绿色产业比重。另一方面，加快绿色低碳科技革命。补贴绿色低碳技术研发和推广应用的企业，将其社会收益内部化为企业私人收益，激励绿色低碳技术创新与应用。完善绿色低碳技术评估、交易体系，加快创新成果转化。推动能源革命，大力发展新能源的同时严格合理控制煤炭消费增长，在安全稳定基础上，逐步利用新能源替代传统能源来降低污染排放系数，实现减污降碳协同发展目标。第三，污染造成居民健康损害，如空气污染会增加患有心肺疾病的风险（Chay 和 Greenstone，2005）；Chen 等（2013）以中国南北方冬季供暖政策为准自然实验，研究发现更高的悬浮微粒导致北方居民平均预期寿命缩短。Ebenstein 等（2015）指出空气污染是中国预期寿命增长低于预期的主要原因。应考虑增加公共健康支出，以降低环境污染对健康和福利的负面影响。

环境规制、融资约束与企业污染减排*

陈诗一　张建鹏　刘朝良

"十四五"规划提出建设人与自然和谐共生的现代化,这要求持续推进污染减排促进经济绿色低碳转型,实现环境与经济协同发展。环境规制是解决环境污染问题的首要制度安排。通过对环境污染排放的外部性进行干预,环境规制弥补了市场机制的不足,提高了排污企业恶化环境质量的成本,促使企业进行污染减排。一般而言,企业可以采取污染治理与压缩产出两种方式减排。企业不同减排方式选择不仅会导致减排效果差异,对企业产出也存在不同影响。当企业通过减产方式减排,企业生产经营将遭受直接冲击,宏观经济可能出现较大波动;而当企业进行积极的污染治理消解环境资源成本上升压力时,企业产出调整的压力减少,经济运行可避免出现较大波动。因此,为实现环境与经济协同发展,在推进污染减排过程中激发企业主动进行环境投资和污染治理至关重要。然而,由于企业污染治理,包括前端生产工艺改进及末端污染净化设施安装等,涉及大量的环境投资,而环境投资普遍具有周期长、前期收益低和风险大的特征(马骏和安国俊,2020),这导致在缺少金融部门支持下,单凭企业内部融资进行环境投资将产生较大的现金流压力与经营风险,企业环境投资与污染治理的激励难以充分实现,因此,企业融资

---

* 原文刊载于《金融研究》2021年第9期。

作者简介:陈诗一,经济学博士,教授,复旦大学经济学院、复旦大学泛海国际金融学院;张建鹏,经济学博士,复旦大学经济学院;刘朝良,经济学博士,复旦大学经济学院。

约束会对企业污染治理、减排方式选择产生影响。当污染企业面临较强的融资约束时,企业可能发现进行环境投资与污染治理的成本较高,从而更倾向于采取减产方式减排,此时推进企业污染减排则会对实体经济产生较大冲击,进而影响经济发展与污染治理的综合效率。

当前我国的环境政策实践向市场激励型转变,环境保护税已全面开征,全国碳排放权交易市场也已开启。市场激励型环境规制能产生污染减排的经济激励,引导企业污染治理和技术创新,蕴含巨大的经济和环境红利。为激发环境规制的引导作用,在推进污染防治过程中,金融部门积极支持和引导十分关键。已有文献对环境规制与企业污染减排之间的关系进行了大量研究(李永友和沈坤荣,2008;郭俊杰等,2019),随着环境问题成为社会关注的焦点,金融发展或融资约束与企业环境表现、污染排放的关系也引起了学者的关注。现实中,我国中小企业普遍存在融资难、融资贵的问题,其中既有市场机制原因又有体制缺陷因素,可能对我国中小企业污染治理和环境规制效果产生影响。对此,结合上述理论分析与文献背景,本文使用倍差法和2004—2013年工业企业污染数据集,以2007年开始实施的排污费提高的环境规制为实证基础,考察我国排污企业污染减排行为及企业融资约束对企业污染减排所产生的影响和作用机制。本文的创新和贡献为:第一,本文从融资约束角度探讨影响环境规制政策效应和企业污染减排的因素,既丰富了现有关于环境规制效应和污染减排的文献,也为我国持续推进污染减排和绿色金融发展提供有益的政策启示;第二,本文研究设计具有一定创新性,使用微观企业污染数据集和倍差法进行研究,所用数据在已有文献中还较少使用,计量方法也有助于识别因果效应。

2007—2013年,我国共有12个省(区、市)将SO_2排污费征收标准从原来的0.63元/千克提高至1.26元/千克,提升幅度高达1倍。通过对企业污染排放、产出调整和污染治理等方面的分析,本文研究发现,排污费提高后，我国排污企业污染排放量大幅降低9.14%，与此同时产出也显著降低4.43%。异质性分析发现，不同规模和不同所有制企业之间表现出明显的减排行为和减排效果差异：大型企业和国有企业污染排放水平和排放强度显著下降，但产出未受显著影响。相反，中小企业和民营企业污染排放水平和排放强度未显著下降，产出受到显著负面影响。基于环境投融资角度的分析揭示，中小企业所面临的融资约束抑制了企业的污染治理，加剧企业的产出调整，最终削弱了企业污染减排效果。上述实证结果在控制住影响企业污染治理的规模和排放强度等混杂因素后仍然成立，表明研究结果具有稳健性。

  本文研究结论为推进经济绿色转型和发展绿色金融提供了有益政策启示：首先，持续推进企业污染减排以促进经济绿色低碳转型，既需要健全和严格执行环境规制，也需要金融部门发挥资金支持和引导作用，从而提升企业污染治理能力。其次，推动我国绿色金融发展，既需要补足我国金融系统的内部短板，缓解中小企业和民营企业的融资难、融资贵等问题，也需要提高绿色金融机构的业务开展能力。绿色金融支持企业污染治理既要避免"一刀切"地规避环境风险，也要防止部分企业的"洗绿"行为，这需要金融部门提高业务能力，包括完善绿色金融标准体系，规范绿色金融业务开展，从而有效鉴别和发现绿色投融资的机会和风险。由于绿色金融业务涉及多学科交叉领域，比如环境资产评估、风险评估和信用认证等，需要会计、咨询和资产评估等相关机构分工协作，发展绿色金融专业性中介服务机构和培育相关人才也很重要。

环境信息公开的绿色创新效应研究*

——基于《环境空气质量标准》的准自然实验

王 馨 王 营

伴随我国绿色低碳循环经济体系的建立健全，绿色创新已成为打好污染防治攻坚战、推进生态文明建设的主动力。为加快推动绿色创新，国家层面出台了《关于构建市场导向的绿色技术创新体系的指导意见》，其中明确指出，推动环境治理从末端应对向全生命周期管理转变。从利益主体来看，环境治理全生命周期管理的实现必须以政府主导为关键、以企业主体为根本、以社会组织和公众共同参与为支撑。为满足环境治理全生命周期管理的要求，加快推进大气污染治理、满足公众需求和提高政府公信力，环境保护部2012年发布了《环境空气质量标准》，并要求各地区根据实际情况和当地环境保护的需要在规定时间之前实施新标准。空气质量新标准实施后，各地空气质量监测实现了实时、无干扰、全覆盖以及直报，极大提高了地方政府环境治理不作为的机会成本，便利了社会公众的环境监督，提升了企业污染排放的惩罚概率。上述多方面压力促使作为创新主体的企业有强烈动机在全生命周期开展绿色技术创新。信息公开是推动绿色创新、促进减污降碳进而最终实现双碳目标

---

* 原文刊载于《金融研究》2021年第10期。
作者简介：王馨，经济学博士，山东财经大学金融学院；王营，经济学博士，山东财经大学金融学院。

的重要力量。

区别于现有命令型环境规制政策的理论文献,《环境空气质量标准》的实施提供了一个崭新视角,不拘泥于强制约束某一类环境利益相关者。该标准旨在监测空气质量状况,为所有环境利益相关者提供科学合理的环境利益诉求工具。同时,区别于现有文献从环境权益交易市场、低碳城市、环保目标责任制、排污收费以及环保补助等角度研究企业绿色创新,本文以《环境空气质量标准》的实施为准自然实验,从企业绿色创新角度分析空气质量新标准实施的微观影响,为宏观环境政策驱动企业绿色创新提供新的理论证据。

本文主要研究思路分为以下三个部分:

一是通过梳理环境规制影响企业创新等文献,结合推动绿色创新发展实践的政策需求,提出针对环保政策与企业创新关系的研究假设。当实施空气质量新标准后,高环境风险企业的绿色创新表现更加积极;地区环保执法越严格,在实施空气质量新标准后,高环境风险企业的绿色创新表现越好;社会公众监督越积极,在实施空气质量新标准后,高环境风险企业的绿色创新表现越好,以降低公众"愤怒成本";媒体监督越积极,在实施空气质量新标准后,高环境风险企业的绿色创新表现越好,以降低被曝光的负面效应。

二是基于以上研究假设,以2007—2017年所有A股上市公司为研究对象,以2012年《环境空气质量标准》的分地区实施为准自然实验,利用多期DID方法对比性地分析了该环境政策实施前后高环境风险行业和低环境风险行业的绿色创新表现差异。研究发现,《环境空气质量标准》实施后,高环境风险行业的绿色创新表现更加积极,既体现在绿色创新数量,也体现在绿色创新质量方面。经过一系列稳健性检验后,上述结论依然成立。通过异质性检验发现,《环境空气质量标准》的绿色创新促进作用在国有企业和非专利密集型企业更加显著。进一步研究发现,随着环境执法力度、公众监督和媒体监督积极性的提高,《环境空气质量标准》的绿色创新效应更加显著;同时,这种绿色创新效应显著改善了当地空气质量。

三是在实证基础上,基于提升环境规制政策效率、增进绿色创新等方面提出政策建议。首先,加强和健全环境规制体系,分类提升环境规制水平。目前我国的环境政策体系尚不完善,即使出台了以促进环境信息透明度为目的的环境治理新标准,仍未能达到环境规制强度水平。基于文中的实证检验,宏观环境政策对高环境风险的企业绿色创新产生正向影响,对于低环境风险的企业绿色创新几乎没有影响。建议根据企业生产经营活动的行业差异化特征制定不同的环境规制政策,对以重工业、轻工业和服务业主导的行业企业应区别对待。此外,应完善环境规制体系和法律体系,建设促进企业转型升级的制度框架,增强绿色创新的制度保障。其次,推动数字技术辅助环境规制对绿色创新的正向激励作用。实施创新驱动发展战略,从内容、技术、模式等各方面提高绿色创新的能力。特别是作为绿色创新的重点环节,从技术层面提升绿色创新的效率尤为重要。例如,以加快绿色创新为目的,部署大数据、云计算、人工智能等先进数字技术在污染产业领域的应用,降低创新成本,提升创新效率,从而激发企业绿色创新潜力,形成更多转型升级的新增长极,增强发展新动能。最后,建立环境规制对企业绿色创新的系统性评估体系。为方便企业和监管者充分掌握绿色创新内容,审慎处理创新过程中可能遇到的复杂问题及不确定性,有必要建立一整套绿色创新的评估制度,增强执行规制政策的前瞻性。

本文主要贡献体现在以下方面:首先,从微观企业绿色创新视角评估了宏观环境政策的有效性,为现有环境规制政策效果研究提供新视角。从制度经济学视角,丰富了宏观环境政策与微观企业行为领域的理论研究。其次,创新性地将《环境空气质量标准》和绿色创新置于同一理论框架,拓展和丰富了企业绿色创新影响因素的相关文献。最后，分析了环保执法、公众监督和媒体监督的调节效应，以及产生的环境效应，这为进一步调动企业环境治理积极性、建立健全绿色低碳循环发展经济体系提供了有益借鉴。

金融政策与经济低碳转型：
基于增长视角的研究*

潘冬阳　陈川祺　Michael Grubb

为实现经济的绿色低碳转型，同时防范环境、气候问题带来的金融风险，我国及世界上许多经济体，近年来纷纷使用金融政策加以支持，即制定"绿色金融政策"。绿色金融政策一般指能够对绿色投融资活动形成激励促进、对非绿色投融资活动形成约束限制，或旨在防范环境、气候相关金融风险的公共政策。

倡导人与自然和谐共处的碳中和目标逐渐成为全球共识，可以预期，绿色金融政策未来会得到进一步发展。然而，与实践中政策快速发展不相称的是，一个最基本的理论议题——"金融政策与实体经济低碳转型之间的关系"，暂未得到充分的理论性探讨。特别是，从经济学"理论模型"上我们尚不十分清楚：（1）金融因素是否及如何影响经济的低碳转型？（2）金融政策能对经济低碳转型起到哪些作用及产生作用的机制是什么？（3）相较于其他绿色经济政策，绿色金融政策的优缺点是什么？如何与其他政策组合搭配？（4）在后疫情时代，金融政策在经济"绿色（低碳）复苏"中将扮演怎样的角色？

为从理论上回答这些问题，本文参考 Acemoglu 等（2012）与 Chu 和

---

* 原文刊载于《金融研究》2021年第12期。
　作者简介：潘冬阳，经济学博士，讲师，中国人民大学应用经济学院；陈川祺，博士研究生，中央财经大学金融学院；Michael Grubb，哲学博士，教授，伦敦大学学院可持续资源研究所。

Cozzi（2014）的做法，将绿色金融相关因素纳入主流宏观经济学的"内生增长"框架，建立了一个适用于分析绿色金融政策问题的经济学理论模型。该模型包含清洁与非清洁（异质性）生产部门、定向技术进步、金融约束与金融政策等新的特征要素。

基于该模型，我们首先通过提出并证明四个理论命题，阐释金融约束对经济低碳转型的潜在影响及金融政策支持转型的作用和机制。其次，采用静态数值模拟的方式，分析对比绿色金融政策与部分财政政策的效果，研究不同政策间组合搭配的方式。最后，在模型中引入疫情冲击，动态模拟分析不同政策情景下经济转型与复苏路径，从而发掘后疫情时代金融政策的角色，并为政策施行提供有益建议。

通过模型推导与数值模拟，我们发现：第一，清洁部门相对非清洁部门若有更强的金融约束，则会推迟经济低碳转型过程，造成环境恶化；绿色金融政策能够缓解清洁部门的金融约束。第二，绿色金融政策可通过直接降低企业金融成本的机制，在短期暂时性地提高清洁部门的产量；如果清洁技术与非清洁技术之间的差距不大，绿色金融政策还可以带来"朝向清洁的技术进步"（即通过提高清洁部门的研发报酬，激励研发人员从非清洁部门转移到清洁部门，推动清洁部门技术的进步），从而在长期内增加清洁部门的产量及其占经济的比重，促进经济实现低碳转型并阻止环境恶化。第三，与特定财政政策工具（包括对清洁机器的补贴、对清洁中间产品的补贴、对清洁技术研发活动的补贴）相比，绿色金融政策在支持经济低碳转型上具有一定的成本效益优势，其能够在花费较低政策成本时带来较高的政策效果。但遗憾的是，金融政策的强度一般有上限（以使"零利率下限"不被突破），因此其效果可能无法像部分财政政策一样可随着政策成本投入的增加而不断提高。考虑到不同政策的优劣势，绿色金融政策可以与清洁技术补贴等财政政策进行组合搭配，以发挥不同政策间的互补作用，降低政策的整体成本，提高整体效果。第四，新冠肺炎疫情冲击可能会推迟经济低碳转型的进程。但如果在疫情后的经济恢复期，适当提高绿色金融政策的力度，则可以在基本不改变政策成本的情况下，将"碳达峰"的时间与低碳转型的路径拉回到没有疫情冲击的情况，实现绿色复苏。实际上，在疫情后如果进一步加大绿色金融政策的力度，还有可能以相对平时更低的成本将碳达峰的时间提前，加快经济低碳转型的进程。

上述这些发现，除了在理论层面回答了关于"金融政策与实体经济低碳转型之间关系"的多个问题，也在实践层面对制定"绿色金融政策"有着多重的现实含义。第一，鉴于金融政策在经济低碳转型中的潜在作用，应继续发展绿色金融政策，并着重探索能够切实减轻绿色（清洁）企业融资约束、降低其金融成本的政策工具。人民银行所推出的"碳减排支持工具"与"支持煤炭清洁高效利用专项再贷款"便是其中的典型代表，可进一步深化研究应用。第二，财政部门可适当安排资金，优先支持绿色金融政策的实施，从而以更低政策成本实现更高的潜在政策效果。第三，金融监管部门与财政部门可以将绿色金融政策与绿色相关财政政策工具进行组合搭配，以提高整体政策效果，发挥政策工具间的互补作用。第四，疫情冲击为加快经济低碳转型提供了机会，政策制定部门可在疫情恢复期强化绿色金融等政策力度。

关于绿色金融政策的理论研究，在当前仍有巨大的需要。仅就本文而言，可以在多个方向进行扩展，例如：（1）探讨最优动态政策（及政策组合）的路径。（2）引入更多财政政策（如税收）、气候（环境）政策（例如排放总量控制），分析更多可行的政策组合方式。（3）引入更多气候环境经济学建模中的重要特征要素，如减排技术、临界点（Tipping point）、惯性等，从而更精确地描述经济与环境的动态。（4）引入更多宏观经济与金融学建模中的重要特征要素，如显性的金融中介部门、金融活动所伴生的风险等，从而更全面地描述金融因素可能产生的影响。（5）探索更多的政策作用机制。（6）在真实世界的参数可得性提高后，对具体国家或地区及具体政策进行更为精确的模拟。

我们为什么需要绿色金融？*

——从全球经验事实到基于经济增长框架的理论解释

文书洋　张　琳　刘锡良

绿色发展是人类进步的必然选择，中国在全球气候变化议题中扮演着越来越重要的角色。尤其是在碳达峰与碳中和的目标下，落实绿色低碳发展不仅是高质量发展的内在要求，也展现了中国的大国担当。在这一背景下，绿色金融受到越来越多的关注。

绿色金融一般泛指与环境保护和可持续发展相关的金融产品、金融市场与金融政策。绿色金融的概念与环境和气候金融近似，同时还包括可持续金融和环境责任投资的部分内容。过去20年中，全球的绿色金融发展进程突飞猛进，绿色金融议题受到越来越多的关注。虽然绿色金融相关的文献数量和占比快速增长，但顶尖的理论性研究成果还较为匮乏，人们甚至很少讨论"为什么需要绿色金融"等基础性问题。根据经济学一般原理，由于污染的外部性问题，环保的主要力量应当是公共部门而非金融系统。然而为什么越来越多的国家选择发展绿色金融？其背后的经济学原理是什么？深入探讨这些问题，是有效制定政策、构建绿色金融理论体系的基础。

---

* 原文刊载于《金融研究》2021年第12期。

作者简介：文书洋，经济学博士，讲师，西南财经大学中国金融研究中心；张琳，经济学博士，副教授，西南财经大学中国金融研究中心；刘锡良，经济学博士，教授，西南财经大学中国金融研究中心。

在现有文献基础上,本文首先使用全球上市公司数据测算各国绿色环保企业的债务占比作为绿色金融的代理指标,结合联合国财政支出数据,分析了全球绿色金融与绿色财政的变化情况。我们发现,在过去20年中,全球政府在环境保护方面的支出总额略有增加,但其占GDP的比例呈下降趋势;同时绿色金融的规模和占比不断提升,并且绿色金融的发展程度与经济体的规模高度正相关。跨国面板数据给出的实证证据表明,绿色金融能够有效促进经济的长期增长,而绿色财政与经济增长表现出明显的先促进后抑制的倒"U"形关系,与绿色金融存在明显的异质性。根据这些经验事实,本文提出"绿色金融是否与传统的公共财政存在差异?"这一问题。

在实证分析基础上,本文基于经济增长框架构建绿色金融的理论模型。该模型是一个包含居民、企业、金融部门和政府的多部门一般均衡增长模型,刻画了经济发展过程中绿色金融、绿色财政与经济增长的动态关系,能够很好地重现上述全球绿色金融发展变化的经验事实。模型证明:首先,绿色金融在长期增长中具有独特的优越性。由于政府部门提供的污染治理(绿色财政)是一种公共品,会随着经济规模的扩大变得"拥挤",因而在经济发展的高级阶段,绿色财政的效果会逐渐减弱。金融机构向企业提供的用于绿色投资的资金(绿色金融)能够弥补绿色财政的不足,实现经济的高质量发展。这一推论可以阐释全球关于绿色财政变化及其与经济发展关系的经验事实,过去20年中,随着经济发展,全球各国政府在环境保护方面的支出总额略有增加,但其占GDP的比重呈下降趋势,绿色财政的力度正在减弱;从回归分析来看,环保财政支出与经济增长存在先促进后抑制的倒"U"形关系。其次,市场环境下,由于污染的外部性问题,企业仅在环境损害达到一定程度之后才会自发进行绿色投资,即绿色金融的自发介入存在规模门槛。这是因为在经济发展初期,企业污染排放对环境的破坏不高,绿色投资带来的收益小于生产投资带来的收益，所以企业不会进行绿色投资。随着经济的发展，生产规模不断扩张，一方面生产性投入的边际收益不断降低，另一方面高污染使得绿色投资更加"有利可图"。此时，企业才会开始关注环境，自发进行绿色投资。因此，与绿色财政相比，绿色金融的发起更加依赖于经济发展程度。这一推论可以阐释关于全球绿色金融发展的经验事实，在过去 20 年中，全球绿色金融的规模和占比不断提升，并且这一期间绿色金融的发展程度与经济体的发展规模高度正相关。再次，适度的绿色金融补贴能够帮助经济实现更好的长期发展。对绿色投资的补贴本质上是将企业绿色投资的部分成本通过政府转嫁给了居民部门，从而激励企业进行治污投资，促进经济增长。然而绿色投资对生产投入的挤占会降低企业产出，且这一作用随着补贴政策增加而加剧，因此存在一个补贴政策的有效区间，仅在这一区间内的绿色信贷补贴政策有助于促进经济增长。最后，绿色金融与绿色财政在污染治理上存在替代效应，在经济增长的稳定性上存在互补效应。这是因为，如果企业降低绿色投资、增加生产投资，虽然能够增加企业期望利润、降低违约风险，但会增加环境风险；而企业期望利润的增加会经由税收途径放宽政府的预算约束，扩大绿色财政的空间，抵消企业绿色投资降低所导致的不利影响。因此，绿色金融与绿色财政存在最优组合策略。在经济发展初期依靠财政投入治理环境，而在发展的高级阶段积极推进绿色金融政策，能够实现更高的经济增速和长期稳态水平。

本文的研究从理论层面回答了"为什么需要绿色金融"的问题，一定程度上为绿色金融的发展提供了基础理论支撑，也为绿色金融理论建模提供了有益参考。同时，本文的政策分析表明，政府能够通过绿色信贷补贴，降低企业进行绿色投资的门槛，优化经济发展；在经济发展的高级阶段，将绿色金融与财政政策相配合，给予绿色信贷适当的补贴，可以有效提升经济发展质量。

未来值得研究的方向是，绿色金融对金融机构自身有什么样的影响？本文论述的核心是讨论绿色金融的宏观效应，并未回答金融机构自身是否存在开展绿色金融活动的内在激励问题。虽然现有研究给出了一些实证证据，但这一问题背后的理论机制分析还需要进一步加强。这一问题关系绿色金融政策的推行，也是未来研究的重要方向。

环境灾害冲击对银行违约率的影响效应研究：理论与实证分析*

王 遥 王文蔚

中国的各类环境灾害事件频发多发，给经济社会发展和人民正常的生产生活秩序造成巨大的负面影响。气候变化进一步提升了环境灾害的规模和频率，使之成为全球面临的共同挑战。随着极端环境灾害事件发生频率与强度的提高，其影响范围逐渐扩散至实体经济领域，导致消费、投资低迷和经济衰退。实体经济与金融体系的联系日益紧密，环境灾害冲击对实体经济的影响也必将传导至金融体系和机构，影响金融稳定，产生金融风险，进一步放大了环境灾害冲击的负面影响。因此，如何从理论和实证层面评估环境灾害对经济金融风险的影响亟待深入研究。

目前，环境风险相关议题已获得广泛关注：国际清算银行（BIS）、央行与监管机构绿色金融合作网络（NGFS）将气候与环境相关风险整合到金融稳定性的监管框架之中，并将相关风险划分为物理风险和转型风险，其中物理风险是指极端环境灾害等导致微观主体的资产和资本存量受到负向不可逆冲击，使得整体经济的运行受到负面冲击，传导至金融体系产生金融风险；而转型风险则是指监管部门出台更加严格的应对气候变化和环境保护政策，使得部分高碳企业的资产受到较大限制，进而

---

* 原文刊载于《金融研究》2021年第12期。
  作者简介：王遥，经济学博士，研究员，中央财经大学绿色金融国际研究院、财经研究院；
  王文蔚，博士研究生，中央财经大学金融学院。

沦为搁浅资产。在此背景下，本文基于物理风险的视角，通过理论模型模拟和基于中国银行业金融机构2008—2018年数据的实证检验，探讨了环境灾害冲击对于银行违约风险的实际影响，并对环境灾害影响银行违约率的作用机制以及进一步影响效应进行分析。

相较于以往研究，本文的创新性主要体现在以下三个方面：第一，就研究主题而言，本文是较早就中国的环境物理风险问题所开展的研究之一。通过理论和实证分析，本文较为全面地检验了环境灾害冲击对于银行违约率的影响效应，在经济体系之外发掘了可能影响中国金融稳定的重要因素，丰富了中国金融风险问题的研究视角。第二，在研究方法上，本文在DSGE建模过程中同时引入灾害冲击因素和金融摩擦机制，进一步突出金融加速器机制对于灾害冲击影响的放大作用，并基于此检验了灾害冲击对包括银行违约率在内的有关经济金融指标的影响。在实证方面，本文利用熵权法，综合多个维度构建环境灾害损失指标，为环境物理风险提供了来自中国的经验证据。第三，本文的理论与实证检验不仅佐证了环境物理风险的存在性，还进一步分析探讨了环境灾害冲击影响银行违约率的一系列衍生后果，包括对企业融资约束及银行放贷意愿的影响，从而丰富了有关融资约束、银行流动性创造等主题的研究视角。

本文的相关分析得出以下基本结论：理论模型模拟结果显示，环境灾害冲击使得银行信贷合同面临的违约率显著提升，导致更高的风险溢价，降低信贷发放规模，并反作用于实体企业，提升了企业的融资成本，企业所面临的融资约束收紧，最终对投资和产出形成更显著的负向冲击，降低了企业的杠杆率水平。与理论模型模拟的结果一致，基于中国数据的实证检验发现环境灾害会显著提升银行的违约率，并通过了一系列稳健性检验。机制检验表明，全要素生产率下降、资产减值损失和宏观经济不确定性水平上升在上述过程中发挥了显著的传导渠道作用。进一步分析表明，环境灾害冲击提升银行体系违约率的效应显著降低了银行的风险偏好水平，使得银行减少放贷规模和主动风险承担水平，降低了银行金融机构的盈利水平，并反作用于实体企业，导致企业面临更为紧缩的融资约束，提升了融资溢价，对企业的日常经营产生负面影响。

本文的主要结论除了丰富有关灾害冲击、金融风险的研究视角外，还具有以下几方面政策启示：第一，应进一步完善应对环境灾害的体制机制建设，更加关注环境灾害对于金融体系的负面冲击效应，下一步应强化意识，在制度设计上充分纳入金融稳定因素。第二，政府部门制定救灾政策应兼顾金融体系稳定，可探索设立灾害金融稳定基金，以防止极端灾害事件冲击可能导致的金融体系挤兑和流动性危机；同时应加强对环境脆弱地区或灾害多发地区的金融机构业务的监管，要求其设立常备灾害准备金，完善灾备中心建设，采取相关激励措施引导金融机构减少对棕色搁浅资产的投资和信贷发放，鼓励金融机构开展绿色金融业务。第三，金融部门在开展业务时要充分考虑可能面临的气候环境风险，定期开展环境压力测试。银行等金融部门在开展信贷业务之前应详尽评估企业自身业务与所在区域的气候环境风险，在信贷定价中充分考虑环境灾害因素。在灾害发生后，金融部门也应通过展期等形式积极帮扶受灾企业，形成企业与金融机构之间的良性互动。

碳定价、双重金融摩擦与"双支柱"调控*

王 博 徐飘洋

中国环境与发展国际合作委员会在《全球气候治理与中国贡献》报告中指出，要加快我国碳定价、碳市场和碳金融机制建设，推动我国碳定价制度渐进完善。2021年7月中旬全国碳排放交易市场上线，而受覆盖面和碳交易价格形成机制难以确定等因素的影响，仅靠设定碳排放总量上限、支持碳交易还不足以实现我国"30/60"目标，长远看来还需加快碳税政策的落地，以弥补碳排放上限政策的不足。与此同时，中国人民银行行长易纲在出席博鳌亚洲论坛2021年年会时指出，要加快研究在对金融机构的压力测试中引入气候变化因素，在投资风险管理框架中纳入气候因素；同时建立金融机构绿色信贷及绿色债券评价体系。未来以宏观审慎政策为主应对气候变化可能带来的系统性风险，以货币政策为主支持绿色发展，同时进一步加强宏观审慎政策和货币政策的协调配合将是碳达峰、碳中和目标实现过程中央行的重点工作。基于以上考量，从碳减排的角度出发，深入研究碳定价政策的减排效果和宏观经济效应、碳定价政策和双支柱政策之间的协调搭配，对实现我国"30/60"目标构建和完善双支柱框架以应对气候转型风险、维护金融稳定及实现经济顺

---

* 原文刊载于《金融研究》2021年第12期。
作者简介：王博，经济学博士，教授，南开大学金融学院；徐飘洋，博士研究生，南开大学金融学院。

利转型升级具有重要的理论和实践价值。

目前有关碳定价政策的研究正不断丰富，但对于不同碳定价政策之间的协调搭配及碳定价政策与金融摩擦和"双支柱"政策之间的循环反馈机制的研究还较为匮乏。本文通过构建包含异质性企业、碳排放的负外部性、银行违约风险的 DSGE 模型，为分析碳减排政策提供了基本的分析框架，并从以下三个方面对已有文献形成补充和扩展：一是从长短期两个方面评估了碳定价政策的影响，并在偶然约束下研究了在碳交易市场中设定碳价上下限对宏观经济的影响；二是通过内生化金融部门违约风险进而构建双重金融摩擦，有效区分了资产价格波动所引发的金融加速器效应与金融部门风险上升所引发的风险规避效应，进而更好地分析了碳定价政策与金融稳定之间的相互反馈机制；三是通过确定性模拟和福利分析评估了碳定价政策与"双支柱"政策在经济转型过程中的有效性。

本文通过构建包含两种碳定价政策、双重金融摩擦和"双支柱"政策的 DSGE 模型，系统考察了碳定价政策对碳减排、经济和金融稳定的长短期影响及"双支柱"政策应对转型风险时的有效性。相关分析得出了三个基本结论：（1）两种碳定价方式在长期均有助于我国经济实现高质量发展，但在短期具有一定的负面影响，在面对碳排放技术冲击，浮动碳价会加剧经济波动，但在碳交易市场中引入价格波动上下限将有助于缓解这一波动。（2）金融摩擦会明显放大气候政策对宏观经济的负面影响，在双重金融摩擦下，金融部门对违约风险的规避所产生的金融加速器效应与金融部门与居民之间的金融摩擦所产生的金融加速器效应具有同等重要的作用。（3）货币当局在执行货币政策以应对气候政策的宏观经济影响时，无须太过关注短期结构性失衡所导致的通货膨胀，而更应关注产出和需求引导，在结构性供需不平衡的状态下，扩大绿色投资、促进绿色生产、引导消费需求才是解决通胀的最好办法。同时，在"双支柱"框架下，宏观审慎政策能有效地缓解气候政策对宏观经济的负面影响，增强金融稳定，提高居民福利。

根据上述分析结论，本文得到以下三方面政策启示：（1）在制定气候政策时，应该将固定碳价与浮动碳价相结合，浮动碳价有助于确保在经济波动中实现我国的"30/60"目标，而固定碳价则可以有效应对碳排放技术的变革，从而减轻因碳排放技术的变动所引发的经济波动，增加经济弹性。（2）金融部门的风险规避效应会显著加剧气候政策的负面影响，因而政府部门应在一定程度上鼓励金融部门进行风险分担，以实现金融服务实体经济的本质，但同时也需注意经济转型过程中金融部门的风险集聚。（3）面对气候政策冲击，需考虑气候政策所导致的金融不稳定和经济波动，注意经济转型过程中所伴随的因短期结构性供需失衡所导致的通货膨胀，通过促进生产，扩大绿色投资，推动供需平衡，从根源上解决产业转型过程中所伴随的通货膨胀。

中国绿色金融政策、融资成本与企业绿色转型*

——基于央行担保品政策视角

陈国进　丁赛杰　赵向琴　蒋晓宇

近年来，中国绿色金融政策陆续出台且支持力度不断强化，政策效果受到广泛关注。绿色金融政策的效果如何？能否成功推进经济的绿色转型？这些问题需要全面而深入的探究。我国近年来的绿色金融政策主要是绿色信贷政策和绿色债券支持政策，而将绿色信贷和绿色债券纳入央行担保品框架成为央行支持绿色发展的重要举措。其中比较重要的绿色债券支持类政策如下：2018年6月，中国人民银行将不低于AA级的绿色债券纳入中期借贷便利（MLF）合格担保品范围，以期实现对绿色资产的金融支持。2021年4月，中国人民银行等部门联合发布的《绿色债券支持项目目录（2021年版）》对绿色债券支持领域和范围进行科学统一界定，这将进一步强化央行担保品类绿色金融政策的支持效果。

截至2021年10月底，我国绿色债券存量近1万亿元，居世界前列，在支持经济绿色转型中发挥着日益重要的作用。但从既有研究来看，绿

---

* 原文刊载于《金融研究》2021年第12期。
　作者简介：陈国进，经济学博士，教授，厦门大学经济学院、王亚南经济研究院；丁赛杰，金融学博士研究生，厦门大学经济学院；赵向琴，经济学博士，教授，厦门大学经济学院；蒋晓宇，金融学博士，中国人民银行金融研究所。

色金融政策效果的研究更多关注绿色信贷政策,对绿色债券支持类金融政策的探究还比较缺乏,且迄今的文献关于绿色金融政策的效果尚未达成一致性的结论。绿色债券纳入央行担保品范围理论上可以提高绿色债券的发行价格,降低绿色企业的融资成本,实现对绿色企业的金融支持。对于棕色企业而言,随着相关政策的出台,其债券融资成本可能会提高,进而倒逼棕色企业通过绿色创新等渠道实现绿色转型,但这些需要深入的机制分析和实证检验。

鉴于此,本文将系统探究绿色金融政策是否对绿色企业形成融资激励,以及倒逼棕色企业绿色转型的效果。理论模型方面,本文通过在 Pástor 等(2021)的模型中引入绿色金融政策因素改进了 ESG 资产定价模型,这一做法更加契合绿色金融政策直接影响债券信用利差的事实,以此分析绿色金融政策、融资成本与企业绿色转型之间相互作用的内在机理。实证研究方面,本文使用 2016 年 1 月至 2019 年 6 月银行间市场的企业债、公司债、金融债和中期票据的一级市场的数据,从债券信用利差的视角检验央行担保品类绿色金融政策对企业的融资激励和倒逼促进效果,然后使用 2016—2020 年上市公司的绿色专利年度数据,分析央行担保品类绿色金融政策影响棕色企业绿色创新的直接效果,以及债券融资成本在棕色企业绿色转型中的作用机制,为相关政策效果提供经验证据。为确保实证研究中因果关系识别的准确性,本文通过改变样本区间、安慰剂检验、政策时滞效应、倾向得分匹配等多种方法,分别对央行担保品类绿色金融政策的融资激励与倒逼促进效果,以及该政策影响棕色企业绿色创新的效果,进行稳健性检验与内生性讨论。

本文的主要研究结论如下:第一,央行担保品类绿色金融政策可以显著降低绿色债券的信用利差,同时会提高棕色债券的信用利差。从融资成本层面分别对绿色企业形成融资激励,对棕色企业的绿色转型形成倒逼促进作用。第二,央行担保品类绿色金融政策的上述效果表现出动态时变性。政策实施初期的政策效果最大，随时间推移逐渐弱化。同时，政策效果存在区域差异，对信用利差的影响在绿色金融改革创新试验区样本中更明显。第三，央行担保品类绿色金融政策通过影响棕色债券的融资成本显著提升了棕色企业的绿色创新，从绿色创新角度看成功倒逼棕色企业绿色转型。

结合上述研究结论，本文为进一步优化绿色金融政策支持效果、推进经济绿色转型提出以下政策建议：第一，可以通过合格抵押品扩容的方式为绿色企业提供金融支持。具体而言，可以将更多符合标准的绿色资产纳入央行合格抵押品范围或者提高绿色资产的抵押率，以进一步强化该类政策的实施效果。第二，可以在既有政策的基础上，实施连续的、递进式的绿色金融政策，以保证政策实施的长久效果。第三，可以对积极进行绿色创新的棕色企业进行融资激励，进一步推动其有序进行绿色转型。

相比于既有文献，本文可能的创新主要如下：（1）将绿色金融政策因素与企业绿色转型纳入考量，从而改进了Pástor等（2021）的可持续投资资产定价模型。现有关于ESG资产定价模型的文献较少考虑到政策因素尤其是绿色金融政策对资产价格的影响。本文通过改进后的ESG资产定价模型为绿色金融政策、企业融资成本与企业绿色转型提供了一个理论分析框架，并阐明了三者之间相互作用的内在机理。（2）相比于已有研究使用单一实证方法可能造成的模型不确定性，本文综合采用双重差分（DID）、三重差分（DDD）、连续DID等实证方法识别了绿色金融政策、债券信用利差与企业绿色转型三者间的因果关系，在一定程度上更好地解决了内生性问题。（3）本文从信用利差和企业绿色创新的双重视角为绿色金融政策的绿色效应提供了双重证据，综合检验了此类政策对债券信用利差的不同影响及政策效果的动态时变性与区域差异性，并验证了促进棕色企业绿色创新的主要机制，为货币政策更好地助力经济绿色转型提供了有益参考。

气候变化冲击下的涉农信用风险[*]

——基于2010—2019年256家农村金融机构的实证研究

刘 波 王修华 李明贤

气候变化是当前全人类面临的重大挑战之一,气候暖化对人类生存环境、经济社会稳定形成了巨大冲击,所引致的经济金融风险已经成为学术界关注的热点问题。《中国气候变化蓝皮书2020》指出,中国是全球气候变化的敏感区,增温速率显著高于全球同期平均水平。瑞士再保险的压力测试表明,如果不采取任何行动,到2050年全球经济因气候变化导致的损失将达到GDP的18%,亚洲经济体将面临更为严重的损失。《2020年全球风险报告》指出,全球未来10年的前五大风险均与环境相关,与气候变化相关的金融风险被认为是系统性金融风险的重要来源之一,防范系统性金融风险需要深入研究与气候变化相关的金融风险。

虽然气候变化对金融体系存在系统性影响,但诸多金融机构并未足够重视气候变化带来的金融风险。在短期内,气候变化趋势难以逆转,如果金融机构未对自身面临的转型风险与物理风险进行评估,并制定相应的风险管理措施,有可能造成经营决策失误和财产损失。中国以间接融资为主,气候变化对商业银行的影响最为突出。商业银行的类型不同,

---

[*] 原文刊载于《金融研究》2021年第12期。
作者简介:刘波,金融学博士,副教授,湖南农业大学经济学院;王修华,金融学博士,教授,湖南大学金融与统计学院;李明贤,管理学博士,教授,湖南农业大学经济学院。

与气候变化相关的风险也有所不同。对于全国性的大型商业银行、股份制商业银行，由于贷款配置在行业、地域上较为分散，气候变化对其的负面冲击有限。农村商业银行、村镇银行等农村金融机构定位于服务"三农"，资产业务主要以信贷为主，且高度集中于县域地理单元与"三农"相关的领域，其信用风险水平更易受气候变化的影响。

农业的投入产出效率高度依赖于气候条件，相比于其他行业，气候变化对农业的影响更为广泛和深刻。虽然总体产量增加，但气象产量仍表现为减产的趋势，气候变化的强烈波动性遏制了农业技术进步带来的生产效益。农村金融机构主要面向农业领域开展业务，气候变化增加了农业产出的不确定性，从而将气候风险传递给了农村金融机构。本文在综合气候变化、农业发展和气候金融三方面文献的基础上，提出了"气候变化—农业发展不确定性—涉农信用风险"的传导机制，并结合农村金融机构的经营地域范围和所服务的主要行业，设计定量研究的实证方案。

在实证研究中，以2010—2019年256家农村金融机构的财务数据为样本，样本农村金融机构包括249家农商行、7家村镇银行，覆盖26个省（区、市）、128个地级市、251个县。本文以年均气温为基础构建量化气候变化程度的指标，将近50年内的年均气温作为参照标准，对年均气温进行标准化处理。标准化年均气温不仅能够刻画气温的波动程度，还能使县域地理单元之间的气候变化程度具有可比性。实证研究包含两个层次：首先，通过固定效应模型评估气温波动对信用风险水平的影响；其次，通过非参数模型、分组回归分析气温波动对信用风险水平的异质性影响。

实证研究的主要结论如下：（1）农村金融机构所在县域地理单元的年均气温波动对其信用风险水平存在显著影响。以近50年的年均气温为基准，年均气温高出其1个标准差时，不良贷款比例将增加0.1365%，气候暖化显著提升了农村金融机构的信用风险水平。(2)如果将年均气温波动细化为四个季度，仅冬季气温的波动对信用风险水平存在显著影响。以近50年的冬季平均气温为基准，当冬季的平均气温高出其1个标准差时，不良贷款比例增加0.0777%。(3)气温波动对信用风险水平的影响具有阶段性特征，随着年均气温波动范围的扩大，信用风险水平对气候暖化的敏感性由弱到强。(4)虽然城商行与农村金融机构均是立足于服务地方的商业银行，但由于城商行的业务覆盖范围更广、服务的行业更为多样，气候变化并未对其信用风险水平产生显著影响。在稳健性检验中，以年度、季度和生长季归一化植被指数（1km）为基础，构建量化气候变化的指标，并将实证模型调整为多维面板固定效应模型。稳健性检验表明，实证研究结论具有较好的稳健性。

本文通过实证研究明确了气候变化对涉农信用风险的冲击方向及程度，不仅为定性研究提供了经验证据，同时也为农村金融机构和金融监管部门应对气候变化冲击提供了决策依据。以研究结论为基础，本文提出以下政策建议：(1)农村金融机构应通过信用风险压力测试，明确气候变化对农村金融机构信用风险的冲击程度，并制定相应的应急预案，提升管理和应对气候风险的能力。(2)行业监管部门应综合考虑农村金融机构的业务结构、服务"三农"的力度，以及风险与气候变化的相关性，对农村金融机构实施差异化监管。(3)金融管理部门需鼓励对融资担保、贷款信用保险等风险管理工具进行创新，为农村金融机构缓释气候风险提供工具支持。

"多言寡行"的环境责任表现能否影响银行信贷获取*

——基于"言"和"行"双维度的文本分析

李 哲 王文翰

2020年,我国提出了碳达峰和碳中和的战略目标。此举彰显出我国引领全球气候治理、构建人类命运共同体的大国担当,也体现了我国加快推进生态文明建设,追求高质量发展的坚定步伐。在我国目前的经济发展阶段,借助经济手段加强环境保护工作不断受到重视。基于这种背景,我国于2007年启动了绿色信贷政策,要求金融机构将企业的环境责任表现纳入信贷决策范围。我国的绿色信贷政策自实施以来,取得了快速发展,但同时也面临着企业"虚构绿色项目,骗取银行信贷资金;借绿色项目名义融资,实际资金挪作他用"等政策执行风险。这种借"环保"之名骗取资本支持的现象威胁到我国绿色金融体系的健康发展,也对我国环境保护市场化机制的深入推进形成不利影响。目前,鲜有文献对此问题进行深入分析,对于该方面的研究亟须展开。

本文所关注的"多言寡行"是指企业环境责任表现上的言行不一,常表现为"口惠而实不至"、"粉饰美化"及"过度宣传"等现象,其

---

* 原文刊载于《金融研究》2021年第12期。
作者简介:李哲,管理学博士,副教授,中央财经大学会计学院,中国管理会计研究中心;
王文翰,博士研究生,中央财经大学金融学院。

背后反映出企业履行环境责任时存在的投机性倾向。我国金融体系主要以银行信贷等间接融资为主,在当前强调发展绿色金融的背景下,重污染企业面临着严厉的融资约束。这种利益机制下,重污染企业很有可能采用"多言寡行"的环境责任表现塑造出与实践不符的绿色声誉,以迎合银行的授信标准,获取融资便利。为此,本文采用文本分析方法,从样本公司公开的年度报告及社会责任报告中手工收集表征企业"言"(环境保护战略规划)和"行"(环境保护实际行动)的数据,识别出企业环境责任表现中的"多言寡行"特征,并以此为基础,着重考察了企业"多言寡行"的环境责任表现对银行信贷决策的影响。研究发现:"多言寡行"的环境责任表现有助于企业获得更多的银行借款。相比于长期银行借款,"多言寡行"对于短期银行借款的正向影响更为明显。《关于构建绿色金融体系的指导意见》(本文简称《指导意见》)的发布抑制了"多言寡行"的银行信贷资源获取效应。原因在于,《指导意见》的出台强化了银行落实绿色信贷政策的考核激励并且改善了绿色信贷政策实施的信息环境,银行更有动力和能力对企业的真实环境责任表现进行甄别。进一步分析发现,相比于环境责任表现"少言多行"及"少言寡行"的企业,企业"多言寡行"的环境责任表现对于银行的信贷资源具有显著的正向影响;"多言寡行"对银行借款的正向影响在无背景关联、价值较低及市场环境更差的企业中体现得更为明显。

本文的潜在贡献主要有以下三个方面:(1)在当前实施绿色信贷的政策背景下,本文研究发现企业有动机采取低成本的印象管理策略("多言寡行")以迎合银行的授信标准,获取更多的信贷资源。本文提供的经验证据有助于加深相关部门对于企业环境行为决策和实践表现的认识。"多言寡行"是种隐蔽的印象管理模式,信贷机构应更加注重"观其行",而不能仅仅"听其言"。结论对于我国银行强化授信对象甄别机制,提高资源配置效率有一定的指导意义。(2)本文拓展了影响企业融资的一种非财务因素。基于我国实施绿色金融的政策背景，结合所度量的"多言寡行"信息披露模式，本文考察了企业环境信息操纵对于银行信贷决策的影响，研究丰富了银行信贷决策影响因素和企业信息操纵领域的研究。另外，本文也为完善我国上市公司环境信息披露制度、强化企业环保绩效考核与监管的必要性提供了新的支持。（3）实证结果证明了《指导意见》对于我国绿色金融发展的重要意义。在这一顶层设计的指引下，我国绿色金融的激励政策不断出台，绿色信贷的实施逐渐由"导向性"走向"实质化"。但相关的学术研究多以政策解读为主，来自数据层面的实证支持尤为缺乏。本文从理论上梳理了《指导意见》影响银行行为的逻辑机制，并实证发现了《指导意见》的发布抑制了"多言寡行"的信贷资源获取效应。本文为《指导意见》如何改善绿色信贷的实施效果提供了微观经验证据。

根据本文的分析结论，得到以下四方面政策启示：（1）本文研究有助于银行等金融机构认识到环境报告可能沦为企业进行印象管理的自利工具。"多言寡行"的环境责任表现是种隐蔽的声誉构建机制，这种言行不一的环保实践模式扭曲了信贷资源的配置环境，带来了绿色信贷政策的执行风险。因此银行进行信贷决策时，应加强对于企业环境责任表现的甄别，在"听其言"的同时更应注重"观其行"。（2）在中央高度重视生态文明建设的背景下，一方面，要深入实施绿色信贷政策，加大对绿色经济的支持力度及对落后产能的淘汰作用；另一方面，要避免走入授信"一刀切"的误区。针对重污染企业，不能盲目进行融资限制，而应平衡惩罚与激励的力度，通过信贷杠杆提高企业对于环保的重视和投入，挖掘企业转型升级的潜力，从而实现环境保护和经济发展的共赢局面。（3）本文结果表明《指导意见》的发布压缩了"多言寡行"企业的资源获取空间，取得了良好的政策效果。但同时，构建绿色金融体系是一项长期工程。为此，各部门应继续相互协作，确保绿色信贷政策实施的精准性和持续性。此外,政府应完善绿色信贷配套保障措施,给予银行一定的风险补偿,提高银行执行绿色信贷政策的积极性和自主性,引导政策执行由"政策驱动"转向"市场驱动"。(4)环境责任表现"多言寡行",本质上是企业通过环境信息操纵而发出的言过其实的绿色信号。因此,监管机构需要完善环境信息披露制度,落实披露责任、细化披露要求、明确披露规范。对于信息披露中存在言行不符的公司进行重点监管,并辅以一定的惩治措施,培育企业规范披露环境信息的良好氛围。

生态法治对债券融资成本的影响*

——基于我国中级环保法庭设立的准自然实验

高昊宇 温慧愉

气候变化是备受关注的社会和发展问题。在市场主导与政府引导相结合的原则下提前进行绿色转型布局、经济发展和减污降碳协同治理，是"既要绿水青山，也要金山银山"的题中之义，也是顺利实现"双碳"目标的必由之路。实现经济增长和"双碳"生态目标相协调的高质量发展，既需要在全面绿色转型中充分发挥金融市场的资源配置导向作用，也离不开强有力的生态环境法治保障。强有力的生态法治保障有助于形成金融市场的绿色导向，同时，为绿色转型注入资本活力是金融服务实体经济的重要体现。深刻理解生态法治引导下金融市场的绿色导向功能及其形成机制，正确认识绿色转型风险，对新时代下完善金融市场功能、促进经济高质量发展具有重要意义。

我国中级环保法庭"从下到上、从点到面"的环境司法专门化探索实践，为研究生态法治建设如何促进金融市场绿色导向、推动绿色转型提供了具有代表性的准自然实验。中级环保法庭是由人民法院依法设立的专门审理环境法律纠纷的审判机构，是环境司法的枢纽所在。与多数立法立规的环境规制政策冲击不同，人民法院环境资源审判庭制度以审

---

* 原文刊载于《金融研究》2021 年第 12 期。
作者简介： 高昊宇，管理学博士，经济学博士，副教授，中国人民大学财政金融学院；温慧愉，博士研究生，中国人民大学财政金融学院。

判和执行作为突破口,为环境治理提供了重要司法保障。

已有文献对环境规制对企业污染治理、清洁转型、经营绩效等方面的经济后果予以高度关注,但相关制度的持续威慑力离不开充分的执行有效性。中级环保法庭设立带来的专业高效的环境司法能力提升,有助于环境诉讼案件的有效审判与执行。近年来伴随着中级环保法庭成立等标志性事件,国家、社会对深化环境司法治理的研究和关注迅速提高,但经济金融领域鲜有研究深入探讨生态法治建设产生的系列经济后果,特别是从资本市场投资者风险定价的视角。有鉴于此,本文的贡献主要在于以下方面。第一,基于现有文献从企业生产和创新活动角度考察环境规制微观经济效应的研究,本文从地区环境司法能力提升资本市场绿色导向功能的视角出发,提供经验证据。第二,本文构建了"外部环境规制—经营成本与环境诉讼风险—外部融资定价与风险"的完整链条,补充了生态法治建设下企业转型风险定价的内在机制研究。第三,本文从推动地区环境司法建设的视角拓展了法与金融的研究。第四,本文对中级环保法庭的地区生态治理效应(范子英和赵仁杰,2019)补充了微观解释,也为我国环境司法和绿色发展实践提供了有益启示。

本文利用我国中级人民法院中级环保法庭设立的准自然实验,基于2008—2019年公司债、企业债和中期票据发行数据,采用渐进三重差分方法,检验生态法治建设对我国信用债券融资成本的影响。研究发现,中级环保法庭设立后,相对低污染行业企业,当地高污染行业企业因环境政策而面临更高的转型风险,其债券信用利差显著增加了0.28%(占样本平均信用利差的12%),表明地区环境司法能力提升带来了资本市场对高污染企业转型风险的定价。环境司法能力提升和生态法治制度完善是加强污染治理的长效机制,设立中级环保法庭显著提高了高污染企业潜在暴露的环境风险,投资者可能基于企业的环境风险和环境表现而产生对企业未来经营业绩下滑和无法按期还本付息风险的消极预期,使得生态法治建设带来的环境规制经济影响外溢到资本市场风险定价层面。此外，本文提出并验证了中级环保法庭设立影响债券融资成本的机制：第一，中级环保法庭强化了生态法治，提高了高污染行业企业的环境诉讼风险；第二，中级环保法庭增加了维权机会，形成对违法排污行为的外部监督压力；第三，中级环保法庭提高了高污染行业企业的生产经营成本；第四，中级环保法庭对高污染行业企业的经营决策形成制约。以上因素都会提高投资者对高污染行业企业要求的风险溢价，提高高污染行业企业的债券融资成本。进一步分析发现，当法治水平较高和地方政府环境治理激励较强时，中级环保法庭的设立对高污染行业企业债券融资成本的影响更大。为缓解中级环保法庭设立的内生性问题，本文采用倾向性得分匹配法，控制更多地区特征，引入更多固定效应，并检验了中级环保法庭设立的动态效应。此外，在采用高污染企业的替代定义、采用双重聚类标准误、考虑债券类型等后，结果依然稳健。

本文在"碳达峰"和"碳中和"进程下的转型风险定价和生态法制建设方面具有重要政策启示。第一，应防范化解环境政策转型风险。在环境政策转型阵痛期，高污染企业环境风险的传导将使得资本市场面临着更为复杂的风险环境。相关企业需要及早应对环境政策转型风险，争取形成绿色发展理念下的比较竞争优势。第二，应在生态法治保障下建立政策引导、市场运作的长效机制。一方面，需要加强生态法治，切实形成环境规制的经济效应，促进金融市场自发形成经济效益与环境效益激励相容的绿色导向，充分发挥绿色转型中的资源配置功能；另一方面，需要对债券市场加以适当引导，培育绿色投资理念，增强绿色投资能力。第三，推动环境司法协调发展，共同助力形成市场化资源配置的绿色导向。生态法治要及早就"碳治理"进行探索，协调推进环境立法和司法建设。未来还需在上层设计、法制建设、社会关注和媒体舆论等多方合力中，加快推动绿色发展变革，实现经济增长与环境保护的双赢格局。

04　银行经营与企业融资

中国银行业结构性全要素生产率增长研究*

朱 宁 刘伟其 于之倩 王 兵

在推动金融供给侧结构性改革过程中，各金融机构作为行为主体一直处于主导地位。当前我国金融体系结构是典型的银行主导型，以间接融资方式配置金融资源为基础，因此银行业成为我国金融结构性改革的重要领域。推动我国银行业的结构性改革，提高金融供给的质量和效率，是我国银行业在新形势下转型发展的迫切要求，有助于银行业更好发挥对实体经济供给侧结构性改革的支持作用。党的十九大报告强调，以供给侧结构性改革为主线，推动经济发展质量变革、效率变革、动力变革，提高全要素生产率。在经济新常态背景下，提高我国银行业全要素生产率（Total Factor Productivity，TFP）增长，既是推进金融结构性改革的应有之义，也是提高经济高质量发展的动力源泉。对于我国银行业的TFP增长，一方面要依靠技术进步，另一方面则要深化金融体制改革，提升金融市场的竞争性和优化配置资源结构的能力。基于此，如何在金融结构性改革背景下有效测算我国银行业的TFP增长水平及精准探索其增长来源是本文亟待解决的问题。

针对我国银行业TFP增长水平的测算和分解，国内外学者已进行了

---

* 原文刊载于《金融研究》2021年第7期。
作者简介：朱宁，经济学博士，研究员，华南理工大学经济与金融学院；刘伟其，经济学硕士研究生，华南理工大学经济与金融学院；于之倩，经济学博士，副教授，广州大学经济与统计学院；王兵，经济学博士，教授，暨南大学经济学院。

大量研究。但对现有文献进行梳理可发现，早期对TFP增长的测算大多使用基于技术效率的TFP增长框架，在TFP增长的分解方面也基本遵循传统的效率变化和技术变化，或基于技术效率衍生出一些新的分解形式，比如规模效率变化、偏向型技术变化等。从金融结构性改革的视角出发，如果按照上述方法对我国银行业进行TFP增长测算可能导致计算结果出现偏差，原因在于技术效率反映的是个体银行的运营水平，所以技术性TFP增长会忽视结构性作用，并不能真实反映整体银行业的TFP增长水平；另外，在TFP增长的分解中，由于缺少基于结构性方面信息支撑，可能导致缺失部分探索TFP增长来源的重要因素，比如结构效率变化（个体银行之间的资源再配置效率改善程度）、制度创新变化（整体银行业的制度环境改善程度）等，甚至可能扭曲相关政策建议。

对此，本文从产业和个体两个维度构建一种加总的Luenberger生产率指标对我国银行业及不同类型银行的结构性TFP增长及来源进行有效评价。在规模报酬可变假设下，本文使用加总的个体银行的生产可能性集构建整体结构性TFP增长模型，并按照传统TFP增长来源分解方式将其分解为整体效率变化和整体技术变化两部分。其中，整体效率变化可以拓展为加总的个体技术效率变化（个体银行自身的运营水平）和结构效率变化（银行业的结构优化水平）两部分，结构效率变化可以继续分解为范围效率变化和规模效率变化；整体技术变化可以由加总的个体技术变化（个体银行自身的纯技术水平变化）和制度创新变化（剔除个体纯技术作用之外的推动技术边界移动的因素）两部分组成。综上所述，本文从三个方面对现有文献进行拓展：（1）使用加总的Luenberger生产率指标，从结构优化的视角对金融结构性改革背景下我国银行业的结构性TFP增长进行测算；（2）从个体银行和整体银行业两个维度对我国银行业的结构性TFP增长进行分解，除了传统的技术变化和效率变化分解外，进一步分解出结构效率变化和制度创新变化；（3）区别于早期使用个体银行技术性 TFP 增长均值来衡量不同类型银行 TFP 增长水平的方法，本文使用结构性 TFP 增长方法对此进行修正。

本文选取 2012—2018 年 62 家商业银行作为样本，并按照利润导向法选择相应的投入、产出指标来进行结构性 TFP 增长测算。为使结构性 TFP 增长模型更具逻辑性，且保证 TFP 测算结果具有可比性，本文以 2012 年作为基期设定方向向量。研究发现，研究期间我国银行业的结构性 TFP 增长表现良好，其中，整体技术进步是银行业结构性 TFP 增长的主要驱动力，而整体效率变化一定程度上出现抑制作用。通过分别对整体技术变化和整体效率变化再分解发现，银行体系的制度创新改善和加总的个体技术进步推动银行业的结构性 TFP 增长；在整体效率变化中，除了规模效率变化提供有限的贡献外，其他部分如加总的个体技术效率变化、结构效率变化和范围效率变化的作用都不明显。与银行业结构性 TFP 增长结果相似，不同类型银行的结构性 TFP 增长也表现良好。从分解来看，整体技术变化是不同类型银行结构性 TFP 增长的主要驱动力，而整体效率变化则产生一定的负面影响。对不同类型银行结构性 TFP 增长进一步分解发现，制度创新变化对于不同类型银行，尤其是股份制银行的结构性 TFP 增长具有显著的推动作用，加总的个体技术变化对股份制银行和地区性银行的结构性 TFP 增长贡献更突出。另外，与中小型银行相比，大型国有银行在范围效率变化和规模效率变化方面表现更佳。

当前，我国经济由高速增长阶段转向高质量发展阶段，是转型升级和结构性改革的关键时期，新旧动能转换不断加速。银行业作为我国金融体系的融资主体，在其中扮演着举足轻重的角色。在金融结构性改革背景下，为进一步推进我国银行业高质量发展，提出四点政策建议：
（1）加快推进我国银行业结构性改革。从范围效率变化和规模效率变化来看，银行机构应着力在业务结构、区域分布等方面形成自身优势和专业化特色，以提高范围效率；中小型银行应根据自身管理能力和资本状况，择机调整经营区域,以实现规模效率改善。(2)优化非利息收入内部结构,提高风险管理水平。特别是部分资金体量较小、风险管理能力较弱的地区性银行,在快速提升非利息收入业务比重的同时产生了大量不良贷款,应进一步强化表外资产风险防控力度,建立风险识别和评估体系以及完整的内控信息反馈机制。(3)充分利用金融科技提高银行产品和服务质量,借助人工智能、区块链、大数据等前沿技术,积极开发个性化、差异化、定制化的金融产品和服务。(4)积极完善金融市场制度建设,进一步深化金融供给侧结构性改革,完善金融环境和基础设施,更好地为金融服务实体经济提供制度保障和支撑。

金融政策竞争中性原则与民营企业融资纾困*

——来自突发公共卫生事件的准自然实验

吕怀立　王文明　鄢姿俏　侯　亮

竞争中性原则是政府用来决定市场竞争机制的制度安排，强调应构建公平竞争机制，反对因企业所有制不同而设置不同的竞争规则。然而，作为信贷市场的主体，商业银行在金融政策的执行上却往往存在着信贷差异，表现出非竞争中性的一面。2020年年初以来，新冠肺炎疫情这一突发公共卫生事件给我国实体企业的生产经营带来巨大冲击。疫情期间，帮助企业应急"输血"，加大货币信贷支持力度成为制定金融政策的重点。因此，新冠肺炎疫情的巨大冲击为我们提供了一个很好的外生实验场景，可以用于检验金融政策竞争中性原则的实现情况及其实现途径。

从信贷维度来看，一些研究认为，由于民营企业被迫承担了更高的融资成本、更短的融资期限和更低的融资额度，使得民营企业在面对宏观经济波动风险时举步维艰。面对来势汹汹的新冠肺炎疫情，融资难、融资贵的问题可能成为疫情下压垮民营企业的最后一根稻草。保持流动

---

* 原文刊载于《金融研究》2021年第7期。

作者简介：吕怀立，管理学博士，副教授，上海大学管理学院；王文明，管理学博士，百人计划研究员，浙江大学管理学院；鄢姿俏，管理学博士，讲师，上海对外经贸大学会计学院；侯亮，会计学硕士研究生，上海大学管理学院。

性合理充裕、加大货币信贷对小微企业、民营企业支持力度成为金融支持疫情防控工作的重点。统计发现，2020年2—3月商业银行的普惠型小微企业贷款规模总体增长较快，大型银行增速均超过30%，股份制银行增速也在20%以上。

一系列金融政策的安排，都意在为受疫情影响较大的民营企业和中小微企业解决资金链紧张的燃眉之急，也进一步促进了金融政策向竞争中性方向靠拢，或许能够极大加快竞争中性原则的落实进程。我们认为，当民营企业经营状况被聚焦关注、支持民营企业的重要性变得特别突出、金融政策向民营企业大幅倾斜时，之前信贷市场执行层面的一些非竞争中性状况能够得到有效缓解。

同时，我们认为当企业面对突发公共卫生事件的外生冲击时，商业信用将成为其获得银行贷款的重要依据，那些为供应链上下游企业提供商业信用支持的民营企业更容易以较低的融资成本获得金融机构的资金支持。这种方式可以看作是金融机构在遇到不利冲击时控制信用风险的一种重要手段，相比于把资金投放到处于供应链上下游的中小企业，投到处于供应链的核心企业更有利于金融机构把控风险。核心企业通过商业信用的方式，给予其供应链上下游企业资金支持，从而在一定程度上也实现了金融机构的风险转移目的。

本文采用双重差分方法，选择在2019年11—12月和2020年2—3月发行的中期票据和短期融资券作为研究对象。研究发现，在面临突发外生事件冲击时，金融政策的竞争中性原则更容易实现，表现为疫情暴发后民营企业的融资成本显著降低；进一步分析表明，金融政策竞争中性原则是通过商业信用的供给来促进融资获取的途径实现的，表现为那些为供应链上下游企业提供更多商业信用支持的民营企业，更容易获得融资便利，融资成本显著降低。我们认为，通过商业信用供给促进融资的模式是一种应对外生冲击的重要机制。进一步检验发现，疫情期间的金融政策并没有导致民营企业出现"脱实向虚"现象，反而降低了其金融化水平，提升了资金使用效率。

　　本文得到以下三方面的政策启示：第一，对民营企业不愿贷、不敢贷的现象并不等于金融政策存在非竞争中性，而是源于金融机构在执行层面的顾虑。因此，解决民营企业融资难、融资贵等问题的政策制定需要充分考虑执行层面的运作。第二，金融市场环境会显著影响信贷配给，要实现信贷资金的优化配置，应着重建立有效的金融市场环境。我们发现，疫情期间央行等部门出台的金融政策有效地改善了民营企业的融资环境，对民营企业提供融资支持并没有导致它们出现资源错配或资金使用效率低下等问题。第三，虽然商业信用供给有利于整个供应链获得资金支持，帮助金融机构在风险可控的情况下落实竞争中性，但这种现象也可能会产生供应链上下游企业的风险传导效应。一旦上游或下游企业出现信用风险或破产风险，必然导致整个供应链出现系统性风险，即实体经济的风险会传导到金融机构，这对风险监管具有参考意义。

高铁时空压缩效应与公司权益资本成本*

——来自A股上市公司的经验证据

郭照蕊　黄　俊

步入高铁时代的中国,"千里江陵一日还"变成了现实,地理时空距离大为缩短。相对于其他交通方式,高铁有着无可比拟的优越性——准时、快速而又安全、环保(汪德根等,2015)。以往文献大多集中于交通基础设施对一国或地区宏观经济的影响,诸如高铁可达性带来的同城效应、投资变化、虹吸效应、重要城市的极化效应等,而较少关注其对资本市场的作用。作为公司财务的核心概念,权益资本成本一直是金融与会计研究领域的热点。具体来说,权益资本成本的高低对资本市场资源配置效率及资金流向有着重要作用,是资本市场发展和相关制度建设的重要考量指标(毛新述等,2012)。同时,权益资本成本是企业投融资项目的甄选及业绩评价的重要标准,对公司的财务及业务决策起着至关重要的作用。因此,研究高铁开通的时空压缩效应对公司权益资本成本的影响对深入认识资本市场的运行与效率、公司投融资决策与业绩评价均大有裨益。

---

* 原文刊载于《金融研究》2021年第7期。
　作者简介：郭照蕊,管理学博士,副教授,上海师范大学商学院；黄俊,管理学博士,教授,上海财经大学会计与财务研究院。

本文以 2007—2018 年中国 A 股上市公司为样本，实证考察了高铁开通能否对所在地上市公司权益资本成本产生影响？如若影响，是否因公司特征的不同而有所差异？高铁开通影响公司权益资本成本的具体路径又有哪些？结果发现，上市公司所在地开通高铁后，由于内外信息不对称程度的降低，公司权益资本成本显著下降。该现象受到一系列公司特征的影响，与多数投资者聚集地距离越远、业务复杂度越高的公司，权益资本成本受高铁开通影响而下降得更明显。随之，研究发现，高铁开通后公司股票流动性的提升及信息披露质量的提高是影响权益资本成本的有效路径。我们进行了包括安慰剂检验、两阶段回归、倾向得分匹配等在内的一系列稳健性分析，本文研究结论保持不变。

与以往研究相比，本文的创新和贡献体现在以下方面：第一，丰富了高铁经济学的研究成果。以往有关高铁的研究较多关注宏观层面，微观层面的研究较少，其对公司权益资本成本的影响更是鲜有涉及。本文系统考察了高铁开通对公司权益资本成本的影响，增进了对高铁开通溢出效应的理解，为认知我国高铁开通的经济后果提供了微观企业层面的证据。第二，拓宽了权益资本成本的研究领域。以往文献较少探讨影响权益资本成本的宏观层面因素，尚未有研究考察交通这一宏观因素对其的影响。本文考察了高铁开通这一交通基础设施对公司权益资本成本的作用，并检验了其影响路径，由此丰富了公司权益资本成本的已有研究。第三，本文的研究也具重要的现实意义。本文研究表明，高铁开通显著降低了所在地公司权益资本成本，证明了高铁开通对当地企业经营的积极作用，这构成了高铁开通影响地区经济的一个微观基础。同时，本文的研究亦表明，高铁的建设不仅方便人们的出行，在增强资本市场资源优化配置功能方面也具有重要作用，这为认识交通基础设施建设对地区经济发展的影响提供了一个新视角。

本文研究也具重要的实践启示：第一，加快交通基础建设是提升实体经济高质量发展的一项重要举措，是供给侧结构性改革的重要方面。交通基础设施建设降低了公司权益资本成本，对所在地公司的财务行为产生积极影响，进而提升了实体经济的发展水平。第二，无论新形势下资本市场运行出现什么样的新特点、新业态，提高上市公司的信息披露质量，降低交易成本，优化资本市场资源配置的效率都应该是培育健全资本市场的基础建设工程。第三，持续重视中心城市、特别是特大城市的带动效应。地理位置无法改变，与特大城市的距离亦无法改变，但不断寻求时空压缩，改变空间结构、分布结构和层次结构可能是一条路径。

半强制股利政策与股权融资成本 *

王春飞 郭云南

法律保护是促使大股东与中小股东进行利益分享的有效手段，而在法律不健全的国家强制股利支付政策可以弥补法律保护不足的缺陷。但从各国监管实践来看，为数不多的国家要求强制分红，比如巴西、智利等国家，相关研究也并不多见。实证研究发现在巴西的强制股利政策的实施非常有效，它虽然提高了公司的股利支付水平，却没有降低公司的投资水平。与巴西等新兴市场国家类似，由于缺少投资者权益的法律保护手段，我国早期上市公司分红比例较少且分红行为不规范，公司连续多年不分红及突击大额分红的情况时有发生，大股东与中小股东之间利益冲突较为严重。鉴于此，我国监管部门从 2001 年开始对上市公司分红行为进行引导，同年支付股利的公司大幅增加，但是也存在许多公司为迎合监管政策进行微股利支付。为了提高分红比例，监管部门在 2006 年直接对分红的比例进行限制并与再融资挂钩，于 2008 年出台《关于修改上市公司现金分红若干规定的决定》（本文简称《决定》）额外限定了分红的形式。值得注意的是，《决定》还重点强调了对分红信息的披露。具体而言，《决定》要求公司在年报中披露利润分配执行情况，明确公司前三年现金分红的数额及其与净利润的比率；同时要求公司在章程中明确现金分红政策及其决策过程，如董事会制定现金分红预案的情况，

---

* 原文刊载于《金融研究》2021 年第 8 期。
作者简介：王春飞，会计学博士，副教授，中央财经大学会计学院；郭云南，经济学博士，教授，对外经济贸易大学国际经济贸易学院。

以确保分红的稳定性；此外还要求监管部门督促上市公司履行信息披露义务。《决定》大大提高了公司现金股利决策的透明度，并有利于投资者形成回报的稳定预期，对于培育资本市场长期投资理念具有重要作用。此后，监管部门在2012年进一步对分红规定进行了完善，因此形成了非常具有特色的上市公司股利监管规定，以期引导上市公司建立持续、清晰、透明的现金分红政策和科学的决策机制，学术界将其称为"半强制"股利政策。

　　从现有研究看，"半强制"股利政策的实施效果似乎并不理想。早期文献发现"半强制"分红政策可能会降低成长型公司的财务灵活性，对成长型公司产生了不利影响；进一步研究发现，"半强制"股利政策虽然能迫使那些高成长、有再融资需求的公司不得不进行派现，却难以约束"铁公鸡"公司派现，并对高派现公司会产生明显的"负向激励"，甚至在一定程度上降低了整体股利支付水平。此外，"半强制"股利政策产生了其他未预期的不利影响，如税收成本，向下操纵应计来规避监管。"半强制"分红政策对提高股东现金股利回报和保护投资者利益所起的作用有限，其合理性值得怀疑。综上所述，以往研究主要从监管成本的角度，发现将分红与再融资挂钩反而会提高融资门槛，从而出现了所谓的监管"悖论"。

　　以往研究主要从监管成本角度来分析，却忽略了一个重要问题——"半强制"股利政策也可能带来监管的收益，我们认为"半强制"股利政策形成股东之间的利益共享机制，并有利于投资者形成稳定的股利预期，从而实现治理的"溢价"。第一，"半强制"分红政策有利于股东之间的利益共享机制的形成。为了防止公司经理层对分散股东的利益侵害，可以加强法律保护或提高股权集中度形成大股东；大股东的存在虽然可以制衡经理层，但也引发了大股东与中小股东的利益冲突，控股股东可能通过减少现金股利支付的方式来提高资本控制权以获取个人私利。

"半强制"股利政策将再融资与股利政策挂钩并强化监管力度,部分公司可能会迫于监管压力或迎合监管政策改变公司的股利政策,提高现金分红的比率。这种迫于监管压力或迎合监管政策的股利政策变化可能会产生一些不利影响,但通过强制分红也可能缓解大股东和中小股东之间的利益冲突,因此,我们认为"半强制"股利支付可以实现股东之间的利益共享,正所谓"有借有还、再借不难",监管部门试图通过强制现金分红来形成良好的股东之间利益共享机制,从而降低股权融资成本。

第二,"半强制"分红政策有利于形成稳定的股利预期。理论认为资产的价值等于其未来现金流的折现,对公司未来现金流的预测可以依赖公司的股利信息。"半强制"股利政策不仅明确了公司的股利支付率,而且对公司股利支付的决策过程以及相关信息披露进行了严格规定,即要求公司在章程中约定股利的分配形式及决策过程,并在年报中详细披露股利的执行情况,以及要求中介机构对股利相关信息披露进行监督,从而有利于投资者形成稳定的股利预期。因此,我们认为,"半强制"股利政策大大提高了公司股利信息的透明度,有助于投资者估计未来现金流的金额和分布情况,从而形成稳定的股利回报预期,降低股权融资成本。

本文利用2008年监管政策提供的良好自然实验机会,主要从"半强制"股利政策的治理效应角度来评估政策产生的经济后果。总体研究发现,与对照组相比,"半强制"股利政策明显降低了受政策影响的公司股权融资成本,与现有文献中监管"悖论"的发现不一致。进一步研究表明,"半强制"股利政策能够提高受影响公司的股利支付水平和股利支付率,并且支付股利公司的股权融资资本成本会明显降低;同时还发现,在代理冲突高的公司中"半强制"股利政策的作用更加明显,这些结果说明将再融资与股利政策挂钩能诱使企业支付更多的股利,从而缓和大股东与中小股东之间的利益冲突,进而降低股权融资成本。此外,我们还进一步研究了"半强制"股利政策的局限性。"半强制"股利政策在会计信息质量高的公司作用更加明显，说明公司整体信息透明度的提高，有利于投资者形成稳定的回报预期，"半强制"分红政策也更加有效；但是会计信息质量低的公司，"半强制"股利的治理效果不明显，说明"半强制"分红政策的治理"溢价"受限于公司的整体会计信息质量。此外，在融资约束较弱的公司，"半强制"股利政策可能产生明显的治理"溢价"，但"半强制"股利政策在融资约束高的公司的作用不明显。

本文的贡献在于：（1）从治理"溢价"的角度来评价"半强制"股利政策的经济后果，并且研究发现与以往研究结论存在明显不同，即"半强制"分红政策可能产生治理"溢价"，丰富了"半强制"股利政策的相关文献。（2）本文通过双重差分法来评价"半强制"股利政策对股权融资成本的影响，不仅可以有效消除"不随时间改变"的不可观测的个体异质性，而且还可以消除受政策影响的个体和不受政策影响的个体在样本期内所经历的共同趋势，结果将更为稳健。（3）本文的研究结论也具有较为明显的现实意义，可以为"半强制"分红的监管政策完善提供借鉴和参考。

改进的效率测算模型、影子银行与中国商业银行效率[*]

李丽芳 谭政勋 叶礼贤

作为我国最主要的金融机构,商业银行在资源配置中起着重要作用,其效率高低对全社会资源配置效率有着直接而重要的影响,处于金融供给侧结构性改革的关键环节。同时,影子银行业务的发展引起了宏观杠杆不断攀升,商业银行处于影子银行业务的枢纽,对稳杠杆和防范金融风险起到关键作用。影子银行业务既为商业银行拓展了收入和利润,为亟须资金的中小企业提供融资,但同时也为高风险领域提供融资,从而导致风险积累。那么,影子银行对中国商业银行的效率产生了什么影响?在理论和实证上,现有文献没有从风险和利润两个角度全面考察影子银行业务对银行效率的影响;在方法上,Wang 等(2014)的规模报酬可变加权两阶段 DEA 模型虽然能够区分期望产出和非期望产出,但无法区分无效投入对效率的影响;在投入与产出的指标上,已有文献只重视不良贷款等"坏"产出对效率的影响,忽视了营业网点扩张所带来的固定资产和职工人数这些可能的"坏"投入对银行效率的影响。那么,银行的同质性扩张究竟是否有助于提升银行效率?这种扩张是否造成了金融资源配置在供给与需求方面的结构性不匹配?上述重要问题,目前还没有

---

[*] 原文刊载于《金融研究》2021 年第 10 期。
作者简介:李丽芳,经济学博士,副教授,暨南大学经济学院;谭政勋,金融学博士,教授,湖南师范大学商学院;叶礼贤,硕士研究生,暨南大学经济学院。

文献进行研究。

本文的主要贡献如下：第一，本文不但建立影子银行影响商业银行效率的理论模型，还首次同时从利润和风险两个角度分析影子银行业务对商业银行效率的影响。第二，已有研究在测算效率时，只区分产出的"好"与"坏"。本文在此基础上首次同时区分投入和产出的"好"与"坏"：把使理想产出增加的投入称为"好"投入，把那些可能使理想产出减少的投入称为"坏"投入，进而改进Wang等（2014）的两阶段DEA模型。第三，本文构建的理论模型和新方法不仅符合中国商业银行的实际情况，更适用于中国商业银行效率的测算，还为新方法建立一套可行的实施方案：首先提出中国商业银行可能存在"坏"投入的观点，其次通过逆DEA模型进一步确认存在"坏"投入变量，最后利用本文的改进模型来测算中国商业银行效率。

理论上，本文构建的模型能够同时分析影子银行业务对利润、风险和效率的影响。从事影子银行业务后商业银行的总风险上升，影子银行业务可为商业银行带来更高的利润，并足够补偿由于从事影子银行业务带来的表内贷款利息收入变化的影响，利润总额趋于增加；但是，影子银行能否有助于效率的提升，取决于利润与风险的相对增加程度。方法上，为了准确测算影子银行和投入的好坏对效率的影响，本文构建了一个新测算模型。与Wang等（2014）不同的是，本文模型不仅考虑产出的"好"与"坏"，还假设在第一阶段既有"好"投入，又有"坏"投入，因此改进了对投入的约束函数。在存在"坏"投入的情况下，本文改进的模型能更准确测算效率。

为了验证前文的理论模型和改进的效率测算模型，本文从多个角度进行了实证分析。首先是数据和投入产出变量的定义。我们选取104家商业银行2007—2017年的数据，共918个观测值。投入指标包括营业成本、固定资产净值和职工人数，以存款作为中间产出指标来测算第一阶段效率，以税前利润、非盈利资产和不良贷款作为第二阶段产出指标。对于投入的"好"与"坏"，我们通过检验后发现：营业成本是"好"投入，而固定资产和职工人数是"坏"投入。对于产出的"好"与"坏"，参照多数文献，把税前利润、非盈利资产作为"好"产出，不良贷款作为"坏"产出。

为了检验是否应该区分投入的"好"与"坏"，我们从不剥离和剥离影子银行业务两种情况进行分析。其结果均表明，无论剥离还是不剥离影子银行业务，不区分投入的"好"与"坏"，均会高估效率，大银行尤其是股份制银行要压缩不利于效率提升的投入，中小银行也要在扩大规模时优化投入。

影子银行业务对银行效率的影响分析也包括两步。首先，不区分投入的"好"与"坏"，即采用传统的测算方法，结果表明，影子银行业务对银行效率产生了较大的影响，而且主要体现在第二阶段。其次，我们区分投入的"好"与"坏"，即采用本文改良后的效率测算模型，结果依然表明，影子银行业务对三类银行的效率均产生积极影响，对工行、农行、中行、建行四大银行和其他股份制银行的影响较大，尤其是股份制银行的效率得到显著提升，对中小银行的影响相对较小。

总的来看，本文得到两个基本结论：第一，固定资产总值和职工人数是不利于效率提升的"坏"投入。如果不区分投入的"好"与"坏"，则会高估中国商业银行效率，尤其是显著高估四大行和股份制商业银行在吸收存款阶段的效率，区分投入的"好"与"坏"后，四大行和股份制商业银行的效率会降低。因此，大型商业银行依靠网点扩张虽然能提高市场份额，但不一定能有效提升效率。第二，影子银行业务同时增加了商业银行的利润和风险，增加的利润能否覆盖所增加的风险，能否提升效率，理论上虽然不能得到明确的结论，但实证结果显示：对于股份制银行，影子银行有利于提升其经营效率；对于中小型商业银行，影子银行对其效率的影响极其微小；对于四大行，影子银行在 2012 年后对其效率的提升效果不明显甚至为负。

根据上述结论和分析，本文建议：第一，大银行可以减缓以营业网点为代表的同质化规模扩张，压缩固定资产投入，裁减冗员。第二，鼓励和扶持中小银行的发展，建立多层次、适应金融服务需求的市场。第三，中小银行可以采取不同于大银行的市场定位，提供多样化、专业化的异质性金融服务。第四，在规范影子银行发展的同时，考虑影子银行对不同银行的影响，在密切关注风险及风险可控的情况下，更好地引导影子银行业务。

高管薪酬延付与银行利润效率*

——基于银行微观视角的研究

王艳艳 王成龙 于李胜 蓝一阳

薪酬延付政策是我国金融监管部门防范银行系统性风险的一项重要举措，旨在防止激励与风险挂钩不足导致银行过度冒险行为。薪酬延付政策在防范化解系统性金融风险、促进经济和金融良性循环中扮演着积极角色。现有文献已对薪酬延付如何影响风险展开较为充分的讨论，然而对薪酬延付如何影响银行经营效率的探讨却较少。

理论上，银行风险与利润效率的关系是协同效应还是挤出效应？现有研究尚未得到一致结论，因而难以通过薪酬延付与银行风险的关系判断薪酬延付对银行利润效率的影响。更为重要的是，关于风险防范政策如何直接影响银行利润效率的文献仍较为匮乏。银行在面对风险防范政策时，其行为可能发生改变，进而产生预期外的经济后果。从激励效应出发，一方面由于薪酬延付的实施增加了银行高管薪酬获取的不确定性，这会削弱管理层努力提升利润效率的动机，并可能导致盈利效率下降；另一方面，管理层出于职业生涯考虑，即便在外部激励"下降"的情况下，为避免职业被替换或向下的调整，可能存在通过改善经营以提升效率的

---

* 原文刊载于《金融研究》2021年第10期。
作者简介：王艳艳，管理学博士，教授，厦门大学管理学院；王成龙，管理学博士，讲师，中南财经政法大学会计学院；于李胜，管理学博士，教授，厦门大学管理学院；蓝一阳，博士研究生，厦门大学管理学院。

内在动机。因此，薪酬延付政策是否以及如何影响银行利润效率有待进一步研究。

2010年银监会颁布《商业银行稳健薪酬监管指引》（本文简称《指引》），规定，银行主要高管延付比例不得低于50%，其他高管及风险管理人员不得低于40%；薪酬延付期至少三年；如果规定期限内风险损失出现超常暴露，商业银行有权将相应期限内已发放的绩效薪酬全部追回，并止付所有未支付部分；商业银行制定的薪酬延付政策同样适用于离职人员。

为检验薪酬延付对银行利润效率的影响，本文以2007—2018年我国商业银行为研究对象，以2010年《指引》的发布为"准自然实验"进行检验。由于各银行对政策的执行时间存在差异，本文采用交错采纳的双重差分模型。之所以选用利润效率，是因为利润效率本质是指企业在既定条件下实现利润最大化的能力。与其他效率定义相比，利润效率强调从银行的盈利能力角度衡量运行效率。对利润效率的衡量，本文采用随机前沿模型分析法（SFA）进行估计，SFA可以将随机误差项和无效率项分离，该方法更适合于中国银行业的研究。

研究发现，与未实施薪酬延付政策的银行比较，实施薪酬延付政策的银行，短期利润效率较实施前有所下降，但长期业绩的稳定性得到改善。机制检验表明，控制风险影响后，薪酬延付政策的实施会导致银行收入减少（而非增加银行支出），说明政策的实施内化了管理层的行为，降低了风险承担行为从而导致收入短期内下降。同时，薪酬延期支付使得管理层更注重长期业绩的持续性，降低了长期业绩的波动性。调节效应结果表明，薪酬延付与盈利效率的负向关系主要体现在股份制银行、未实施股权激励及应收款项类投资发展不充分的银行中。这说明，不同银行的管理层动机差异会影响薪酬延付与银行利润效率的关系，实施股权激励及适度的应收款项类投资有助于缓解薪酬延付带来的利润效率损失。

本文研究结果表明，以降低风险为初衷的银行高管薪酬延付政策的实施确实抑制了管理层的风险行为，虽然使得银行利润效率一定时期内有所下降，但增加了银行长期业绩的稳定性。

  本文的主要贡献在于：首先，从银行微观视角研究了薪酬延付政策对其利润效率的影响。现有研究多从监管视角检验薪酬延付政策是否能够有效防控风险，本文进一步从银行微观视角补充了该政策对利润效率和盈利稳定性的影响。其次，本文研究利用外生事件冲击，在缓解效率和风险之间的内生性影响后，拓展了现有关于风险应对与效率之间关系的研究。前期研究大多从资本视角对银行风险与效率的关系进行探讨。实际上，风险防范与银行效率之间存在很强的内生性，本文在控制风险影响的基础上利用薪酬延付政策这一外生事件，深入分析了直接影响银行利润效率的因素和可能路径。最后，本文发现推行股权激励等方式能够缓解薪酬延付带来的利润效率下降，为政策的有效实施提供一定借鉴意义。

税率"锚定效应"与企业投资决策*

郑登津 孟庆玉 袁 淳

党的十九大报告指出，随着经济结构的不断优化，我国需要进一步深化投资改革，发挥投资对优化供给结构的关键性作用。而企业投资是我国投资中重要的组成部分，理解高管投资决策的理性和非理性影响因素将有利于深化供给侧结构改革，促进我国经济又好又快的发展。同时，我国也多次强调要保持宏观政策连续性稳定性可持续性，政策如果"急转弯"将不利于企业未来生产经营的稳步增长。正如有关决策者非理性特征的研究中，心理学家发现当决策环境存在不确定性时，人们并非如新古典经济学中的假设一般，能够客观地预期未来各种情况发生的概率，而是有选择性地过度依赖某些信息，在此类初始锚值的影响下进行不充分的调整并决策的过程被称为"锚定效应"。目前，尚未有研究考察高管的这一非理性心理是否会对企业投资决策产生影响。鉴于此，本文试图探究高管在投资决策中是否存在"锚定效应"？

产生"锚定效应"的前提是决策环境存在不确定性，且有"锚值"可制约个体决策。为满足上述条件，本文从影响企业投资决策的重要因素——税率层面进行研究，以往研究主要研究税率高低及波动性等理性层面（Fazzari 等，1988；付文林和赵永辉，2014；Hanlon 等，2017；

---

* 原文刊载于《金融研究》2021 年第 11 期。
  作者简介：郑登津，会计学博士，副教授，中央财经大学会计学院；孟庆玉，会计学博士，讲师，中国民航管理干部学院经济管理系；袁淳，会计学博士，教授，中央财经大学会计学院。

Jacob 等，2016），忽略了税率锚定非理性层面对投资决策的影响。目前我国整体的税收体系还在不断完善、一些政策变化波动有时偏大、各地征税强度差异较大等，政策连续性也在不断提高，在此背景下，企业的投资决策环境也会充满不确定性（Tversky 和 Kahneman，1974；才国伟等，2018；孟庆玉等，2020）。当企业面临的实际税率处于较大波动状态时，高管无法理性预测各种状态发生的概率或者根本无法估计出所有可能的状态，难以准确估计未来的实际税率，若此时企业承担的实际税率高于企业历年承担税负的"常态"，加重了管理层对企业高税负承担的感知，高管可能会过度依赖税负高这一显眼的信息且非理性地预测未来税率也较高，最终导致高管对税率的非理性锚定行为。一旦高管对税率产生锚定行为，将直接影响到企业的投资决策。

因此，本文以 2003—2018 年沪深两市所有 A 股非金融上市公司为初始样本，研究税率"锚定效应"对企业投资决策的影响，结果发现：高管在投资决策中存在显著的税率"锚定效应"，当高管锚定企业当期的高税率时，即企业当期的税率高于自身样本期税率均值（内在锚）或当年同类型企业税率均值（外在锚）时，未来的投资支出均存在显著下降，且内在"锚定效应"强于外在锚定效应。进一步地，我们发现投资中的税率"锚定效应"还因高管的个人特质和公司特征的不同而有所差异。具有财税背景的、任期更长的、年龄更大的高管，将能够有效抑制投资中税率锚定的非理性行为。当公司的税率波动性越大时，高管面临的税率不确定性也越高，投资中的税率锚定效应更加显著。最后，我们发现投资决策中的税率"锚定效应"带来的投资不足，最终显著降低了公司的经营业绩和企业价值。论文结论揭示了投资中税率"锚定效应"这一非理性行为带来的负面经济后果。

与现有研究相比，本文潜在的贡献如下：第一，高管的非理性因素是影响高管投资决策的重要因素，但已有研究主要考察了高管过度自信这一非理性因素对企业投资决策的影响（Pikulina等，2017）。Kahneman（2003）认为高管除了过度自信之外，还存在着非理性锚定行为，现有的研究尚未考察投资中的"锚定效应"这一非理性因素，本文则从税率锚定的视角，研究了高管对高税率的过度锚定对企业投资的抑制作用，丰富了影响投资决策的非理性因素的实证研究。第二，多数学者对于研究对象锚定值的设定仅局限于研究对象本身，通常为计算其他公司相应研究对象的平均值（祝继高等，2017；陈仕华和李维安，2016；许年行和吴世农，2007），鲜有从研究对象的影响因素这一角度设定锚定值。本文则从税率这一影响投资决策的重要因素角度，研究税率"锚定效应"对高管投资决策的影响，并发现内在"锚定效应"强于外在锚定效应，丰富了"锚定效应"的相关研究，为行为经济学理论提供证据支持。第三，本文从"锚定效应"的角度丰富了税负对投资决策影响的研究。以往的文献主要从税率本身高低研究税率对投资的影响，当公司实际税率低，相较市场大环境，承担税负情况轻时，企业会加大投资；也有文献研究表明税率不确定性能够抑制企业投资，上述文献均证明了高管会理性地考虑税率对企业投资的影响（Fazzari等，1988；Jacob等，2016；孟庆玉等，2020）。在传统税负投资理论中，未来公司实际税率不高或者较低时，企业未来应加大投资支出，但本文则引入心理学上一个重要的概念——"锚定效应"，是对传统税收投资理论的补充，丰富了所得税税率影响投资这一领域的研究。第四，本文的结论不仅对企业的投资实践具有启示作用，也对充分发挥投资在优化供给结构中的关键性作用、推进供给侧结构性改革及在改革中注重保持宏观政策连续性、稳定性和可持续性，都有着启示意义。

05　金融市场

中债估值识别了债券信用风险吗？*

——基于跳跃视角的实证分析

史永东　郑世杰　袁绍锋

自 2007 年公司债发行伊始，我国信用债市场进入了高速发展时期。截至 2020 年末，我国信用债市场余额已高达 38 万亿元人民币，是仅次于美国的世界第二大信用债市场。与此同时，信用债违约也在逐年增加，据 Wind 数据库统计，2020 年债券违约数量为 150 只，较 2015 年增长 555.56%，违约金额达 1 697.02 亿元，为 2015 年的 13.94 倍。信用债作为金融市场的重要组成部分，其违约激增必然会对系统性金融风险防范产生不利影响。提前识别并预警债券的违约风险，既可保护投资者利益，增强信用债的吸引力，强化债券市场的投融资功能，也能降低信用债市场的信息不对称性，抑制高风险企业的过度融资，并通过价格机制的资源配置功能，降低企业杠杆率和系统性金融风险。

信用债市场中传统的信用风险识别工具是信用评级。在我国债券市场中，评级机构多采用"发行人付费"的模式。在该付费模式下，信用评级存在固有的利益冲突。为增加收入和市场份额，评级机构往往会迎合发行人需求，刻意调高信用评级，从而导致信用评级难以识别债券违

---

* 原文刊载于《金融研究》2021 年第 7 期。
作者简介：史永东，经济学博士，教授，东北财经大学应用金融与行为科学学院、金融学院；
郑世杰，博士研究生，东北财经大学金融学院；袁绍锋，经济学博士，中国金融期货交易所。

约风险。在信用评级难以发挥信用风险识别功能的情形下，同样作为信息中介的债券第三方估值能否准确揭示债券预期违约风险？回答这一问题对完善债券市场信息环境建设和防范系统性风险具有重要的现实意义。

目前，我国债券市场中主流的估值工具是中债估值，它由中债估值中心在每个交易日结束后发布。中债估值具有以下优势：第一，不同于传统的信用评级，中债估值采用的是"投资者付费"模式，独立性更高；第二，中债估值中心直接隶属于中央结算公司，该公司负责发债企业信息的披露，同时也是债券的中央托管和结算单位，从而为中债估值接触发债企业相关信息提供了便利条件；第三，不同于KMV模型，中债估值不仅包含了发债企业的财务信息，还综合了债券的市场信息，并且每日发布，实时性更好；第四，中债估值被监管机构广泛应用于交易定价、风险评估和公允价值计量等方面。因此，相对于传统的信用风险识别工具，中债估值可能更加有效地反映了债券的价值信息。

在债券信用风险研究中，公司价值跳跃往往作为揭示债券违约风险的一个前瞻性指标，这是因为公司价值跳跃会增加债券违约的概率，使债券持有人面临更大的不确定性。相关研究也表明，股票、期权等资产价格或收益率的跳跃在反映发债企业相关信息的同时，也能够影响债券的信用利差。在信用评级难以有效识别债券信用风险的背景下，对于更加有效反映债券价值信息并得到监管机构充分认可的中债估值，其短期的变化或跳跃可能会成为投资者判断债券信用风险的重要参考。因此，本文从跳跃的视角探究中债估值对债券信用利差的影响及二者的作用机制，以此说明中债估值对债券信用风险的识别作用。

具体来说，本文以2011—2018年中国A股上市公司发行的一般公司债为样本，基于期权定价理论，对中债估值跳跃如何影响债券信用利差进行了实证研究。结果表明，中债估值跳跃能够显著提高债券信用利差，其中，中债估值下跳提高了信用利差，上跳降低了信用利差，且下跳对信用利差的影响程度大于上跳。在采用工具变量、因果识别等一系列稳健性检验后，结论依然成立。异质性分析发现：中债估值跳跃对信用利差的作用在机构投资者中较强，同时在信息不对称性严重、流动性差及违约风险高的债券中也较强。进一步分析表明，中债估值跳跃的概率及程度与债券的风险特征密切相关，中债估值能够向投资者传递公有和私有信息；中债估值跳跃提高了股票分析师的预测表现，改善了信息环境。

　　本文的主要贡献为：首先，当前有关债券信用风险识别的研究主要停留在信用评级，鲜有文献从第三方估值的视角对该问题进行探讨。本文首次分析了中债估值对于债券信用风险识别的作用，为债券信用风险识别的研究提供了新视角。其次，本文发现中债估值不仅可反映债券信用风险信息，还能在现有公共信息的基础上为投资者提供增量的私有信息，这对于目前缺乏信用风险有效识别工具的中国债券市场具有重要现实意义。再次，本研究发现中债估值跳跃可以提高股票分析师预测表现，这说明中债估值对股票市场信息环境的完善也有一定促进作用。最后，本文的研究结论还具有一定政策含义，债券第三方估值具有缓解中国债券市场中债券评级难以反映债券信用风险信息的作用，能够为不同缔约主体及政府监管部门防范债券违约风险、治理违约事件、运用市场化的手段保护债权人利益提供理论参考。

杠杆投资者融资交易行为模式研究*

——来自A股市场的经验证据

康文津　顾　明

　　自2010年证监会推出融资融券方案以来，A股市场上融资交易和融资余额都出现了较为显著的增长。目前A股市场上融资余额总量已经达到万亿元的水平，其对于中国股市的重要性日趋增加，研究杠杆投资者的融资交易行为模式及其对于A股定价机制的影响具有重要意义。为此，本文基于抵押约束模型实证检验了杠杆投资者的融资交易行为模式和市场回报率、流动性等重要指标之间的相关关系。研究发现，滞后股票收益与杠杆投资者的净融资交易额之间存在着显著的正相关关系，说明我国杠杆投资者总体而言是追涨杀跌的趋势追逐者。股票价格下跌对融资交易的影响显著大于股票价格上涨所带来的影响，且这种不对称性在很大程度上是由市场收益而非个股异质性收益所引起的。

　　具体而言，本文利用超过1 000只可以融资融券的股票对个股做时间序列回归，将本周净融资交易额（Net Trading）回归到上周股票收益。研究发现，滞后股票收益与杠杆投资者的净融资交易额之间存在着显著的正相关关系：当股票价格在第t周增加时，杠杆投资者将在第t+1周

---

* 原文刊载于《金融研究》2021年第7期。
　作者简介：康文津，金融学博士，教授，上海财经大学金融学院；顾明，金融学博士，副教授，厦门大学经济学院。

产生显著的融资净买入；当价格下跌时，第 t+1 周产生显著的融资净卖出。为了量化这种影响，本文样本公司平均市值约为 250 亿元，10% 的股票价格涨跌将导致杠杆投资者在接下来的一周对该股有 4 400 万元左右的融资净买入或净卖出。

接下来，本文检验股票价格上涨和下跌对杠杆投资者交易行为的影响是否存在差异。Brunnermeier 和 Pedersen（2009）的抵押约束模型表明，由外生正向或负向冲击引起的资产价格上涨或下跌对于杠杆投资者会产生显著不同的影响。当市场因正面消息上涨时，由于杠杆投资者投资组合市值增加，他们理论上可以借入更多的资金进行额外的融资购买，但是实际上他们并不会立即进行风险资产的购买，而是等待合适的时机再进行相应的买入。当资本市场由于负面消息冲击而下跌时，杠杆投资者面临着投资组合市值缩水，抵押约束收紧，甚至可能会有被强行平仓的风险。此时，他们需要通过及时出售所持有的风险资产来降低杠杆比例。因此本文假设，股票价格下跌对杠杆投资者融资交易行为的影响强于股票价格上涨时的影响。

本文实证结果同样表明，股票价格变化与杠杆投资者融资交易行为之间存在着显著的不对称性，即股票价格下跌对于杠杆投资者融资交易行为的影响约为同幅度股票价格上涨影响的两倍。为了量化这种影响，本文以 250 亿元的样本公司平均市值为基础，若股票价格上涨 10%，接下来一周内杠杆投资者会进行约 3 200 万元的融资净买入；而如果股票价格下跌 10%，杠杆投资者在下一周会进行约 5 850 万元的融资净卖出。股票价格变化与杠杆投资者融资交易行为之间的不对称性支持了 Brunnermeier 和 Pedersen（2009）抵押约束模型的预测。此外，本文还发现当公司股票处于相对的"美好时期"时，由于负面冲击所造成的股票价格变化和杠杆投资者融资交易行为之间的不对称性会更大，支持了 Acharya 和 Viswanathan（2011）提出的理论预测。

此外，本文还探讨了基于杠杆投资者融资交易行为的股票收益可预测性。研究发现，杠杆投资者的融资交易行为与未来股票周度收益之间存在负相关关系。当调整后净融资交易额每增加一个标准差将导致个股年收益率下降约7%。这种负相关关系主要是由融资净卖出所引起的。

打造一个"规范、透明、开放、有活力、有韧性"的资本市场是我国股票市场建设的长期目的。基于前文的研究成果，本文对如何进一步提高我国A股市场的活力与韧性提出以下两点政策建议。一是本文的研究说明应该进一步加强对于广大投资者，尤其是融资融券投资者的教育工作，使其尽量摆脱对"追涨杀跌"交易方式的依赖。对于融资融券投资者，相关监管机构需要辅以相应的事前、事中、事后监管措施。二是在股票市场处于相对美好或是平静的状态时，要防止投资者由于过分乐观而累积过高的杠杆。应当以"晴天修屋顶"的态度，密切关注场内融资总量和杠杆使用程度。

在总结以往融资融券机制运行经验的基础之上，通过加强市场监管，加强投资者教育，更好地把握金融市场的运行规律，可以对中国股市未来的发展产生正面的推动作用。从微观层面上来说，这将有助于降低中国股票市场过高的波动性，提高我国A股市场上投资者所面对的风险收益比例，增强投资过程中的获得感。从宏观的层面上来说，这能够让中国股票市场更有活力、更具韧性，能更有效地抵抗各种潜在的外来冲击，从而为我国实体经济的转型升级作出更大贡献。

市场摩擦对特质风险溢价的影响效应*

——基于 A 股主板市场的实证分析

李少育　张　滕　尚玉皇　周　宇

相对国外发达市场而言，A 股的市场摩擦仍然较为严重，信息不对称、交易成本、买卖限制、卖空机制、外部冲击等市场摩擦因素对股票收益率的影响较大。在防范和化解系统性风险的过程中，进一步分析市场摩擦如何作用于特质风险定价效应具有重要的理论和现实意义。这不仅有助于从新角度解释一些典型的市场异象（如"特质波动率之谜"和特质偏度风险溢价），而且能够为投资组合管理和证券市场监管与发展提供建议。

大部分关于股票发达市场的研究主要从风险偏好和流动性视角解释特质风险和股票收益率的负相关关系（Mitton 和 Vorkink，2007；Barberis 和 Huang，2008；Bali 和 Cakici，2008）。关于中国股票市场的研究已经揭示了特质风险和股票收益率的负相关关系，并且认为代表异质信念的换手率（左浩苗等，2011；Long 等，2018）、代表投资者博彩偏好的特质偏度（郑振龙等，2013）及与流动性相关的套利限制因子（虞文微等，2017；Gu 等，2018）是解释特质风险和股票收益率负相关的重

---

* 原文刊载于《金融研究》2021 年第 8 期。
作者简介：李少育，经济学博士，副教授，华南师范大学国际商学院；张滕，经济学博士，讲师，西南财经大学证券与期货学院；尚玉皇，经济学博士，教授，西南财经大学中国金融研究中心；周宇，硕士，西南财经大学证券与期货学院。

要因素。然而，鲜有文献尝试检验市场摩擦因素本身的定价效应，并分析其对特质风险溢价的作用和机制。

本文试图研究多维度市场摩擦因素的定价效应，并分析其如何影响中国资本市场上特质风险（特质波动率、特质偏度及特质偏度的替代变量）和预期收益率的相关关系。基于2001—2015年中国A股主板股票相关数据，本文先引入适应中国股市特征的连续和非连续市场摩擦变量来代理信息不对称、交易成本、价格冲击、涨跌停板限制、做空机制限制、期货交易限制和外生冲击因素；然后通过Fama-French三因子和五因子模型提取股票的特质波动率和特质偏度，利用Fama-MacBeth横截面回归，验证市场摩擦的定价效应及对特质风险溢价的影响效应，并分析市场摩擦通过流动性影响特质风险溢价的机制；最后，本文从稳健性角度引入加权市场摩擦因子来验证特质风险与横截面股票收益的相关关系的变化，并从投资组合角度判断出市场摩擦下股票的特质风险溢价特征。

从理论上分析，市场摩擦体现在市场的交易难度中，与流动性息息相关。市场摩擦能够通过流动性机制影响特质风险的定价效果：（1）信息不对称的市场摩擦程度较大，则信息传播的延迟性越长，交易时间成本增加，流动性降低，越来越多的投资者没法及时调整头寸，从而使得特质风险的累积定价效应增大。（2）基于制度性成本和交易成本的市场摩擦程度越高，股票流动性越低，股票的特质风险越小。（3）当面对较大的价格冲击时，股票的特质风险变小。（4）在缺少做空机制的市场摩擦下，股票的价格弹性受到约束而使得交易速度变小，股票的特质风险减弱。（5）基于限制股指期货交易的市场摩擦会降低股票的流动性，股票的特质风险也会显著降低。（6）全球性金融危机的外部冲击促使投资者产生避险行为，风险资产的交易意愿降低，交易次数减少。因此，基于外生冲击的市场摩擦会降低流动性，减小特质风险。在后五种情况中，给定原有定价比例，如果特质风险变小，则其定价系数的绝对值会增大，从而增强了特质风险的定价效应。根据以上理论分析,本文提出以下两个假说。

假说1:基于信息不对称、交易成本、买卖限制、卖空限制、风险对冲和外部冲击的多维度市场摩擦因素具有定价效应。

假说2:多维度的市场摩擦因素通过降低流动性的机制增强了特质风险(特质波动率或特质偏度)的定价效应。

实证结果表明,市场摩擦和特质风险因子(特质波动率和特质偏度)都具有定价效应。各市场摩擦因素分别影响了交易时间、交易频率、交易次数、交易意愿和交易速度,股票流动性显著减少,进而增强了特质波动率的负向定价效应,部分解释了"特质波动率之谜",但市场摩擦对特质偏度因子溢价的影响较为微弱。同时,本文通过投资组合分析发现基于特质波动率和特质偏度因子的投资策略具有超越CAPM、三因子和五因子模型的绝对收益,并印证了市场摩擦对特质风险因子绝对收益的影响作用。

通过实证分析,本文得到以下几点结论与启示:一是我国股票市场依然存在"特质波动率之谜",在引入特质偏度的情况下,市场摩擦确实存在定价效应,并能够部分解释"特质波动率之谜"。为了防范市场摩擦本身的风险及交叉风险,应该注重完善上市公司信息披露的及时性、全面性、准确性;进一步放开我国的融资融券市场限制、期货市场交易限制和涨跌停板限制;在防范国际市场的系统性和传染性风险的过程中,容易引起特质风险,因此,既要注意市场流动性的及时补充,也要注意市场流动性的引导与控制。二是我国股市存在特质偏度风险因子的定价效应。市场摩擦会削弱特质偏度的风险溢价,应该加强股市的退出机制建设,继续进行更广泛和深入的投资者教育,培养广大投资者的理性投资理念。三是基于三因子和五因子模型构建的特质波动率组合及特质偏度风险因子的投资组合可以获得超过CAPM模型、三因子模型和五因子模型的绝对收益率,从而对市场投资者构造投资组合具有参考意义。

市场操纵降低了中国股票市场的信息效率吗*

——来自沪市 A 股高频交易数据的经验证据

孙广宇　李志辉　杜　阳　王　近

中国 A 股市场已经走过了三十多年的发展历程，规模上不断发展壮大，总量已经稳居全球第二的位置，仅次于美国股票市场。截至 2020 年底，A 股市场共有 4 154 家上市公司，总市值达 80 万亿元，超过 GDP 的 70%，全年股票筹资额达 16 676.54 亿元。从股票二级市场成交量和成交额来看，2020 年股票市场成交量为 166 403.00 亿股，股票成交额为 2 060 174.09 亿元，均比 2019 年有大幅提升。上述一系列数据表明我国股票市场在规模层面已经取得了长足的进步，然而，近年来违法违规交易行为依然屡禁不止，市场发展质量仍然有待提高。据统计，2020 年证监会查处的市场操纵行为非法获利高达 4.16 亿元，严重损害了广大投资者的合法权益。因此，查处市场操纵行为，提升股票市场公正水平，对于新时代资本市场的健康发展至关重要。

信息效率，又称价格发现效率，是资本市场有效性最直接的体现，

---

* 原文刊载于《金融研究》2021 年第 9 期。
　作者简介：孙广宇，经济学博士，讲师，浙江工商大学金融学院；李志辉，经济学博士，教授，南开大学经济学院；杜阳，经济学博士，博士后，中国银行博士后科研工作站、中国人民大学博士后科研流动站；王近，经济学博士，兴业基金管理有限公司风险管理部。

它主要衡量证券价格吸收信息的速度、反映信息的多少及证券价格与价值的偏离程度。信息效率的变化直接影响资源的有效配置和资本市场质量。因此，信息效率的变化不仅是投资者关注的热点，同时也是市场监管者关心的重点。综观现有文献，我们可以发现，影响信息效率变化的因素非常广泛，从公司层面来看，透明度、交易成本是影响信息效率的重要原因；从市场层面来看，卖空限制、市场行情、网络媒介、分析师跟踪也是影响信息效率的重要因素；从国家层面来看，市场化程度、法制水平、经济政策不确定性同样会导致信息效率变化。

另外，最近一些学者从投资者视角展开研究发现，机构投资者、外国投资者、投资者情绪是导致信息效率变化的重要诱因。然而遗憾的是，学者们尚未从违法违规交易者视角出发，分析市场操纵与信息效率的关系。事实上，市场操纵者通常具有资金优势、持股优势和信息优势，操纵过程会对股票价格形成产生重要影响。相关研究认为被操纵股票在操纵期间的买卖价差、波动率、超额收益率和成交量显著增加，而在操纵之后会出现价格反转。

市场微观结构理论也认为，证券价格形成过程与交易者类型及其交易方式等密切相关，并把市场中交易者类型分为知情交易者和非知情交易者。在股票价格形成过程中，一方面，市场操纵者有时扮演着知情交易者的角色，其利用信息优势，通过价值投资，让股票价格更接近其真实价值，提升了信息效率；另一方面，市场操纵者有时又扮演着非知情交易者的角色，其利用资金优势和持股优势，通过价格投机，让股票价格与内在价值偏离，降低了信息效率。可见，市场操纵对信息效率的影响方向并不明晰，如何客观评价市场操纵对股票信息效率的真实影响？与此同时，市场操纵对信息效率的影响机理是什么？这些问题是本文研究的重点。

有鉴于此，本文以尾市交易操纵为研究对象，尝试对沪市A股可疑的尾市交易操纵行为进行识别与监测，并基于监测结果论证市场操纵对信息效率的影响方向和机制。另外，从防范市场操纵的视角出发，本文还比较了上市公司所有权差异、信息披露质量差异、市场行情差异下的市场操纵对信息效率影响的异质性。本文可能的边际贡献主要体现在以下两点：第一，目前学术界关于信息效率影响因素研究中，鲜有从市场操纵者视角出发，本文承接前人研究，并受市场微观结构理论启发，认为市场操纵者兼有知情交易者和非知情交易者的交易策略，对股票价格形成与信息效率有重要影响，同时进一步厘清市场操纵通过影响流动性和波动性，导致信息效率变化的作用机制。第二，市场操纵监测模型最新研究中，过往学者局限于价格这个单一指标进行建模监测，本文则同时把成交量、收益率、买卖价差、换手率偏离指标纳入模型考量范围内，进而提升了市场操纵监测的严谨性。

本文基于构建的尾市交易操纵识别模型，实证分析了市场操纵对信息效率的影响。本文得出以下研究结论：（1）基准分析表明市场操纵对信息效率存在不利影响；（2）影响机制分析发现，市场操纵后股票的流动性和波动性的异常变化是其影响股价信息效率的关键传导路径；（3）稳健性分析发现，市场操纵对信息效率的不利影响不因市场操纵类型和信息效率指标而改变；（4）拓展性分析发现，在国有企业、上市公司信息披露质量较高情形下，市场操纵对信息效率不利影响程度较小。

以上研究结论对改善我国股票市场信息效率，提升股票市场质量具有一定的政策启示。一要着力增强对股票市场违法违规交易行为的监测和发现能力。随着各种新型操纵手段的出现，违法违规交易行为呈现出越来越强的隐蔽性和复杂性，可充分发挥大数据、云计算及人工智能等新兴技术手段所带来的优势，构建更加完善的监测体系。二要加大处罚力度，提升违法违规行为的成本。

宏观经济信息与金融市场关联性*

——来自混频动态条件相关系数模型的证据

周开国　邢子煜　杨海生

2018年3月政府工作报告明确指出"强化金融监管统筹协调",协调监管的理念在监管层和实务界逐渐成为共识。2018年12月中央经济工作会议指出,"防范金融市场异常波动和共振"对金融市场间的关联关系具有清晰的认识是有效实施协调监管的基础和关键。金融部门作为实体经济的血脉,"增强金融服务实体经济的能力"要求金融市场与宏观经济协调匹配。一个信息灵通、运行良好的金融市场应能有效反映宏观经济的全方位特征。充分利用宏观经济信息,准确估计金融市场的动态关联性,对于实施跨市场协调监管、高效监测和预警市场间的风险共振具有重要意义。

尽管关于金融市场关联性已有大量研究,但绝大多数文献仅关注资产价格间统计意义上的联系,鲜有讨论这种关联现象背后的经济根源与机制。宏观经济信息作为公共信息,某些因素是驱动各项资产价格协同变动的关键,一方面宏观经济信息发布会引发资产价格短期跳跃,另一方面宏观经济信息反映了经济的整体运行状态。忽略宏观经济信息的作

---

* 原文刊载于《金融研究》2021年第11期。
作者简介:周开国,金融学博士,教授,中山大学岭南学院、广州新华学院经济与贸易学院;
邢子煜,金融学博士研究生,中山大学岭南学院;杨海生,经济学博士,副教授,
中山大学岭南学院。

用而只关注市场间统计上相关关系的做法可能会造成我们对市场关联的认知存在一定程度的偏差。宏观经济信息是否能够帮助我们更好地理解金融市场之间的关联关系？众多宏观经济变量中哪个才是最重要的？宏观经济信息在任何时期总是有效的吗？这些问题的答案对更加充分利用宏观经济信息捕捉金融市场间的关联关系具有重要意义。然而，金融市场的高频价格数据与宏观经济变量的低频特征难以同时纳入传统的金融市场关联性分析框架，突破这种数据缺陷造成的两难境地是充分利用宏观经济信息分析金融市场关联性的关键。

本文借鉴 DCC-MIDAS 模型，将宏观低频变量纳入金融市场间高频相关性的分析框架，并采用协方差矩阵估计精度比较方法，给出了宏观经济信息对金融市场相关性影响的直接证据；分析了宏观经济信息模型和市场长期波动率信息模型对金融市场间动态条件相关系数的估计效率差异；系统讨论了各宏观经济变量对金融市场相关性影响的周期性特征；弥补了现有文献中关于多市场相关性讨论的不足。研究结果有助于我们更准确地把握引起金融市场共振的因素，更好地理解宏观经济对金融风险的影响机制，为在不同冲击下准确实施跨市场协调监管提供可行思路，并为结合宏观经济信息和金融市场数据构建金融风险混合实时监测指标提供了参考框架。

本文采用 2006 年 1 月至 2018 年 6 月中国工业增加值、M_2、居民消费价格指数、经济政策不确定性指数等月度数据，共计 150 个样本点，以及相应样本期内股票市场、货币市场、外汇市场、债券市场的日度收益率数据，共计 3 258 个样本点进行研究，得到以下结论。

第一，工业增加值和货币供应量对金融市场关联性具有显著的负向影响，经济政策不确定性和通货膨胀水平则相反。宏观经济信息引入金融市场关联性分析框架的方式并不会对结果稳健性产生影响，但相较于间接方式，直接引入宏观经济信息的方式在金融市场局部关联性高点识别与估计实时性方面都更具优势。第二，宏观经济信息作为金融市场关联性的长期成分，可以比其他基于市场信息的模型获得至少1.45%的效率提升。实体经济运行状况、经济政策不确定性和货币供应量是影响金融市场关联性较为重要的因素，而通货膨胀的重要性相对较低。第三，工业增加值和通货膨胀对金融市场关联性的影响相对稳健，货币供应量和经济政策不确定性呈现出周期性特征。在经济上行期，宽松的货币政策更容易引发金融市场关联性提升，而经济政策不确定性则具有一定的抑制作用，此时工业增加值和货币政策信息带来的效率提升更为明显。在经济下行期，经济政策不确定性和货币政策信息带来的效率提升更高。

  本文研究结论对防范系统性风险和统筹协调监管具有借鉴意义。第一，跨市场协调监管要重视宏观经济因素在市场间关联性分析中的作用，提前防范金融市场关联性的上行。可逐步形成一套系统的金融市场风险共振监控指标。第二，在跨市场协调监管实践中，关注经济周期动态，根据所处经济周期阶段灵活运用政策工具，以宏观政策遏制金融市场风险共振，动态调整监控指标中各宏观变量的比例权重。第三，关注宏观经济信息在金融市场联动中的渠道作用，发挥其经济信号作用；谨防市场恐慌性情绪的跨市场传递和利用信息发布引导投资者情绪。

限购政策是否降低了上市房地产企业价值？*

——基于强度双重差分法的经验研究

梁若冰　张东荣　方　心　林细细

2016年底中央经济工作会议首次提出"房子是用来住的、不是用来炒的"这一概念，2021年《中华人民共和国国民经济和社会发展第十四个五年规划和二〇三五年远景目标纲要》正式将"房住不炒"纳入指导未来中长期经济发展的政策文件，表明中央政府对于推动金融、房地产同实体经济均衡发展，有效遏制房地产市场过热的决心。

随着经济的快速发展和城市化，在过去的20年里，中国主要城市的房价迅速上涨。据国家统计局统计，全国35个大中城市的住房均价由2002年的2 267元/平方米上涨到2019年的15 356元/平方米。为了抑制房地产市场的过度投机，稳定土地价格、房价和价格预期，自2010年以来，地方政府发布了一系列的限购政策。截至2011年底，已有46个城市对住房数量、户籍、贷款比例等采取限制政策。此后，由于房地产市场日趋稳定，这些政策在2014年在大多数城市被取消。然而，由于

---

* 原文刊载于《金融研究》2021年第8期。
　作者简介：梁若冰，经济学博士，教授，厦门大学经济学院；张东荣，经济学博士，厦门大学经济学院；方心，经济学硕士，厦门大学经济学院；林细细，经济学博士，副教授，厦门大学经济学院。

2015年和2016年房价出现新一轮快速上涨，到2019年，60个城市又开始新一轮的购房限制。尽管各个城市采取的具体措施有所不同，但这些政策的主要目标均为通过抑制住房市场的需求来抑制快速上涨的房价。限购政策作为稳定和调控房地产市场的主要手段，对房地产企业及房地产市场产生何种影响值得探究。

本文利用2008—2013年和2015—2019年房地产上市企业的数据，构建了强度双重差分（DID）模型，实证分析了两轮限购对房地产上市公司市场价值的影响，并分析了主要的影响渠道。由于上市房地产企业在不同城市开发的房地产项目有所差异，因此限购政策的实施对各企业的影响也不尽相同。为此，本文采用累积强度指标来识别房地产企业受到限购的差异性作用，其主要原理就是根据各企业在各城市开发的住宅项目在其总开发项目中的比重，确定住房限购政策对不同企业的差异性影响。

首先，本文利用各城市上市房地产企业销售额所占比例构建限购强度指标，并利用强度DID模型进行实证分析，发现两轮限购均显著降低了房地产企业的市场价值。同时，本文还分析了不同限购政策的异质效应，发现：在第一轮限购中，户籍限制、全市限购与仅购两套房等政策是有效的；相比之下，在第二轮限购中，市区限制与转售限制的影响最为显著。

其次，本文分析了上市房地产企业的经营绩效数据，发现两轮限购对盈利能力和营运能力均无显著影响，但第一轮限购对企业偿债能力有显著负向影响，说明该政策可能提高了上市房企的经营风险，而第二轮限购则主要降低了企业的发展能力指标。

再次，本文进一步分析了限购对城市房地产市场的影响，发现第一轮限购对房价指数及其增长率无显著影响，而第二轮则有效遏制了房价上涨的趋势。因此，由于两轮政策对房地产市场的影响不同，对股票投资者预期的影响也不同。

最后，本文分析了深沪股市的日度数据，发现两轮限购对相关上市房地产企业的股票日收益率有显著的负向影响，这表明限购对上市房企价值的影响主要是通过投资者预期引起的。基于前述对房地产市场与企业经营绩效的分析，一个合逻辑的推断是：第一轮限购通过提高企业经营风险而改变了投资者预期，从而降低了上市房企的股市表现以及市场价值；第二轮限购通过遏制房价上涨而改变了企业发展能力，从而降低了投资者对上市房企的市场预期，并最终降低了后者的市场价值。

本文的研究结论对于理解我国房地产市场的发展形势及房地产政策的当前调整与未来效果具有一定启示意义。本文发现两轮限购政策均通过改变投资者预期改变了上市房企的市场价值，体现了限购政策对稳预期发挥的作用，其中第一轮只是改变了投资者的风险预期，而第二轮更是从实体层面改变了投资者预期。从两轮限购政策的比较看，第二轮限购在强化"房住不炒"政策方面对房地产市场与股票市场均产生了实质性的影响，因而作用的力度更大，也更持久。本轮房地产调控政策的核心就是将在未来相当长一段时间坚持实施"房住不炒"政策，这对于改变两个市场的投资者预期，促使房价与股价回归基本面有着重要作用：既有利于抑制住宅市场的投机炒房行为，从而使房价回归理性，体现其居住属性的实际价值；也有利于投资者正确认识房企的股票市场表现，从而促使房企股价回归基本面。

06　国际经济与贸易

反倾销如何影响跨国并购

杨连星

近年来,全球经济增长放缓,反倾销贸易壁垒日益成为诸多国家贸易保护采用的主要手段。党的十九届五中全会提出要"积极营造良好外部环境,推动构建新型国际关系和人类命运共同体"进而构建更高层次的开放型经济体制,"十四五"规划纲要也指出"坚持实施更大范围、更宽领域、更深层次对外开放,依托我国大市场优势,促进国际合作,实现互利共赢"。全球经济发展外部环境的不确定性进一步加剧,根据商务部数据,2020年中国出口产品共遭遇28个国家(地区)132起贸易救济立案调查,涉案金额约131亿美元。与此同时,中国企业跨国并购呈现快速发展趋势。据联合国贸发会议《世界投资报2020》统计,2019年中国对外直接投资流量1 369.1亿美元,继续保持全球第二位,连续8年居全球前三,跨国并购已经成为中国企业对外直接投资的主要形式。由此,中国遭遇的贸易壁垒是否引致了企业跨国并购的迅速增长,企业应如何理性判别和应对贸易壁垒带来的跨国并购的机遇和风险,这些问题引起了理论和政策部门的极大关注和重视。

贸易壁垒对于企业对外直接投资存在多重影响。已有理论表明,资本跨国流动对国际贸易具有完全替代性,资本流动主要来源于贸易壁垒。早期针对日本的样本研究发现,反倾销促进了日本企业在欧洲和美国的

---

* 原文刊载于《金融研究》2021年第8期。
作者简介:杨连星,经济学博士,副教授,华东师范大学经济学院。

跨国投资，企业通过跨国并购方式替代产品出口，进而节省运输成本及关税成本（Barrell 和 Pain，1999）。但也有研究发现，较强的贸易壁垒使得企业对外投资受到极大管制，对来自贸易摩擦对象国的各种企业国际化形式，东道国往往采取"全面谨慎"的原则，使得通过投资跨越贸易壁垒的方式难以实现，只有发达国家跨国公司倾向于选择利用跨国并购的方式来规避反倾销政策。进一步从行业层面来看，当存在反倾销时，技术密集型行业比劳动密集型行业更有可能采取跨国并购的模式。

针对跨国并购影响因素的研究，大多从东道国或母国自身特征方面考量，对"国家、行业及企业"影响研究较为缺乏，因而本文着重从国家间的"贸易壁垒"角度入手，探究"贸易壁垒"因素对跨国并购的影响。本文选取中国企业跨国并购案例样本，结合世界银行反倾销数据库，实证估计反倾销对于中国企业跨国并购的影响差异。与已有研究相比，本文创新主要体现在以下两个方面：首先，已有文献研究大多聚焦于国家宏观与行业层面，鲜有探究反倾销如何影响了微观企业跨国并购及其理论机理。本文通过构建多层面的反倾销与跨国并购指标，全面考量了反倾销与微观企业跨国并购规模、数量、成功率等指标的影响关系及其内在影响机制，有效丰富和拓展了相关领域的研究视角。其次，已有研究尚未将跨国并购的规模、成功率与并购类型等特征指标与反倾销之间的关系进行逐一探究，比较而言，本文对此进行了整合与总结，相关研究内容完善了反倾销与跨国并购多维度指标之间的复杂影响关系。因此，本文在贸易壁垒激励效应的研究领域具有一定的拓展性与创新性。

基于中国企业 1996—2016 年跨国并购案例样本数据及反倾销数据，结合相关理论模型，本文发现：第一，特定国家—行业对反倾销并不能引致针对特定东道国行业层面的跨国并购，这可能是因为如果贸易制裁国对中国某出口行业进行贸易制裁，其目的在于保护国内该行业的市场份额及生产销售，因而双方直接进行的同行业的跨国并购可能很难实现，无论是在政策上还是行业本身的"抵制效应",都使得难以直接达成跨国并购协议。第二,不同层面反倾销对微观企业跨国并购存在显著抑制效应,但一定程度上能显著提高微观企业的并购成功率,其中,行业层面反倾销的贸易保护政策显著抑制了被制裁国企业的跨国并购规模,反倾销会带来"成本增加问题"及产品价格的"不确定性",进而抑制微观企业跨国并购。第三,行业层面反倾销更多抑制的是跨行业的跨国并购,即反倾销目的在于保护特定行业在其本国的市场份额,由此有可能导致跨行业并购的风险会进一步提升,反倾销加大了对"上下游企业"的并购风险,跨行业并购相对阻力更大,整合并购协同成本更高。第四,行业层面反倾销对微观企业跨国并购的激励效应,可能与反倾销遭遇国出口竞争力存在紧密关联。

基于上述结论,本文有以下政策启示:首先,出口国企业可以充分利用跨国并购来规避反倾销贸易保护政策。通过跨国并购行为不仅可以有效避开反倾销贸易制裁,而且在东道国特定行业市场中依然能保留一定的市场份额,甚至能扩大自己的市场占有率。其次,同行业并购策略有助于规避反倾销引致的跨国并购风险,进而提升企业并购成功率。在遭遇反倾销贸易壁垒时,企业可采用以同行业为主的横向并购,规避贸易壁垒引致的跨国并购风险。最后,根据企业自身状况,制定符合实际的跨国并购策略。中国企业实施海外并购时更应从多方面慎重考虑,权衡利弊,科学评估目标企业价值、自身实力及并购后联合企业价值,避免出现好高骛远和冲动盲目的情况。

关税冲击与中国进口行为*

张国峰　陆　毅　蒋灵多

作为促进贸易高质量发展的重要内涵之一，扩大进口是转变经济增长方式、进一步完善经济政策的重要内容。中国政府出台了一系列扩大进口的贸易政策，明确提出将优化进口结构、扩大进口规模上升到国家战略层面。在诸多进口贸易政策的鼓励下，2018年中国进口总额高达2.14万亿美元，比2001年增长8.77倍。

然而，近些年，中国正面临深刻变化的外部环境。以美国为首的贸易保护主义对中国企业生产经营造成了诸多不利影响。为捍卫世界贸易组织体制和自身合法权益，中方不得不对原产于美国的部分进口商品加征关税进行抵制。那么，中国反制关税是否精准有力地打击了美国产品输华？中国总进口贸易及国内产业链是否遭受明显冲击，反制关税是否影响中国扩大进口的基本方针？上述问题的探讨不仅有助于中国更好地应对错综复杂的国际环境，同时也为进一步深化实施扩大进口的对外开放战略提供重要的理论指导。

本文运用多期双重差分模型考察反制关税对中国进口的影响。双重差分模型是进行政策效果评估时应用最为广泛的研究工具。美国于2018年3月23日起对进口钢铁和铝产品全面征税。截至2019年12月底，中

---

* 原文刊载于《金融研究》2021年第10期。

作者简介：张国峰，经济学博士，副教授，对外经济贸易大学国际经济贸易学院；陆毅，经济学博士，教授，清华大学经济管理学院；蒋灵多，经济学博士，讲师，对外经济贸易大学国际经济贸易学院。

美双方一共进行了三轮进口关税调整。2019年9月以后,一系列排除清单和暂停加征关税清单陆续公布,尤其是在第一阶段经贸协议达成之后。由于中国分批次对美国产品征收反制关税,政策冲击的时间点并不唯一,因此需要采用多期双重差分模型。此外,美国对中国产品加征关税的冲击、产品的月度周期与年度周期等因素均已被控制。

本文研究内容主要包括三部分。首先,从进口额、进口数量和进口价格三方面考察中国关税冲击对自美进口贸易的影响。其次,分析关税冲击对中国总进口贸易的影响及中国进口贸易转移现象。最后,从上下游产业链视角探讨关税冲击的影响,并从产品进口需求弹性、产品技术复杂度、进口企业所有制三方面分析关税冲击的异质性影响。

本文采用的2017年1月至2020年6月月度贸易数据来自中国海关总署。由于数据未包含企业名称与代码信息,只能识别HS8分位产品层面的总进口。中国对美国产品加征进口关税的相关数据来源于中国财政部网站,具体包括加征关税的HS8分位产品清单、加征税率、公布清单日期、关税生效日期等信息。美国对中国产品加征进口关税的相关数据来源于美国贸易代表办公室。此外,本文匹配了中国与美国的HS8分位产品编码、中国投入产出表(IO)行业代码与中国海关产品编码(HS8),以控制美国对中国产品加征关税冲击,并分析中国加征进口关税的上下游产业链传导效应。

研究发现:(1)中国对美反制关税精准有力,中国自美进口额和进口数量显著下降。随着关税排除清单的实施,进口下降幅度有所减缓。(2)中国总进口及国内产业链并未受到明显冲击,反制关税的影响总体可控。随着中国不断调低MFN关税税率,对美进口贸易转移至经济规模较大的贸易伙伴国。(3)尽管富有弹性产品、非燃料初级产品及高技术产品对美进口,以及民营企业对美进口均受到一定冲击,但这些产品和企业的总进口并未受到波及,总体外贸形势依然稳中向好。

本文研究结论政策启示如下。首先，中国加征反制关税虽然抑制了中美贸易，但并未对中国整体进口贸易产生明显冲击。这意味着，反制关税形成了精准有力的局部打击效果，有助于敦促美国维护多边贸易体制、遵守世界贸易组织规则，即反制关税的初衷及效果均与中国扩大开放的外贸方针相一致。其次，有必要通过配套措施降低反制关税的负面影响。有关部门可更积极地开展排除清单工作，降低反制关税对国内产业的冲击，尤其是寻求商品替代来源难度大、产业冲击明显或社会后果严重的情形。同时，政府可以搭配使用税收优惠、补助补贴、资金支持等政策，缓解反制关税对中间投入品成本的拉升效应，为企业寻找新的商品替代来源争取时间。此外，"一带一路"倡议的推进和《区域全面经济伙伴关系协定（RCEP）》的签署为促进对外贸易伙伴多元化和产品多样化提供了良好的机遇。

本文的边际贡献主要涉及以下方面。第一，与现有文献采用的数值模拟分析不同，本文基于中国实际进口数据分析反制关税的实施效果。第二，本文分析了反制关税对对美贸易和整体进口贸易的影响，有助于了解反制关税的局部影响和整体效应。第三，本文分析了上下游产业关税的影响，并探讨了行业与企业层面的异质性影响。

长期来看，中美贸易摩擦会对中国产业链稳定、产业转型升级、企业自主创新等方面均产生一定影响，有待下一步深入探讨。

劳动力成本对中国加工贸易规模及转型升级的影响[*]

毛其淋 盛 斌

早在 1984 年,我国就签署了《制定最低工资确定办法公约》,然而在相当长的一段时期内并未有官方的最低工资标准。1993 年劳动部颁布了《企业最低工资规定》,提出中国开始实施最低工资制度。随后在 1994 年,第八届全国人民代表大会常务委员会第八次会议通过了《中华人民共和国劳动法》,明确了最低工资的法律地位,这标志着中国正式实施最低工资制度,大多数省(区、市)在 1995 年前后正式公布了第一个月的最低工资标准。2004 年,劳动和社会保障部通过并实施了《最低工资规定》,将最低工资制度推广至全国各地。

最低工资制度的实施会明显提升企业的用工成本,进而导致加工贸易企业长期以来享有的低成本红利逐步消失。近年来,加工贸易转型升级问题已引起高度关注。党的十七大报告明确要求要加快转变外贸增长方式,立足以质取胜,调整进出口结构,促进加工贸易转型升级。2010年底,商务部会同国家发展改革委等六部委研究出台了《促进加工贸易转型升级的指导意见》,明确了推动转型升级的指导思想、原则、目标及相关政策。2016 年 1 月,国务院印发了《关于促进加工贸易创新发展

---

[*] 原文刊载于《金融研究》2021 年第 10 期。
作者简介:毛其淋,经济学博士,教授,南开大学跨国公司研究中心,经济学院;盛斌,经济学博士,教授,南开大学跨国公司研究中心,经济学院。

的若干意见》，再次明确提出要着力吸引更高技术水平、更大增值含量的加工制造和生产服务环节转移到中国，加快加工贸易转型升级，进一步向全球价值链高端跃升。因此，从最低工资上涨与劳动力成本上升的视角研究中国加工贸易规模变动与转型升级问题具有较好的理论价值和现实意义。

从理论上看，最低工资上涨和劳动力成本上升主要从以下几个方面影响加工贸易升级：第一，最低工资上涨会导致资本相对于劳动力的价格出现下降，而要素相对价格的变化会促使企业对要素投入决策进行调整，进而激励企业采用更多的资本替代劳动力，同时会倒逼加工贸易企业加大研发创新力度来应对用工成本的提升。第二，最低工资上涨可能会激励企业加大对员工的在职培训力度，而员工在职培训的增加对企业加工贸易升级具有积极的影响。第三，最低工资上涨还会通过资源再配置途径对加工贸易升级产生影响。最低工资标准上涨引致的劳动力成本冲击会淘汰一部分不符合要求的低竞争力企业，强化市场的优胜劣汰机制，有利于形成良性的产业竞争，进而改善资源再配置效率，对加工贸易转型升级产生积极的作用。

本文基于2000—2013年企业级微观数据，以中国《最低工资规定》的出台作为准自然实验，采用双重差分法系统地研究了劳动力成本上升对企业加工贸易规模及转型升级的影响。本文研究主要有三点发现。第一，劳动力成本上升虽然缩小了企业加工贸易规模，但通过倒逼机制促进了加工贸易企业转型升级。第二，机制检验表明，劳动力成本上升促进了加工贸易企业增加固定资产投资、扩大研发创新和在职培训的投入力度、提高生产效率，进而推动了企业加工贸易升级。第三，本文还在城市层面研究了劳动力成本、资源配置与加工贸易升级的关系，结果表明，劳动力成本上升显著促进了城市加工贸易升级，这当中，出口市场份额再配置是劳动力成本上升促进城市加工贸易升级的重要途径。

本文研究具有重要的政策启示。长期以来，中国加工贸易的快速发展在很大程度上得益于廉价的劳动力成本优势，然而，中国加工贸易存在"量"大"质"低的典型特征，往往缺乏自主品牌与核心技术，多数处于"贴牌生产"阶段，导致出口扩大主要由大量低附加值的初级加工制成品支撑。本文研究发现，尽管劳动力成本上升不利于加工贸易规模扩张，但通过"倒逼机制"显著促进了企业加工贸易升级，并且通过改善资源再配置效率的途径推动了城市加工贸易升级。这意味着，我国可以通过适度提升最低工资标准和完善工资保障制度的方式，促使加工贸易企业减少甚至抛开对低成本劳动力战略的过度依赖，转向通过加强研发创新和提升效率途径走出"低技术陷阱"，进而推动加工贸易企业实现转型升级，以此提升其在全球价值链中的地位和俘获产品出口附加值的能力。

本文的贡献主要有以下三个方面。第一，本文或许是国内外文献中率先系统全面地研究了最低工资制度和劳动力成本上升对中国加工贸易的影响，在一定程度上丰富了最低工资经济效应的评估文献。第二，本文在开放型经济和全球价值链的大背景下构建了加工贸易转型升级的综合指标评价体系，并深入检验了劳动力成本上升驱动加工贸易转型升级背后的传导机制。第三，本文不仅从微观层面考察劳动力成本上升对企业加工贸易升级的影响，还从宏观层面研究劳动力成本上升对城市加工贸易转型升级的影响，揭示了出口市场份额再配置在其中发挥的作用，这在一定程度上丰富了最低工资上涨或劳动力成本上升的资源再配置方面的研究。

服务贸易开放、市场化改革与中国制造业企业生产率*

彭水军　舒中桥

在信息化时代，服务作为一种中间投入，已经成为决定企业比较优势的主要因素之一，其获取的难易程度会影响下游制造业企业的竞争力。制造业服务化也已成为一国制造业转型升级、占领价值链高端地位的重要手段。但总体来看，我国制造业增加值主要来自制造加工环节，制造业服务化水平有待进一步提高（彭水军等，2017）。2015年发布的《国务院关于加快发展服务贸易的若干意见》（本文简称《意见》）中指出，中国服务贸易发展较快，但总体上国际竞争力相对不足。为了加快制造业转型升级，同时促进服务业发展，我国相继推出了一系列重大举措，力求通过积极发展服务型制造业和生产性服务业，促进中国制造业转型升级、向价值链高端攀升，实现由制造大国向制造强国的转变。因此，在我国服务业竞争力相对较弱的情况下，探讨不断深化的服务贸易开放政策是否有利于促进服务业的发展，是否有利于提升中国制造业企业的生产效率、加快促进中国制造的价值链升级，无疑具有重要的现实意义。此外，《意见》的指导原则之一是"构建公平竞争的市场环境""发挥市场在服务贸易领域资源配置的决定性作用"。国内已有大量研究表明，

---

* 原文刊载于《金融研究》2021年第11期。
　作者简介：彭水军，经济学博士，教授，厦门大学经济学院；舒中桥，博士研究生，厦门大学经济学院。

市场化程度对中国宏观经济增长和微观企业效益等均具有显著影响（毛其淋和许家云，2015），因此市场化改革对服务贸易开放效果很可能存在重要的调节作用，然而目前鲜有文献对此进行探究。

有必要指出的是，现有关于中国服务贸易开放问题的研究大多都使用了2007年以前的早期数据，如张艳等（2013）构建了一个包含金融、分销和电信三个部门信息的服务贸易限制指数，并基于1998—2007年中国制造业企业数据进行研究，发现服务贸易开放促进了中国制造业企业生产率的提升，且对出口企业的促进作用更加显著。孙浦阳等（2018）同样使用了1997—2007年中国工业企业数据，并从外资进入和中间品视角进行研究，认为允许外资参股的政策通过成本渠道提升了行业贸易福利，且对一般贸易更为明显。但毛其淋和方森辉（2020）却指出，当外资政策由禁止进入变更为允许进入，竞争效应会大于技术溢出效应，从而对本土企业生产率造成负面影响。我们认为，研究结论存在差异的原因在于：首先，中国在2007年前后两个阶段的服务贸易进出口数据存在较大差距；其次，贸易开放过程中，我国企业价值链地位和产品质量不断提升（祝树金等，2018；Aichel和Heiland，2018），国内产品对进口中间品的替代效应逐渐增强（Koopman等，2012；Kee和Tang，2016）。大部分已有研究主要关注出口企业，忽略了现阶段国内非出口企业的产品质量提升后，在产品市场形成的对进口产品的竞争力逐渐增强。

相对于已有研究，本文的贡献主要体现在以下几点：第一，构建了一个微观企业生产理论框架，将服务作为制造业企业的重要生产投入，从理论上分析了在考虑国内产品替代性的情况下，服务贸易开放如何影响制造业企业的劳动生产率；此外，本文基于国内改革与对外开放政策协调角度，研究了市场化对服务贸易开放的调节作用。第二，采用更具有时效性的中国2012年工业企业数据库和World Bank服务贸易限制指数（STRI），不仅将 Beverelli 等（2017）的研究拓展到企业层面，更是对其中无法解释的实证结果进行了深入探讨，从而得出新的结论，服务贸易开放促进了中国制造业出口强度较大企业的生产率的提升，但抑制了非出口企业生产率的提升，且对国企及非东部地区中的出口企业生产率的促进效应更为显著，而对非国企及东部地区的非出口企业的不利冲击更大。第三，本文继续探讨了市场化对我国服务贸易开放效果的调节作用，发现国内市场化程度对服务贸易开放政策具有双重效果，表现为市场化扩大了服务贸易开放对出口强度较大企业的正向促进作用，减弱了服务贸易开放对非出口企业的负面冲击。第四，本文还发现，市场化主要通过 FDI 渠道调节服务贸易开放对企业生产率的影响。

本文的结论区别于绝大部分已有文献，对我国深入推进改革开放具有一定的借鉴意义，也为双循环发展提供了一定程度上的政策启示：对外循环要以开放促发展，对内循环要扩大内需，因此既要保证出口企业在开放中获益，又要防止非出口企业受到开放带来的负面竞争过大。近年来，我国的产品、服务和工程质量都得到明显的提高，有效促进了经济社会的发展。本文的研究结论表明，在当前，由于中国国内制造业产品竞争力的提升，贸易政策对中国的影响已然发生一些变化，影响机制和结果更为复杂，需要更好地协调国内市场化进程和服务贸易自由化政策之间的关系。首先，服务贸易对出口企业和非出口企业的影响具有差异性，在进行贸易开放的同时，需要注意避免对非出口企业产生过大冲击，在发展经济外循环的同时，保护经济内循环格局的建设。其次，进一步促进市场化改革，从而降低服务贸易开放过程中可能带来的对非出口企业的负面冲击，还能放大服务贸易开放对出口企业生产率的促进作用。本文发现，市场化主要通过 FDI 途径发挥调节作用，因此应重视 FDI 政策的合理适度开放。最后，进一步缩小东部较发达地区和非东部欠发达地区的市场化程度差异，避免服务贸易自由化影响区域发展。

提高出口退税能够"稳就业"和"稳外贸"吗？*

王君斌　刘河北

近年来，全球贸易保护主义的抬头加剧了各国之间的贸易摩擦。为应对贸易摩擦对我国经济的不利影响，财政部和国家税务总局先后出台《关于调整部分产品出口退税率的通知》（财税〔2018〕123号）和《关于提高部分产品出口退税率的公告》（财政部　税务总局公告2020年第15号），决定进一步提高部分产品的出口退税率。我国也多次强调宏观经济政策"稳中求进"，做好"六稳""六保"工作，而稳就业则被放在了首位。此外，出口退税是鼓励企业出口、促进国内经济发展和扩大就业的重要手段，也是开拓国际市场、提高产品竞争力的重要工具。1994年我国分税制改革以来，出口退税的税率、规模和占出口总额的比重都处于上升趋势，出口退税力度不断加大。因此，探讨出口退税政策对我国就业和外贸的影响，具有理论和现实意义。据此，本文以中美贸易摩擦为例，探讨我国出口退税政策在稳就业、稳外贸及应对贸易摩擦中的作用机制，并在动态随机一般均衡（DSGE）框架下展开。

本文首先研究了我国就业和净出口的周期特征，基于1994—2020年季度数据的检验证据发现：就业的波动较平稳，净出口则呈现高波动特征，

---

* 原文刊载于《金融研究》2021年第12期。
作者简介：王君斌，经济学博士，副教授，西南财经大学财政税务学院；刘河北，经济学博士，讲师，广西财经学院海上丝绸之路与广西区域发展研究院。

就业和净出口均呈现较弱的顺周期特征。这些周期特征不仅与其他国家存在显著差异,与现有文献的结果相比也存在较大不同。

其次,为了解释我国就业和净出口的周期特征,本文构建了一个含有不完全金融市场和价格不完全传递的对称两国开放经济宏观经济模型。利用中美两国宏观数据进行校准,数值模拟发现:在本国出口退税冲击和他国技术冲击下,构建的模型能够较好地拟合我国就业和净出口的周期特征。其中财富效应和由贸易条件变化引起的支出转移效应是主要的内在传导机制。对本国而言,他国技术冲击将形成一种跨国的正向需求冲击,导致本国产出、就业和净出口上升,形成共动性,产出与就业、净出口的相关系数均为正,但由于不完全金融市场和价格不完全传递的存在,他国财富效应对本国产出、就业、净出口的影响将被削弱,这意味着产出与就业、产出与净出口的相关系数是一种弱正相关关系。另一方面,出口退税冲击改变了两国进出口商品的贸易条件,提高出口退税率将使本国出口商品价格下降,进而形成支出转移效应。同样受到不完全金融市场和价格不完全传递的影响,本国提高出口退税率引致的支出转移效应也将被削弱,使产出与就业、净出口呈现弱正相关关系。

在厘清出口退税作用机制的基础上,本文以中美贸易摩擦为例进行反事实实验,探讨在以下两种情形下,我国提高出口退税率能否起到稳就业和稳外贸的作用。数值模拟发现:我国单方面提高1%出口退税时,就业增长0.05%,净出口增长0.28%,而后逐渐递减并呈现较强的持续性,提高出口退税能够稳就业和稳外贸。这是因为出口退税冲击改变了出口商品与进口商品之间的相对价格,提高出口退税相当于降低了我国出口商品的价格,贸易条件恶化,由贸易条件变化引起的支出转移效应,使他国家庭增加对本国商品的购买需求,本国出口相应地增加。出口需求上升导致就业增加。

对我国而言,美国提高进口关税是一种负向的需求冲击。当我国提高 1% 出口退税和美国提高 1% 进口关税时，我国就业增长 0.03%，净出口增长 0.16%，而后逐渐递减并呈现较强持续性，勒纳中性不成立，此时出口退税在稳就业和稳外贸中的作用尽管被削弱，但依然有效。这是因为在我国出口退税冲击和美国进口关税冲击的共同作用下，我国宏观变量呈现一正一负交替变化，但宏观变量的变化幅度不一样。由于模型中两国参数校准值不同及不完全金融市场和价格不完全传递的存在，使得我国出口退税冲击对宏观变量的影响幅度大于美国进口关税冲击，此时这两个冲击的叠加净效应是非零的，即存在真实效应。

因此，基于以上两种情形的分析可知，我国的出口退税政策不仅能够在一定程度上对冲、抵消他国提高关税对我国就业和净出口的不利影响，而且能够产生正向的净效应。尽管提高出口退税政策的净效应较小，但确实发挥了稳就业和稳外贸的作用。更进一步，采用贝叶斯估计方法也佐证了以上结论是稳健的。

本文的边际贡献体现为以下两点：一是拓展了国内文献在我国就业和净出口周期特征方面的研究。本文构建的两国开放经济模型，不仅能够较好地解释我国就业和净出口的周期特征，而且将我国的出口退税政策纳入其中，并探讨了相应的内在机制。二是构建的两国开放经济模型，能够反事实地模拟和评估不同情形下我国提高出口退税率在稳就业和稳外贸方面的政策效果，具有一定的现实借鉴意义。

从长远来看，贸易摩擦将不可避免，但无论是什么形式的贸易摩擦，出口退税政策作为我国主要的外贸调节工具之一将发挥相应的对冲作用。

07　普惠金融与社会发展

企业履行社会责任的共赢效应：
基于精准扶贫的视角*

潘健平　翁若宇　潘　越

2013年，习近平总书记在湖南省调研时首次提出了"精准扶贫"，要求对深度贫困人群实施精准识别、精准帮扶，做到因地施策和因人施策，从而化解不同地区由于不同原因所产生的贫困问题。许多企业主动承担社会责任并积极参与到精准扶贫中。2016—2020年仅深交所的上市公司就累计投入约699亿元，帮助187万贫困人口成功脱贫。

企业履行社会责任的动机可以被归纳为以下三种。第一种是利他性动机，这是企业为了回馈社会、不求回报的奉献行为。第二种是管理者私利动机，基于这种动机，承担社会责任成为管理者利用企业资源来提升个人社会形象和地位的工具。第三种是战略性动机，企业积极履行社会责任是为了获取声誉和政治资本等战略性资源。虽然目前有关企业社会责任的研究已经较为丰富，但是大部分研究关注的都是慈善捐赠这种货币形式的援助，对于技术援助、教育援助等非货币形式的研究仍然十分匮乏。此外，关于慈善捐赠的研究主要关注企业"捐不捐"和"捐多少"，并没有考查慈善捐赠的捐赠效果，而大部分研究基于企业从中受益的结果推断企业履行社会责任的动机是非利他的，甚至是企业自利的工具，

---

* 原文刊载于《金融研究》2021年第7期。
　作者简介：潘健平，经济学博士，讲师，东南大学经济管理学院；翁若宇，经济学博士，讲师，厦门国家会计学院；潘越，管理学博士，教授，厦门大学经济学院金融系。

这可能在一定程度上扭曲企业履行社会责任的初衷和动机。

本文以2013—2018年沪深A股非金融上市公司作为研究对象，手工收集并整理了企业实施精准扶贫的相关数据，考察企业实施精准扶贫的动机及所产生的社会福利效应是否有别于传统的慈善捐赠。本文的研究发现：第一，对扶贫企业而言，实施精准扶贫缓解了企业的融资约束，从而提升企业的经营业绩和股东财富。第二，对于被扶贫地区而言，企业的精准扶贫在未对地区生态环境造成危害的前提下，显著提高了地区的经济发展和居民可支配收入的增长速度。第三，本文发现企业实施精准扶贫并不是为了掩盖企业的不当行为或转移投资者对于其资本市场表现低迷的关注，因而排除了管理者实施精准扶贫的私利动机。以上实证结果表明企业实施精准扶贫是利他性动机与战略性动机的结合，能够实现企业、社会和环境三者的共赢。

本文的结论具有一定政策含义。第一，实施精准扶贫是继开发式扶贫之后建设全面小康社会过程中实施的重大战略举措。在过去的开发式扶贫中，由于兴建基础设施需要的资金较大、投资回收期较长，因此，扶贫的任务主要由政府承担。但是，随着扶贫工作的日益深入，贫困人口的分布在地理上呈现出分散化的特征，以政府为主导，让多元主体广泛参与的精准扶贫战略展现出了扶贫的效率优势。本文的研究发现实施精准扶贫能够实现企业、社会与环境三者之间的共赢。因此，我国的反贫困经验表明，全世界的其他贫困地区在脱贫减贫的过程中，要让企业深度嵌入帮扶群体中，充分发挥企业在产业、技术和人才等方面的优势，借助于市场机制，最大限度地提高扶贫资金的使用效率。第二，全面脱贫以后，如何实现精准扶贫与乡村振兴的有效衔接成为重要研究问题。中共中央、国务院在《关于实现巩固拓展脱贫攻坚成果同乡村振兴有效衔接的意见》中指出，要坚持政府推动引导、社会市场协同发力。在脱贫攻坚的过程中，企业所发挥的作用有目共睹。而在未来服务乡村、振兴乡村的过程中，企业应该系统化、常态化地建立服务乡村振兴的长效机制，主动将产业优势和人才优势嵌入乡村，与当地的经济发展相融合，这不仅可以服务国家乡村振兴的重大战略，而且能够通过资源互补获得更好的发展机会。

本文的贡献主要体现在以下两个方面。第一，本文从企业实施精准扶贫的视角澄清了企业履行社会责任的动机。现有研究基于企业从慈善捐赠中受益的结果推断企业履行社会责任的动机是非利他的，甚至是企业自利的工具。本文发现企业在实施精准扶贫的过程中有着较为明显的利他性动机，这说明企业履行社会责任的出发点之一是提高社会福祉，而不仅仅是为自身谋利，这为准确地理解企业履行社会责任的动机提供了新的理论视角和实证证据。第二，本文借助企业实施精准扶贫这个事件厘清了企业履行社会责任的结果究竟是单方获益还是多方共赢。许多研究发现企业履行社会责任只能实现单方获益。Chen等（2018）发现履行社会责任的成本是企业的盈利能力下降及股东利益的受损。Lu等（2021）的研究进一步发现不仅是国企，民营企业的盈利能力和股东价值都出现显著下降。这说明企业履行社会责任虽然能够改善社会福利，但是其代价是股东利益的受损。与他们的研究结论有所不同，本文发现企业履行社会责任在增加股东财富的同时，也促进了被扶贫地区的经济发展和居民增收，同时当地的生态环境也没有恶化，从而验证了通过实施精准扶贫而履行的社会责任能够产生共赢效应，这为进一步理解企业履行社会责任所产生的社会福利效应提供了新的视角。

"活在当下"还是"未雨绸缪"?

——地震对中国城镇家庭储蓄和消费习惯的长期影响

章 元 刘茜楠

2000—2019年,地震、洪水、风暴、干旱等自然灾害在全球范围内造成约2.97万亿美元的经济损失,导致至少123万人丧生。自然灾害的频发和突发对社会经济持续增长造成了严重威胁,有关自然灾害的影响及其应对成为社会各界普遍关注的热点问题。经济学文献认为,家庭为了应对未来的自然灾害冲击会采取预防性储蓄措施,利用储蓄来熨平负向冲击导致的收入意外下降,从而实现消费平滑。但自然灾害的种类很多,包括地震、洪水、干旱、飓风、病虫害等,不同灾害的可预测性、破坏程度、可规避程度、发生频率及冲击的后果都不尽相同,因此将其混在一起研究可能导致有偏的结果。

全球有27亿人口生活在地震带上,过去20年地震与海啸造成的死亡人数占自然灾害造成总死亡人数的56%。但现有经济学文献关于地震对家庭储蓄和消费行为的影响研究并不充分。本文认为,地震与洪水、干旱等自然灾害的一个重要区别是其不仅会给家庭财产或收入造成损失,还会带来死亡威胁,而这会提高地震带居民的死亡风险预期,并引发恐

---

* 原文刊载于《金融研究》2021年第8期。

作者简介:章元,经济学博士,教授,复旦大学中国社会主义市场经济研究中心;刘茜楠,经济学博士研究生,复旦大学中国社会主义市场经济研究中心。

惧和焦虑等负向情绪。已有文献从理论上证明了更高的死亡风险会降低个体的耐心程度,使得人们更倾向于当前消费。相关心理学研究则进一步指出人类会通过增加享受型消费来摆脱死亡威胁带来的恐惧和焦虑等负向情绪。因此,本文认为相比"预防性储蓄"假说,"活在当下"假说更能够刻画居住在地震带上并遭受过地震冲击的家庭的消费和储蓄行为,并提出如下经济机制解释地震冲击对地震带居民储蓄和消费习惯的长期影响:地震经历在长期内并不会影响家庭的收入水平,但它带来的死亡风险和心理冲击会使地震带居民更多地进行享受型消费,从而降低了家庭储蓄率。

中国的国土面积占全球大陆面积的7%,却承受了全球33%的大陆强震。因此,中国为研究地震对居民储蓄和消费习惯的影响提供了很好的样本。本文基于来自国家统计局的2002—2009年城镇住户调查(UHS)中18个省(区、市)的样本,保留了户主5岁以后一直居住在本地的家庭,并使用户主5岁后经历的4.5级及以上地震频率作为家庭遭受地震冲击程度的度量指标。本文实证发现,在控制城市、年份、年龄组固定效应及家庭、户主和城市特征后,户主经历地震频率的回归系数显著为负,户主每多经历1次地震,其家庭储蓄率降低约0.2个百分点。机制分析发现,户主经历的地震频率在长期内对家庭可支配收入没有显著影响,但是对消费支出有显著的正向影响。本文进一步将国家统计局定义的八大类消费进行细分,并分别定义了宽口径和窄口径的享受型消费,结果发现户主经历的地震频率在长期内显著提高了家庭的享受型消费,如文化娱乐、养生保健、美容、奢侈品支出等,但是对非享受型消费没有显著影响。上述结果表明,地震冲击通过提高城镇家庭的享受型消费进而降低了家庭储蓄率。本文充分考虑了遗漏变量和迁移导致的内生性问题,并采取多种方式进行稳健性检验,例如,控制城市的文化、地理环境等特征变量、采用户主7岁以后经历的地震频率或户主经历的6级以上强震频率作为核心自变量、利用倾向得分匹配法（PSM）得到的配对样本进行回归、利用1992—2000年UHS样本进行回归、排除地震损失带来的直接影响及溢出效应的影响、采用不同的聚类标准误等，都发现上述结论是稳健的。另外，本文基于其他劳动力调查样本实证检验发现，个体经历的地震频率越多，其受到负向情绪的影响显著越大，并且自我控制力显著越低。这也再次说明地震冲击使得当地居民更容易产生恐惧和焦虑等负向情绪，并会降低他们的自我控制力，这在一定程度上解释了地震带居民更倾向于享受型消费的原因。

  本文的研究结论在理论和现实层面都具有一定的意义。从理论层面看，一是丰富了地震影响居民消费和储蓄行为的文献，关于此问题的研究尚未达成一致结论，本文认为"活在当下"假说更适合刻画地震经历对中国家庭储蓄和消费习惯的长期影响，为上述研究提供了来自中国城镇家庭的细致微观证据，也为心理学领域关于死亡威胁对个体消费行为影响的研究提供了来自现实而非实验场景的证据。二是为理解中国家庭储蓄率的决定因素提出了一个消费习惯角度的解释，也为享受型产品生产或服务企业的选址提供一定的启示。从现实层面看，中国经济的一个典型特征是高储蓄率和低消费率，党的十九届五中全会提出要坚持扩大内需战略基点，把实施扩大内需战略同深化供给侧结构性改革有机结合起来，畅通国内大循环，促进国内国际双循环，全面促进消费。本文的研究结论提示要激发居民的消费潜力，可在倡导正确价值观的前提下，从培养居民文化娱乐性消费习惯的角度出发进行政策设计；此外，新冠肺炎疫情的暴发对全球经济形成巨大的负向冲击，本文的结论有助于预测这一负向冲击对居民消费和储蓄率的影响，同时也提示疫情期间人们培养起来的使用口罩和消毒等物资的习惯可能在长期内对居民储蓄率产生影响。

金融素养与家庭储蓄率*

——基于理财规划与借贷约束的解释

吴卫星 张旭阳 吴 锟

近年来居民储蓄和消费的变化引起广泛关注。2021年3月《中华人民共和国国民经济和社会发展第十四个五年规划和2035年远景目标纲要》指出：深入实施扩大内需战略，增强消费对经济发展的基础性作用和投资对优化供给结构的关键性作用，建设消费和投资需求旺盛的强大国内市场。家庭财务健康状况会影响扩大内需政策的效果。研究发现，家庭的财务优化程度受限于金融素养水平。金融素养与退休计划有着很强的正向关系（Van Rooij 等，2011），缺乏金融素养的家庭退休后的储蓄往往不足，且积累过多的负债，不善于利用金融创新工具（Lusardi 和 Mitchell，2007；Campbell，2006）。根据生命周期假说，理性人在工作期间会不断进行储蓄，退休后使用储蓄度过晚年，一生中消费是平滑的。然而现实中，居民在临近退休前会减少其工作及娱乐相关的花费，不断降低自身的杠杆，减少消费贷款并增加流动性储蓄（Olafsson 和 Pagel，2018）。这种"临时抱佛脚"的做法说明居民在工作期间并没有积累充足的储蓄来满足退休生活的需要。

---

* 原文刊载于《金融研究》2021年第8期。
　作者简介：吴卫星，理学博士，教授，对外经济贸易大学应用金融研究中心；张旭阳，金融学博士，讲师，北京工商大学经济学院；吴锟，金融学博士，副教授，北京物资学院经济学院。

家庭储蓄率是否合理，最终会影响到家庭的资产和负债状况。关于金融素养对家庭金融决策的影响，目前多集中在家庭的资产端或负债端。而家庭的资产配置和负债行为侧重于存量概念，储蓄率更接近于一个流量指标。本文实证研究了金融素养与家庭储蓄率之间的关系，使用工具变量解决内生性问题，通过理财规划与借贷约束的视角探讨金融素养与家庭储蓄之间的作用机制。本文发现：（1）金融素养与家庭储蓄率呈倒"U"形关系，当金融素养由低升高时家庭储蓄率会随之升高，而后随着金融素养水平的不断提高储蓄率会步入下降通道。（2）理财规划意识和借贷约束分别是影响储蓄率上升和下降的渠道。金融素养由低逐渐升高时，家庭的理财规划意识增强，通过提高储蓄率来保障家庭资金充足。当金融素养增加到一定程度，理财规划意识抑制消费的作用减弱，同时借贷约束缓解会帮助家庭增加消费。从而解释了金融素养与家庭储蓄率的倒"U"形关系。本文进一步揭示，金融素养与储蓄率之间的倒"U"形关系，并不代表金融素养水平高的家庭出现储蓄不足或者过度消费的可能性增大。实证发现金融素养越高的家庭具有较稳定储蓄的可能性越大，而出现"月光"的概率越低。当家庭金融素养提升后，理财规划意识对增加储蓄率的作用不显著，而对于资产的优化配置作用显著。家庭理财规划的注意力可能由增加储蓄率转移到了对储蓄资金的保值升值上。

现阶段，如何提振内需同时避免过度消费，受到政府和业界的关注。储蓄率并不像永久性收入假说那样，人们在确定的最优值上储蓄，而是有异质性的。前人的研究包括房价、社保、老龄化、收入不平等、高等教育改革等，说明外部环境会影响到家庭的储蓄，本文研究家庭内部的因素，即金融素养水平，也可以影响到储蓄率。金融素养作为影响家庭金融决策的重要变量，对储蓄和消费并不是简单的线性影响，总体呈倒"U"形关系。金融素养水平高的家庭融资约束降低，会将更多精力放到优化资产配置方面，提高资金运作效率，合理安排消费。最优储蓄的概念是相对的，金融素养水平低的家庭往往缺少规划、借贷约束强，提高储蓄对他们来说是更合适的选择。

根据上述分析结论，得出以下三方面的启示。（1）金融市场对家庭的作用可能是相对的，考虑金融素养后会对储蓄率的高低有新的认识。按照金融素养水平的不同，将储蓄率偏低的家庭分为两类，一类是金融素养水平低的家庭，其缺乏理财规划意识；而另一类是金融素养水平高的家庭，其拥有较稳定储蓄，资产配置更加多样化。这两类家庭储蓄率下降的成因不同，应区别对待。（2）金融市场的波动起伏、消费种类和形式不断丰富给金融素养水平低的家庭带来的更多是外部风险。需要关注这类人群面临的金融困境。本文发现理财规划对于金融素养水平低的家庭储蓄率提升作用更显著。因此对储蓄率偏低且金融素养水平偏低的家庭，及时普及财务规划知识，有助于改善家庭财务健康状况。（3）家庭拥有较高的金融素养水平，可以较好地分散外部市场波动和获取投资收益，面对风险也有较多金融工具来缓冲，意味着家庭在金融市场上有比较优势。此时，家庭会进行资金的再配置，增加当下的消费。总体来看，普及金融教育对于不同金融素养水平人群均有积极意义。

新型农村社会养老保险参与决策中的同群效应*

张川川　朱涵宇

社会保障体系建设是实现国民收入再分配、保障国民基本生活福利、维护社会安定和建设社会主义和谐社会的重要举措。2000年以来，我国社会保障体系快速发展，相继实施了新型农村合作医疗保险、城镇居民医疗保险、新型农村社会养老保险（新农保）和城镇居民社会养老保险等一系列重大的社会保障项目，于2012年实现了社会医疗保险和社会养老保险在制度上的全覆盖，建成了世界上覆盖人口规模最大的社会保障体系，取得了举世瞩目的成就。

社会保障制度具有实现收入再分配和风险分担的作用，但是能够在多大程度上发挥上述作用却高度依赖于政策的参与度。尽管我国已经实现了社会保障体系的全面覆盖，但是对于采取自愿参与原则的社会保障项目，政策目标人群的参与率远低于100%。过低的参保率严重限制了社会保障制度在实现收入再分配和风险分担方面能够发挥的作用，妨害了社会保障制度保障人民群众基本生活的功能。

理清微观个体参与社会保障项目的决策机制，是科学制定社会保障政策、健全社会保障体系和最大化社会保障制度功能的前提。但是，针

---

* 原文刊载于《金融研究》2021年第9期。
　作者简介：张川川，经济学博士，百人计划研究员，浙江大学经济学院。朱涵宇，经济学博士研究生，北京大学国家发展研究院。

对社会保障项目参与决策的严谨研究却并不多见。社会保障项目的低参与率现象并不是中国所独有的，也普遍存在于其他国家。Currie（2006）在总结使用其他国家数据所做研究的基础上，认为信息传递、污名效应和交易成本等是影响个体参与社会保障项目的重要因素。然而，许多社会政策的参与率仅仅略高于50%，上述因素并不能够完全解释如此低的参保水平。在最近两项研究中，Alsan和Yang（2018）、Zhang（2019）分别考察了移民政策和文化观念对社会政策参与率的影响。然而，移民政策和文化因素仅能解释特定政策和文化背景下的个体参保决策，无法解释世界范围内普遍存在的低参与率问题。

本文旨在考察同群效应在社会保障项目参与中的作用。同群效应对个体决策存在着广泛的影响，已有研究也表明社会医疗保险的参与决策同样存在同群效应（Duflo和Saez，2002；Liu等，2014）。我们以新农保为例，对社会保障项目参与决策中的同群效应进行实证检验。新农保是参与率较低的社会保障项目之一。中国政府于2009年启动新农保政策，并于2012年底实现了全国覆盖。但是，2014年新农保政策适保人群的参与率仍很低，使用中国家庭追踪调查（CFPS）数据计算的符合条件的60岁以下人群的参与率约为62.2%。

使用CFPS数据，我们估计了同村居民参与新农保的比例对个体参保决策的影响。基于传统的普通最小二乘（OLS）方法的估计结果显示，同村居民参保率每增加1个百分点，个体参加新农保的概率显著增加0.76个百分点。为了解决OLS估计存在的内生性问题，我们参照Case和Katz（1991）、Duflo和Saez（2002）的做法，使用同村居民平均年龄作为同村居民参保率的工具变量（IV），进行了工具变量估计。正如Duflo和Saez（2002）所指出的，在控制了个体自身年龄的情况下，同村居民的年龄能够较好地满足工具变量的外生性假设。工具变量估计结果显示，同村居民参加社会养老保险的比例每增加1个百分点，个体参保率显著增加 0.42 个百分点，IV 估计结果同 OLS 估计结果一致。

理论研究表明，同群效应可以通过信息传递和社会规范两个机制发挥作用（Manski，1993，2000；Bikhchandani 等，1998）。本文接下来对上述两个可能的机制做了考察。为了验证信息传递机制是否存在，我们检验了同群效应随时间的变化，发现同群效应随着新农保政策实施时间的增加而显著下降，表明信息传递是同群效应发挥作用的重要机制之一。我们还发现，受访者越是依赖于从邻居处获取信息，而非从电视、网络、广播和报刊等媒体处获取信息，其参保决策受到同村居民参保率的影响越大，这再次验证了信息传递机制的存在。为了检验社会规范的作用，我们利用村庄是否存在大姓度量当地的宗族文化，检验了存在宗族文化的村庄同群效应是否更加显著。结果确实显示，宗族文化越强的村庄，同群效应越大。由于宗族是一个具有较强凝聚力的组织，并且宗族内部具有相对统一的社会规范，上述发现表明社会规范可能是参与决策中同群效应的影响机制之一。

我们进一步考察了同群效应中可能存在的异质性效应。将样本按照年龄、性别、学历进行分组，分别估计了不同群体中的同群效应。结果发现，同村男性群体的参保决策对男性群体和女性群体的参保决策均有显著影响，而各年龄组、学历组人口的参保率只影响同组人口的参保决策。这表明，男性群体的参保行为对其他群体具有相对较强的示范和引领作用。

总结而言，本文研究表明同群效应在社会保障项目参与决策中发挥着重要作用，信息传递和社会规范是同群效应发挥作用的重要机制。此外，同群效应并不是对称的，有些群体的参保行为具有更强的示范作用。上述发现对有关个体决策中同群效应的研究做了重要补充，也为社会保障项目参与决策影响因素的研究提供了新的分析视角。

本文政策启示如下：首先，加强政策宣传和增加政策透明度，能够有效提高社会保障项目的参与程度；其次，通过政策干预，有针对性地提高具有较强示范引领作用人群的参与率，有助于提高项目的整体参与程度。

学区房溢价的影响因素：
教育质量的视角*

张　勋　寇晶涵　张　欣　吕光明

2021年7月，中共中央办公厅、国务院办公厅印发的《关于进一步减轻义务教育阶段学生作业负担和校外培训负担的意见》提出，要"积极开展义务教育优质均衡创建工作，促进新优质学校成长，扩大优质教育资源"和"充分激发办学活力，整体提升学校办学水平，加快缩小城乡、区域、学校间教育水平差距"。那么，如何实现义务教育优质资源的均衡化？准确理解优质教育资源的形成机制十分关键。

理论上，优质教育资源可能形成于学校的教育质量，也可能来源于生源质量。一方面，学校的教育质量以学校的教学硬件和师资水平的优良程度为代表，教育质量越高教育资源越优质；另一方面，生源质量越高，同群效应越大，学生成绩可能提升越多，教育资源也越优质。尽管有大量研究证实优质教育资源可以带来学区房溢价，但对优质教育资源主要来源的探讨仍然相对缺乏。

本文从学区房视角探讨优质教育资源的来源。随着我国房地产市场逐步成熟，居民"用脚投票"机制直接影响住房价格，可根据教育资源的优质程度来选择住房。这意味着，优质教育资源可以被资本化，由此

---

* 原文刊载于《金融研究》2021年第11期。
  作者简介：张勋，经济学博士，教授，北京师范大学统计学院；寇晶涵，博士研究生，福特汉姆大学经济学系；张欣，经济学博士，副教授，北京师范大学统计学院；吕光明，经济学博士，教授，北京师范大学统计学院。

带来了学区房溢价。进一步地，由于优质教育资源取决于教育质量和生源质量，这两个因素的资本化效应之和即为学区房的总溢价。如果能够量化学区房中这两个因素的溢价，便可获知其分别在多大程度上影响了教育资源的优质性。

本文利用北京市二手房成交数据和来自中国教育经费统计数据库学校层面教育质量信息，量化教育质量对优质教育资源的解释力，进而得以探讨教育质量的可量化经济价值。具体地，本文采用特征价格模型和边界固定效应方法，将优质资源校的学区与该学区边界房屋交易样本进行配对，从而控制不可观测变量的影响，计算出每套学区房相对于可比非学区房的溢价。在此基础上，根据优质资源校及周边的薄弱学校的质量差异，量化教育质量在学区房溢价中的作用。

本文力图在以下几个方面有所贡献。

一是理论方面，本文利用学校层面的教育质量信息，结合房地产市场的住房交易数据，对优质教育资源所带来的学区房溢价中教育质量的解释力进行了量化，进而探讨优质教育资源的形成机制，对讨论教育质量与学区房溢价关系的文献进行了有益补充。

二是实证方面，目前已有的探讨教育质量与学区房溢价关系的文献，未能对教育质量与学区房溢价的真实关系作出回答。我国特有的制度背景使量化学区房溢价中的教育质量因素成为可能：不同于多数欧美国家的教育经费来源于物业税，我国教育投入主要依靠地方政府的一般性财政支出。因此，采用中国学校层面的教育质量数据研究学区房溢价效应，可更好地识别从教育质量到住房价格的因果效应，从而能更准确地量化教育质量与学区房溢价的关系，探讨优质教育资源的背后形成机制。

三是借助北京市三个教育强区（西城区、东城区和海淀区）的异质性分析，讨论优质教育资源的形成机制，为平抑高企的学区房价格提供政策上的有益参考。如果是教育质量不同引发了教育资源优质程度的差别（学区房溢价的高低），那么为缓解学区房溢价，应采取措施尽可能使教育质量均等化，如促进教育全要素（包括教师）有序流动等；相反，如果来自生源质量差异，那么提升代际流动性可能才是平抑学区房溢价的根本。

本文的实证结果表明，以学校物质资本和教师人力资本所表征的教育质量是学区房溢价，即优质教育资源的主要来源，解释了总体学区房溢价的64.71%，这种解释力在考虑了新建小学、教育改革和民办学校资源差异等潜在的内生性问题后依旧稳健。进一步通过量化北京市的三个教育强区中教育质量的解释力，发现优质教育资源既可能形成于优质生源集聚，也可能源于教育经费投入长期累积所带来的教育质量的提升。

政策层面上，2020年底，我国已有2 809个县（市、区）通过义务教育基本均衡发展认定，累计占比达到96.8%，如期实现了95%的国家教育事业发展"十三五"规划目标。在此背景下，如何围绕义务教育优质均衡的2035年教育现代化目标并结合"房住不炒"定位，稳步推进义务教育均衡化改革，推动教育要素在区域、学校间有序合理流动，成为亟待解决的重要问题。根据本文研究，学校层面的物质资本投入和人力资本质量是带来学区房溢价的主要原因，横向改革则有助于平抑学区房溢价。因此，以义务教育均衡化改革为契机，加强薄弱学校的关键物质投入，促进优秀教师的有序流动和引进优秀师资能够显著提升教育质量，对实现教育资源均衡发挥重要作用。当然，本文的研究并不意味着教育需要做到绝对公平。在公共财政所保障的优质教育资源的基础上，居民可以自主选择更丰富的教育资源。此外，考虑到生源质量在学区房溢价中的重要性，加大多校划片力度，减弱房产对优质学校的依附关系，增加代际流动性，推进机会平等化，也是平抑高企的学区房价格的重要手段。

风险分散与中国混合型基本养老保险制度改革研究*

彭浩然　程春丽

20世纪90年代,中国基本养老保险制度从完全的现收现付制向社会统筹与个人账户相结合的"统账结合"模式转轨,其中社会统筹部分依然实行现收现付制,个人账户实行基金积累制。改革的初衷是期望混合基本养老保险制度能够发挥现收现付与基金积累两种制度的优势,实现社会互济与自我保障相结合、公平与效率相结合。但是,由于未解决好制度转轨成本,社会统筹基金收不抵支,地方政府为了确保当期养老金发放,挪用个人账户的资金,造成个人账户有名无实,形成空账。随着个人账户空账规模越来越大,相关政策制定者与研究者开始反思我国是否应该选择或继续坚持"统账结合"的混合基本养老保险制度。一些学者甚至建议废除个人账户,重新实行完全的现收现付制。时至今日,个人账户问题依然困扰着我国基本养老保险制度改革。当前亟须回答以下两个重要问题:第一,中国实行混合型基本养老保险制度的理论基础是什么;第二,社会统筹账户与个人账户的最优比例如何确定。

面对日益严重的人口老龄化,许多国家都在考虑改革其基本养老保险制度。从国内外文献来看,研究者对现收现付制的质疑和担心主要来

---

* 原文刊载于《金融研究》2021年第11期。
作者简介:彭浩然,经济学博士,教授,中山大学岭南学院;程春丽,经济学博士,助理教授,中山大学岭南学院。

自人口老龄化背景下其能否保持财务平衡及对宏观经济的负面影响，而对基金积累制的担心则主要体现在较高的投资风险、再分配功能较弱等方面。客观来讲，现收现付制和基金积累制都面临着各自的风险，并不存在孰优孰劣的问题。现收现付制的内含回报率取决于社会工资总额的增长率，劳动力供给数量和劳动生产率都会对其有影响。在许多发达工业国家，股票市场的投资回报率要高于社会工资总额的增长率。从回报率的平均值来看，似乎是基金积累制占优势。但是，这种分析忽视了回报率的波动性。仅仅从回报率的高低就判定应该从现收现付制向基金积累制转轨并不合适，还需要考虑不同制度的风险因素、运行管理费用，以及制度转轨成本问题。

由于现收现付养老保险可以被视为一种准资产，所以从风险分散角度考虑，无论个体参加哪种形式的养老保险制度，都可以视作其为退休后获取养老金而所作的投资。从分散养老风险的角度可以很好地理解我国基本养老保险制度的"统账结合"模式。基于这一思路，本文构建了一个两期消费模型，研究一位有代表性参保人在现收现付制与基金积累制之间如何进行资产分配，以实现终身效用最大化。这位参保人将面临三种主要风险：劳动力供给数量、工资增长率和资本投资回报率。在理论研究的基础上，本文运用中国数据进行模拟测算，定量研究了我国基本养老保险制度的最优统账比例，并进行敏感性分析。最后，我们根据求得的最优统账比例，结合外生给定的养老金替代率目标，计算基本养老保险的筹资规模。本文研究发现，我国基本养老保险最优统账比例取决于现收现付制的内含回报率和基金积累制的投资回报率的随机特性；在现阶段应以现收现付制占主导地位，引入小规模个人账户基金积累制可以分散人口老龄化给现收现付制所带来的风险。同时，本文还发现中国基本养老保险要维持40%～45%的替代率水平，其财务可持续性会面临较大挑战。

无论是在理论上还是实践中，基本养老保险制度选择问题一直颇具争议，并不存在一种绝对占优的养老保险制度适合所有的国家。现收现付制与基金积累制都面临着各自风险。由于不同国家的人口结构、劳动生产率、资本市场的完善程度都存在较大差异，各国政府应根据所面临的环境和应对风险的能力审慎选择合适的基本养老保险制度。中国现阶段彻底否定或推翻"统账结合"模式存在一定困难。无论我国基本养老保险个人账户是真实积累还是记账式，实现基本养老保险制度财务可持续性都是政策制定者所追求的目标，关键问题是如何在长期实现基本养老保险资产端与负债端的匹配。从长远来看，随着人口老龄化程度的加深及职工工资增长速度放缓，现收现付制的内含回报率会逐渐降低。如果要实现给定的养老金替代率目标，就必须提高养老保险基金的投资回报率，否则就会面临较大的养老金收支缺口。因此，要实现基本养老保险制度的可持续发展，一方面要通过各种家庭政策，建立生育友好型社会，以提高人口生育率；另一方面，必须重视基本养老保险基金的投资运营。在此基础上，配合养老保险制度的参量式调整，比如延长退休年龄等，才能实现养老保险资产端与负债端的匹配。

城市服务多样性与劳动力流动[*]

——基于"美团网"大数据和流动人口微观调查的分析

张文武　余泳泽

随着中国经济步入高质量发展新阶段，在全域人口红利消退和区域人口红利释放并存的社会背景下，城市间人才争夺和劳动力竞争逐渐成为新时代的焦点，城市依靠什么吸引和留住人才赋予了劳动力配置研究新的视野和角度。在中国新型城镇化推进过程中，"以人为核心"的理念正在成为城市人才引进和管理政策的重要特征，满足消费者差异化偏好和个性化需求的城市特征也将成为影响劳动力流动的重要因素。作为城市便利性和舒适度的重要支撑，城市服务的生产能力、类别多寡和供给方式为生活在本地的劳动者创造了福利提升的诸多路径。在城市对劳动力需求和人才竞争逐渐"白热化"的背景下，城市服务供给的多样化和便利性究竟对劳动力迁移居住发挥着怎样的作用？城市服务多样性能够吸引和留住什么样的人才？回答这些问题无疑具有积极而丰富的现实意义。

在高质量发展新阶段人民对美好生活追求的内涵逐渐延展，城市服务的供给能力和多样性逐渐成为劳动者迁移居住决策的重要考虑，尤其

---

[*] 原文刊载于《金融研究》2021年第9期。
作者简介：张文武，经济学博士，教授，南京财经大学国际经贸学院；余泳泽，经济学博士，教授，南京财经大学国际经贸学院。

是进入和居住在城市的人口正在朝着年轻化、知识化的结构演进,对生活丰富性和舒适性追求倾向所形成的地区集聚特征愈加凸显。在此背景下,城市如何通过提供舒适性条件和宜居宜业的综合服务吸引人才、留住人才成为新的治理导向。然而遗憾的是,除了少数学者从房价、公共服务等方面进行探讨以外(张莉等,2017;周颖刚等,2019;宋弘和吴茂华,2020),现有研究对城市服务多样性影响劳动力流动的关注不多,尤其是结合城市服务互联网化供给模式现实,从个人微观层面展开城市服务多样性如何影响劳动力流动迁移决策的分析亟待扩展补充。

本文利用"美团网"大数据和2017年中国流动人口动态监测数据,构建城市服务多样性指标,研究其对个体劳动力流动的影响,并结合城市环境和区域特征分析讨论。在选择城市与省会之间地理距离作为工具变量进行内生性问题处理之后,研究结果证实了城市服务多样性对劳动力流动的显著影响。具体来说,对于流动人口而言,城市服务多样性每增加1%,劳动力打算从该城市流动迁出的概率降低3.23%。即控制了个人和城市特征及遗漏变量等引起的内生性问题后,城市服务多样性越高,劳动力选择流动的可能性越低。根据年龄节点和技能水平将样本进行分组回归,结果进一步展示了不同劳动力群体对城市服务多样性的敏感差异。相较于中老年群体,年轻化人口在城市服务多样性越高城市中流动迁出的概率越小,初步表现为城市服务类别每增加1%,中青年劳动力流动迁出的概率降低4.62%。就不同技能水平群体所受到的影响来看,无论是对高技能水平劳动力还是较低技能水平劳动力,城市服务多样性带来的舒适性福利都很重要,只是相对而言高技能水平劳动力的敏感度更高。我们进一步引入城市环境的调节效应及区域差异性进行了扩展讨论,发现城市信息化建设和市场化水平对城市服务多样性吸引留住人才具有正向放大作用。即城市移动互联网等信息技术建设和市场化水平提高,会进一步丰富劳动力居住在城市获得相应产品和服务的渠道,从而降低劳动力流动迁移的意愿和概率。另外，区域差异性的结果显示，中西部地区劳动力流动所受城市服务多样性的影响相比东部地区较小，结合年龄、技能水平交叉项的系数进一步表明，现阶段仍然表现为能力较强或者年龄较轻的劳动力选择在东部城市停留；相较于中小城市的流动人口，大城市劳动力流动对城市服务多样性的敏感性更高，显示出城市服务多样性所反映的舒适性福利正在成为大城市抽取中小城市"人口红利"的重要通道。

本文的研究发现为城市"抢人大战"背景下吸引人才、留住人才的劳动力竞争提供了新的政策启示。城市经济正在步入高质量发展新阶段，劳动力空间再配置的内涵已不仅局限在规模流动和跨区域迁移的"量变"层面，而是朝着劳动力结构优化和效率提升的"质变"方向延伸。城市吸引和留住高质量劳动力的优势不仅仅取决于生产环节的"谋生渠道"，还依赖于生活领域的舒适性福利提升。城市管理者和政策设计者应从实际出发，培育发展更加符合个人福利偏好的市场形态；通过构建更加多样化的城市服务供给体系等途径，逐步提高城市劳动要素质量；特别是有必要结合第七次人口普查的良好数据基础，对城市的人口结构、空间分布、集聚特征等展开纵横向对比分析，研判劳动力流动的长期趋势，从城市服务供给侧改革和需求侧管理"双向发力"打造综合竞争优势。

网红直播打赏收入影响因素的
实证研究*

廖 理 王新程 王正位 张晋研

随着经济的发展与居民财富的增加，居民的财富支配成为了重要的实践与研究话题。近年来，网红经济的快速发展使直播打赏成为一种新型的财富支配方式，这种现象引起了社会广泛关注。作为新时代的一种新的经济形态，网红经济既是机遇，也意味着挑战。一方面，网红经济能够刺激消费，增强经济活力。另一方面，网红为争夺流量不择手段，可能侵犯消费者权益，带来不良社会风气，因此网红经济的持续健康发展亟待正确的价值引导和监管约束。2021年7月12日，文化和旅游部公布了《网络表演经纪机构管理办法（征求意见稿）》。该办法针对"网络表演行业"，以规制经纪机构为中心，从规范资质、人员及打赏行为等多个角度草拟了规定。"网络表演行业"的核心收入源于观众打赏，网红娱乐平台与网红主播会按照一定的比例对观众打赏进行分成，可见，打赏这一新型个人财富支配方式在"网红经济"中扮演着重要角色。探索打赏背后的影响因素和经济规律不仅对网红娱乐平台的可持续发展至关重要，且可为相关制度的落实和完善提供有益参考，有助于引导"网红经济"持续健康发展。然而，受限于数据的可获得性，目前尚未有学

---

* 原文刊载于《金融研究》2021年第8期。
作者简介：廖理，经济学博士，教授，清华大学五道口金融学院；王新程，金融学博士，香港大学经济及工商管理学院；王正位，金融学博士，副教授，清华大学五道口金融学院；张晋研，金融专业硕士，清华大学五道口金融学院。

者对此进行探究。

本文依托从 5 家网红经纪机构获取的独特数据,实证分析了网红主播直播打赏收入的影响因素。这 5 家网红经纪机构提供了其签约的 41 位直播同款游戏的网红主播 2019 年每场直播收入与直播时长的面板数据。本文所有实证分析均使用普通最小二乘法模型,在研究网红主播对观众的娱乐陪伴时,核心因变量为网红主播直播收入的对数和单位时间内直播收入的对数,核心自变量为网红主播直播时长的对数,模型中还加入弹幕数量、直播经验、网红主播与时间固定效应作为控制变量。在研究打赏的"羊群效应"时,核心因变量为非头部打赏者单位时间内打赏金额的对数,核心自变量为头部打赏者单位时间内打赏金额的对数。

相关分析主要揭示了以下两点:第一,网红主播对观众的娱乐陪伴会使其更多更快地获得打赏收入。首先,网红主播直播时间越长,其每场直播收入越高;其次,打赏强度随着直播时长的增加而相应提升,打赏强度是指单位时间内网红主播获得的打赏收入。一个合理的解释是,网红主播对观众的娱乐陪伴使观众的精神需求得到了满足,观众更容易产生打赏行为,因此网红主播获得了更多的打赏收入。本文还通过删除头部主播的方式剔除了 MCN 机构"造星"活动的影响,验证了结论的稳健性。第二,观众的直播打赏存在"羊群效应",头部打赏者与非头部打赏者的打赏显著正相关。为了排除伪回归的顾虑,本文还使用主播直播经验进行了异质性检验。

本文的发现在一定程度解释了网红经济扩张迅速的原因,对引导网红经济健康发展也具一定启发意义。首先,主播与观众及观众之间相互影响,共同促进了网红经济的快速增长。一方面,网红主播对观众的娱乐陪伴使其获得了打赏收入,而观众对其进行打赏与支持则可能会增强主播直播的动力,使其进一步增加直播时长。另一方面,头部打赏者与非头部打赏者的打赏行为彼此影响,使主播收入不断增长。因此,网红经济具有"马太效应"。其次,"羊群效应"的存在还印证了《网络表演经纪机构管理办法(征求意见稿)》中第十二条的合理性。即网络表演经纪机构不得以虚假消费、带头打赏等方式诱导用户消费,不得以打赏排名、虚假宣传等方式炒作网络表演者收入。

本文的创新意义主要体现在以下几点:第一,本文开创了网红主播直播打赏收入影响因素的微观视角实证研究,对未来网红经济的研究和监管具有启发意义。第二,本文是目前较早使用网红主播收入数据的实证研究,借助特有的网红经纪机构数据完整地记录了网红主播每场直播的收入与直播时长,研究结论可信度较高,可为有关机构引导和规范网红经济健康发展提供参考。第三,本文通过区分头部打赏者和非头部打赏者的打赏金额,可以验证观众打赏中"羊群效应"的存在;探究网红主播收入的影响因素也为"超级明星效应"提供了新的经验证据。

本文所采用的样本数量与维度有限,要探索网红经济的一般规律,更好引导其健康发展,仍有诸多问题需要进一步研究。

08　公司治理与公司金融

董事会断裂带与企业薪酬差距*

徐灿宇 李烜博 梁上坤

企业高管与普通员工之间的薪酬差距不仅影响企业的经营绩效,还关系社会分配的公平与稳定。董事会作为公司内部治理的核心,探索其监督职能发挥的影响因素将有助于从根本上理解薪酬差距的成因与后果。区别于已有文献从董事会独立性等个体特征角度进行研究,本文引入管理学研究中的断裂带理论,基于董事会内部认同和差异的视角,试图从整体上考察董事会内部结构对企业薪酬差距的影响。

随着公司运营时间的延长,董事会内部可能因为各类因素出现立门派、站队等现象,从而形成不同的小团体。同一个小团体内部成员相互认同、彼此交流频繁,而不同小团体间差异较大、交集互动较少。小团体之间具有不同的逐利动机,并存在着管理理念、管理方式及认知程度等方面的差异,这给董事会整体有效性和监督职能的发挥带来了不小的挑战。管理学领域将上述董事会内部存在多个小团体的现象称之为董事会断裂带,并发现断裂带普遍存在(Lau 和 Murnighan,1998)。董事会断裂带的强度越大意味着小团体之间的差异越大,董事会内部分化、站队现象越严重,越会对董事会职能的发挥产生严重影响。基于此,本文尝试从激励设计角度探讨董事会内部小团体的存在是否会影响董事会的监督职能,进而影响企业薪酬差距。

---

* 原文刊载于《金融研究》2021年第7期。
作者简介:徐灿宇,管理学博士,博士后,华东理工大学商学院;李烜博,博士研究生,新加坡管理大学会计学院;梁上坤,管理学博士,教授,中央财经大学会计学院。

以 2005—2019 年中国 A 股上市公司为样本，本文立足董事会断裂带这一崭新角度，探索董事会中小团体的差异性对于薪酬差距的影响和后果。研究发现，董事会断裂带的存在会导致企业薪酬差距扩大；进一步分解董事会断裂带的类型后发现，由深层特征形成的断裂带对于薪酬差距的影响强于由表层特征形成的断裂带；区分公司所在行业的竞争程度后发现，外部的行业竞争有助于缓解董事会断裂带造成的薪酬差距扩大；从经济后果来看，由董事会断裂带造成的薪酬差距对于企业业绩具有显著的负向影响。在进行多项稳健性测试后，这些发现保持稳定。

本文的研究有以下三个方面可能的贡献。

第一，本文从董事会断裂带的角度丰富了有关薪酬差距治理的研究。已有文献对于薪酬差距成因的探索大多指向管理者权力理论，并将高管权力视为给定的条件，对于造成高管有权力自定薪酬的原因则探索不足，因此难以从根源上回答如何限制高管权力以缩小薪酬差距。本文的理论分析及实证发现表明，董事会断裂带导致的董事会监督职能受损是高管权力的来源之一。因而，对于薪酬差距的治理应关注董事会断裂带的形成。

第二，本文推进了董事会断裂带度量方式和经济后果的研究。度量方式上，本文考虑了独立董事、内部董事、财务经历、董事性别、兼职董事等八个董事特征的显著影响，有助于更准确地识别出断裂带的形成，并进行了计量优化，克服子群体数量的限制，使断裂带的测量更为准确。经济后果上，以往文献从公司绩效、企业价值、跨国并购展开研究，大多集中于董事会的咨询职能，而对董事会监督职能的研究尚不深入。本文探讨董事会断裂带对董事会监督与薪酬差距的影响，对此形成了有益补充。

第三，本文的研究对于完善公司薪酬激励机制、提升董事会监督效力也有一定的现实意义。有关企业内部治理与激励机制的最优契约理论认为，通过有效的契约安排可以使高管薪酬与股东财富紧密联系起来，激励高管为股东利益最大化行事。然而该理论成立的前提之一是董事会能进行有效的谈判，因此对于董事会运行效率的探索将有助于完善公司内部治理、健全激励约束机制。本文的研究表明，董事会断裂带会造成董事会监督职能受损，引发的薪酬差距不具有激励效果，甚至对企业业绩产生负面影响。因此，在安排董事成员时注意人物特征的合理搭配，实现多元化的同时防范断裂带的形成，强调董事会的整体目标以缓解子群体内部认同的危害，将有助于实现有效的董事会监督与薪酬激励。

　　本文的研究也具有一定的现实启示。一方面，本文的研究为完善上市公司治理水平、保持企业活力提供了新思路。多样化的董事会特征虽然给企业带来更多的资源和信息优势，但随着特征越来越多样及时间的推移，董事会成员可能基于相似特征而断裂成不同的小团体，小团体的存在直接影响着董事会的有效性和职能发挥。因此，公司在享受多样化特征所带来的诸多优势的同时也应该注意并防范董事会内部小团体的形成和所带来的危害。公司应该建立相应的董事会追责制度，全面监督董事会运作过程，做到责任落实到人，以震慑并抑制公司治理主体、董事会中断裂带导致的负面影响，进而从根源上完善治理水平、保持企业活力。另一方面，在薪酬差距治理实践上，本文对董事会内部监督、高管权力来源的探索和研究，有助于从根本上抑制薪酬差距的扩大。研究发现，董事会断裂带引发的董事会监督职能受损，是高管权力膨胀与薪酬差距扩大的原因。因此，公司要防范断裂带的形成，强调董事会整体目标以缓解子群体内部认同的危害，这对于提升董事会监督效力、完善薪酬差距治理具有现实意义。

失业保险与公司财务杠杆*

彭 章　施新政　陆 瑶　王 浩

随着劳动力要素市场化配置改革的推进，劳动力市场化程度日渐加深，劳动力流动性越来越高，劳动者更换职业更加频繁必然导致更多的暂时性失业。在这样的大趋势下，失业保险将发挥越来越大的作用。失业保险作为一项重要的劳动保障制度，它可以保障失业人员的基本生存需要，维护社会公平稳定，对个人和社会都有重大积极意义。但失业保险对企业的影响尚不明晰。本文以资本结构为视角，研究了失业保险金水平与企业财务杠杆的关系。

近期研究发现，劳动力因素与财务杠杆有密切联系，但现有研究大多以美国为背景。美国劳动力市场与中国劳动力市场有着巨大差异，鲜有学者关注我国劳动力因素如何影响公司杠杆率。理论上，失业保险金水平对企业财务杠杆的影响颇有争议。第一，失业保险金上升可能导致企业杠杆率下降。当失业保险金上升时，员工失业后获得的补偿更多，员工对失业风险更不敏感，员工要求的失业风险溢酬降低，公司劳动力成本下降。劳动力成本下降使得公司自由现金流增多、盈利能力增强，公司更有可能偿还债务，更倾向于运用内源融资替代债务融资，导致财务杠杆下降。本文称该渠道为"劳动力成本渠道"。第二，失业保险金

---

* 原文刊载于《金融研究》2021年第8期。
作者简介：彭章，经济学博士，助理教授，中央财经大学财政税务学院；施新政，经济学博士，副教授，清华大学经济管理学院；陆瑶，经济学博士，教授，清华大学经济管理学院；王浩，贝恩创效管理咨询（上海）有限公司。

的提高可能通过降低经营杠杆来提升财务杠杆。失业保险金的提高降低了劳动力成本和解雇员工的成本，公司经营杠杆下降，在总杠杆一定的情况下公司可以选择更高的财务杠杆。本文称该渠道为"经营杠杆渠道"。第三，失业保险金的提高可能使公司提升杠杆率更容易，导致杠杆率上升。Agrawal 和 Matsa（2013）发现保守的财务政策能够减少员工的失业风险，因此当失业保险金增加时，员工对失业风险容忍程度更高，公司倾向于采取更高的财务杠杆以享受税盾等杠杆带来的利益。本文称该渠道为"员工谈判渠道"。

为检验我国失业保险金水平与企业财务杠杆的关系，本文运用我国上市公司 2009—2019 年的数据进行实证分析，发现失业保险金每上升1%，公司财务杠杆平均下降 0.021~0.038 个百分点。接下来对劳动力成本渠道进行检验发现：失业保险金与员工工资，特别是非高管员工的工资呈负相关；更低的员工工资导致了更低的财务杠杆、更多的内源融资、更高的债务偿还概率。这些结果均与劳动力成本渠道一致。进一步检验显示，该作用在位于高失业率省份的企业和国有企业中更为显著。此外，本文还发现，失业保险金主要降低了长期负债率而非短期负债率。

本文还进行了一系列稳健性检验。首先，为了处理内生性问题，本文分别运用 2011 年实施的《社会保险法》和 2017 年实施的《关于调整失业保险金标准的指导意见》作为自然实验，运用双重差分模型和工具变量法进行实证检验，所有结果均与主要结果一致。接下来，我们还将失业保险金水平和最低工资水平单独放入模型中回归以排除多重共线性问题的影响。此外，在更换模型设定、排除投资水平的干扰、更换样本的情况下，主要结果仍然成立。

本文的学术贡献体现在以下三方面：第一，本文丰富了我国劳动力与金融领域（labor 和 finance）的研究。目前，劳动力与金融领域的研究大多以美国等发达国家为背景，我国的研究仍然处于起步阶段。 不同国家国情不同，同样政策可能导致不同结果，我国是劳动力大国，针对我国的研究有重要意义。Agrawal 和 Matsa（2013）运用美国数据发现失业保险金水平提高导致公司财务杠杆上升，而本文得出了与之相反的结论，这说明评估我国劳动力政策的影响时不能够照搬其他国家的结果，应当结合我国实际情况进行分析。第二，本文从公司层面补充了我国失业保险研究。现有的失业保险研究基本是个人、行业、地区层面的研究，鲜有文献从公司角度研究失业保险的作用。我国学者对失业保险的研究也往往从其促进再就业功能进行探讨，鲜有文献探讨失业保险对公司金融、公司财务的影响。本文以公司资本结构为切入点研究了失业保险金水平与公司劳动力成本、财务杠杆的关系，是对我国失业保险领域相关研究的有益补充。第三，本文结果对我国上市公司资本结构研究有一定贡献。一方面，本文结果表明劳动力政策也会影响公司资本结构，补充了上市公司资本结构决定因素的相关文献；另一方面，我国上市公司资本结构决策是更加符合权衡理论还是啄食次序理论一直都是争论的焦点，本文结果表明其更符合啄食次序理论，这为我国上市公司资本结构研究提供了新证据。

本文也具有一定政策启示：本文发现提高失业保险保障力度能够降低企业劳动力成本和财务杠杆。因此，完善失业保险政策、提高失业保险保障力度不仅有利于员工，而且能够间接降低企业劳动力成本，缓解财务风险，从而有利于整个社会经济的高质量发展。

上市企业员工满意度与创新*

——来自"中国年度最佳雇主100强"的经验证据

许红梅　倪骁然　刘亚楠

人力资本是企业最重要的生产要素之一。如何充分激发员工的工作热情，实现对人力资本的有效利用，是企业实现可持续发展的关键。那么，营造让员工满意的工作氛围是否有利于企业长期发展？本文试图通过考察员工满意度与企业创新之间的关系来回答这一问题。

创新是一类高度依赖于人力资本的复杂活动。Hall（2002）提供的证据表明，支付给高技能员工的薪酬占到了企业研发费用的一半以上。可见，员工在企业创新过程中扮演着关键角色。然而，关于员工满意度与企业创新之间的关系，现有理论有着不同的预期。一方面，利益相关者理论认为，提升员工满意度可以给员工带来额外的补偿与激励，这能够提升员工在企业经营活动中的参与感，降低员工通过追求短期业绩获得回报的心理预期，形成容忍失败、立足长远的认知。鉴于创新项目的高风险性与长期性，员工满意度的上述作用将有助于提升创新水平乃至企业价值。另一方面，员工满意度的提升也可能给企业创新乃至企业绩效带来负面影响。由于代理问题的存在，经理层可能会通过许诺高工资、高福

---

* 原文刊载于《金融研究》2021年第9期。
作者简介：许红梅，管理学博士，副教授，华南师范大学国际商学院；倪骁然，经济学博士，副教授，厦门大学经济学院、王亚南经济研究院；刘亚楠，硕士研究生，华南师范大学国际商学院。

利等提高员工满意度的方式换取更高的支持度、获取私利或享受安逸生活。如果员工满意度的提升反映了上述效应的存在,这将不利于企业创新。此外,旨在提升员工满意度的项目会产生高额的成本,当这一成本大于其带来的收益时,会有损于企业绩效。因此,如果提升员工满意度方面的成本过高,企业将难以在创新项目上进行足够的投入,这同样不利于创新。

本文在中国情境下,对员工满意度与企业创新之间的关系进行实证检验。在转型时期,越来越多的企业开始重视从多个维度(如激励体系、培训体系、企业文化、企业形象、工作环境和组织管理等)提升员工满意度,以充分挖掘人力资本潜力。不过,面对经济下行压力,降低劳动力成本、避免过多额外投入依然是企业确保持续经营的有效措施。厘清员工满意度与企业创新的关系,对于处在转型时期的中国企业具有重要的现实意义。特别是在我国正在以创新驱动为抓手,努力实现高质量发展的阶段,这一研究也具有重要的政策价值。

智联招聘与北京大学社会调查中心于2011年起发起了"中国年度最佳雇主"评选,每年定期发布"中国年度最佳雇主100强"榜单。本文以上述评选为基础,以2011—2017年沪深两市的A股上市企业为研究对象,考察上市企业员工满意度对创新的影响。研究发现,在全样本中,"100强"公司比其他公司的专利申请总数高30.6%左右。由于"中国年度最佳雇主100强"评选委员会并未公布参加评选但落选的企业名单,在本研究中,我们采用"100强"企业作为处理组,其他未在"100强"榜单之上的A股上市公司作为对照组。在以1∶1最邻近配比得到的PSM样本中,"100强"企业比其他企业的专利申请总数高约47%。此外,我们进一步区分了专利类型,发现以上效应主要体现在对发明专利和实用新型专利的提升上。进一步检验说明,员工满意度可以通过影响企业创新失败容忍度来提高企业创新水平,且可以显著提升企业创新效率和全要素生产率。

本文主要有以下两个方面的贡献。

首先,本文丰富了劳动力与创新方面的研究。过往研究考虑了员工持股、员工薪酬差距和员工所得税等与薪酬相关的因素如何影响企业创新。不过,员工满意度在薪酬因素之外,还与文化体系、培训体系、组织体系等非薪酬因素有关,本文提供了与上述研究不同的视角。具体来看,本文以入选"中国年度最佳雇主100强"榜单衡量员工满意度,考察了其对企业创新的影响。

其次,已有研究从劳动保护的视角讨论了员工对企业行为的影响。然而,劳动力市场上的政策变化虽然可以从法律层面提升对员工的保护力度,但由于相对强制性的要求会直接增加企业经营压力,企业主观上善待员工的意愿未必显著提升,员工满意度也未必会有明显变化。我们主要考察员工对企业激励体系、文化体系、培训体系和组织体系的综合感知如何影响其对企业的人力资本投资。因此,本文与以往聚焦劳动力市场政策变化的研究存在显著区别。

本文也具有一定的政策价值。目前中国经济由高速增长阶段转向高质量发展阶段,人们对美好生活有了更高的诉求,需要在工作中获得更高的认同感。因此,以往企业以牺牲员工福利为代价的用人方式已经难以为继。本研究为这一观点提供了实证证据,本文结果有以下启示:现代企业不仅要依靠员工的汗水,还要重视员工多方面的诉求,提升其工作满意度,从而更好地发挥人力资源潜力,提升员工创新效率。本文的发现能够为转型国家中的企业转变用工方式、更好地挖掘人力资源潜力以促进创新提供参考。

管理者能力与资本市场稳定*

张 路 李金彩 袁振超 岳 衡

经过近30年的发展,中国A股市场已经成长为全球第二大资本市场。然而,和西方成熟的资本市场相比,我国股市暴涨暴跌的问题仍然较为突出。股价大幅下跌给投资者带来巨额财富损失,不利于资本市场稳定,甚至会危及实体经济发展。如何抑制股价大幅下跌风险成为理论界和实务届共同关注的热点话题。探寻股价大幅下跌风险的抑制机制对维护资本市场稳定和国家经济发展具有极其重要的现实意义。

综观现有的国内外研究,学者们认为管理者隐藏坏消息是股价大幅下跌风险的主要原因。他们主要从降低代理成本和缓解信息不对称的角度进行探讨,管理者的行为大多被限制在委托代理理论的分析框架中,按照同质化的理性人对他们的决策行为进行分析,将企业行为差异归为不同企业治理因素的异质性。事实上,管理者处于企业经营活动的核心,他们的感知能力、认知能力和价值观等个人特征都将显著地影响企业决策(Hambrick 和 Mason,1984)。然而,现有文献尚未从管理者能力如何影响股价大幅下跌风险这一视角展开讨论。对于现代企业而言,管理者能力是管理者有效率地利用企业资源创造价值的能力(Demerjian 等,2012)。相比能力低的管理者,高能力管理者可以准确理解技术和行业

---

* 原文刊载于《金融研究》2021年第9期。
作者简介:张路,会计学博士,副教授,中国农业大学经济管理学院;李金彩,会计学硕士,北京首都机场餐饮发展有限公司;袁振超,会计学博士,副教授,深圳大学经济学院;岳衡,会计学博士,副教授,新加坡管理大学会计学院。

发展趋势，有效预测产品需求，提高项目投资效率，高效组织员工工作，还可以降低信息不对称引起的道德风险。因此，管理者能力的高低，对企业经营目标的实现与否具有决定性的作用。

本文利用2007—2020年的中国A股上市公司数据试图探究管理者能力对资本市场稳定的影响。我们参考Demerjian等（2012）的研究成果，使用DEA-Tobit模型计算管理者能力。参考既往文献，使用负收益偏态系数和企业股票收益上下波动两个指标衡量企业股价大幅下跌风险。研究发现管理者能力与企业股价大幅下跌风险显著负相关，即管理者能力可以有效地抑制企业股价大幅下跌风险，稳定资本市场。在此基础上，本文做了一系列横截面检验，结果表明管理者能力对企业股价大幅下跌风险的抑制作用在非国有企业、大股东持股比例较低和外部制度环境水平较低的企业中更为显著。最后，本文讨论了管理者能力降低股价大幅下跌风险的作用机制，发现随着管理者能力的提高，企业经营风险（以业绩波动性和诉讼情况衡量）显著降低，企业治理水平（以管理费用率、可操纵性应计和信息透明度衡量）显著提高。上述发现为管理者能力通过降低经营风险和改善公司治理水平，进而降低未来的股价大幅下跌风险提供了直接证据。此外，本文还做了一系列稳健性检验，发现研究结果没有发生改变。

本文的研究具有重要的理论贡献和现实意义。在理论层面，一方面，现有对股价大幅下跌风险的研究文献多将管理者局限在委托代理框架中，而去分析探讨管理者的自利行为对企业的负面影响。本文试图从管理者能力的角度分析管理者的正面效应，发现管理者能力对股价大幅下跌风险的抑制作用，补充了研究企业股价大幅下跌风险影响因素的文献。另一方面，从管理者异质性的角度分析企业行为逐渐成为学术界关注的热点。相比年龄、性别和学历等人口统计学因素，管理者能力是管理者异质性的综合体现。本文研究结论明确了管理者能力作为企业资源对企业经营发展的重要作用，丰富了管理者能力经济后果的研究。在实践层面，本文的研究结论表明，相关政策制定部门要切实采取措施激发和保护管理者能力，从而有效降低股价大幅下跌风险，维持市场稳定，促进资本市场平稳健康发展。

卖空机制、双重治理与公司违规*

——基于市场化治理视角的实证检验

徐细雄 占 恒 李万利

2010年3月启动的融资融券交易制度打破了长期以来只能做多不能做空的"单边市"格局,是我国资本市场的重要制度创新,其实施效果也备受关注。研究表明,卖空机制(融券交易)一方面有利于股市及时融入负面信息,提高股价的信息含量、矫正高估的股价、降低股价的波动,进而改善我国资本市场效率。另一方面,既然卖空机制加剧了公司负面信息的发现和扩散并显著影响上市公司股价表现,这也可能进一步影响公司行为。因此,近年来学术界开始关注卖空机制对公司决策行为产生的影响。有研究发现,卖空交易会对公司信息披露形成有效的外部监管,提高管理层信息披露的真实性。

当前我国资本市场法制建设尚不完善,公司违规行为频繁发生,打击了投资者信心,破坏了资本市场运行效率。公司违规行为的有效约束是保护投资者利益、促进资本市场高效运行的重要基础。与其他投资者相比,卖空者更有动力跟踪和监督管理层的不当行为,并通过卖空交易威慑管理层,从而形成有效的外部监督。这是由于卖空制度允许卖空者

---

* 原文刊载于《金融研究》2021年第10期。
作者简介:徐细雄,管理学博士,教授,重庆大学经济与工商管理学院;占恒,博士研究生,重庆大学经济与工商管理学院;李万利,管理学博士,助理教授,湖南大学金融与统计学院。

基于公司存在的负面信息做空公司并从中获利，使得公司隐藏的违规负面信息通过卖空交易向市场传递风险信号，进而可能引发监管关注并加大股价下跌压力，导致公司面临严重的声誉损失和市值缩水。因此，管理层出于维护公司市值的考虑会约束自身的不当行为。然而，现有文献对卖空机制与公司违规行为之间的内在逻辑关系尚未给予充分论证。

基于此，本文试图从市场化治理视角探讨卖空机制对公司违规行为的影响效应和机制，并利用我国证券市场融资融券制度的准自然实验场景进行实证检验。运用 A 股上市公司 2008—2017 年数据并采用部分可观测 Bivariable Probit 模型和双重差分模型，本文实证发现，卖空机制不仅显著降低了标的公司的违规倾向，也明显提升了其违规稽查概率。同时，卖空机制还显著缩短了违规稽查时间。这意味着，卖空机制对公司违规的治理效应主要是由事前威慑及事后惩罚两类机制实现。此外，标的公司违规发生年份融券力度明显增加，这表明卖空者确实具有信息优势且对公司违规行为具有较强敏感性。进一步检验揭示，卖空机制主要通过内部公司治理效率和外部市场信息效率两条路径对公司违规行为发挥双重治理作用。具体来讲，放松卖空约束强化了大股东和独立董事等内部治理主体对公司违规行为的监督干预，从而抑制了事前违规倾向；同时，卖空机制也增加了外部资本市场中的分析师关注及违规负面信息的传播效率，进而提升了违规行为的事后稽查概率。最后，本文还发现，卖空机制的违规治理效果受到违规监管环境（法制监管、内部控制和行业违规）和标的公司个体特质（公司成长性、市值规模和股价波动性）的调节作用的影响。

本文的贡献主要体现在以下几个方面：第一，拓展了卖空机制对实体经济后果的研究。以往针对卖空机制的研究主要聚焦在资本市场定价效率，近年来开始关注卖空交易对信息披露质量、公司盈余管理、投融资策略选择及企业创新等公司内部决策行为的影响。本文将研究内容拓展至公司违规领域，丰富和拓展了对卖空机制所引发经济后果的理解。第二，深化了卖空机制对公司违规行为治理效果及内在机理的研究。不同于以往研究，本文突破单一的信号传递理论视角，尝试从资本市场信息效率和内部公司治理效率二维视角构建分析框架并实证揭示了卖空机制对违规行为的双重治理作用。研究发现，卖空机制对违规行为的治理作用并不局限于改善外部资本市场的信息效率，提升违规稽查概率；它也对内部治理行为产生重要影响，明显增强了大股东和独立董事等治理主体对公司违规行为的监督干预积极性，因而有利于抑制公司违规倾向。此外，本文还发现卖空制度显著缩短了违规行为的查处时间，特别是标的公司违规发生年份的融券力度明显增加。这表明，卖空者确实具有及时有效识别市场中公司违规行为的信息优势。第三，本研究也具有较强的实践意义。本文实证揭示了卖空交易在抑制公司违规中发挥了市场化治理效应。这表明，卖空机制正在成为增强投资者保护的一种有益补充，引入卖空交易这一市场化治理机制，对抑制公司违规行为、增强投资者利益保护具有重要的现实意义。

根据上述分析结论，得到以下三方面政策启示：（1）作为一种市场化监督机制，卖空机制引发的公司负面信息传递会对上市公司违规行为产生事前和事后的双重治理效应，这为监管部门提供了一种改进市场违规行为治理效率的新思路。（2）卖空机制的实施有助于增强大股东自我约束及内部监督行为，同时也改善了独立董事监督履职效率。这对改善中国公司治理水平具有重要的启示和实践价值。此外，卖空机制的治理效应的发挥也在一定程度上依赖于公司个体特征和治理环境因素，因此在制定实施卖空标准时应适当考虑不同类型的公司特征和治理因素，使卖空机制的市场化治理价值能够得到更充分发挥。（3）对于投资者来说，关注卖空交易也有助于其合理评估公司风险，进而优化其投资决策。

金字塔式控股结构与上市公司资本运作的机会主义倾向*

郑志刚　郇　珍　黄继承　赵锡军

金字塔式控股结构在世界很多国家和地区是十分典型的企业集团组织方式。所谓的金字塔式控股结构指的是上一级公司的实际控制人通过持有下一级公司控制性股份，层层控制，实现对处在末端公司的控制。金字塔式控股链条下的母公司、子公司和孙公司组成实际控制人控制的庞大企业集团和所谓的"资本系族"。

作为实现和加强公司控制的方式，金字塔式控股结构的典型特征被描述为控制权与现金流权的分离。这里所谓的控制权反映的是实际控制人在上市公司股东大会上以投票表决方式实现的对重大事项决策的影响力，而现金流权则反映的是以实际投入上市公司出资额为表征的责任承担能力。二者的分离则意味着承担责任与享有权利的不对称，形成一种经济学意义上的"负外部性"。如同经理人的经营权与股东的所有权"分离"导致"经理人与股东之间的代理冲突"一样，在金字塔式控股结构下，控制权和现金流权二者的"分离"导致作为控股股东的实际控制人有动机和能力掏空转移子、孙公司资源，使外部分散股东利益受损，成为"股东之间代理冲突"的典型形式。

---

* 原文刊载于《金融研究》2021年第11期。

作者简介：郑志刚，经济学博士，教授，中国人民大学财政金融学院；郇珍，经济学博士，中国农业发展银行山东省分行；黄继承，管理学博士，副教授，中国人民大学财政金融学院；赵锡军，经济学博士，教授，中国人民大学财政金融学院。

围绕金字塔式控股结构负外部性的研究，以往文献更多关注控股股东以资金占用等方式来"隧道挖掘"上市公司资源的机会主义行为这类负外部性。本文则关注金字塔式控股结构下上市公司控股股东及其背后实际控制人资本运作的机会主义倾向，从纵容市场炒作和资本运作这一新的视角揭示金字塔式控股结构存在的负外部性。

在我国资本市场，金字塔式控股结构无论在国企还是非国企都很常见。但由于国有上市公司资本运作行为更多地受到国企改制、产业政策、供给侧结构性改革等国家宏观经济政策的影响，相比较而言，资本运作作为金字塔式控股结构负外部性的例证在非国有上市公司中更为典型。本文选取非国有上市公司作为研究对象，实证考察金字塔结构的复杂程度对控股股东及其背后实际控制人机会主义性质资本运作行为的影响。借鉴以往文献，本文分别从反映投机性的"彩票股"、企业金融化水平及关联资本运作倾向等方面展开考察。研究表明，随着金字塔结构复杂程度的增加，处于金字塔式控股结构中的上市公司的控股股东及其背后实际控制人倾向于进行更加频繁的市场炒作和资本运作，而这没有带来投资者预期的改善和绩效提升，反而使其演化为以控股股东及其背后实际控制人财富短期快速增值为目的的机会主义行为。

本文对公司治理文献，特别是金字塔式控股结构外部性研究文献的贡献主要体现在以下几方面。第一，除了以往文献揭示的"隧道挖掘"行为，本文的研究表明，金字塔结构的负外部性还体现在纵容控股股东及其背后实际控制人机会主义性质的资本运作行为上，增加了金融市场的波动。本文由此构成金字塔式控股结构文献的重要补充和扩展。第二，本文从企业金字塔式控股结构这一新的视角出发，揭示了非金融企业金融化及我国国民经济出现的"脱实向虚"现象背后的诱因。研究表明，金字塔控股结构的复杂程度也会显著影响企业金融资产的配置。在金字塔式控股结构下，受权责不对等的激励扭曲的影响，控股股东更偏好进行金融资产的配置，以在短期内实现实际控制人财富增值。第三，本文的研究表明，是否处于金字塔控股结构下的资本系族中，成为上市公司具有"彩票股"特征的重要影响因素，从而构成"彩票股"影响因素文献的重要补充和新的扩展。所谓"彩票股"指的是，同时具备"低股价""高历史日收益率"与"高换手率"三个特征的股票。本文研究表明，金字塔结构下控股股东及其背后实际控制人资本运作的机会主义倾向，吸引更多具有博彩偏好的投资者进行股票投机买卖。

  本文还具有一定的现实意义。本文研究表明，处于金字塔式控股结构下的上市公司热衷资本运作和市场炒作的偏好，一方面将加剧股票市场的波动性，增加系统性金融风险，另一方面则导致资本"脱实向虚"，使实体经济投入不足，不利于实体经济的发展壮大。未来，我国资本市场也许可以借鉴成熟资本市场的发展经验，抑制上市公司金字塔结构复杂化趋势，促使我国资本市场有效助力实体经济发展。

控股股东股权质押与员工持股计划"工具化"*

——基于 A 股上市公司的实证研究

邱杨茜 黄娟娟

2013 年《中共中央关于全面深化改革若干重大问题的决定》提出"允许混合所有制经济实行企业员工持股，形成资本所有者和劳动者利益共同体"，随后证监会在 2014 年发布了《关于上市公司实施员工持股计划试点的指导意见》，引起各界的广泛关注。上述政策颁布以来，实施员工持股计划的公司逐渐增加。员工持股计划的设立和实施大多得到了控股股东积极参与或主导，近年来甚至出现提供借款担保、发布"兜底式公告"推行员工持股计划的现象。为什么控股股东会积极推行员工持股计划？员工持股计划的激励效果是否会受到控股股东动机的影响？这是值得探究的重要问题，且对日后员工持股计划制度设计和改进完善具有深远的影响。已有研究指出，公司会出于降低现金工资和缓解融资约束、反收购、管理层防御、业绩操纵等需求而推行员工持股计划，进一步看，设立员工持股计划的动机也影响了激励效果。现有关于控股权配置与激励问题的研究主要考察的是股东权力（持股比例）的影响力，而股东权

---

* 原文刊载于《金融研究》2021 年第 11 期。

作者简介：邱杨茜，经济学博士，助理教授，厦门大学经济学院金融系；黄娟娟，管理学博士，副教授，厦门大学经济学院金融系。

力只是控股股东影响激励的必要条件而非充分条件，只有弄清楚控股股东因何影响激励计划推行，才能够更有针对性地在制度设计上加以改进。

近年来，控股股东股权质押可能引起的诸多问题也成为我国资本市场的监管重点。本文以控股股东股权质押产生的控制权转移风险作为切入点来考察控股股东与员工持股计划推行的关系。控股股东的股权质押是控股股东为缓解自身资金需求的质押行为，但是股票价格下跌时如果不能及时补仓或解除质押，就会面临被强制平仓甚至控制权转移的风险。相关研究表明，股权质押情形下控股股东有动机进行市值管理、维持股价稳定，并可能存在弱化激励、减少股利、降低创新、盈余管理等经济后果。本文认为员工持股计划从市值管理和内部人利益绑定两个方面满足了股权质押下控股股东维持股价稳定的重要需求：一方面，大股东机会主义使得股权质押的控股股东有动机寻找有效的市值管理工具，主动影响公司的股价水平；另一方面，控股股东质押加剧了两权分离，质押融资所体现的资金匮乏或潜在的资金需求，有可能需要大股东积极涉入激励制度，实现与管理层和骨干员工等内部人的利益捆绑。对控股股东而言，员工持股计划不同于高管股权激励，股票主要来源于二级市场购买，计划设立有效地释放了内部人购买公司股票的积极信号；员工持股计划的激励对象既包含普通员工，也包含公司高管，他们在努力工作提升公司价值的同时，也希望在计划期内因股价走高而获利，易于形成控股股东、管理层、员工三方的"内部人利益同盟"，从而缓解控制权转移的长短期风险；员工持股计划是一种实施成本较低、计划周期较短、面临监管更少且几乎没有业绩门槛的激励方式，在实施利益捆绑上具有更高的便利性。

为了考察控股股东质押对员工持股计划的推行和激励效果的影响，本文利用2013—2018年A股上市公司的样本进行实证分析后发现：前期存在控股股东股权质押的公司、股权质押率越高的公司，推行员工持股计划的概率显著更大；股东压力的调节效应表明，控股股东所面临的控制权转移风险越大，推行员工持股计划的概率也越高；有股权质押的公司推行员工持股计划的累计超额收益率为正，且与无质押的样本组没有显著区别，可见控股股东利用员工持股计划进行短期市值管理是有效的；但是对于提升公司长期价值和经营业绩没有显著促进作用。针对公司治理结构的进一步研究表明，控股股东的权力大小对股权质押下推行员工持股计划有显著正向调节作用，而董事会和独立董事则没有发挥出显著的调节作用。为了缓解内生性问题，本文将2017年9月证券业协会发布的《证券公司参与股票质押式回购交易风险管理指引（征求意见稿）》及同期沪深交易所分别发布的《股票质押式回购交易及登记结算业务办法（2017年征求意见稿）》作为股权质押管理趋严的政策冲击，进行了DID分析、PSM-DID分析，结论稳健；本文又以样本公司所处地区的平均质押率为工具变量，分别实施两步法和MLE工具变量法检验，分析结果均支持本文结论。

本文研究结果的借鉴意义在于：第一，控股股东作为员工持股计划制定的主导者和参与者，其所面临的市值下跌控制权转移风险，会导致其基于自利因素推行员工持股计划，尤其是质押率较高的时候更是如此。此时员工持股计划可能与股东的市值管理、维持股价稳定等动机和短视行为有关，弱化了激励的作用。第二，员工持股计划因其设立灵活、锁定期短、限售要求较低、监管宽松等特征，容易被控股股东利用，公司内部治理机制在这种情况下无法起到有效的抑制作用。上述问题值得引起监管部门和投资者的重视。一方面，员工持股计划的制度设计可以进一步完善，比如适当拉长员工持股计划的禁售期、增加员工持股计划的卖出信息披露等，以降低该计划的"工具化"可能；另一方面，加强外部治理机制的作用，以降低控股股东在公司决策中因自利行为带来的影响。

本文的贡献主要体现在以下两个方面：第一，本文拓展了股权质押的研究。学术界现有对于股权质押经济后果的研究包括对控股股东占款的影响（郑国坚等，2014；李旎和郑国坚，2015）、对股价崩盘风险的延后效应（谢德仁等，2016）、对创新投入的挤出效应（李常青等，2018）、对现金股利的削减作用（廖珂等，2018）等，本文补充了股权质押对市值管理和内部人利益绑定行为存在显著影响的经验证据，证实控股股东股权质押对公司的激励方案推出存在显著的影响，而该情形下推出的员工激励计划对公司长期市值和经营业绩提升作用有限，拓展了股权质押的经济后果研究。第二，现有关于控股权配置与激励问题的研究主要停留在股东与高管股权激励层面，并且更多地关注股东权力（持股比例）的影响。本文为该研究方向补充了来自员工持股计划的新经验证据，并且关注控股股东影响激励问题的重要动机（避免控制权转移风险），为控股股东涉入激励的相关理论提供了直接有力的验证。

放松卖空管制能够抑制并购商誉泡沫吗?

孙诗璐 张斐燕 郑建明 刘艳霞

近年来,在我国资本市场上,并购热潮下产生的商誉泡沫已成为当前重要的金融风险要素之一,引起了股东、监管部门及其他利益方的担忧。因此,在防范化解金融风险的背景下,谨防商誉泡沫已成为实务界和理论界广泛关注的热点话题。在实践中,并购重组作为公司重大投融资决策之一,管理层会深度介入其整个流程,不仅直接参与并购方案的制订和实施,还会对并购标的选择、估价等在内的并购全过程发挥主要决策权,因此,管理层自身动机对并购活动产生直接影响,其中包括并购商誉形成的规模和数量。基于委托代理理论,并购决策中的代理冲突导致管理层更加关注其私人利益(如股票期权、社会声誉等),从而不惜牺牲并购中创造的股东财富。进一步,代理问题的存在,会驱使管理层更可能凭借其信息和决策优势来提高并购频率和扩大并购规模,甚至不惜支付较高的溢价完成并购重组,从而导致商誉高估,助推商誉中非理性估值泡沫成分。那么,如何控制和防范商誉泡沫呢?除了已有研究关注到的内部控制、外部审计等治理机制外,从根本上抑制商誉估值泡沫还应有赖于基础性市场机制创新。

---

* 原文刊载于《金融研究》2021年第11期。

作者简介:孙诗璐,管理学博士,讲师,北京化工大学经济管理学院;张斐燕,经济学博士,讲师,北京化工大学经济管理学院;郑建明,教授,经济学博士,对外经济贸易大学国际商学院;刘艳霞,副教授,管理学博士,北京化工大学经济管理学院。

融资融券机制的实施是中国资本市场的一项制度创新。卖空的相关研究主要集中在两个领域。首先是卖空对股票流动性、稳定性和效率的影响。其次是卖空对公司财务决策的影响,例如盈余管理、投资决策和创新。研究表明,卖空具有价格发现功能,作为有效的外部公司治理机制可以减少盈余管理、提高企业投资效率、增加创新支出和产出等,然而鲜有研究探讨卖空是否可以抑制并购决策引起的商誉泡沫的形成。基于此,本文运用我国沪深两市所有 A 股上市公司 2007—2017 年的年度样本数据,将卖空管制逐步放松作为外生冲击事件,实证检验了放松卖空管制对并购商誉泡沫的影响,结果发现:(1)放松卖空管制以后,超额商誉显著下降,商誉资产也显著下降,这表明卖空机制对商誉泡沫产生了明显的抑制效应;(2)相比于国有控股公司,民营控股公司中放松卖空管制抑制商誉泡沫的作用更明显;(3)卖空通过吸引分析师关注、增加对管理层激励的途径来抑制商誉泡沫;(4)在市场化水平较高、行业竞争程较低情形下,卖空机制抑制商誉泡沫的效应更强;(5)卖空通过抑制商誉泡沫防范股价崩盘风险及提高企业盈利能力。

本文得到的贡献在于:首先,并购商誉泡沫是近年来我国资本市场最为重要的现象之一,本文则基于资本市场中放松卖空管制政策,为如何抑制商誉泡沫提供了新思路,丰富了并购商誉方面的相关文献。其次,作为一种外部治理机制,卖空机制对并购这一重大投融资决策发挥了有效的治理作用,已有文献以并购绩效为视角揭示了卖空机制的治理效应,但忽略了卖空机制对商誉估值泡沫这一并购中重要隐形经济后果的影响,而本文则填补了这一新领域的研究空白。最后,本文为试图寻找到化解商誉泡沫的有效手段提供了现实依据,为相关部门制定关于并购重组的政策法规及推进我国的放松卖空管制政策提供了有益参考,也为当前我国资本市场制度的建设提供了重要启示。

中小股东积极主义对债券持有人财富的溢出影响[*]

——基于网络投票数据的实证研究

曾爱民　吴　伟　吴育辉

提高直接融资比重，促进多层次资本市场健康稳定发展，是党的十九大报告提出的重要战略目标之一。截至 2020 年 12 月末，中国债券市场托管余额达到 117 万亿元，已超过中国同期 GDP 规模，成为仅次于美国的全球第二大债券市场。然而，自 2014 年超日债违约、刚性兑付被打破后，债券违约事件频繁发生，引起了投资者和监管部门对中国债券市场违约风险的重视。因为债券违约不仅会损害投资者利益，而且可能进一步引发系统性金融风险。如何确保债券市场健康发展，提高债券市场服务实体经济的效率，防范化解债券违约风险，已成为深化多层次资本市场改革过程中需要解决的重要问题。具体到企业层面，债券违约与发行企业财务业绩、偿债能力和信息不对称程度等因素息息相关。因此，寻求改善公司信息不对称的相关制度建设，以及提升公司业绩和增强财务稳健性的各种治理机制，对保护债券持有人财富具有重要意义。

中小股东通过网络投票等方式积极参与公司重要决策是近年来公司

---

[*] 原文刊载于《金融研究》2021 年第 12 期。
作者简介：曾爱民，管理学博士，教授，浙江工商大学会计学院；吴伟，管理学硕士，浙江工商大学会计学院；吴育辉，管理学博士，教授，厦门大学管理学院。

治理机制的重要变革之一。中小股东通过网络投票等方式积极参与公司治理能否产生积极影响？一方面，郑国坚等（2016）指出，由于中小股东存在缺乏远见、专业性不足等问题，且其利益联盟具有较强的不稳定性，因此中小股东参与治理可能会导致公司经营管理混乱。另一方面，有研究指出中小股东利用网络投票等方式积极参与公司治理具有抑制经理代理成本，促进企业技术创新等多方面的积极作用（例如，胡茜茜等，2018；李姝等，2018；郑志刚等，2019）。可见，现有研究主要考察了中小股东治理对公司及其自身利益的影响，但鲜有考察其对外部利益相关者的影响。

鉴于此，本文从公司最重要的外部利益相关者之一——债券持有人的视角出发，收集了2008—2018年深交所全部上市公司的股东大会网络投票数据，尝试探究中小股东积极主义对债券持有人财富的溢出效应，并对其内在机理以及调节作用进行检验。结果表明：第一，中小股东基于主观利益的积极主义行为，其客观后果能显著增加其所在公司的债券持有人财富。在控制内生性影响之后，该作用依然存在。第二，进一步探究其内在机理发现，中小股东积极主义虽无法显著影响公司的信息披露质量，但能通过提升公司业绩和增强财务稳健性的双重路径，对债券持有人财富产生正向溢出影响。第三，当公司内部治理环境较差，投资者具备学习效应，以及媒体外部信息渠道畅通时，中小股东积极主义对债券持有人财富的正向溢出效应更为显著。

本文的创新和贡献主要体现在以下几个方面。第一，区别于现有研究聚焦考察中小股东积极主义对公司及其自身利益的影响，本文通过检验互联网背景下中小股东积极主义对债券持有人财富的溢出效应，为监管部门保护债券持有人利益，促进债券市场健康发展提供了新思路。第二，本文分别从公司业绩、财务稳健性及信息披露质量三重视角出发，探究了中小股东积极主义对债券持有人财富产生影响的作用机理，有助于深化对中小股东积极主义如何发挥治理效应的理解，同时也丰富了投资者利益保护的相关理论体系。第三，本文通过检验中小股东积极主义的潜在影响因素，为优化中小股东网络投票的治理效应提供了方向。

基于上述研究结论，本文提出政策建议：首先，要进一步加强对中小股东的教育和引导，避免其在股票市场上过度投机和盲目跟风，善于"用手投票"，充分发挥中小股东新型治理主体的积极作用。其次，监管部门应进一步优化制度环境，为中小股东积极参与企业治理保驾护航；同时公司应当为中小股东参与决策提供便利条件，努力发挥中小股东建言献策等积极作用。

Journal of Financial Research

Brief Edition

(Volume II · 2021)

01 Macroeconomics & Monetary Policy

China's Interest Rate System and Market - Based Reform of Interest Rate

YI Gang

(The People's Bank of China)

Interest rate is the price of funds and an important variable in the macro-economy. It has great significance for macroeconomic equilibrium and resource allocation. In theory, the natural interest rate equals to the real interest rate when aggregate supply and demand reaches equilibrium. In practice, interest rate directly affects saving and consumption behavior of households, investment and financing decisions of enterprises, as well as import export and balance of payments, and in turn plays an important role in guiding macroeconomic operation. The equilibrium interest rate is determined by market supply and demand, reflecting a combined effect of saving, investment and financing behavior of market entities, such as enterprises, households and financial institutions, in the financial market. In the long run, the interest rate level is supposed to approach the natural interest rate. The central bank should adjust the policy rate to comply with the economic principle, the need of macroeconomic management and cross-cycle policy design. Now China's real interest rate is slightly lower than its economic growth rate and is at a relatively reasonable level. China keeps on promoting the market-based reform of interest rate, which not only adapts to China's actual conditions, but also basically conforms to international practices. While orderly lifting previous restrictions on interest rate, China attaches great importance on the establishment of market-based interest rate system, promoting the critical role of the market interest rate in guiding macroeconomic operation.

China has already established a relatively comprehensive market-based interest rate system. The central bank mainly uses monetary policy tools to adjust liquidity of the banking system, and releases policy rate signals. With the assistance of interest rate corridors, the central bank guides market benchmark interest rate fluctuating around the policy rate, and then transmits to the loan interest rate through the banking system, guiding the supply and demand of funds and the allocation of resources, and achieving monetary policy goals. Recently, the People's Bank of China launched an electronic trading mechanism for the Standing Lending Facility(SLF), to better consolidate the ceiling of the interest rate corridor. In China's market-based interest rate system, some important interest rates may include: the open market operation interest rate as the central bank's short-term policy rate, the medium-term lending facility (MLF) interest rate as the medium-term policy rate, loan prime rate (LPR) , reserve interest rate, and Shanghai Interbank Offered Rate (Shibor) , etc. In addition, the benchmark deposit rate has played an important role in the past, which has provided an important reference for financial institutions to set their own deposit rates. Now the 1 - year benchmark deposit rate in China is 1.5% , financial institutions could either add or minus basis points to the benchmark to set their own deposit rates. This is kind of a "golden - rule level" , which meets the need of cross - cycle policy design.

China's yield curve has approached to be mature. In a market - based interest rate system, the benchmark yield curve has great importance, and could provide pricing reference for various financial products and market entities. The yield curve reflects the interest rate term structure from short - term to long - term, and is composed of a series of major market benchmark interest rates. The short end of the yield curve is the overnight and 7 - day repo interest rate DR. The central bank could inject base money through open market operations, which directly affect the short - term market benchmark interest rates. The long end of the yield curve is the Treasury bond yield, formed by market transactions, which is mainly based on market expectations of future macroeconomic trends. The investors and policy makers could observe important market information through the Treasury bond yield. A mature yield curve can play an active role in reflecting changes in macroeconomic growth and inflation. In recent years, the compilation and release of China's Treasury bond yield curve has become more mature and the yield curve is widely used. At the same time, the correlation between China and the United States' Treasury bond yields has increased. However, considering the size, turnover rate, and bid - ask spread of the Treasury market, there is still room for improvement in the market basis of China's Treasury bond yield curve compared with the developed markets.

In addition, the asset purchase tool is an operation when the central bank has limited choice during financial crisis. Central banks should avoid implementing the asset purchase tool for too long, for it will cause many problems. If it must be implemented, central banks should adhere to three principles: aiming to help the market back to normal, moving ahead of the market as much as possible, and reducing the scale and duration of asset purchase as much as possible. At present, China has the conditions to implement a normal monetary policy for a longer period, and there is no need to implement asset purchase operation right now.

The People's Bank of China will further deepen the market - based interest rate reform, improve the formation and transmission mechanism of market - based interest rates, promote central bank policy rate system, and strengthen the cultivation of market benchmark interest rates. Meanwhile, the PBC will also continue to strengthen financial regulation, improve business environment, promote hard budget constraints, forestall financial risks, and provide a more favorable condition for further market - based interest rate reform.

Great Achievements in Building a Moderately Prosperous Society in All Respects in the New Era and Prospects for the Country's New Journey: Statistical Monitoring and Analysis Based on the China Balanced Development Index

XU Xianchun　LIU Wanqi　PENG Hui　ZHANG Zhongwen

(School of Statistics, Southwestern University of Finance and Economics; Tsinghua China Data Center, School of Economics and Management, Tsinghua University; School of Statistics and Management, Shanghai University of Finance and Economics)

On the occasion of the centenary of the founding of the Communist Party of China (CPC), the building of a moderately prosperous society in all respects for the benefit of more than 1.4 billion people is not only a solemn commitment made by China's party to its people and history but also a key step in realizing the Chinese dream of the great rejuvenation of the Chinese nation. This study focuses on the statistical monitoring and analysis of the core contents of the Tsinghua China Balanced Development Index during the building of a moderately prosperous society in all respects since the 18th CPC National Congress. These contents include data relating to economic development, social governance, cultural construction, poverty alleviation, the people's livelihoods, and the ecological environment. The results comprehensively reflect China's great achievements. Further to this study's use of the monitoring results to examine the country's new journey, it analyzes the problems and challenges presented by the comprehensive construction of a modern socialist country. Based on our results, this study suggests countermeasures to address the main contradictions affecting China's society in the new era and help start its new journey toward the comprehensive construction of a modern socialist country.

The construction of the China Balanced Development Index is based on the principal contradictions affecting Chinese society in the new era. The index links the need to improve people's lives with imbalances and inadequacies in the country's development and meets the requirements for a comprehensive system to monitor the country's progress in building a moderately prosperous society in all respects. First, the China Balanced Development Index measures comprehensive criteria for the improvement of people's lives, which cover four areas: economic development, social progress, the ecological environment, and people's well - being. Second, based on the idea of no one being left behind on the path to a prosperous society benefiting all people, the China Balanced Development Index embodies the whole population and uses the Poverty Incidence Rate indicator to measure the progress of poverty alleviation in different regions. Third, the construction of the China Balanced Development Index embodies all regions, fully addressing the problems of development imbalances between different regions and between urban and rural areas.

Our results show historic achievements in building a moderately prosperous society in all respects since the beginning of the new era: economic development continues to advance, the level of social governance continues to improve, cultural soft power is becoming increasingly prominent, poverty is successfully alleviated, people's living standards are significantly enhanced, and the ecological environment is improving markedly.

Based on our analysis of the data from the China Balanced Development Index, this study finds the following problems and challenges: regional differences need to be further narrowed, the imbalance between urban and rural development remains prominent, the ability to innovate does not meet the requirements of high - quality development, imbalances and inadequacies in the people's disposable incomes remain prominent, the equalization of basic public services needs to be further ameliorated, and governance of the ecological environment needs to be further improved.

This study suggests some potential solutions to the above problems. First, adhering to the strategy of promoting major regional development and building a new pattern of regional coordinated development. Second, vigorously implementing China's rural revitalization strategy and promoting the integrated development of the country's urban and rural areas. Third, strengthening the construction of technological innovation and diffusion systems and continuously improving the national innovation capability. Fourth, ameliorating the income distribution policy to further narrow the income distribution gap. Fifth, making deeper pension, medical care, and education reforms, while promoting the equalization of basic public services. Finally, further modernizing the governance of the ecological environment to achieve sustainable development.

Forecasts of Macroeconomic Variables in China: Combination Forecasts of Surveys and Models

LIANG Fang   SHEN Shihan   HUANG Zhuo

(International School of Business & Finance, Sun Yat-sen University; University of California, Los Angeles; National School of Development, Peking University)

This paper uses the forecast combination method to predict the GDP growth and CPI growth in China. It also compares the out-of-sample performance of predictive model forecasts, expert forecasts, and combined forecasts in predicting GDP and CPI growth, and analyzes forecast errors to explore whether the forecast combination method can improve forecasting accuracy in different economic periods.

We choose several predictive models from multiple perspectives. First, we use the regime-switching model (RSM) to reflect the dynamic patterns of GDP and CPI growth rates during stable and volatile periods. Second, we use the mixed data sampling (MIDAS) model to incorporate the information content of monthly data to improve the accuracy in predicting quarterly macro variables. Third, we use the mixed-frequency error correction model (MF-ECM) to consider the cointegration relationships between variables. To use a multi-dimensional and high-frequency macroeconomic dataset in prediction, we also resort to the mixed-frequency vector autoregression (MF-VAR). In addition, since the growth rates of GDP and CPI are both first-order single integral time series, the autoregressive integrated moving average model (ARIMA) is included as a benchmark.

We use the forecasts of macroeconomic variables in the "Langrun Forecast" program to construct our expert forecast data. We choose the "Langrun Forecast" mainly for two reasons. First, it contains forecasts from various institutions and covers a long time period. Second, the forecasts included are all provided by well-known academic institutions or leading commercial organizations, which ensures the reliability and continuity of the data.

Based on forecast series provided by models and experts, we use a variety of methods to carry out combination forecasts and explore whether forecast combination helps improve forecast accuracy. Specifically, the combination methods include simple averaging, weighting by forecasting errors, and the Bayesian model averaging method based on the Bayesian information criterion.

The predictive information set includes fixed asset investment, total retail sales of consumer goods, total export value, total import value, industrial added value, M_2 supply, Shanghai Composite Index volatility, national interbank market interest rate, financial institution RMB loan balances, newly started area of commercial housing, generated electrical energy, consumer expectation index, and national housing prosperity index. We use a multi-dimensional and high-frequency macroeconomic information set to make predicts.

In the out-of-sample comparison, expert forecasts generally outperform model forecasts. The empirical results show that the expert forecasts contain almost all the information predicted by the models, indicating that the experts have considered the predictive content of the models when making forecasts. Furthermore, we find that the accuracy of expert predictions is significantly higher than model predictions during periods of economic instability (2008—2010), as experts can adjust expectations timely by grasping the actual economic environment and the direction of economic policies, and thus obtain more accurate forecasts. In addition, combined forecasting improves forecast accuracy. The robustness tests show that the improvement of forecast accuracy by combination forecasting does not depend on a specific benchmark, and changes in the length of the estimation window do not affect the main findings.

This paper contributes to the existing literature mainly in two ways. First, previous studies that use forecast combination methods to predict China's macroeconomic variables focus on a specific combination forecasting model and discuss its predictive performance. Few studies have considered survey forecast information in the combination forecasting. Compared with model forecasts, expert forecasts are more sensitive to macroeconomic conditions and policy releases, and therefore can continuously update predictive information during forecasting, which improves forecast accuracy. This paper combines expert forecasts and model forecasts by using combination forecasting methods, and examines whether expert predictive information and model forecasting results can help to improve forecasting accuracy simultaneously. Second, this paper compares the forecast performance of expert forecasts and econometric models in different economic periods. We find that expert forecasts significantly outperform model forecasts during periods of economic volatility, and explains the reasons for the difference across economic states.

Spillover Effects of U. S. Monetary Policy, China's Asset Price Fluctuations and Capital Account Control

WU Liyuan ZHAO Fuyang WANG Chan GONG Liutang

(Institute of World Economics and Politics, Chinese Academy of Social Science; School of Economics, Central University of Finance and Economics; School of Finance, Central University of Finance and Economics; School of International Economics and Management, Beijing Technology and Business University; LMEQF, Peking University)

A bulk of empirical studies have confirmed the spillover effects of U. S. monetary policy on China and other emerging market countries. The U. S. Federal Reserve resumed its quantitative easing policy in 2020. This resulted in the federal funding rate falling to zero, a dramatic expansion of the Federal Reserve's balance sheet, and a global flood of liquidity. Currently, the U. S. economy is gradually recovering, and inflation is rising. It is therefore expected that the Federal Reserve will soon tighten monetary policy and increase the federal funding rate. This implies that emerging market countries, including China, may once again experience a shortage of liquidity and interest rate hikes, in contrast to the current extremely fluid monetary policy. This raises the following three key questions. What are the spillover effects of U. S. monetary policy on China's economy? What is the mechanism of such spillover effects? What policies could stabilize the fluctuations caused by these spillover effects? This paper aims to answer these questions with reference to the Federal Reserve's interest rate hike in 2016.

Based on Davis and Presno (2017), we contruct a small open economy dynamic stochastic general equilibrium model (DSGE) with financial friction and a real estate market. We thereby propose the causative mechanism as follows: The increase in U. S. interest rates generates externalities in the flow of capital, which accelerates the decline of domestic asset prices. This triggers the first feedback channel, which is driven by financial friction, leading to the synergistic decline of domestic investment and asset prices. Thus, the expected return on domestic assets is reduced, which triggers a second feedback channel and further increases capital outflows.

In addition, we use welfare analysis to determine the optimal level of capital account control and its effect on the independence of monetary policy. This reveals the optimal level of capital account control should be moderate, as such control has two opposing effects: capital account control can effectively alleviate the influence of foreign interest – rate shocks on economic fluctuations while it can also decrease the efficient allocation of national wealth. The optimal level of capital account control must therefore balance macro – prudence and efficiency. What's more, we find that appropriate policies for capital account control help to enhance the independence of monetary policy.

In contrast to previous studies, we simultaneously replicate and explicate, within a unified framework, the characteristics of China's macroeconomy subsequent to the U. S. Federal Reserve's interest rate hike in 2016. We also propose a mechanism for the interaction between the feedback channels of capital flow externalities and financial accelerators, which links the spillover effects of U. S. monetary policy with asset price fluctuations. This confirms that China's real estate market is a key channel via which U. S. monetary shocks affect China's economy.

Based on the above findings, we make the following policy recommendations. First, capital account control should be gradually transformed to capital account management. This requires the gradual liberalization of long - term capital account restrictions and the establishment of a regular mechanism for the management of abnormal capital flows. Second, more market – oriented dynamic measures for capital account management should be explored, such as risk reserves, Tobin taxes, and macro – prudential taxes. Third, while the opening of the capital account is gradually and steadily promoted, policies should be developed to increase reform depth and risk prevention. Increasing reform depth requires the marketization of the RMB exchange rate formation mechanism and the opening of the financial market, whereas increasing risk prevention requires the gradual implementation of policy experiments in lower risk fields.

Nowcasting China's Quarterly GDP Using Mixed - Frequency Data

WANG Xia   SI Nuo   SONG Tao

(School of Economics, Renmin University of China; Lingnan College, Sun Yat - sen University; School of Economics, Xiamen University)

As GDP can comprehensively reflect the economic condition of a country or a region, GDP predictions are carefully scrutinized by many institutions. However, because GDP is usually only calculated on a quarterly frequency and released after a delay of 3 weeks, classical forecasting models cannot provide accurate and timely GDP predictions. However, some macroeconomic variables that are highly correlated with GDP, such as industrial added value, import and export volumes, and the total retail sales of consumer goods, are released monthly with a much smaller delay. The incorporation of this monthly information into GDP prediction could therefore improve the timeliness of GDP forecasting, enable the correct evaluation of economic conditions, and facilitate the formulation of appropriate macroeconomic regulations. However, the incorporation of these monthly indicators into economic forecasting models will require the solution of key problems associated with these indicators' underlying data, namely its mixture of data frequencies, the ragged - edge behavior of real - time data, the presence of data revision, and the periodic absence of data.

To deal with the problems of absent data and ragged - edge data, we nowcast China's GDP based on Zheng and Wang's (2012, 2013) mixed - frequency dynamic factor model for year - on - year growth rates. Compared with mixed data sampling (MIDAS) and mixed - frequency vector autoregression

(MFVAR) models, the mixed - frequency dynamic factor model accounts for missing data in addition to dealing with ragged - edge data, and thus makes full, accurate, and timely use of the data. In addition, a year - on - year growth rate model is more useful in China, as the National Bureau of Statistics announces only year - on - year growth rates for most macroeconomic indicators, and policymakers focus on year - on - year GDP growth rates. Moreover, as year -on - year growth rates are based on data for the same month or quarter each year, they can mitigate effects due to seasonality, which is not generally accounted for in official year - on - year economic growth data released in China (and is another reason why a year - on - year growth rate model is appropriate for China). Thus, once new data are released, we can immediately update our nowcasting result. This means that we can nowcast the quarterly GDP growth rate in real time using the most up - to - date data and thus provide a reliable and timely economic prediction for decision - makers. Our results also show that the mixed - frequency dynamic factor model provides more accurate predictions than the MIDAS and the MFVAR models.

In addition to developing GDP nowcasting, we derive some other important results. First, in contrast to GDP data, which are announced quarterly, in April, July, October, and January, with an approximately 3 - week delay, we can estimate the quarterly GDP growth rate on a monthly basis. For example, we estimate the year - on - year growth rate of GDP from February to April, which is crucial information for decision - makers and for economic modeling. Second, in addition to determining the smoothed estimator of a common factor, we also obtain the smoothed estimator of the idiosyncratic factor. The sum of these factors is then used to derive a smoothed estimate of the monthly year - on - year growth rate of real GDP. Third, we circumvent the missing data problem, which is due to the restriction of statistical rules, the effect of the Spring Festival, and other factors, by estimating the missing data from the observations of other indicators, which affords a complete time series of data.

In summary, our GDP nowcasting method enables daily (rather than quarterly) forecasting of China's quarterly GDP growth rate, which means that we can incorporate the latest information about economic conditions into our forecasts. Thus, we can provide more timely and reliable economic predictions to policymakers. From the perspective of macroeconomic regulation, these economic predictions may allow policymakers to generate real - time updates of its judgments on current economic conditions and thereby formulate more timely and suitable macroeconomic policies. From the perspective of microeconomic decision - making, these economic predictions may enable enterprise managers to understand the current economic situation more clearly and in a timely fashion, and thereby to efficiently adjust investment plans and development strategies. Thus, we believe that our nowcasting - based economic predictions will be invaluable for developing more effective national - level macroeconomic control and enabling better market - level microeconomic decisions.

Does Human Capital in the Financial Sector Affect Real Economic Growth in China?

LIU Guanchun   SI Dengkui   LIU Fang

(Lingnan College, Sun Yat-sen University; School of Economics, Qingdao University; Institute for the World Economy, Shanghai Academy of Social Sciences)

The fundamental purpose of the financial sector is to serve the real economy. Currently, China's economic development is characterized by a "cold" real economy and a "hot" virtual economy. The financial sector is favored by social elites, while the real sector exhibits a sluggish trend. The mainstream explanation for this disconnect is that human capital has been overallocated to the financial sector, stifling innovation in the real sector and thus leading to a decline in real economic growth. However, given the information asymmetry between creditors and borrowers, increasing human capital in the financial sector also helps eliminate credit contract frictions, and result in credit expansion, which promotes real economic growth. To provide theoretical and practical reference for deepening financial supply-side structural reform and realizing an innovation-driven growth regime, this paper investigates how the allocation of human capital between the financial and real sectors affects real economic growth in China.

In theory, the financial sector's human capital has ambiguous effects on real economic growth. On the one hand, it hinders real economic growth through the following channels: (i) crowding out labor and capital in the real sector; (ii) transferring profit from the real sector, weakening entrepreneurship, and reducing the intrinsic incentives of productive activities; and (iii) lowering the overall entrepreneurial ability. On the other hand, it promotes real economic growth through the following channels: (i) strengthening the ability of the financial sector to absorb social deposits via financial product innovation and industrial competition; (ii) alleviating the information asymmetry between creditors and borrowers and accurately identifying the ability of firms to repay loans; and (iii) improving the allocation of credit among firms with different financing constraints.

This paper constructs a two - sector growth model consisting of banks and firms to investigate how the financial sector's human capital affects real economic growth. It then tests the model using the 2008 Chinese Economic Census dataset and data from prefecture - level cities from 2003 to 2015. The theoretical analysis shows that there is an inverse U - type relationship between human capital in the financial sector and real economic growth which is driven by capital crowd - in and innovation crowd - out effects. A series of empirical analyses supports the model's predications. In particular, our simple counterfactual calculation suggests that the real economic growth rate will increase by about 0.45% when human capital is efficiently allocated between the financial and real sectors, and the contribution increases as China's economy grows. This paper obtains similar findings using the Chinese Industrial Database over the 2011—2013 period and confirms that the financial sector's human capital increases a firm's access to external financing and reduces capital misallocation among firms.

In sum, these findings demonstrate that increasing human capital in the financial sector does not absolutely promote or inhibit real economic growth,suggesting that there is an optimal allocation threshold of human capital between the financial and real sectors. Therefore, to maintain long - term and high - quality economic growth, it is important to optimize human capital allocation. This paper's theoretical analysis and empirical findings have important policy implications. First, because talented employees are drawn to the financial sector for its high salaries, policymakers should improve modes of income distribution. Second, it is essential to restrict the blind expansion of the financial sector and strengthen its functions of providing financial services to the real sector. The " financial sector transfers 1. 5 trillion yuan of profits to the real sector" policy implemented in 2020 in response to the COVID - 19 Pandemic not only helps reduce the financing cost of firms, but may also help to optimize the allocation of human capital.

This paper makes three contributions to the literature. First, it is the first to examine how human capital in the financial sector affects China's real economic growth. Other studies focus on the growth effects of the allocation of human capital between rent - seeking and productive sectors, whereas this paper explores the effect of human capital allocation between the financial and real sectors. Second, this paper examines the influence of human capital allocation in the financial sector on real economic growth and the mechanism that underlies this influence. Although there are several related theoretical studies, this paper uses empirical evidence to confirm that the financial sector's human capital is conducive to expanding credit scale. Third, this paper enriches the understanding of the link between financial development and economic growth. Previous studies focus on the scale expansion and structural adjustment of the financial system, whereas this paper adopts the perspective of human capital allocation, which provides a new explanation for the inverse U - type relationship between financial development and economic growth.

Does the Liquidity Coverage Ratio Regulatory Requirement Affect the Efficiency of Monetary Policy Transmission? Evidence from China's Banking Industry

ZHUANG Yumin   ZHANG Yi

(School of Finance, China Financial Policy Research Center, Renmin University of China; Bank of China)

The painful lessons of the 2008 financial crisis illustrate that relying solely on capital regulation does not guarantee that commercial banks will be sufficiently resilient. In this regard, the Basel Committee on Banking Supervision (BCBS) put forward a global liquidity regulatory framework as an important part of Basel Ⅲ. Specifically, BCBS strengthened its liquidity framework by developing two minimum standards for funding and liquidity: the liquidity coverage ratio (LCR), which emphasizes short-term liquidity and the ability to prevent fire sales; and the net stable funding ratio (NSFR), which is aimed at reducing funding risk.

Once brought forth, liquidity regulation has raised a fierce debate about its potential impact on commercial banks and the transmission of monetary policy. Although the theoretical banking literature provides a logical framework for liquidity regulation design, no research yet empirically reveals its potential impact, especially the impact of the LCR regulatory requirement. How did commercial banks respond to the LCR regulatory requirement? Does the LCR regulatory requirement affect the transmission efficiency of monetary policy? If so, how can we coordinate liquidity regulatory rules and monetary policy? To the best of our knowledge, these questions have not yet been fully addressed.

From both theoretical and empirical perspectives, our paper sheds light on the coordination mechanism between liquidity regulation and traditional monetary policy tools under a macroprudential regulatory framework.

Our paper theoretically redefines the liquidity shortage cost function based on the LCR regulatory requirement and incorporates it into a classical Monti-Klein model to illustrate the potential impact of the LCR regulatory requirement on monetary policy transmission efficiency. Our model indicates that the existence of liquidity shortage costs is an essential prerequisite for the monetary policy transmission process. Thus, the LCR regulatory requirement may influence the efficiency of monetary policy transmission by changing the marginal cost of a liquidity shortage. However, this effect depends on commercial banks' liquidity management behavior.

Using a semi - annual sample of 65 major commercial banks in China between 2015 and 2019, we empirically test our theoretical predictions. The results show that liquidity regulation has a significant impact on the efficiency of monetary policy transmission, which depends on banks' liquidity management behaviors when facing a possible LCR shortfall. To be specific, commercial banks, which actively adjust their funding structures and strengthen the quality of their liabilities, not only enhance their short - term liquidity profiles, but also improve the efficiency of monetary policy transmission. However, some urban and rural commercial banks with lower LCRs tend to hoard liquidity assets to fulfill LCR requirements, which may reduce the efficiency of monetary policy transmission.

Based on the aforementioned findings, this paper features some policy implications. We suggest that regulators should objectively evaluate the potential impact of liquidity regulation on monetary policy transmission efficiency, closely monitor commercial banks' liquidity management behaviors, and flexibly introduce a variety of regulatory settings to ensure banks' resilience and stability and improve monetary policy transmission efficiency. We also recommend that commercial bank managers should properly adjust the structure of assets and liabilities to cope with the potential impact of LCR regulatory requirements.

The main contributions of this paper are as follows. First, we expand the application range of the Monti - Klein model and reveal the micro mechanism of monetary policy transmission. Second, we provide empirical evidence for the potential impact of the LCR regulatory requirement, which compensates for the current gap in the liquidity regulation research. Third, we reveal the nexus between liquidity regulation and monetary policy transmission with both a theoretical framework and empirical evidence, which may help future researchers understand the potential impact of the liquidity regulation specifically and macroprudential policy generally.

However, this paper is subject to some limitations in terms of data quality and the length of the sample time period. How the LCR affects the interbank market and other monetary policy transmission channels are important questions that require further exploration. For future research in this area, we hope to describe the behaviors of commercial banks more accurately under multiple regulatory constraints, which may enhance the micro - mechanism design of two - pillar policy coordination in China.

Income Gaps, Credit Constraints, and House Price Fluctuations

CHEN Jinzhi WEN Xingchun SONG Lu

(School of Government Audit, Nanjing Audit University; School of Banking and Finance, University of International Business and Economics; National Academy of Development and Strategy, Renmin University of China)

Income gaps, credit constraints, and housing prices are long - established and prominent topics of social concern. International Monetary Fund (IMF) figures from September 2020 report a record high global real house price index of 167. 26 (using the first quarter of 2000 as the base period). The data show a rising trend in 47 of the 63 sampled countries and regions. Furthermore, since the U. S. subprime mortgage crisis, many scholars have investigated the potential relationships between income gaps and credit constraints. Numerous papers show that relaxation of credit constraints contributes significantly to rising house prices. Although this finding raises a natural question of how income gaps influence house prices through credit channels, this question is rarely mentioned in the literature.

Theoretically, because different income groups have different housing demands, changes in income distribution should significantly affect house prices through the amplification effect of credit leverage. Therefore, this paper aims to establish a general framework to interpret house price changes through the channel of income gaps affecting credit constraints. It shows that income gaps, credit constraints, and house prices are closely related. Specifically, an income gap reduction improves the relative income levels of low - income groups, which relaxes their credit constraints for house purchases. The relaxation of credit constraints makes the (aggregate) housing liquidity premium decrease. However, low - income groups have higher housing marginal utility, and access to external financing increases the housing market weight of low - income groups that have rising incomes. Thus, relaxation of credit constraints raises the housing marginal utility for society as a whole, which offsets the negative impact that liquidity premium decreases have on house prices, and ultimately increases house prices overall. This paper's findings are further supported by empirical analysis of cross – country panel data, which shows that the rising share of income going to low – income groups has significantly stronger effects on credit constraints and house prices than does growth in the incomes of high - income groups.

This paper makes three main contributions. First, existing explanations of the effects of income gaps on housing prices are mainly based on static analyses; because our model introduces the effects of credit constraints, this paper incorporates dynamic characteristics. Second, previous studies often use representative agent models to investigate the relationships between credit constraints and house prices. This paper enriches the research dimension by including analysis of heterogeneous agents. Third, the literature mainly studies the relationships between income gaps and house prices directly from the empirical level but does not conduct in – depth analysis of the transmission mechanism. In contrast, the construction of this paper's heterogeneous agent model enables a clear description of the transmission mechanisms between income gaps, credit constraints, and house prices. Importantly for policy makers, our results provide new insights into the factors that cause house prices to rise.

Finally, this paper has real - world importance. At present, China's real estate market trends are different in first - and second - tier cities than they are in third - and fourth - tier cities. CREIS data show approximately 10% growth in the land supply and transaction volumes of China's first - and second - tier cities in 2020. In contrast, the data show the land supply and transaction volumes of

China's third - and fourth - tier cities decreasing by half in the same year. China's real estate market is deeply tied with bank credit, government revenue, and social investment. If the market encounters a sudden and severe decline, it will inevitably lead to serious systemic financial risks. As far as the current situation is concerned, the proposal of " six priorities and stability in six areas " shows the Chinese central government's concern about the population's livelihood, employment, financial stability, and investment expectations. Narrowing the income gap is itself an important means to protect the basic population's livelihood. This paper shows the further importance of narrowing the income gap to expand the scale of society's use of financing, prevent house prices from collapsing, and stabilize investment expectations. With particular relevance to the "Gray Rhino" real estate market, which is characterized by slowing economic growth and exhaustion of land resources, mechanisms should be considered to prevent the systemic financial risks caused by a " hard landing" of the real estate market. Management of the real economic function of the real estate industry is particularly important at present because the industry has the characteristics of large - scale, long industrial chains, growing employment, and increasing fiscal contributions. Relative to some short - term policies, more analysis should be applied to the basic aspects of income distribution and its influence on the domestic market and the domestic economic cycle.

Do Innovative Lending Facilities Affect Bank Loan Interest Rates?

DENG Wei   SONG Min   LIU Min

(School of Accounting, Zhongnan University of Economics and Law; Economics and Management School, Wuhan University)

In the past few years, the People's Bank of China (PBC) has created a series of lending facility tools represented by mid - term lending facility (MLF) tools to help guide commercial banks to reduce their financing costs and promote high - quality economic development. Compared to the lending facility tools introduced by the Federal Reserve and other central banks during the crisis, the MLFs are intended as normal monetary policy tools rather than temporary rescue tools. The MLFs are designed to provide base money to commercial banks, support the proper growth of credit, and the reduction of commercial bank loan interest rates.

Due to a lack of suitable causality identification strategies, it remains controversial whether lending facility tools have an effective impact on the interest rates of commercial bank loans. In particular, in China, where a variety of monetary policy tools coexist, the complex effects of different monetary policy tools affect and overlap with each other. This complexity presents difficulties for the study of the policy effects of lending facility tools. So far, empirical research on the impact of China's lending facility tools on bank loan interest rates remains rare. Based on the quasi - natural experiment created by the introduction of MLFs by the PBC, this paper uses hand - collected data from the 2009 to 2017 annual reports of 100 commercial banks to conduct an empirical study of whether China's lending facilities have an effective impact on commercial bank loan interest rates. The main conclusions of this paper are as follows. First, after the creation of the MLFs, the greater the eligible collateral held by commercial banks, the lower the interest rates of their loans. This effect increases over the studied period, showing that lending facilities can significantly affect commercial bank loan interest rates and have an increasing policy effect over time. Second, the PBC's MLF operation expands the amount of borrowing from the PBC and the lending provided by commercial banks. This increased lending effectively reduces commercial bank loan interest rates, showing that the MLF tools work through the channel of eligible commercial bank collateral.

The contributions of this paper are as follows. First, by using hand - collected eligible collateral data from commercial banks, this paper demonstrates the transmission mechanism by which MLFs affect bank loan rates. Previous empirical studies of the impacts of lending facility tools in China do not consider the eligible collateral of commercial banks or demonstrate how lending facilities exert their policy effects through such banks. Given that China's lending facilities have required that participating commercial banks provide eligible collateral, our use of hand - collected eligible collateral data provides original micro - level evidence that the MLFs work through the collateral channel. Second, by studying the policy effects of the MLF tools from the perspective of commercial bank loan interest rates, this paper verifies the effectiveness of the MLFs, thereby enriching the literature. Our results show that the PBC can effectively decrease commercial bank interest rates by using lending facilities to provide large - scale, low - cost funds to commercial banks, and that the effects are enhanced over time.

The findings of this paper have implications for collateral management in China's monetary policy and its implementation of lending facilities. First, the PBC can use lending facilities to influence commercial bank loan interest rates by adjusting lending facility scales, interest rates, and eligible collateral ranges. The PBC's lending facilities help improve the formation mechanism of the loan prime rate (LPR) formation mechanism and reduce social financing costs. Second, The

MLF is a hybrid monetary policy tool that is both quantitative and price based. In practice, the PBC mainly operates the MLF by adjusting its size. In contrast, the MLF's interest rate has undergone small changes, with an overall downward trend. As a result, the extent to which the MLF interest rate affects commercial bank loan interest rates is unclear. Therefore, to improve the effectiveness of China's lending facilities, it is important to further explore how the policy effects of the MLF's functional mechanisms are affected by different scales of operation and lending facility interest rates.

The Global Financial Cycle and Cross - border Capital Flows

TAN Xiaofen   YU Mengwei

(School of Finance, Central University of Finance and Economics)

The cross - country co - movement of financial conditions is a notable feature of the development of global financial integration. This phenomenon, called the global financial cycle, can be interpreted as a set of push factors, including US monetary policy and global risk aversion. If a country's capital flows are mainly driven by the global financial cycle, the country is more likely to experience sudden surges and stops in capital inflows that are not related to domestic fundamentals. In addition to amplifying the fluctuations of a country's capital flows and financial cycle, the global financial cycle may also increase the volatility of a country's economic cycle if the global financial cycle is not aligned with a country's specific macroeconomic conditions. For example, if a loose global financial condition coincides with a country's economic prosperity, this may lead to excess capital inflows into the country, which in turn leads to asset price bubbles and excess credit creation. Asset price bubbles and excessive credit growth are the best predictors of financial crises.

Understanding the impact of the global financial cycle on cross - border capital flows is particularly important given the current complex international situation. Previous studies show that in periods of stress, capital flows are mainly driven by global factors. For example, the COVID - 19 pandemic has led to unprecedented capital outflows from emerging markets, mainly because of the sharp increase in global risk aversion and uncertainty. Although many emerging economies have experienced outflows during the COVID - 19 pandemic, some have been much more affected than others. So how can we explain this heterogeneity? Could macroeconomic fundamentals and structural factors explain it? The global financial cycle is an uncontrollable exogenous shock to a country, but a country can enact policies to adjust fundamentals and structural factors. Therefore, answering the above questions could help to improve policies for capital flows management.

First, this study uses principal component analysis to generate a global factor (GF) variable, extracted from 42 major stock market indexes, as a proxy for the global financial cycle.

Second, the study examines the impact of the global financial cycle on capital inflows during the 1997—2017 period. We find three main patterns. (i) An increase in GF reduces capital inflows significantly, and this impact exists for all of the sub - items of capital inflows, namely foreign direct investment, portfolio equity, portfolio debt, and banking loans. (ii) In the 2008 global financial crisis, the portfolio inflows (including equity and debt) of emerging economies became more sensitive to the global financial cycle. However, due to the safe - haven effect, the portfolio inflows of advanced economies were less sensitive to the global financial cycle. In both advanced economies and emerging market economies, banking loans were extremely sensitive to the global financial cycle, which confirms the importance of cross - border banks during periods of global financial market volatility. (iii) In the post - 2008 financial crisis period, portfolio debt inflows are more sensitive to the global financial cycle than in the pre - crisis period.

Third, we explore why the global financial cycle affects the capital flows of countries unequally. We make the following conclusions. (i) When a country is in a period of economic prosperity (with relatively high economic growth and interest rates), the impact of the global financial cycle on capital inflows is relatively weak. (ii) When a country has a high level of capital account liberalization or financial development, the impact of the global financial cycle on capital inflows is relatively strong. (iii) The effect of the global financial cycle is stronger in fixed exchange rate regimes than in more flexible (although not necessarily fully flexible) regimes.

Finally, using a mediation effect model, we find that US monetary policy shock is an important driver of the global financial cycle, which affects cross-border capital inflows.

Policy makers could respond to the global financial cycle in the following ways. First, they could strengthen the monitoring and analysis of cross-border capital flows. Policy makers must not only pay attention to the scale of cross-border capital flows but also to the structure of the capital flows. Bank loans and debt flows have a greater effect on financial stability and have to be monitored carefully. Second, sound macroeconomic fundamentals and reasonable institutions can help a country absorb external shocks. Specifically, countries should (i) adopt sustainable and stabilizing macroeconomic policies that enhance economic and market resilience; (ii) open up capital accounts gradually and impose capital controls when necessary; and (iii) improve the flexibility of exchange rates, although they do not need to be fully flexible.

Interest Rate Differential, the Dollar Index, and China's Capital Flows

MIAO Yanliang HAO Yang FEI Xuan

(State Administration of Foreign Exchange Investment Center)

Understanding the drivers of China's cross - border capital flows is critical for maintaining financial stability and curbing financial risks in China. Cross - border flows are generally driven by both push and pull factors. Conventional wisdom holds that these can be best captured by interest rate differentials across countries. However, interest rate differentials are not the only driver of China's cross - border flows. Empirical studies suggest that speculation on potential price movements in bilateral exchange rates (i. e. , currency speculation) is also an important motivation. In history, as both the interest rate and the RMB exchange rate are not fully market - driven in China, there may be other factors that have affected China's cross - border flows.

To shed light on this important issue, we focus on the role of the U. S. dollar index (DXY). Leveraging the time - varying parameter vector auto - regression (TVPVAR) method, we find that the DXY is the most critical factor in determining China's cross - border flows. This finding is robust to a variety of sample periods and model specifications. Why is the exchange rate more important than the interest rate? And why is the multilateral dollar exchange rate more critical than the bilateral exchange rate of the RMB against the U. S. dollar? We refer these questions as " the conundrum of China's cross - border capital flows". To resolve this conundrum, we examine the channels through which the DXY affects capital flows and propose a novel framework to explain China's cross - border flows.

Our empirical results suggest that the DXY influences capital flows through two main channels. The first is via exchange rate expectations. For a long period, the RMB exchange rate was either pegged or crawling pegged to the U. S. dollar, resulting in the low flexibility of the RMB. In this condition, when factors other than China's economic fundamentals make the U. S. dollar appreciate, the RMB is expected to depreciate, which leads to the outflow of speculative capital. Similarly, when the U. S. dollar depreciates, the RMB is expected to appreciate, which attracts capital flows. Therefore, when the bilateral RMB exchange rate against the U. S. dollar cannot make timely adjustments based on fundamentals, the DXY becomes a leading indicator of RMB exchange rate expectations, thereby driving capital flows. The second channel is through risk appetite. Studies document that the U. S. dollar cycle is highly correlated with the global risk appetite and the DXY is becoming the best representation of global investors' risk appetite. As the world's most important financing currency, the value of the U. S. dollar affects the willingness and ability of major global financial institutions to provide liquidity through the balance sheet effect.

If the DXY drives China's cross - border capital flows, what drives the DXY? Our results show that the China - U. S. interest rate differential increasingly explains and even leads the DXY. The China - U. S. interest rate differential first and foremost reflects the differentiation of the economic fundamentals of the two economies. As China's spillovers become stronger, however, the China - U. S. differential also drives and reflects economic differentiation between the U. S. and other major economies, including Europe and Japan. Accordingly, the China - U. S. interest rate differential could still explain and lead the DXY, despite the index not including the RMB.

Our most critical contributions are uncovering a novel factor that determines China's capital flows—the DXY—and showing that it is more important than interest rate differentials. However, we also find that China - U. S. interest rate differentials can explain the DXY. The explanation for these seemingly contradictory findings lies in the historical inflexibility of the RMB's bilateral exchange rate, which does not fully reflect shifts in economic fundamentals in a timely and adequate manner. This lagging and insufficient response can be corrected through two channels. One channel is through capital flows driven by interest rate differentials, a traditional channel frequently highlighted in the literature and by policymakers. We emphasize a brand new and more critical channel: the exchange rate speculation channel arising from the lack of exchange rate flexibility. China's economy drives the DXY due to its increasing spillovers to Europe and Japan. The DXY in turn drives China's cross-border flows by affecting exchange rate expectations and global risk appetite. When changes in the bilateral exchange rate are lagging and insufficient, currency speculation and changes in risk appetite could lead to large and volatile capital flows. Therefore, increasing exchange rate flexibility would not only increase monetary policy independence but also significantly reduce the overshooting of capital flows.

Openness and Money Demand: Measuring the Opportunity Cost Effects of International Financial Markets

QIN Duo　LU Shan　WANG Huiwen　Sophie van Huellen　WANG Qingchao

(School of Oriental and African Studies, University of London; School of Statistics and Mathematics, Central University of Finance and Economics; School of Economics and Management, Beihang University; Expedia Group)

Standard money demand models neglect the direct effects of economic openness. This omission is problematic when domestic opportunity cost variables fail to fully reflect the dynamics of international financial markets. Examining the effect of this omission is of great practical importance given the ever-increasing openness of China's economy. We propose composite international financial indices (CIFIs) to measure the latent variables that are omitted in standard money demand models. Using techniques from machine learning and measurement theory, we develop a novel model-based approach to construct CIFIs that combines both unsupervised and supervised dimension reduction methods. The choice of the popular error-correction model for the money demand function leads us to construct two types of CIFIs: long-run and short-run CIFIs.

We collect a large set of around 100 financial input indicators to construct CIFIs using monthly data for the 1993M9—2015M6 period. These input indicators are obtained from 21 economies, covering almost all of China's major trading partners. The CIFI construction algorithm contains two stages of aggregation. First, it produces composite financial input indicators by aggregating groups of financial indicators. These groups are formed using clustering methods under the unsupervised learning approach. Second, it uses supervised dimension reduction methods to aggregate the composite financial input indicators following the principle of partial least-squares (PLS). The algorithm produces short-run CIFIs by targeting money growth rates, whereas it forms the target of long-run CIFIs using the error-correction term of standard money demand models. The second supervised aggregation stage sets the input indicators as leading indicators by construction, allows for dynamic dis- synchronization among them, and performs dynamic backward selection of different lags to make the dynamic input forms of the leading indicators as simple as possible. Concatenation is imposed on the resulting CIFIs during regular data updates.

Experiments with CIFI-enhanced money demand models yield positive outcomes. Our key findings are as follows: (i) We find strong evidence of the effects of foreign opportunity costs on China's money demand based on the statistical significance and constancy of the coefficients of CIFIs and overall comparisons of model explanatory power; (ii) the effect of the short-run CIFIs is particularly robust, as evidenced by the 2007—2008 US-led financial crisis; however, in the enhanced error-correction term of the long-run CIFIs, a temporary coefficient variation toward insignificance is observed, which is interpreted as resulting from the emergency measures taken by the People's Bank of China in response to the crisis; (iii) model performance comparisons of the CIFIs produced with and without the first step of unsupervised dimension reduction show the necessity of this step in that it helps reduce redundant information in large financial datasets; (iv) tracing the compositions of CIFIs back to individual financial input indicators yields various patterns and features that enable the identification of the sources of the aggregate foreign opportunity cost effects.

The explicit links between disaggregate input indicators and aggregate CIFIs provide valuable tools for policymakers to monitor external financial shocks from different geographical regions and markets and assess their aggregate risks in real time. Our CIFI algorithm opens a novel route of model-based composite construction. This route also sheds light on why the conventional route of principal component-based factor analysis is insufficient to construct composite indices for macro-modeling.

Measuring and Analyzing Coordinated Development between the Manufacturing Industry and the Real Estate Industry in China

PI Jiancai   SONG Daqiang

(School of Economics, Nanjing University)

Currently, the high - end development of China's manufacturing industry has become a high priority for the country. The development of the manufacturing industry requires efficient cooperation between the producer services industry and the life services industry. Overall, benign coupling and coordination have been achieved between the producer services industry and the manufacturing industry in China. As the real estate industry is an important contributor to the life services industry, the degree of coupling coordination between the real estate industry and the manufacturing industry will directly affect the transformation and upgrading of China's manufacturing industry. The average sale price of commercial housing in 35 large and medium - sized cities in China increased substantially from 2004 to 2016. In the context of the rapid heating of China's real estate market, it is important to judge whether the country's manufacturing industry and real estate industry have achieved coordinated development. This article measures and analyzes the coordinated development of these two industries and thus provides an important reference for formulating policies to promote benign interactions between the two industries.

We manually collect data on 29 subdivided manufacturing industries and the real estate industry in various provinces of China from 2004 to 2016 and measure the degree of coupling coordination between the manufacturing industry and the real estate industry using a coupling coordination degree model. Meanwhile, using the input-output table, we measure and compare the overall driving effects of the manufacturing industry and the real estate industry on each other, identify the best degree of coupling between the two industries from the perspective of the internal mechanism, and use the panel threshold regression method to calculate the value range of the best degree of coupling coordination between the two industries. Furthermore, we examine the impact of the coordinated development of the manufacturing industry and the real estate industry on total factor productivity (TFP) and the economic growth rate through empirical testing. Additionally, considering that during the development of China's real estate industry, China has issued a series of real estate control policies, we use a progressive difference - in - differences (DID) method to analyze the impact of external shocks on the degree of coupling between the two industries.

We obtain five main results. First, the interaction between the manufacturing industry and the real estate industry changed from uncoordinated development in 2004 to coordinated development in 2016. Second, the coordination degree between the two industries in Central and Western China is slightly higher than that in Eastern China. Third, around 2012, the overall development level of the real estate industry exceeded that of the manufacturing industry in Eastern, Central, and Western China. Fourth, in Eastern China, there is a significantly negative relationship between economic performance and the coordination degree between the manufacturing industry and the real estate industry due to the overheated real estate market in this region. Fifth, the purchase restriction policy has improved the degree of coupling between the manufacturing industry and the real estate industry. These findings have the following three policy implications: (i) it is necessary to fully consider the driving effects of the manufacturing industry and the real estate industry on each other when formulating industrial policies; (ii) it is necessary to strengthen market supervision and create a favorable environment for the healthy development of the manufacturing industry and the real estate industry; and (iii) the implementation of purchase restriction policies cannot follow a one - size - fits - all approach as this decreases the positive economic effects of the coordinated development of the manufacturing industry and the real estate industry.

This article makes four contributions to the literature. First, studies often focus on the impact of real estate prices on the manufacturing industry but rarely investigate the coordinated development of the manufacturing industry and the real estate industry, as this article does. Second, this article clarifies the interaction mechanism between the manufacturing industry and the real estate industry. Third, this article gives the best degree of coupling between these two industries from the perspective of the internal mechanism. Fourth, we discuss the impact of the external shock of a real estate purchase restriction policy on the degree of coupling between the two industries.

A possible extension for future research is to compare the coordinated development of the manufacturing and real estate industries in China and developed nations to further investigate the importance of benign interactions between industries for high - quality economic development.

02 Financial Stability & Risk Management

A Study on Financial Contagion: A Simulation Based on the Chinese Banking Sector Data

MA Jun　HE Xiaobei

(National School of Development, Peking University)

The debt to GDP ratio has increased significantly worldwide in the post COVID-19 Pandemic, making maintaining financial stability a great challenge to regulatory authorities globally. As conventional stress testing models do not consider the contagion of financial risks and thus tend to underestimate the impact of shocks on financial resilience, the central banks in advanced economies have started to develop macroprudential stress test models with specific focus on financial contagion channels. However, studies on the contagion effects within China's banking sector remain very limited. This paper aims to fill this gap and lay the foundation for China's macroprudential stress test framework. Based on the granular balance sheet data of listed Chinese banks, we present a micro - founded model to capture the financial contagion effects within the Chinese banking sector. We focus on the mark - to - market price channel of fire sales, as it is proven to be a critical contagion channel during financial crises. We calibrate the demand curves of multiple asset classes using the bond data, model banks' optimization problems in fire sales with regulatory constraints and simulate the model to exogeneous shocks.

Specifically, we model both the first - round and the second - round effects of financial risks spreading in the banking sector. The first - round effect is the direct impact of a shock on banks, characterized by banks' losses (e. g. , credit losses) and the changes in banks' capital adequacy ratios due to the losses. The second - round effect is the financial contagion effect that arises from banks' responses. When a bank breaches its capital requirement due to the initial shock, it has to sell financial assets to boost the capital adequacy ratio. This behavior causes mark - to - market losses of other banks with common asset holdings, which may cause them to breach capital requirements and start another round of fire sale. That depresses asset prices further and generates greater mark - to - market losses. The second - round effect is the contagion channel through which financial risks are amplified and spread in the banking sector.

We also model banks' optimal behaviors in response to shocks. To minimize losses of fire sales, banks consider multiple factors when choosing assets to sell. The first is the risk weight of the assets, as assets with higher risk weights weigh more in calculating capital adequacy ratios. The second is the market depth of the asset. Illiquid assets are typically sold at price discounts which can be quite drastic amid fire sales. Selling illiquid assets leads to greater investment losses and banks need to sell more to meet the capital requirements. The third is the banks' balance sheet structure. Given the price discounts at fire sales, a bank suffers greater losses from selling a class of assets if that asset class accounts for a Large share on the bank's balance sheet.

Our results and policy implications are as follows. First, market depth is critically important in the transmission of contagion risks. As the depth of the Chinese bond market grew from 2017 to 2019, the financial contagion effects were attenuated over the period. In other words, the banking sector in China became more resilient during these three years. Second, individual banks' optimal behaviors may amplify the financial contagion effects. This is because banks all choose to sell the same kind of relatively liquid assets and hence cause sharp price falls of that particular asset, which causes greater mark - to - market losses of other banks holding the common asset. Third, an external shock can generate contagion effects in a non - linear pattern. It is therefore very difficult to discern the emergence and the end of financial risks, which poses a serious challenge for regulators to decide when to act or exit. Forth, it is essential for the regulators to build a macroprudential stress test framework that captures the financial contagion effects. A conventional static bank stress test only captures the direct effects of shocks, and our results suggest that this will greatly underestimate the impact of shocks.

Our paper contributes to the literature in three ways. First, we consider multiple asset classes with different levels of market depth and estimate their demand curve based on the data from the Chinese bond market. That forms the basis upon which we model banks' optimal behaviors in response to shocks. Second, we model banks' optimization problem with regulatory constraint, and analyze the key factors contributing to banks' optimal behaviors. This lays the micro - foundations for stress testing models, which has been omitted in the literature. Third, we investigate quantitatively the effects of financial contagion when banks face the constraint of capital adequacy ratio. The simulation results can help regulators identify the sources of emerging financial risks and assess their impact on the financial system.

Liquidity Illusion and High Leverage Ratio Dilemma

ZHANG Chengsi   LIU Zehao   HE Ping

(School of Finance, Renmin University of China;
School of Economics and Management, Tsinghua University)

The Fifth Plenary Session of the Nineteenth Central Committee of the Communist Party of China reveals significant attention to stabilizing the financial system and buttressing the bottom line of systematic risks. Excessive leverage is a potential factor that triggers systemic risks in economic operations, so it is necessary to take a deeper investigation into it. In response to China's rising leverage in recent years, studies have attempted to find its causes from several perspectives, but have yet failed to explain the essential reasons for the formation of leverage resulting from lack of liquidity under the credit currency system. Moreover, the obvious reverse trend between the leverage ratio and the value support of liquidity during 1999 to 2018 has been undervalued by the academia and lacks theoretical explanation.

To this end, this paper constructs a model of preference shocks and liquidity shocks under the credit currency system, deduces the relationship between the value support of liquidity and the formation mechanism of leverage, explains the nature and impact of insufficient liquidity under the credit currency system, and clarifies that the high leverage accompanying insufficient liquidity is caused by the lack of value support of liquidity. Insufficient value support of liquidity depresses economic entity's ability to pay for short – term consumption and stimulates long - term investment. Over - investment brings about the impulse to borrow, thus driving the increase in leverage.

This paper proposes that the value support of liquidity depends on the real value of the currency that can be used for payment when the economic entities need to purchase goods and services. From a national perspective, the currency issued by the central bank is its debt held on behalf of the country, whose value is determined by the debtor's future cash flow (the country's fiscal revenue) and the guarantees provided by the debtor (the reserve assets held by the central bank) . In this sense, real liquidity is supported by central bank's reserve assets and government's fiscal revenue. More importantly, the imbalance between the supply and the demand of value support of liquidity can cause the leverage ratio to rise, which may in turn bring about large fluctuations in the economy and even trigger a financial crisis. Therefore, it is necessary to change the motivation and the logic of macro policy implementation. Increasing the number of nominal currencies cannot solve the leverage problem caused by the lack of value support of liquidity. Only by increasing the number of reserve assets corresponding to the issued currency to inject additional value support of liquidity can the liquidity shortage dilemma be solved. Only by solving the constraints imposed by the lack of value support of liquidity on the sustained and healthy economic development can China achieve its strategic goal of accelerating the construction of a new development pattern during the "14th Five - Year Plan" period.

To solve the problem of insufficient value support of liquidity supply, it is essential to re - examine the coordination mechanism of the monetary policy and the fiscal policy under the dual - cycle system. In the domestic big cycle, the problem of excessive investment caused by the shortage of value support of liquidity has affected the smoothness of consumer consumption, which is in conflict with China's goal of boosting domestic demand. To maintain ample value support of liquidity in the whole society, fiscal policies must balance tax rates and maintain reasonable tax revenues. Large - scale and continuous tax cuts cannot be over emphasized. Monetary policy needs to pay attention to both nominal liquidity and the value support of liquidity. In the domestic and international dual cycle, it is necessary to adhere to the concept of openness and expand the scale of international trade. The foreign exchange income from international trade increases central bank's base currency investment through foreign exchange funds and converts into central bank's reserve assets, both of which enhances the value support of liquidity. Since exports are not completely endogenous and there is uncertainty in foreign exchange income, the changes in the monetary base input of the foreign exchange account channel should be closely monitored, and reserve requirements and open market operations should be used timely to hedge its impact. In addition, although the increase in reserve assets can increase the value support of liquidity, there is an optimal scale. Excessive reserve assets will lead to insufficient domestic consumption and cause welfare losses. In this condition, taxes can be reduced appropriately to increase consumption and improve welfare while maintaining a reasonable level of value support of liquidity. In summary, forming a good coordination between the monetary policy and the fiscal policy in the control of the value support of liquidity can stabilize the macro - leverage ratio from the root cause and improve the overall social welfare.

Local Government Implicit Debt and the Pricing of Chengtou Bonds

LIU Xiaolei   LYU Yuanzhen   YU Fan

(Guanghua School of Management, Peking University; Anderson School of Management, UCLA; Claremont McKenna College)

The recent explosion of Chinese local government debt has raised alarm among investors and regulators. According to China's National Audit Office's government debt report, Chinese local governments had accrued implicit and explicit debts totaling 17.89 trillion renminbi (RMB) by June 2013. The lack of a systematic measurement system for Chinese local government debt has long been a problem, especially for city - level governments, as their debt is mostly implicit. *Chengtou* bonds, a unique type of bond that combines the features of municipal and corporate bonds, are deeply rooted in the history of the Chinese government's administrative system reform. Lacking the authority to independently issue debt due to the 1994 Budget Law, Chinese local governments set up local government financing vehicles (LGFVs) to issue so - called *chengtou* bonds. While these bonds are commonly understood as carrying an implicit government guarantee, the identity of the implicit guarantor is unclear.

In this article, we examine to what extent local government implicit debt affects the pricing of *chengtou* bonds. We further explore variations in the implicit guarantor that is recognized by the market. We first construct a measure for city - level local government implicit debt. As debt owed by LGFVs accounts for a large portion of city - level governments' debt, using the public disclosures of bond - issuing firms, we total all of the outstanding interest - bearing debt of

LGFVs under the jurisdiction of a local government to obtain a proxy for total implicit city - level debt. We then divide the total interest – bearing debt by local government revenue, local gross domestic product (GDP), and local fixed - asset investment to obtain three local government implicit debt ratios.

We first hypothesize that if the market believes that *chengtou* bonds carry an implicit government guarantee, local government implicit debt ratios should be related to the yield spread of *chengtou* bonds. Consistent with this hypothesis, we find that higher local government implicit debt ration are associated with higher yield spreads of *chengtou* bonds at the city level. This result holds in both the secondary and primary market samples.

Next, we explore the time - varying identity of the implicit guarantor using default events and government policy changes. In April 2011, Yunnan Highway, a LGFV owned by Yunnan Province, defaulted on some outstanding bank loans. Although the crisis was not directly related to *chengtou* bonds and was finally resolved with government intervention, this event may have significantly impacted investors' recognition of the risks associated with *chengtou* bonds. We find that the relationship between the city - level government implicit debt ratios and the yield spreads of *chengtou* bonds did not exist prior to the Yunan Highway default event and became significant only afterwards. This result is consistent with the arguement that investors initially believed the central government to be the guarantor of *chengtou* bonds and ignored the implicit debt burden of local governments. Investors only began paying attention to city - level government implicit debt after the 2011 default event.

In October 2014, the State Council issued Directive No. 43 to clarify the relationship between local governments and LGFVs. This document makes it clear that city governments can swap their LGFVs' debt for municipal bonds issued directly by provincial governments. We thus hypothesize that after the issuance of Directive No. 43, provincial government implicit debt ratios become important in the pricing of *chengtou* bonds issued by city - level LGFVs. Indeed, we discover that provincial government implicit debt ratios are significantly positively related to *chengtou* bond yield spreads after October 2014.

In summary, our evidence suggests that the identity of the implicit guarantor of city - level *chengtou* bonds has shifted over time from the central government to city - level governments, and more recently, to city - plus province - level governments.

Although implicit guarantees reduce the borrowing costs of local governments, due to the lack of formal legal protection, the pricing of *chengtou* bonds is significantly affected by market events and government regulations that shift market perceptions regarding the identity of the implicit guarantor. The uncertainty related to the implicit guarantee creates unnecessary risk and may potentially increase local governments' borrowing costs in comparison to them raising debt independently.

Policy Continuity, Non - financial Enterprises' Shadow Banking Activities, and Social Responsibility Activities

HAN Xun   LI Jianjun

(School of Economics, Beijing International Studies University;
School of Finance, Central University of Finance and Economics)

With the development of China's diversified shadow credit market, the non - financial enterprise sector has begun to act as a substantial credit intermediary, becoming the main shadow banking intermediary. The characteristics of shadow banking, such as high leverage, high risk, and information asymmetry, create high uncertainty in the cash flows of the economic entities involved in shadow banking, which intensifies the risk in both the virtual and real economies. Therefore, exploring the economic consequences of the shadow banking activities of non - financial enterprises has important theoretical and practical implications and may help to prevent funds from diverted out of the real economy as well as other systemic financial risks.

Using data of non - financial A - share listed companies from 2006 to 2017, this paper attempts to examine the impact of non - financial enterprises' shadow banking activities on their social responsibility activities, and it further explores the mechanism through which policy continuity affects the interaction between enterprises' shadow banking and social responsibility activities.

This paper's main contributions are as follows. First, it expands the research on non - financial enterprises' shadow banking activities. Second, it enriches the understanding of the effects of policy continuity on micro enterprise behavior and attempts to identify the mechanism through which policy continuity affects the relationship between non - financial enterprises' shadow banking and social responsibility activities. Third, it examines the two channels of relative risk between the finance and entity economies and signal transmission.

The results show that non - financial enterprises' shadow banking activities inhibit social responsibility activities, and this effect is more significant in enterprises with strong market arbitrage motivation, low levels of cooperate governance, and weaker external financing ability. Increased policy continuity weakens the negative relationship between non - financial enterprises' shadow banking and social responsibility activities. The driving mechanisms are as follows. First, increasing policy continuity increases the relative risk of finance investment in the real economy, which weakens the negative effect of non - financial enterprises' shadow banking business on social responsibility activities. Second, an increase in policy continuity enhances the positive information signal that enterprises send to the public through their social responsibility activities.

This paper not only enriches the research on shadow banking, non - financial enterprise financialization, and other academic fields, but also it has important implications for policy makers seeking to improve policy continuity and stability, restrain a shift " from real to virtual" economies, and prevent systemic financial risk agglomeration. Accordingly, this paper puts forward the following policy suggestions. First, strengthen the information disclosure on the financial assets held by non - financial enterprises and enhance the transparency of financial statements. Second, improve the corporate governance structure of non - financial enterprises and strengthen their awareness of corporate social responsibility. Third, enhance the stability and continuity of policies and guide the formation of reasonable expectations. Fourth, continuously promote the structural reform of the financial supply side, optimize the financing structure, strengthen the functional supervision of the shadow banking system, and guide the finance sector to better serve the real economy.

Implicit Leverage Constraints, Liquidity Risk, and Investor Sentiment

ZHU Xiaoquan　CHEN Zhuo

(School of Banking and Finance, University of International Business and Economics; PBC School of Finance, Tsinghua University)

　　The Administrative Measures for the Operation and Management of Publicly Offered Securities Investment Funds, implemented in August 2014, require the leverage of fixed - income funds to be below 140% but give no explicit requirement for the leverage of equity funds. In practice, equity funds barely invest on margin and even set aside a high proportion of cash reserves (Simutin, 2014; Boguth and Simutin, 2018). This self - imposed zero - leverage constraint is implicit and motivates funds to indirectly gain leverage by holding high beta stocks when funding conditions deteriorate. Based on this intuition, this paper uses actively managed equity - oriented open - end funds from 2003 to 2019 to explore the implications of the aggregate mutual fund beta.

　　We aggregate all actively managed equity funds in China to a hypothetical large fund and calculate the value - weighted average market beta of its aggregate A - share holdings. Following Brunnermeier and Pedersen (2009), we conjecture that a priced liquidity risk factor drives the dynamic of the aggregate mutual fund beta. The time series of the aggregate mutual fund beta contains useful information on the tightness of implicit leverage constraints for Chinese mutual funds and reflects the liquidity condition in the stock market. Furthermore, we investigate whether loadings on changes in the aggregate mutual fund beta predict returns in the cross - section. We find that exposure to the monthly change in the aggregate mutual fund beta unconditionally fails to predict returns at the firm and fund levels. In contrast, such exposure negatively predicts stock and fund returns following periods of low sentiment or low liquidity. The negative price of the change in the tightness of implicit leverage constraints is consistent with the notion that an asset that pays off when implicit leverage constraints are tighter provides capital when the capital is most valuable. As a result, the strong performance of stocks and funds with low exposure to implicit leverage constraints following periods of low sentiment or low liquidity can be rationalized as compensation for liquidity risk. However, short - sale constraints prohibit the positive relationship between leverage tightness exposure and stock returns after periods of high sentiment.

By exploiting the staggered implementation of pilot marginable stocks in China, our study compares the cross - sectional pricing power of changes in implicit leverage constraints among pilot and non - pilot stocks. We find that the distorted risk-return relationship is more pronounced among stocks that are ineligible for margin trading. This confirms our conjecture regarding conditional pricing, namely, that in high - sentiment regimes, short - selling constraints lead to active leverage constraints and thus affect the pricing kernel. Next, recent papers document that funds oriented toward small - and medium - cap stocks exhibit a stronger liquidity preference in deteriorating funding conditions (Li et al. , 2015; Zhang et al. , 2017). We construct the fund - beta - based implicit leverage constraint using funds investing in small - and medium - sized stocks and document that this aggregate beta measure captures the dynamics of funding liquidity in a more timely manner.

This study extends the literature in two ways. First, we propose a measure for implicit leverage constraints. Different from developed markets, retail investors have long been important market participants in the A - share market. Meanwhile, the recent emergence of high - frequency trading, together with retail investors' noisy trading, may invalidate turnover as an effective proxy for market funding conditions (Baker and Wurgler, 2007) . The proposed aggregate risk - taking measure of mutual funds can be used as a market - based forward - looking signal of market illiquidity. Second, we explore the interaction between implicit and explicit leverage constraints. We show that the distorted risk-return relationship between leverage tightness exposure and stock returns is more pronounced among stocks that are ineligible for margin trading, especially after periods of high sentiment. These findings provide direct evidence of the conditional pricing of liquidity risk.

However, semi - annual snapshots of fund holdings fail to capture the daily trading activities of active funds, thus contaminating our liquidity measure. We mitigate this concern by dropping funds with a high probability of window dressing, and our main findings remain unchanged. In addition, it is possible that other forces overlap with our sentiment channel; for example, the timing ability of fund managers and investor inflows / outflows may affect the aggregate fund beta. Furthermore, it is relevant to investigate whether mutual fund herding during high - sentiment periods affects price efficiency. We leave these questions for future research.

Controlling Shareholders' Share Pledging and Leverage Manipulation in High - Leverage Companies: Evidence from China

XU Xiaofang   TANG Taijie   LU Zhengfei

(Business School, Beijing Technology and Business University; Guanghua School of Management, Peking University)

Share pledge financing has become common in China's capital market; however, it often brings great risk, especially in high - leverage companies. Once a firm's stock price falls sharply after share pledging and touches the unwinding line, its controlling shareholder will be under great pressure and may lose control rights. Therefore, the controlling shareholder often has a strong motivation to drive the company to conduct market value management to prevent the stock price from crashing to the liquidation line; this is commonly achieved by changing accounting policy or adjusting the firm's information disclosure behavior. However, research on the impact of shareholder equity pledging on the quality of accounting information mainly focuses on income statements (especially the information quality of earnings) and seldom deals with balance sheets.

To reduce the risk of debt default and the forced liquidation of the pledged shares, the controlling shareholder, out of self - interest, may lead the company to cover up bad news using leverage manipulation after equity pledging. Leverage manipulation refers to reducing the leverage level presented on the balance sheet, via the use of financial activity arrangements (e. g. , off - balance sheet liabilities) and other accounting methods (Xu and Lu, 2020). Leverage manipulation is an appropriate proxy for the quality of balance sheet information because the higher the leverage level is, the lower the balance sheet information quality is. Additionally, the delisting system plan announced by Shenzhen Stock Exchange and Shanghai Stock Exchange in 2012 added delisting conditions, such as a firm's net assets being negative (with a negative value at the end of one year, the end of two consecutive years, and the end of three consecutive years corresponding to a delisting risk warning, listing suspension, and termination of listing, respectively) , making it difficult for listed companies to avoid delisting by merely manipulating profits. Therefore, controlling shareholders who have pledged equity in high - leverage firms often have strong incentives to drive firms to manipulate leverage to reduce the risk of control transfer due to the leverage indicator being suspended or terminated from listing.

Based on the balance sheet information of A - share non - financial listed companies with high leverage in China from 1999 to 2019, this paper empirically tests the influence of controlling shareholders' share pledging on the possibility and extent of corporate leverage manipulation. We find that high - leverage companies with share pledging by controlling shareholders are more likely to engage in leverage manipulation, and the higher the pledge ratio, the greater the degree of leverage manipulation. Our conclusions remain unchanged after a series of robustness tests considering any potential endogeneity problems. We also find that these influences are more pronounced in high - leverage companies with lower growth, greater pressure on short - term debt servicing, more media attention, and higher stock price crash risk.

The research contributions of this paper are as follows. First, it expands the literature on the influencing factors of leverage manipulation. The few studies on the influencing factors of leverage manipulation are mainly from the perspective of company characteristics (e. g. , leverage ratio and financing restrictions); however, this paper focuses on the equity pledging of controlling shareholders. Second, it enriches the literature on the economic consequences of share pledging. Unlike previous studies, this paper focuses on balance sheet information and investigates the impact of equity pledging from the perspective of leverage manipulation. The results show that the manipulation of balance sheet information is an important economic consequence of leverage manipulation. Furthermore, the study provides empirical evidence that can serve as a reference for policymakers to prevent corporate leverage manipulation and standardize the share pledging of controlling shareholders. The findings also suggest the need to further regulate the equity pledging of controlling shareholders, especially in high - leverage companies with a high pledge ratio, and to guard against the adverse effects of leverage manipulation on systemic financial risks. The results indicate that to prevent limited credit funds from entering high - liability pledgers with leverage manipulation and improve the efficiency of credit resource allocation, it is necessary to strengthen the monitoring of the quality of balance sheet information.

Financialization and Labor Share: Firm - level Evidence from China

LUO Mingjin   TIE Ying

(International Development Cooperation Academy/Institute of International Business, Shanghai University of International Business and Economics)

Globally, the last four decades have been characterized by a continuous decline in the labor income share, which has attracted the attention of many scholars. However, using a sample of China's listed firms, we observe that China's labor income share did not decline significantly after the 2008 financial crisis and even showed an upward trend. We also observe surges in the rapid deepening of the financialization of nonfinancial firms in China during the same period. Intuitively, we find a positive link between firms' financialization and labor income share after the crisis. This raises the question of whether the newly emerging and rapidly spreading financialization of firms in China may be an important reason for the growth of labor income share after 2010. If so, what is the mechanism? Is it sustainable? These are the questions we try to answer.

Using a sample of China's listed firms from the 2007 to 2017 period, we investigate the relationship between the financialization of Chinese listed firms and their labor income share. We find that the financialization of Chinese listed firms has a positive effect on their labor share, which is inconsistent with the findings of a negative correlation between the two in studies using samples of firms in developed countries.

We argue that the spillover effect of financialization on workers' wages and its inhibition of productivity is the explanation for our results. The results of our mediation analysis are as follows. Financialization has a positive spillover on employees' income (i. e. , the profit spillover effect); however, it also inhibits labor productivity (i. e. , the technology inhibitory effect) . These two channels can help explain the positive relationship between financialization and labor share in China. Our analysis of heterogeneous samples shows that the positive effect of firms' financialization on labor share is especially dominant among firms from areas with higher minimum wage and more skilled workers.

Further analysis finds that the classic principal - agent framework fails to explain financialization in China. Instead, the role of financialization in promoting labor share stems from the excess returns in China's financial market. Financialization is a rational choice for firms when there are excess returns in the financial market, but it also damages productivity. Therefore, the positive relationship between financialization and labor share is unsustainable. In the long run, profit - oriented financialization in China may not only damage the actual income of workers but also damage the industrial foundation, and thus it may be referred to as a " sweet poison".

We make three contributions to the literature. First, we extend the research on the relationship between financialization and labor income share to the micro level. Unlike others who have used samples of firms from developed countries, we, focusing on China, propose and identify a "profit spillover" effect and a "technology inhibition" effect of firms' financialization on labor income share. Second, previous studies of firms' financialization have paid insufficient attention to endogeneity problems. In this paper, we try to overcome this problem by using the frontier synthetic instrumental variable method and the event method to confirm the causal relationship between the financialization of firms and labor share. Third, breaking out of the classic principal - agent framework, we identify " another style" of firms financialization, which occurs when there are excess returns in the financial field. This insight not only helps to improve the understanding of firms' financialization but also has important practical value.

We conclude that the pulling effect of firms' financialization on China's labor income share is based on the specific condition of excess returns, so it is not only unsustainable, but it may also result in long - term damage. Thus, the economic trend " from the real to the virtual" caused by the rapid development of firms' financialization must be guarded against.

03 Green Finance

Environmental Tax, Double Dividend and Economic Growth

NIU Huan   YAN Chengliang

(School of Economics, Central University of Finance and Economics)

In a long time, China's rapid economic growth was at the cost of pollution, which also has caused serious medical burden of environmental diseases and the loss in health human capital. The phenomenon of "pollution before wealth" restricts sustainable and high - quality economic development. More seriously, we may confront the risk of falling into an "environmental poverty trap". On Jan 1st 2018, China implemented environmental tax to guide polluters to reduce emissions, which is of great significance for building a "Beautiful and Healthy China". Two problems associated with environmental tax are worth exploring. First, it is of theoretical and practical significance to discuss whether environmental tax will realize " double dividend ". Second, confronted with the problems of "pollution before wealth" and "old before wealth", it is a worthy study whether environmental tax can help to get rid of the "environmental poverty trap".

This paper constructs an overlapping generation model (OLG), which includes environmental taxes, pollution and life expectancy. The study has shown that environmental taxes have an inverted U - shaped or monotonically increasing relationship with the pollution and per capital income under certain parameters. This relationship indicates that the lower tax rates may increase pollution and excessive tax rates may reduce per capital income. The corresponding mechanism is that while the "negative revenue effect" of environmental taxes leads to a decline in capital accumulation, the "health effects" of environmental taxes increases life expectancy and capital accumulation. The effect of environmental taxes on the environment and the economy is transmitted through capital accumulation. The government has more revenue by increasing tax rates in environment to increase expenditure on environmental governance, which makes it easier for the economy to generate green dividends. Further, we find that there is a certain tax rate interval to achieve a "double dividend", which is in line with the green development concept of "lucid waters and lush mountains are invaluable assets". Under the endogenous growth framework, there are multiple equilibrium points, that is, a stable balanced growth path and an environmental poverty trap. On the balanced growth path, the environmental tax rate and economic growth have an inverted U - shaped relationship.

The contributions of this paper are as follows: First, this paper introduces life expectancy with the concept of "prevention is greater than cure" and emphasizes the time lag of pollution and public health on health. This paper enriches the mechanism of environmental taxes on consumption and savings from the perspective of "life cycle" by introducing life expectancy. Second, under the neoclassical growth framework, the existence of "double dividend" provides theoretical foundation for the green development concept. Third, Under the endogenous growth framework, we find that environmental policies can explain the phenomenon that some countries have realized the model of "environmental Kuznitz curve", while others falled into the "environmental poverty trap", which enriches the theoretical mechanism for explaining income disparity among countries.

The policy recommendations mainly include following points: First, there is an optimal environmental tax rate in the economy, that is, an excessively low environmental tax rate may aggravate pollution, and an excessively high environmental tax rate may will inhibit economic growth. Chinese environmental tax only accounted for 0.14% of total tax revenue in 2019, so the environmental tax rate should be appropriately increased. Local governments make a comprehensive consideration of the environmental carrying capacity, pollutant status and economic development goals when formulating differentiated environmental tax rates. We will focus on raising environmental tax rates for industries with high pollution and carbon emissions, and achieve the goal of coordinated pollution reduction and carbon reduction. Second, according to the pollution accumulation equation, pollution depends on investment, emission intensity and governance efficiency. It is necessary to increase investment in environmental governance, reduce pollution emission intensity through upgrading technology and restructuring industrial structure, and improve governance efficiency by updating environmental governance equipment and technology. Third, pollution causes health damage to residents, so the government should increase people's health and consumer welfare caused by pollution through increasing public health spending.

Environmental Regulation, Financing Constraints, and Enterprise Emission Reduction: Evidence from Pollution Levy Standards Adjustment

CHEN Shiyi　ZHANG Jianpeng　LIU Chaoliang

(School of Economics, Fudan University)

With the continuous deterioration of the environment, environment protection and pollution reduction have received worldwide recognition. For China, pollution reduction not only contributes to the construction of ecological civilization, but also helps promote the green transformation of the economy. Besides environmental regulation, support and guidance from the financial sector are also very important for pollution reduction.

From 2007 to 2013, 12 provinces or municipalities in China gradually doubled the SO_2 levy standards from the original 0.63 yuan/kg to 1.26 yuan/kg. Using 2004—2013 China's Environmental Statistios Dataset (CESD) and the sequential adjustments of levy standards as a quasi-natural experiment, this paper applies the difference-in-differences method to examine how the adjustments of levy standards and firms' financing constraints affect firm behaviors and pollution control. Empirical results show that the increase in pollution charge reduces pollution emission by 9.14% while also significantly lowering outputs by 4.43%. The results remain robust in a series of tests. Heterogeneity analysis indicates that large enterprises and state-owned enterprises have carried out effective pollution control, achieving significant reduction in pollution emission intensity without significant drop in outputs. Small and medium-sized enterprises (SMEs) and private enterprises, however, have reduced outputs, and their effect of pollution control needs to be improved. Using credit loan and interest expenditure data, this paper makes further analysis from the perspective of environmental financing. Results show that environmental financing constraints lead to heterogeneous pollution control effects. While implementing the policy, SMEs face substantial environmental financing constraints, which significantly restrains their pollution treatment, aggravates the output adjustment, and ultimately weakens pollution reduction. Controlling for confounding factors (e. g. enterprise size and enterprise pollution emission intensity) that affect enterprise' incentives to reduce pollution does not change the findings.

Enterprises have two options to reduce emission: output reduction and pollution treatment. Pollution treatment usually involves installing pollution disposal equipment, updating production process, and the R&D of green technology which require substantial environmental investment. However, green investments are usually long - term and highly risky with low early return. Relying on internal financing for green investments exerts large pressure on enterprises' cash flows and operational risks. Therefore, when stringent environmental regulations are implemented, there is rising financing demand. If the financial sector ignores this demand, enterprises facing rising emission costs and tight external environmental financing constraints will choose to sacrifice their outputs. This choice not only brings negative economic consequence, but also deviates from the goal of green transformation of production.

The innovation and contribution of this paper are as follows. First, this paper points out that financing constraints affect the outcome of enterprise emission reduction, which enriches the literature on environmental regulation and enterprise pollution reduction, and provides policy enlightenment for the promotion of pollution reduction and the development of green finance. Second, the findings facilitate our understanding of the relationship between environmental regulation and Porter Hypothesis. The literature has long been focusing on whether environmental regulation can stimulate enterprises' green R&D innovation and efficiency improvement. This paper shows that appropriate financial support helps enterprises promote environmental investment. Third, this paper cleans and processes the data of CESD which has not been widely used in academic literature, providing useful experience for applying CESD.

This paper has the following policy suggestions. First, in promoting pollution reduction, we should not only strictly implement environmental regulations, but also pay attention to financial support from the financial sector, so as to improve the pollution treatment capacity of enterprises. Second, to boost environmental investment, the financial sector not only needs to complement the internal weaknesses of China's financial system through ways such as channel funding and reducing borrowing cost for SMEs, but also needs to promote the development of green finance. In providing financial support for enterprise pollution control, uniform environmental risk aversion to polluters is undesirable and enterprises' "green washing" behaviors should be prevented. This requires the financial sector to enhance green finance operations and effectively identify the opportunities and risks in green investment.

The Impact of Environmental Governance Policy on Green Innovation: Evidence from China's Quasi - Natural Experiment

WANG Xin　WANG Ying

(School of Finance, Shandong University of Finance and Economics)

In response to environmental conditions and the need for environmental protection, the former Chinese Ministry of Environmental Protection's Ambient Air Quality Standard (2012) establishes requirements for management of the whole environmental governance lifecycle to accelerate the treatment of air pollution, meet public needs, and improve the credibility of the government. Since the implementation of the new standard by all regions within the required schedule, local air quality monitoring realizes real - time, interference - free, and comprehensive coverage with direct reporting. The standard greatly increases the opportunity cost of local government inaction in environmental governance, facilitates environmental supervision by the public, and improves the probability that pollution emissions by firms will be punished. These pressures provide a strong motivation for enterprises, as the main source of Chinese innovation, to carry out whole - lifecycle green technology innovation. Environmental information disclosure creates an important force promoting green technology innovation and pollution and carbon reduction to achieve the double carbon target.

This paper is divided into three parts. First, we review the literature regarding the impact of environmental regulations on innovation by firms and combine it with the needs of policy promoting the development of green technology innovation. Given this context, we propose research hypotheses regarding the relationships between environmental protection policy and green technology innovation by firms. Since the implementation of the new standard, we find that green technology innovation by high environmental risk firms has become increasingly positive in response to stricter regional environmental protection law enforcement and more active media supervision. Second, taking all A - share listed firms in China from 2007 to 2017 as the research object and the staggered implementation of the Ambient Air Quality Standard in 2012 across cities as the quasi - natural experiment, we use a multi - period difference - in - differences (DID) method to analyze the differences between high and low environmental risk firms in green technology innovation before and after the implementation of the new standard. After the implementation of the new standard, we find that the green technology innovation of high environmental risk firms becomes more positive, as measured by both the quantity and quality of green innovation. The validity of this conclusion is confirmed by a series of robustness tests. The heterogeneity test finds that the new standard's effectiveness in promoting green technology innovation is more significant for state - owned firms and non - patent - intensive firms than for privately owned firms and patent - intensive firms. Further research shows that the effects of the new standard on green technology innovation are significantly enhanced by improvements in environmental law enforcement and the intensity of public and media supervision. Third, the positive effects of the new standard lead to significant local air quality improvements. Our findings lead us to some policy suggestions. First, the authorities should strengthen and improve the environmental regulation system by classifying and improving the levels of environmental regulation. Second, the authorities should promote the positive advantages of using digital technology to assist environmental regulation in support of green innovation. Third, the authorities should establish a systematic approach to evaluate the effects of environmental regulation on enterprise green innovation. Fourth, a set of evaluation systems can be established to help firms and regulators recognize the content and complexity of green innovation and prudently manage the problems and uncertainties that may be encountered in the innovation process. Such evaluation systems can enable more prospective implementation of regulatory policies to encourage green innovation.

  We contribute to the literature in several ways. First, from the perspective of institutional economics, we enrich the related theoretical research in the field of macro - environmental policy and micro - behaviors. The environmental regulation literature mainly studies the impacts of command - based and market - based regulation policies on pollution transfer, energy conservation, and emission reduction by firms and on environmental protection investment in general. We evaluate the effectiveness of macro - environmental policy from the perspective of green technology innovation by firms, thereby providing new evidence in the study of existing environmental regulations. Second, we creatively place the Ambient Air Quality Standard and green technology innovation into the same theoretical framework, thereby expanding and enriching the relevant literature on the factors that influence green technology innovation by firms. Third, we analyze the regulatory and environmental effects of environmental law enforcement, public supervision, and media supervision. The results provide a useful reference to further motivate firms in their support for environmental governance and establish a sound system for the development of a green and low - carbon circular economy.

Financial Policy and Low - Carbon Transition of the Economy: A Growth Perspective

PAN Dongyang   CHEN Chuanqi   Michael Grubb

(School of Applied Economics, Renmin University of China; School of Finance, Central University of Finance and Economics; Institute for Sustainable Resources, University College London)

Given the global net - zero target for carbon emissions and awareness of the role of investment and finance in a low - carbon economic transition, financial regulators in many countries have started to promote green investment by developing so - called green financial policy to alleviate the barriers to and increase the incentives for green investment. For example, central banks provide refinancing for banks that conduct green lending. Discussion and development of green financial policy have increased in recent years as climate change and environmental degradation have intensified. In 2016, China promulgated the Guidelines for Establishing the Green Financial System, in which several green financial policy tools were first proposed. Financial regulators worldwide have started to take action, particularly since the founding of the Network of Central Banks and Supervisors for Greening the Financial System in 2017.

The growth of green financial policy is expected to continue; however, many questions remain about the theoretical relationship between green financial policy and the low - carbon transition of the physical economy, which is the ultimate purpose of this policy. Do financial factors affect the low - carbon transition? If so, how? What can financial policy do for the transition? Compared with other policies, what are the advantages and disadvantages of green financial policy?

Moreover, given the current COVID-19 pandemic, what can green financial policy do for the "green recovery" that is being called for by many? This study aims to answer these questions.

We build a macroeconomic growth model of directed technical change. In this model, the production sector is divided into two parts—clean and non-clean—to analyze the transition of industrial structure and its environmental impact. We introduce financial constraints and financing costs to analyze the role of financial policy. The model is also extended with the shock of the COVID-19 pandemic to analyze the green recovery.

Using the model, we first show the specific roles of financial policy in supporting the low-carbon transition by giving and proving four formal propositions. This clarifies the mechanisms through which financial factors can play a role in the low-carbon transition. Second, we numerically analyze the effect of green financial policy and compare it with the effects of other green economic policies. This reveals the advantages and disadvantages of green financial policy and can help policymakers choose appropriate policies. Third, we simulate the dynamics of the economy under different policy scenarios with and without the COVID-19 Pandemic shock. This shows what the pandemic and different policy mixes could bring to the green transition and economic recovery.

This study finds that (i) stronger financial constraints in the clean sector relative to the non-clean sector delay the low-carbon economic transition and cause environmental degradation, and green financial policy can alleviate these financial constraints. (ii) Green financial policy can increase the output of the clean sector and, under certain conditions, facilitate the low-carbon transition of the economy and prevent environmental degradation. (iii) Financial policy is cost-effective compared with some fiscal policies that promote the low-carbon transition; there is space for mixing policies. (iv) Increasing the intensity of green financial policy in the aftermath of the pandemic would be beneficial for achieving a green recovery and may accelerate the low-carbon economic transition at a cost lower than expected.

Our work has significance for both research and policy. In terms of research, this study discusses the role of financial policy in the low - carbon transition from the economic growth perspective using a theoretical model. It extends the horizon of financial development theory from the sustainability perspective and provides a theoretical basis for future empirical research on the effects of green financial policy. Our growth model, which includes factors related to green finance, could also be a useful tool for future research. In terms of policy, this paper provides a theoretical basis for analysing green financial policy and provides policymakers with the following practical information: the mechanisms by which green financial policy works, the advantages and disadvantages of such policy, the way to effectively mix different policies and policy recommendations for the post - pandemic era.

Why Do We Need Green Finance? Global Empirical Facts and Theoretical Explanations in an Economic Growth Framework

WEN Shuyang　ZHANG Lin　LIU Xiliang

(Institute of Chinese Financial Studies, Southwestern University of Finance and Economics)

Green development is a must for human progress, and the role of finance in green development is receiving more attention. "Green finance" generally refers to financial products, markets and policies related to environmental protection and sustainable development. In academia, the concept of green finance is closely related to environmental and climate finance and overlaps sustainable finance and socially responsible investing (SRI) . In the past two decades, the development of global green finance has significantly advanced, and green finance issues have received increasing attention. However, theoretical research in this field lags behind. Although the number and proportion of studies have grown rapidly, and the economic theory of green finance is weak. Scholars struggle to rigorously answer the fundamental question of why we need green finance. According to the general principles of economics, the externality of pollution indicates that the main force of environmental protection should be the public sector rather than the financial system. However, more and more countries are choosing green finance. What is the economic intuition behind this phenomenon? An in-depth discussion of these issues forms the basis for effective policymaking and the development of green finance theory.

This study uses data on listed companies worldwide to estimate the debt ratio of green enterprises in various countries as a proxy indicator of green finance. Then, combining that with fiscal expenditure data from the United Nations, we examine the changes in global green finance and government expenditures on environmental protection. The results show that in the past 20 years, total global government expenditures on environmental protection have slightly increased, but the ratio of this expenditure to GDP has a downward trend. Meanwhile, the scale and ratio of green finance to GDP have continued to increase, and the development level of green finance has been in line with the economy. Further cross - country panel data analysis shows that green finance effectively promotes long - term economic growth, showing obvious heterogeneity with green fiscal investment. On the basis of these findings, we ask whether green finance differs from traditional public finance in terms of economic principles?

This study builds a multisector general equilibrium growth model that includes residents, enterprises, financial sector and government. It depicts the dynamic relationship between green fiscal investment, green finance and economic growth and reproduces the abovementioned facts. The theoretical analysis shows that, First, green finance has advantages for long - term growth. It can mitigate the deficiency of public services subject to congestion and achieve high - quality economic development. Second, there is a scale threshold above which firms voluntarily choose to protect the environment by using green finance without government intervention. Subsidies for green credit can promote firms' green investment and enable the economy to reach a higher steady state. Third, a combination of green financial and fiscal policies to guide fiscal investment in the initial stage of economic development and gradually strengthen the promotion of green finance in later stages can speed economic growth, achieve a higher steady - state capital stock level, and meet the goal of high - quality economic development. This study answers the question of why we need green finance from the economic theory perspective. It addresses the basic theoretical shortcomings in the field of green finance, providing basic theoretical support for the development of green finance and a useful analytical framework for further theoretical research on green finance.

This article also has implications for future research. For instance, the next important academic question to address is how green finance affects financial institutions. Although this article discusses the macroeconomic benefits of green finance, it does not explore whether financial institutions have inherent incentives to engage in green finance. There is some empirical evidence in the literature, but the theoretical basis of this problem is still unclear. Whether the implementation of green finance policies can be incentive compatible is an important direction for future research.

The Impact of Environmental Disasters on the Bank Default Rate: Theoretical and Empirical Analysis

WANG Yao   WANG Wenwei

(International Institute of Green Finance & Institute for Finance and Economics, Central University of Finance and Economics; School of Finance, Central University of Finance and Economics)

China has experienced frequent environmental disasters with huge negative impacts on economic and social development. The real economy and financial sector are becoming more closely aligned, and the impact of environmental disasters on the real economy will inevitably be transmitted to the financial system and institutions, affecting financial stability, generating financial risks, and generally amplifying the negative impact of environmental disasters. From the perspective of physical risk, this paper discusses the actual impact of environmental disasters on banks' default risk through dynamic stochastic general equilibrium model simulations and empirical tests using data from China's banking institutions from 2008 to 2018.

This article's main contributions are as follows: First, it is one of the first theoretical and empirical studies on China's environmental risks. Second, in terms of research methods, this article simultaneously introduces disaster shock factors and the financial friction mechanism, highlighting the amplification effect of the financial accelerator mechanism on the impact of disaster shocks. Further, this article examines the impact of disaster shocks on relevant economic and financial indicators, including bank default rates. In terms of empirical research, this article uses the entropy method to construct environmental disaster loss indicators on multiple dimensions, providing empirical evidence from China of environmental risks. Third, the theoretical and empirical tests not only support the existence of environmental risks but also further analyze and explore a series of derivative consequences of environmental disasters on banks' default rates, including the impact on corporate financing constraints and banks' willingness to lend. This enriches the research perspectives on topics such as financing constraints and bank liquidity creation.

The simulation results of the theoretical model show that environmental disasters significantly increase the default rate of bank credit contracts. This leads to higher risk premiums and reduces the scale of credit issuance, undermining enterprises and increasing their financing costs. Eventually, the tightening of financing constraints significantly negatively affects investment and output, reducing enterprises' leverage. Consistent with these results, the empirical tests show that environmental disasters significantly increase banks' default rates, and these findings pass a series of robustness tests. The mechanism test shows that the decline in total factor productivity, asset impairment loss and the increase in macroeconomic uncertainty are all significant transmission channels in this process. Further analysis shows that the environmental disaster effect of increasing the default rate significantly reduces the risk appetite of banks, reducing the scale of lending and risk - taking. This then restricts enterprises through tighter financing constraints and higher financing premiums, negatively affecting their operations.

The main conclusions of this paper have the following policy implications: First, the systems and mechanisms to deal with environmental disasters should be improved and more attention given to the negative impacts of environmental disasters on the financial system. Next, awareness should be strengthened, and financial factors fully incorporated into the system. Second, government departments should consider the stability of the financial system when formulating disaster relief policies. Specifically, they should explore establishing disaster financial stability funds to prevent financial system runs and liquidity crises caused by extreme events. The supervision of financial institutions should include a standing disaster reserve, improving the construction of disaster recovery centers, adopting relevant incentives to guide financial institutions to reduce investment and credit for brown stranded assets, and encouraging financial institutions to engage in green finance. Third, the financial sector must fully consider climate and environmental risks and conduct environmental stress tests on a regular basis. Before launching a credit business, banks and other financial departments should thoroughly assess the climate and environmental risks of the business and region and fully consider environmental disaster risks in credit pricing. After a disaster occurs, the financial sector should also actively assist disaster – stricken enterprises through extensions and other benign interactions.

Carbon Pricing, Dual Financial Friction and Dual Pillar Regulation

WANG Bo   XU Piaoyang

(School of Finance, Nankai University)

At the Boao Forum for Asia 2021 Annual Conference, Yi Gang stated that "we should accelerate research on the introduction of climate change factors in stress tests of financial institutions and incorporate climate factors into the investment risk management framework. At the same time, we will step up support for carbon emission reduction by leveraging commercial bank ratings, deposit insurance rates, and a macro - prudential assessment framework. The central bank will focus on macro - prudential policies to deal with the potential systemic risks brought by climate change with monetary policies to support green development…and further strengthening the coordination between macro - prudential policies and monetary policies will be the key work in the process of achieving the 30/60 carbon target. " Therefore, research on the economic impact of carbon trading and carbon tax policies is of great significance. Additionally, the impact of climate policy and the roles of financial friction and the dual - pillar policy in the economic transformation process must be thoroughly discussed. Realizing China's 30/60 goals, constructing and perfecting the two - pillar framework to deal with climate transition risks, maintaining financial stability and achieving a smooth economic transformation and upgrade are of great theoretical and practical value.

This study makes three main contributions to the literature. First, it evaluates the macroeconomic effects of carbon pricing from both short - and long - term perspectives. It also explores the exogenous macroeconomic shocks of carbon price fluctuations within upper and lower limits. Second, we effectively distinguish between the financial accelerator effects of asset price volatility and risk aversion. Third, we combine the two - pillar and climate policies to evaluate the effectiveness of the two - pillar policy using certainty simulation and welfare analysis. This approach is an effective way to improve the two - pillar framework approach to dealing with the risks of economic transformation.

Dynamic stochastic general equilibrium modeling shows that, first, two kinds of carbon pricing can contribute to high - quality long - term economic development in China, despite some short - term negative effects. Floating carbon prices intensify economic fluctuations, but a lower limit on the market price helps alleviate these fluctuations. Second, financial friction magnifies the negative economic impact of climate policies. Under dual financial friction, the financial accelerator effect caused by the financial sector avoiding default risk is as important as the financial accelerator effect caused by the financial friction between the financial sector and residents. Third, in response to the economic effects of climate policy, monetary authorities should not overly focus on short - term inflation; rather, they should focus on output and demand. With a structural imbalance of supply and demand, expanding green investment, promoting green production and guiding consumer demand are the best ways to resolve inflation. Moreover, under the two - pillar regulation, macroprudential policies can effectively mitigate the negative economic impact of climate policies, enhance financial stability and improve residents' welfare.

The following policy recommendations are offered: First, combining fixed and floating carbon pricing will help achieve the 30/60 carbon target. A fixed carbon price can effectively cope with carbon technology changes, reducing their economic impact. Second, risk aversion in the financial sector will significantly exacerbate the negative impact of climate policies. Therefore, the government should encourage the financial sector to share in the risks and provide financial services to the real economy. However, attention should be paid to risk concentration in the financial sector. Third, macro - prudential policy should be used to address the financial instability and economic fluctuations that result from climate policy. Monetary policy should address structural supply - demand imbalances. For short - term structural supply - demand imbalances that lead to inflation, monetary authorities should promote production, expand green investment, promote supply-demand balance and address inflation at the root.

China's Green Finance Policy, Financing Costs and Firms' Green Transition: A Central Bank Collateral Framework Perspective

CHEN Guojin　DING Saijie　ZHAO Xiangqin　JIANG Xiaoyu

(School of Economics/Wang Yanan Institute for Studies in Economics, Xiamen University; Research Institute, the People's Bank of China)

In recent years, China has introduced successive green finance policies, intensifying policy support for the green transition of the economy. The effectiveness of these policies and how they promote the green transition of the economy has attracted a great deal of attention.

In this paper, we integrate the green finance policy and green transition into the sustainable investment asset pricing model and analyze the effects of green finance policy on the expected returns of risky assets and firms' green innovation. Next, using the quasi-natural experiment of the central bank including green bonds as qualified collateral, we provide empirical evidence of the effects of green finance policy from the perspectives of financing costs and corporate green innovation. We also conduct various robustness tests, such as changing the sample interval, a placebo test, policy delay effect, and propensity score matching to address potential endogeneity in our empirical investigation.

This study's main findings are as follows. (i) The central collateral framework policy reduces the credit spreads of green bonds and increases the credit spreads of brown bonds, demonstrating that the green finance policy creates financing incentives for green firms and pressures for the green transition of brown firms, respectively. (ii) These effects are stronger in the green finance reform and innovation pilot zone but gradually weaken over time. (iii) The central collateral framework policy significantly enhances the green innovation of brown firms through financial pressure that forces them to engase in green transition.

According to these findings, we propose three policy implications for the central bank to better promote the green transition of the economy. (i) The central bank should continue to provide financial support for green firms through the expansion of collateral. Specifically, expanding the green assets those qualify as collateral or increasing the mortgage rate of green assets can further strengthen the policy effects. (ii) The central bank should implement the continuous and progressive green finance policy and further expand the green finance reform and innovation pilot zone to promote green transition. (iii) The central bank should provide financing incentives for brown firms that actively engage in green innovation.

This paper makes the following contributions to the literature. (i) With the introduction of green finance policy and firm's green transition decision, we extend the sustainable investment (ESG) asset pricing model of Pastor et al. (2021) . ESG asset pricing models rarely consider the impact of financial policy, especially green finance policy, on asset prices. Using the extended ESG asset pricing model, this paper provides a unified theoretical framework for green finance policy, firms' financing costs and firms' green transition. (ii) To address potential concerns about model uncertainty caused by a single empirical methodology, we use a combination of difference - in - difference (DID) , triple differences (DDD) and continuous DID methods to identify the causality between green finance policy, bond credit spreads and firms' green transitions, resolving the endogeneity problem. (iii) This paper provides evidences of the green effects of green finance policy from the perspectives of credit spreads and firms' green innovation. We comprehensively test the heterogeneous effects of the policy on bond credit spreads and the dynamic time - varying and regional differences in the policy effects. We verify the mechanisms that force brown firms to engase in green transition.

Climate Change and the Credit Risk of Rural Financial Institutions

LIU Bo   WANG Xiuhua   LI Mingxian

(Economic College, Hunan Agricultural University;

College of Finance and Statistics, Hunan University)

The potential economic and financial risks of climate change have become a hot topic in academia. The *Global Risks Report*(2020) states that the top five global risks in the next 10 years are environmental and that the financial risk associated with climate change is an important source of systemic financial risks. Avoiding these risks requires comprehensive investigation of the financial risks related to climate change. Although climate change has a systematic impact on the financial system, many financial institutions are not paying enough attention to the financial risks induced by climate change.

Agricultural production is the first sector affected by climate change because the input-output efficiency of agricultural production is strongly correlated with climatic conditions. As rural financial institutions handle the finance needs of the agricultural sector and climate change increases the uncertainty of agricultural output, the potential climate risk is transmitted to rural financial institutions. This paper proposes the following transmission mechanism based on the climate change, agricultural development and climate finance literature: climate change → uncertainty in agricultural production → agricultural credit risks. This paper further proposes an empirical research scheme using the market location and primary business of rural financial institutions.

In the empirical study, we exploit a panel of financial data from 2010 to 2019 that includes 249 rural commercial banks and 7 rural banks from 26 provinces, 128 prefecture cities and 251 counties. Using the average annual temperature of each county, we construct an index to quantify the degree of climate change. The average annual temperature over the past 50 years is used as a reference to standardize the average annual temperature. After standardization, the average annual temperature illustrates the fluctuations in temperature and enables comparisons of the degree of climate change between counties. The empirical study has two levels. We first investigate the influence of temperature fluctuations on credit risk using a fixed effects model. Next, we use a nonparametric model and grouped regression to analyze the heterogeneous effect of temperature fluctuations on credit risk.

The results lead to the following conclusions. (i) Temperature fluctuations of the county where a rural financial institution is located significantly affects its credit risk. Using the average annual temperature over the past 50 years as a reference line, when the average annual temperature is 1 standard deviation above the reference line, the proportion of nonperforming loans increases by 0.1365%. Hence, climate change significantly increases the credit risk of rural financial institutions. (ii) If the average annual temperature fluctuation is subdivided into four quarters, only the temperature fluctuation in winter significantly affects credit risk. Taking the average winter temperature over the past 50 years as a reference standard, when the average winter temperature is 1 standard deviation above the reference standard, the proportion of nonperforming loans increases by 0.0777%. (iii) The effect of temperature fluctuation on credit risk level has phased characteristics. As the range of the average annual temperature fluctuation expands, the sensitivity of credit risk to climate change increases from weak to strong. (iv) Although city commercial banks, rural commercial banks and rural banks all serve local economic development, climate change does not significantly affect the credit risk of city commercial banks because their business is more dispersed among regions and industries. In a robustness test, we measure climate change using the normalized difference vegetation index (1 km) and use a multi - way fixed effects model, and the results remain unchanged.

Through empirical examination, this paper detects the direction and degree of the effect of climate change on agricultural credit risks. The findings provide not only empirical evidence for qualitative research but also implications for rural financial institutions and regulators to respond to climate change. The following countermeasures are suggested based on the research conclusions: carrying out stress testing, implementing differentiated supervision and innovating risk mitigation tools to prevent agricultural credit risks.

Corporate Environmental Responsibility and Bank Credit: Text Analysis of Words and Deeds

LI Zhe   WANG Wenhan

(School of Accountancy & China Management Accounting Research Center, Central University of Finance and Economics; School of Finance, Central University of Finance and Economics)

China officially launched its green credit policy in 2007. Green credit requires financial institutions to consider enterprises' environmental responsibility in their credit decisions. China's green credit policy has developed rapidly since its implementation. However, some enterprises obtain capital support by addressing environmental protection in name only, threatening the healthy development of China's green financial system and creating an unfavorable factor in China's environmental protection marketization mechanism. Therefore, this paper focuses on the "more words than deeds" phenomenon in enterprises' environmental protection practices and investigates its influence on banks' credit decisions. The results will help credit institutions to recognize the implementation risks of green credit policy. This paper provides a new decision - making reference for ensuring the healthy development of green credit.

Using text analysis to collect environmental performance data from the reports of listed companies, this paper identifies the characteristics of more words than deeds enterprises and empirically tests the effect of the more words than deeds approach on bank credit. The findings are as follows. (i) The more words than deeds approach helps enterprises obtain more bank loans. (ii) Compared with long - term bank loans, the positive effect is more obvious for short -

term bank loans. (iii) The promulgation of the Guiding Opinions has restrained the positive influence of the more words than deeds approach on bank loans. (iv) Further analysis shows that compared with enterprises that do not use the more words than deeds approach, the environmental responsibility performance of enterprises with more words than deeds has a significant positive impact on the credit resources of banks. This positive impact is more obvious in enterprises with no political connections, lower value and a worse market environment.

The potential contributions of this paper are as follows. (i) Under the current green credit policy, this paper deepens understanding of corporate environmental behavior decision - making and practices. (ii) This paper enriches research on the factors that influence bank credit decisions and on corporate information manipulation. In addition, this paper provides new support for improving the environmental information disclosure of listed companies in China. (iii) The Guiding Opinions is the systematic framework of China's current green financial policy. However, most of the related academic research focuses on policy interpretation, with a lack of empirical support at the data level. This paper provides micro - level empirical evidence of how to improve the implementation of green credit.

The policy implications of this paper are as follows. (i) Financial institutions should recognize that environmental reports may be used by enterprises for impression management. Therefore, when making credit decisions, banks should strengthen the scrutiny of corporate environmental responsibility performance. (ii) In practice, implementing the green credit policy is necessary; however, the financing of heavily polluting enterprises should not be blindly restricted. Instead, a balance of punishments and incentives can achieve a win-win balance of environmental protection and economic development. (iii) Building a green financial system is a long - term project. Therefore, all departments should continue to cooperate with each other to ensure the appropriate and sustainable implementation of the green credit policy. (iv) Regulators should improve the environmental information disclosure system and focus on the supervision of companies whose words and deeds are inconsistent, supplemented by certain punishment measures.

The Impact of Environmental Rule of Law on Bond Financing Cost: Evidence from Environmental Courts in China

GAO Haoyu　WEN Huiyu

(School of Finance, Renmin University of China)

With climate change becoming a social and development issue of great concern, carbon emission peak and carbon neutrality have become critical tasks in China at this stage. How to promote green transformation and achieve high - quality development has received broad discussion. Strong protection of environmental rule of law is indispensable to facilitate green orientation in financial markets under the " market -led and government - guided" principle. Moreover, bringing capital vitality to green transformation is an important embodiment of improving the level of financial servicing entity economy. Hence, to explore the coordinated development of economy and ecology and improve the functions of financial markets in the new era, it is of great practical significance to examine the real effects of the environmental rule of law construction in enterprises and financial markets.

Based on a quasi - natural experiment on the establishment of specialized environmental courts (EC) in China's Intermediate People's Courts, we exploit the staggered difference - in - difference - in - differences (DDD) method to examine the impact of the environmental rule of law on the cost of bond financing, utilizing a data set of corporate bonds, enterprise bonds and medium - term notes issued from 2008 to 2019. We find that after the establishment of the intermediate EC, local firms in high - pollution industries face higher transition risks due to environmental policies. Their credit spreads significantly increase by about 28. 4 basis points (about 12% of the average credit spreads) in our sample, indicating that improved regional environmental justice capacity promotes the capital market pricing of the transition risks induced by environmental policy. We then propose and empirically test the underlying mechanisms of the effect of EC establishment on bond financing cost. We find that the environmental rule of law enhanced by EC raises the bond financing cost of firms in high - pollution industries by aggravating the exposure of environmental litigation risks, strengthening external environmental monitoring, increasing operating costs, and sub - optimizing resources allocations in operating activities. Further analysis finds that the impact of EC establishment on bond financing costs is greater in the sample with better legal environments and stronger government incentives for environmental governance. To address the endogeneity of EC establishment, we adopt the propensity score matching method, control for more regional characteristics, add more fixed effects, and investigate the dynamic impacts of EC establishment. In addition, the conclusions remain robust to the use of alternative measures of high - pollution firms, the use of two - way clusters, and the consideration of bond types.

This paper contributes to several strands of literature. First, based on prior literature on the economic effects of environmental regulation, this study provides empirical evidence on how regional environmental justice capacity enhancement promotes the green - oriented function of capital markets. Second, this paper supplements the pricing mechanisms of firms' transition risks under the construction of environmental rule of law. Third, the paper contributes to the literature on law and finance from the perspective of promoting environmental justice efficiency.

This paper has important policy implications in the pricing of transition risks and the construction of environmental justice under the process of carbon emission peak and carbon neutrality. Strong protection of environmental rule of law plays an important role in promoting long - term coordination of policy guidance and financial markets' operation, and cultivating green investment philosophy and ability. Under advanced regional environmental rule of law represented by the establishment of EC, firms need to promptly prevent and resolve transition risks and improve environmental performance to achieve comparative competitive advantages in the new era of high - quality development. In the future, the effects of environmental rule of law on improving ecological governance and accelerating the green transformation of the economy should be further strengthened in the joint efforts of legislation, justice, law enforcement, government, and public concerns.

04　Banking Operation & Financing

Structural Total Factor Productivity Growth in China's Banking Sector

ZHU Ning　LIU Weiqi　YU Zhiqian　WANG Bing

(School of Economics and Finance, South China University of Technology; School of Economics and Statistics, Guangzhou University; School of Economics, Jinan University)

To effectively promote the high - quality economic development of China's financial sector, the new direction of China's financial reform must include financial structural reform. Indirect financing is the typical financing mode of China's banking system, and thus the banking sector has a key role in financial structural reform in China. In this context, total factor productivity (TFP) is a crucial index for evaluating the performance of financial structural reforms and their ability to generate high - quality economic growth. Therefore, as financial structural reform of China's banking sector is deepening, a method is required to scientifically evaluate and explore the source of the sector's structural TFP growth.

Previous studies typically evaluate TFP growth and decomposition based on technical efficiency. However, technical efficiency examines only the efficiency of individual firms and does not examine the efficiency of an overall sector (or industry). Moreover, the lack of a structural effect may mean that examination of the decomposition of TFP growth could lead to important information on the source of TFP growth being missed. This could include information on structural efficiency change, which involves the improvement of resource reallocation efficiency among individual firms, and information on institutional innovative change, which involves the improvement of the environment of overall banking system. Thus, policy suggestions developed without consideration of the above information could be inappropriate.

To address the above-described research gap, this paper constructs an aggregate Luenberger productivity indicator based on industrial and individual levels of productivity to effectively evaluate and explore the source of structural TFP growth in various banks in China and across China's entire banking sector. First, based on the assumption of variable returns to scale, this paper uses all of the production possibility sets of individual banks to construct an aggregate structural TFP growth model and decomposes this model into overall efficiency change and overall technological change. Overall efficiency change is then decomposed into aggregate technical efficiency change and structural efficiency change, and structural efficiency change is further decomposed into scope efficiency change and scale efficiency change. Additionally, overall technological change is decomposed into aggregate technological change and institutional innovation change.

This paper samples data from 2012 to 2018 from 62 Chinese commercial banks and selects input and output variables according to a profit-oriented approach to evaluate structural TFP growth. To ensure that a reasonable structural TFP growth model is obtained, a direction vector is set using data from 2012 as the base period. This shows that China's banking sector has good structural TFP growth during the study period, with the average annual growth rate being 1.24%. Overall technological progress is found to be the main driver of structural TFP growth, whereas the overall efficiency change has a somewhat negative effect on structural TFP growth. The decompositions of overall technological change and overall efficiency change clearly show that institutional innovation change and aggregate technological progress promote the structural TFP growth of China's banking sector. In addition, all of the components make limited contributions to overall efficiency change. Similar to the findings regarding the effects on China's entire banking sector, it is found that three types of banks perform well: state-owned banks, joint stock banks and local banks. Overall technological change is the main driver of the structural TFP growth of various types of banks, whereas overall efficiency changes have negative effects on structural TFP growth. Furthermore, institutional innovation changes make significant contributions to the structural TFP growth of various types of banks, particularly to that of joint stock banks. Thus, aggregate technological changes have positive effects on the structural TFP growth of joint stock and local banks. In addition, large state-owned banks outperform joint stock and local banks in terms of scope efficiency change and scale efficiency change.

This paper makes the following policy suggestions for financial structural reform based on the results above, which may promote high-quality economic development of China's banking sector. (i) It is imperative that financial structural reform is accelerated, given the current shortcomings in scope efficiency change and scale efficiency change. (ii) The strengthening of risk management in China's banking sector must be urgently addressed, as non-performing loans lead to negative technical efficiency change. (iii) Full use should be made of financial technology to optimize the structure of banking products, as technological progress is the main driver of the development of China's banking sector. (iv) Further improvements must be made to the financial environment and infrastructure, and institutional guarantees and support must be provided to financial services in the real economy because institutional innovation improvement is essential for structural TFP growth.

Competitive Neutrality and Non - State - Owned Enterprises' Access to Debt Financing: A Quasi - Natural Experiment during the COVID - 19 Pandemic

LYU Huaili   WANG Wenming   YAN Ziqiao   HOU Liang

(School of Management, Shanghai University; School of Management, Zhejiang University; School of Accounting, Shanghai University of International Business and Economics)

Competitive neutrality involves maintaining a level playing field for competition between public (SOE) and private (non - SOE) enterprises, such that they follow the same rules when competing for business. However, in China commercial banks are the principal players in the credit market, and they commonly practice credit discrimination when they implement financial policies, which is a deviation from competitive neutrality. As such, prior research clearly recognizes that in comparison to SOEs, non - SOEs are at a substantial disadvantage when accessing the credit market.

In response to COVID - 19 Pandemic shock, China introduced a series of financial policies to provide increased monetary and credit support to real sectors, especially to non - SOEs. Thus, we explore whether and how such financial policies affect competitive neutrality following the spread of the COVID - 19 pandemic, which represents a unique exogenous experimental scenario.

We use a sample of medium - term notes and commercial papers issued around the time of the outbreak of the COVID - 19 pandemic to conduct difference - in - differences tests of the realization of competitive neutrality via financial policy. We find that compared with SOEs, non - SOEs experience a significantly larger reduction in the costs of debt financing during the pandemic period, which suggests that government intervention leads to improved competitive neutrality. Our analyses also show that the reduction in debt-financing costs for non-SOEs is proportional to the amount of trade credit they provide to their partners along the supply chain. Thus, the supply of trade credit by key non-SOEs to other non-SOEs along the supply chain reduces the COVID-19 pandemic-generated financial constraints on these other non-SOEs, thereby serving as an important mechanism to promote the realization of financial policy that ensures competitive neutrality. Furthermore, we find that the supportive financial policies implemented during the pandemic period reduce non-SOEs' level of financialization and improve their efficiency of fund utilization.

Our study makes several contributions.

First, it explores an important approach to achieving competitive neutrality via financial policy. Our findings indicate that the credit discrimination against non-SOEs that previous studies document results not from the financial policies themselves, but from commercial banks' partial implementation of these financial policies. These findings highlight better ways to realize competitive neutrality via financial policy.

Second, our study contributes to research on credit discrimination and ownership discrimination. Our findings suggest that the financial policies promulgated by the central bank and other institutes effectively improve the financing environment for non-SOEs during the pandemic period, and the resultant financial support to non-SOEs does not result in resource misallocation or the inefficient use of raised funds. In fact, the improved financing environment for non-SOEs significantly alleviates the credit and ownership discrimination that they usually experience in the debt market.

Third, our study enriches understanding of the complementary relationship between commercial credit and bank debt. We find that a non-SOE's financial support of its non - SOE trade partners along the supply chain serves as a positive signal, which increases the probability that these trade partners will obtain loans from commercial banks on favorable terms in the event of extreme shocks.

Fourth, our study provides insights into the financial risks embedded within the financial system, which should be monitored by regulators. For example, although the supply of commercial credit may enable non - SOE trading partners along the entire supply chain to obtain financial support and assist financial institutions in implementing policies to ensure competitive neutrality and maintaining controllable levels of credit risks, there is also a risk that this supply may generate contagious financial distress. That is, if non - SOEs in the supply chain default on their loans or declare bankruptcy, this may have a spillover effect on the entire supply chain, leading in extreme cases to financial crisis.

The Spatiotemporal Constraint Effect of High - speed Railway and Corporate Equity Capital Cost: Empirical Evidence from China's A - share Listed Companies

GUO Zhaorui   HUANG Jun

(School of Business, Shanghai Normal University; Institute of Accounting and Finance, Shanghai University of Finance and Economics)

China has made remarkable progress in high - speed railway construction over the past decade, and it now ranks first in the world in terms of total mileage. Compared with other modes of transportation, high - speed railway has many advantages, being faster, safer, and more environmentally friendly. However, little attention is paid to its effect on the capital market. As a core concept in corporate finance, the cost of equity capital has always been of interest to researchers. At the micro level, this cost is an important criterion for the selection and performance evaluation of investment and financing projects and is vital for financial and business decisions. At the macro level, it plays an important role in efficient resource allocation and capital flow, and is an important indicator of the development of the capital market and the construction of relevant institutions (Mao et al., 2012). Therefore, understanding the spatiotemporal constraint effect of high - speed railway on the cost of equity capital will provide useful insights into the operation of the capital market, corporate investment, financing decisions, and performance evaluation.

Taking China's A - share listed companies from 2007 to 2018 as a sample, this paper empirically investigates whether the opening of a high - speed rail has an impact on the equity capital cost of local listed companies. If so, is the impact different according to the companies' characteristics? What are the specific paths by which the opening of a high-speed rail affects the cost of equity capital? The results show that the cost of equity capital decreases significantly after the high-speed rail opens near the listed companies due to the reduction in internal and external information asymmetry. This phenomenon is affected by a series of company characteristics. The more distant the company is from the majority of investors, and the higher the company's business complexity is, the more the cost of equity capital is affected by the opening of the high-speed rail. Subsequently, we find that the improved company stock liquidity and information disclosure quality after the opening of a high-speed rail both affect the cost of equity capital. A series of robustness checks, including placebo tests, a two-stage regression, and propensity score matching, confirm the results of this paper.

The contributions of this paper are as follows. First, it systematically investigates the impact of high-speed railway on the cost of equity capital, which improves our understanding of the spillover effect of high-speed rail operations and provides micro-enterprise evidence of the economic consequences of high-speed railway in China. Second, this paper investigates the effect of high-speed railway on the cost of equity capital, and then examines the channels of influence, enriching research on companies' cost of equity capital.

Our findings have the following practical implications. (i) Accelerated construction of transportation infrastructure will ensure the high-quality development of the real economy. (ii) No matter what new characteristics and new forms of business appear in the operation of the capital market under the new situation, improving listed companies' quality of information disclosure, reducing transaction costs, and optimizing the efficiency of capital market resource allocation should be basic construction projects to cultivate the capital market. (iii) Geographical location and distance from megacities cannot be changed, but the continuous search for spatiotemporal compression and changes in the spatial structure, distribution structure, and hierarchical structure enlarges the driving effect of central cities, especially megacities, i. e. Beijing, Shanghai, Guangzhou, and Shenzhen.

Semi - Mandatory Dividend Policy and Cost of Equity

WANG Chunfei　GUO Yunnan

(School of Accountancy, Central University of Finance and Economics; School of International Trade and Economics, University of International Business and Economics)

Legal protection is an effective method for encouraging large shareholders to share benefits with small and medium shareholders. In countries where laws are incomplete, mandatory dividend policies offset the deficiencies of inadequate legal protection. Nevertheless, mandatory dividend policies have only been adopted in a few countries, including Brazil and Chile, and there are few studies of these regimes. Chinese regulatory departments have offered guidance to listed companies in terms of dividend payout since 2001. In that year, there was a significant increase in the number of companies paying dividends, but in many cases only meager dividends were paid in response to the regulatory policies. To increase the dividend payout ratio, in 2006, China's regulatory departments directly restricted dividend payout ratios and linked them to refinancing. The Decisions on Amending Some Provisions on Cash Dividends by Listed Companies (hereinafter referred to as the "Decisions")was promulgated in 2008, and it made additional specifications to dividend payout modes. It is noteworthy that the Decisions highlighted the disclosure of information about dividend payouts. Thereafter, in 2012, the regulatory departments further improved the dividend rules, formulating fairly characteristic dividend payout regulatory rules, which are called semi - mandatory dividend policies in academic papers.

The implementation of semi - mandatory dividend policies has not resulted in the ideal division of dividends. The literature shows that semi - mandatory dividend policies may decrease the financial flexibility of growth companies and have adverse effects on these companies. Some studies suggest that semi - mandatory dividend policies have hardly any effect on " mean" companies' distribution of cash dividends, while forcing high growth companies that need refinancing to distribute cash dividends. As significant "negative incentives" for companies with high cash dividends, these dividend policies have even led to a certain decrease in the overall cash payout ratio. In addition, they have other unexpected adverse effects, for example tax costs. Most research focuses on regulatory costs and generally confirms the so - called regulatory "paradox".

These studies of semi - mandatory dividend policies adopt the perspective of regulatory costs and ignore an important issue: semi - mandatory dividend policies may also create regulatory benefits. In our opinion, these policies constitute a mechanism of profit sharing between shareholders and are beneficial because they help investors to develop stable expectations about dividends and thus realize governance "premiums".

This paper uses the new regulatory policies in 2008 as a natural experiment. It evaluates the economic consequences of semi - mandatory dividend policies from the perspective of their governance effects. It finds that these policies significantly reduce the equity costs of corporations, which is inconsistent with the findings in the literature that the policies result in a regulatory "paradox". Further analyses show that the effect of semi - mandatory dividend policies is stronger in companies with substantial agency conflicts. In addition, this paper examines the limitations of semi - mandatory dividend policies. It finds that the governance effects of semi - mandatory dividends are not evident in companies with low - quality accounting information or companies that are subject to strong financing constraints.

The contributions of this paper are as follows. First, the economic consequences of semi - mandatory dividend policies are evaluated from the perspective of governance "premiums", which enriches the literature about these policies. Second, this paper assesses the effects of semi - mandatory dividend policies on equity costs using the difference - in - differences method, making the findings of this paper robust. Third, the findings of this paper may be used as references for modifying and improving the regulatory policies for semi - mandatory dividend payouts.

Improved Efficiency Measurement Model, Shadow Banking, and the Efficiency of Chinese Commercial Banks

LI Lifang   TAN Zhengxun   YE Lixian

(School of Economics, Jinan University; Business School, Hunan Normal University)

Shadow banking can increase the profits of commercial banks and provide funds to small and medium - sized enterprises to induce economic development. However, shadow banking also finances high - risk projects, such as real estate, which leads to risk accumulation in commercial banks. Although shadow banking simultaneously affects commercial banks' profit and risk, studies only focus on its effect on the former, and there is a lack of research on the impact of shadow banking on the profit and risk of commercial banks from both theoretical and empirical perspectives. Moreover, in the last two decades, Chinese commercial banks have expanded rapidly by opening more branches, which may lower bank efficiency. Studies neglect the impact of "bad" inputs on bank efficiency, which may lead to errors when estimating Chinese bank efficiency. Therefore, investigating the impact of shadow banking and "bad" inputs on bank efficiency may provide important practical insights for the supply - side reform of the financial system.

This paper examines the impact of shadow banking and "bad" inputs on Chinese bank efficiency. We establish theoretical models to investigate the impact of shadow banking from the profit channel and the risk channel. By simultaneously distinguishing "good" and "bad" inputs and outputs, we extend the two - stage DEA model of Wang et al. (2014) that simply distinguishes between "good" and "bad" outputs. Additionally, we empirically examine the impact of "bad" inputs and shadow banking on the profit, risk, and efficiency of Chinese commercial banks. This paper makes the following four main contributions to the literature. First, we construct a theoretical model and investigate the impact mechanism of shadow banking on bank efficiency from the perspectives of profit and risk. Second, we extend the bank efficiency measurement model of Wang et al. (2014) by establishing a new two - stage DEA model that simultaneously distinguishes between "good" and "bad" inputs and outputs under the assumption of weighted variable returns to scale. Third, we develop a new system to analyze the efficiency of Chinese commercial banks. We first suggest that there are "bad" inputs in Chinese commercial banks. Next, we identify these "bad" inputs by using an inverse DEA model and apply the strong free disposability assumption in our model based on a thorough discussion of strong free disposability, week - free disposability, and non - free disposability. We then apply this new model to examine the efficiency of Chinese commercial banks. Finally, for the first time, we compare the impact channels and the impact extent of shadow banking on Chinese bank efficiency using a frontier considering the impact of shadow banking as the standard to measure the frontier minus the impact of shadow banking. The results show that our new theoretical model, the efficiency measurement model, and the new system to analyze the efficiency of Chinese commercial banks are more suitable for the analysis of Chinese commercial banks.

Additionally, we empirically analyze the impact of shadow banking on bank efficiency using data from 104 Chinese commercial banks from 2007 to 2017. The results show that shadow banking simultaneously increases bank profit and risk. Furthermore, we find that fixed assets and the number of employees are the "bad" inputs that can be compressed. The model that only differentiates outputs overestimates the efficiency of Chinese commercial banks, especially the four major banks and joint - stock commercial banks, indicating that the expansion of branches of large commercial banks does not improve bank efficiency. The results indicate that shadow banking is generally beneficial to the efficiency of large commercial banks, especially joint - stock commercial banks, but has very little impact on small and medium - sized commercial banks.

Our findings have two important implications. First, large commercial banks should promote the supply - side reform of the financial industry by compressing the input of fixed assets and reducing staff numbers, whereas small and medium - sized banks should target a different market position by providing a wide variety of services. Second, allowing commercial banks to develop a moderate degree of shadow banking while controlling its risk. Thus, compressing "bad" inputs and regulating shadow banking are important to increase effective financial supply, improve the financial supply structure, and increase bank efficiency.

Effects of China's Compensation Deferral Policy on Bank Profit Efficiency: Evidence from the Bank Level

WANG Yanyan   WANG Chenglong   YU Lisheng   LAN Yiyang

(School of Management, Xiamen University; School of Accounting, Zhongnan University of Economics and Law)

China's compensation deferral policy is a debt incentive reform designed to help banks avert systemic risks. It aims to reduce the probability of bank risk - taking behaviors caused by the mismatch of incentives and risks. The reform plays important roles in averting and defusing major risks and promoting a virtuous cycle between economy and finance. The literature thoroughly discusses how compensation deferral affects risks, but there is less discussion on how compensation deferral affects bank profit efficiency.

Prior research does not consistently conclude whether the relationship between bank risks and bank profit efficiency is based on a synergy effect or a crowding - out effect. It is difficult to assess the impacts of China's debt incentive reform on bank profit efficiency through the relationship between compensation deferral and bank risk - taking. More importantly, there remains a lack of evidence regarding how risk prevention policy affects bank profit efficiency. The bank behavior changes when responding to the policy, their behaviors change, resulting in unexpected economic consequences. From the perspective of the incentive effect, the pay level of a bank's management is directly linked to the bank's profit efficiency. Hence, the implementation of compensation deferral will increase the uncertainty of executive interests, and thus weaken management's motivation to improve profit efficiency. However, because of career concerns, bank managers need to prevent declines in profit efficiency after reforms are imposed, otherwise their careers could be negatively affected. Furthermore, if management cannot identify underlying risks, it is usually difficult for a bank to effectively increase income or save costs. Further study is needed on whether and how compensation deferral affects a bank's profit efficiency.

Using a 2007 to 2018 sample of Chinese commercial banks, this paper uses the difference - in-differences method with staggered adoption to study the effects of compensation deferral on bank efficiency and the mechanisms causing the effects. The results show that the implementation of compensation deferral internalizes management behavior and reduces a bank's risk - taking activities. Compensation deferral may result in the reduction of a bank's profitability by decreasing revenue rather than increasing costs, and thereby causing profit efficiency to decline. However, the parallel trend test shows that the effect on profit efficiency is reversed at the fifth year after compensation deferral is implemented. Hence, the policy makes management pay more attention to the persistence of long - term performance, which helps reduce long - term performance volatility. Further analysis finds that the negative relationship between compensation deferral and bank efficiency mainly exists in joint stock banks (JSBS). This paper also finds that the implementation of equity incentives and the acceptance of moderate ARIX holdings can help weaken the negative relationships between bank efficiency and compensation deferral. Our paper shows that although compensation deferral negatively affects short - term bank performance, it also causes management to pay more attention to the stability and persistence of long - term bank performance. From the profitability perspective, our findings provide theoretical evidence for the effects of China's deferral compensation policy on the prevention of risks and stabilization of growth.

This paper makes several contributions. First, it explores the impact of compensation deferral reform on profit efficiency from a bank's micro - perspective. Previous research mostly examines whether compensation deferral can effectively avert and defuse risks from a regulatory perspective. This paper supplements the previous evidence on how the compensation deferral reform affects profit efficiency and stability from a bank's micro - perspective. The paper also analyzes the mechanisms by which compensation deferral affects bank profit efficiency from the cost and benefit dimensions, thereby providing a more comprehensive and in - depth understanding of how compensation deferral affects bank behavior. Second, this paper uses an exogenous shock to mitigate the endogeneity issue. It examines how changes in a bank's real behavior in response to the compensation deferral reform affect the bank's profit efficiency. Most studies discuss the relationship between risk and efficiency from the perspective of bank capital. However, there is strong endogeneity between risk prevention and bank profit efficiency. This paper uses the exogenous shock caused by the introduction of compensation deferral to control the impact of risks and analyze the mechanisms that directly affect a bank's profit efficiency. Third, this paper finds that the implementation of equity incentives can alleviate the decline in profit efficiency caused by compensation deferral. Given that the compensation deferral reform plays a positive role in averting risks and stabilizing growth, our conclusions provide a reference on how to avert risks while limiting the consequential costs to profit efficiency.

The Tax Rate Anchoring Effect and Enterprise Investment Decisions

ZHENG Dengjin MENG Qingyu YUAN Chun

(School of Accountancy, Central University of Finance and Economics; Economics and Management Department, Civil Aviation Management Institute of China)

When studying irrational decision - making characteristics, psychologists find that people are unable to objectively predict the probability of various future situations when the decision - making environment is uncertain. Instead, as expected under neoclassical economics, people selectively over - rely on some pieces of available information. The resulting process, in which inadequate adjustments and decisions are made under the influence of initial "anchor values", is called "the anchoring effect". However, few studies examine whether this irrational psychology affects investment decisions made by corporate executives. Therefore, this paper explores whether there is an anchoring effect that affects executive investment decisions.

The premises of the anchoring effect are that decisions carry uncertainty and that decision - making can be influenced by anchor values. This paper studies the anchoring effects of tax rates, which are an important factor in enterprise investment decision - making. When the effective tax rate is volatile, executives are unable to rationally predict all possible outcomes and accurately estimate future effective tax rates. If the existing enterprise effective tax rate is higher than the normal tax burden, executives may over - rely on the conspicuously heavy current effective tax burden and irrationally predict that future effective tax rates will be high. This irrational anchoring of executive expectations on existing tax rates will directly affect enterprise investment decisions.

Therefore, this paper examines the impacts of tax anchoring effects on enterprise decisions. As its initial sample, our analysis uses data regarding all of the non - financial A - share listed companies in the Shanghai and Shenzhen stock markets from 2003 to 2018. The results reveal significant irrational tax rate anchoring behaviors that influence corporate investment decision - making and significantly reduce future investment expenditure. At times when the current enterprise tax rate is higher than either the contemporary average tax rate (inner anchor) or the equivalent corporate tax rate (external anchor), future investment spending is shown to decline significantly. In such cases, the inner anchoring effect is found to be much stronger than the external anchoring effect. Furthermore, this paper finds that the effects of tax rates on investments vary according to specific executive and corporate characteristics. With increasing age and tenure, executives with fiscal and tax backgrounds are all more able to effectively restrain irrational tax rate anchoring behaviors in their investment decisions. The influence of tax rate anchoring on investments increases with the volatility of the corporate tax rate. Overall, this paper finds that the underinvestment caused by the tax rate anchoring effect significantly reduces a company's operating performance and enterprise value. This conclusion reveals the negative economic consequences of tax rate anchoring in investment decision - making.

The potential contributions of this paper to the literature are as follows. First, irrational executive behaviors are important factors that affect senior investment decision - making. From the perspective of the tax rate anchoring effect, this paper enriches the empirical study of the influence of irrational factors on investment decisions. Second, from the perspective of tax rates, which are an important factor in investment decisions, this paper studies the impact of the tax rate anchoring effect on investment decision - making by senior executives.

It thereby enriches relevant studies on the selection of anchor values in the anchoring effect, and thus provides evidence in support of existing behavioral economics theories (Zhu Jigao et al. , 2017; Chen Shihua and Li Weian, 2016). Third, the literature mainly studies the direct impacts of tax rates and tax rate uncertainty on investments (Fazzari et al. , 1988; Jacob et al. , 2016; Meng Qingyu et al. , 2020). This paper supplements traditional tax investment theory by enriching research on the influence of tax burdens on investment decisions from the perspective of the anchoring effect. Fourth, the conclusions of this paper have implications for the investment practices of enterprises. Solving the problem of tax rate anchoring in investment decision - making will help improve investment efficiency. Maintenance of the continuity and stability of macro tax policy will promote healthy and sustainable enterprise development.

05 Financial Market

Does China Bond Valuation Identify the Credit Risk of a Bond? An Empirical Analysis Based on a Yield - Jump Perspective

SHI Yongdong   ZHENG Shijie   YUAN Shaofeng

(School of Applied Finance and Behavioral Science/School of Finance/Research Centre of Applied Finance, Dongbei University of Finance and Economics; China Financial Futures Exchange)

Credit debt is a vital part of the financial market, and an increase in credit defaults has a negative effect on the prevention of systemic financial risks. Thus, the advance identification of default risks has numerous positive effects: it protects the interests of investors, enhances the attraction of credit debt, strengthens the investment and financing functions of the bond market, reduces information asymmetry in the credit bond market, inhibits excessive financing of high - risk enterprises, and reduces leverage ratios and systemic financial risk (via the resource allocation functions of pricing mechanisms).

The traditional tool used to identify credit bond risk is the credit rating, and ratings agencies in China typically use an "issuer - paid" approach for their assessments. However, this approach involves an inherent conflict of interest, as ratings agencies often increase revenue and market share by deliberately upgrading issuers' credit ratings, which makes it difficult to identify the actual default risk of such issuers' bonds. In these circumstances, a key question is, can a third - party valuation of such bonds accurately reveal their expected default risk? The answer to this question is of great practical significance for optimizing the construction of the bond market information environment and preventing systemic risk.

At present, the mainstream valuation of China's bond market is the ChinaBond valuation, which is issued by the ChinaBond Pricing Center Co., Ltd., after the end of each trading day. A ChinaBond valuation has the following advantages. First, in contrast to a traditional credit rating, a ChinaBond valuation adopts the "investor - paid" approach to assessment, which is more independent than the "issuer - paid" approach. Second, the ChinaBond Pricing Center Co., Ltd. is directly affiliated with the China Central Depository & Clearing Co., Ltd., which discloses information about bond issuers and acts as the central custodian and clearing house for bonds. Thus, the China Central Depository & Clearing Co., Ltd. provides objective conditions for the ChinaBond Pricing Center Co., Ltd. to use to obtain relevant information. Third, in contrast to the Kealhofer, McQuown, and Vasicek model, ChinaBond valuations integrate the market information of bonds with the financial information of bond issuers, and it is released daily to ensure better real - time performance. Fourth, ChinaBond valuations are widely used by regulators for transaction pricing, risk assessment, and fair value measurement. In addition, studies find that the price or yield jumps of assets, such as stocks and options, reflect relevant information on bond issuers and the expected default risk of their bonds, and affect the credit spread. Thus, short - term changes or jumps in a ChinaBond valuation could enable investors to judge the credit risk of bonds.

Accordingly, this paper determines the utility of a ChinaBond valuation for the identification of credit risk by exploring its effect on bond credit spread and the mechanism of this effect in terms of jumps in valuation. Specifically, based on the data of ChinaBond valuations provided by the ChinaBond Pricing Center Co., Ltd. from 2011 to 2018, this paper studies how a jump in a ChinaBond valuation affects bond credit spread. The results show that a jump in such a valuation significantly affects the bond credit spread: an upward jump decreases the credit spread, and a downward jump increases the credit spread. In addition, a downward jump has a greater effect than an upward jump, and a heterogeneity analysis shows that a jump in the valuation of credit spreads has a greater effect on institutional investors and on bonds with severe information asymmetry, poor liquidity, and high default risk. Further research shows that a valuation jump contains private information, in addition to public information, and can be used by stock analysts to improve their forecasting performance.

The key contributions of this paper are as follows. First, current research on the identification of bond credit risk focuses on credit ratings, and few studies discuss this issue from the perspective of third - party valuation. Thus, this paper's analysis of the role of a ChinaBond valuation in credit risk identification provides a new perspective for related research. Second, this paper finds that a ChinaBond valuation not only gives credit risk information on bonds but also provides investors with private information that complements existing public information. This is invaluable for China's bond market, which lacks effective tools for the identification of credit risk. Third, the conclusions of this paper have profound policy implications, as they reveal that third - party valuations can provide more credit risk information than credit ratings. Thus, third - party valuations can serve as a theoretical reference for various contracting parties and government regulatory authorities for guarding against the risk of bond default or for managing a default event, or as a market - based means to protect the interests of creditors.

The Trading Behavior of Margin - Leveraged Investors: Evidence from Chinese Stock Markets

KANG Wenjing　GU Ming

(School of Finance, Shanghai University of Finance and Economics; School of Economics, Xiamen University)

Since the introduction of the margin trading system in the Chinese A - share market in 2010, the trading volumes and holding balances of margin investors have increased significantly. Today, margin investors hold approximately 1 trillion yuan of A - share stocks, and these investors are thus a key part of the market. There is therefore a need for a better understanding of the trading behavior of margin investors and its effect on the pricing mechanisms of the A - share market. To this end, we exploit the unique data availability of the Chinese A - share market to conduct in - depth analyses of the trading of margin investors to determine how their trading affects market returns and liquidity.

We refer to the predictions of collateral constraint models and hypothesize that margin investors are trend - followers; thus, there should be asymmetry in the relationship between stock price changes and leveraged investors' trading behavior. We observe a significant trend - following pattern in the behavior of margin investors in Chinese stock markets: these investors buy after a stock price increases and sell after a stock price decreases. We find that a stock price decrease has a greater effect on margin investors' trading activity than a similar stock price increase. We further show that this asymmetry is mainly driven by market - level returns.

Specifically, we conduct stock - level time - series regressions in which the weekly net buying activity based on margins is regressed on the lagged weekly stock returns. We find that a significantly positive relationship exists between leveraged net buying activity and past stock returns: if the stock price increases in week t - 1 , there is a significant increase in the net buying activity by leveraged investors in week t; analogously, if the stock price decreases in week t - 1 , there is a significant increase in the net selling activity by leveraged investors in week t. We quantify the magnitude of this effect based on the average size of our sample firm (approximately 25 billion RMB) and thus calculate that a 10% stock price change in a given week will lead to a 0.25% (or 44 million RMB) change in the total market cap trading by leveraged investors in the following week.

Next, we test whether there is any difference between the effects of stock price increases and decreases on leveraged investors' trading behavior. Brunnermeier and Pedersen (2009) suggest that a loss spiral may occur in some price - decrease circumstances, where an initial price decrease caused by an exogenous shock can lead to leveraged speculators experiencing losses on their existing positions, causing them to de - leverage by selling, which causes further price decreases, and thus continued selling. In addition, when a market increases in value and leveraged investors can borrow more, they are free to choose whether to make additional stock purchases, but when a market decreases in value and leveraged investors are affected by funding or collateral constraints, they are compelled to sell their portfolio holdings, especially if they receive margin calls. Therefore, we hypothesize that the effect of stock price decreases on leveraged investors' trading behavior is stronger than the effect of stock price increases on their trading behavior.

We find that there is indeed significant asymmetry in the relationship between stock price changes and leveraged investors' trading behavior: specifically, the effect of a stock price decrease on leveraged trading activity is approximately twice the effect of a stock price increase of the same magnitude on leveraged trading activity. This means that a 10% price increase of an average stock in a given week will lead to net buying of approximately 0.13% of the market cap by leveraged investors in the following week, whereas a price decrease of 10% will lead to net selling of 0.24% of the market cap by leveraged investors in the following week. Notably, these differences are statistically significant, and thus provide direct support for the predictions of the Brunnermeier and Pedersen (2009) collateral constraint model. Furthermore, we find that the asymmetric relationship between stock price changes and leveraged trading behavior strengthens in good economic times, which is consistent with the theoretical predictions of Acharya and Viswanathan (2011).

We also explore the return predictability of leveraged trading activity. We observe that a significantly negative relationship exists between net leveraged buying activity and subsequent stock returns. In addition, we find that the negative relationship between leveraged investors' trading activity and their subsequent weekly stock returns is primarily attributable to the selling behavior of margin investors.

Overall, our paper provides strong empirical support for collateral constraint models. We also provide policy recommendations on how the resilience of Chinese stock markets could be improved.

The Effects of Market Frictions on Idiosyncratic Risk Premium: An Empirical Study of the Main Board of China's A Stocks

LI Shaoyu   ZHANG Teng   SHANG Yuhuang   ZHOU Yu

(International Business College, South China Normal University;

School of Securities and Futures/Institute of Chinese Financial Studies,

Southwestern University of Finance and Economics)

Due to asymmetric information, trading costs, buy and sell constraints, lack of short - sales mechanisms, and exogenous shocks, the effects of market frictions on stock returns are more serious in China's A - share stock market than in developed foreign stock markets. Therefore, it is reasonable to ask how market frictions affect the pricing effect of idiosyncratic risks in China. In practice, answering this question would support the improvement and development of the capital market in China and help investors construct reasonable investment strategies. The question also suggests a new theoretical perspective: using market frictions to explain market anomalies (e. g. , the idiosyncratic volatility puzzle and idiosyncratic skewness premium).

Many studies of non - Chinese markets (e. g. , Mitton and Vorkink, 2007; Barberis and Huang, 2008; Bali and Cakici, 2008) use risk preferences and liquidity to explain the idiosyncratic volatility puzzle. However, studies show that there is a negative relationship between idiosyncratic risk and stock return in the Chinese stock market. Heterogeneous belief (e. g. , Zuo et al. , 2011; Long et al. , 2018) , gambling preferences (Zheng et al. , 2013) , and limited arbitrage (Yu et al. , 2017; Gu et al. , 2018) contribute to this negative relationship (puzzle). However, studies of both foreign and domestic markets ignore the effects of market friction.

We attempt to investigate the pricing effects of various dimensions of market friction and explore the mechanism through which pricing factor affects idiosyncratic risk. Our samples are drawn from the main board of China's A - share stock market for the 2001 to 2015 period. We first introduce continuous and discrete market friction variables to represent the dimensions of information asymmetry, trading costs, price shocks, price limit constraints, short - selling constraints, future trading constraints, and exogenous shocks. Second, the idiosyncratic volatility and idiosyncratic skewness variables are derived from a three - factor regression and five - factor regression, respectively. Then, they are used in a Fama - MacBeth cross - sectional regression to test the pricing effects and how these effects influence idiosyncratic risk premiums. We try to discuss the effects of the market friction factors on idiosyncratic risk premiums via liquidity channels. Third, we use a weighted market friction index in a robustness test of the empirical results and conduct a portfolio analysis to infer the characteristics of idiosyncratic risk premiums under different market frictions.

Empirical studies indicate that the idiosyncratic risk factors, including idiosyncratic volatility, idiosyncratic skewness, and market frictions, have significant premiums. Market frictions enhance idiosyncratic volatility via decreased liquidity in the form of trading time, trading frequency, trading number, trading demand, and trading speed. Market frictions weakly influence idiosyncratic skewness. We also find that the absolute returns of portfolio strategies based on idiosyncratic risk factors outweigh those of CAPM, the three - factor model, and the five - factor model. Furthermore, the returns of portfolio strategies based on idiosyncratic risk factors are impacted by market frictions, which confirms the findings of the regressions.

We make two contributions to the literature. First, we partially explain the effect of market frictions on idiosyncratic volatility and to identify the driving mechanisms as stock liquidity (trading time cost, trading frequency, trading hours, trading inclination, and trading speed), although the effect of the market frictions on idiosyncratic skewness is relatively weak. Second, we find that portfolios constructed using idiosyncratic risk variables have higher absolute returns than the CAPM, three - factor, and five - factor portfolios. As a result of market frictions, the absolute return of a portfolio based on idiosyncratic volatility shrinks. The findings indicate that market liquidity is indispensable to avoid market crashes when managing systematic and contagious risks from international markets. It is also necessary to control for the spread of liquidity, and we should be cautious in assessing the individual stock risks incurred by the overflow of liquidity. In particular, it is necessary to develop policies for directional liquidity injection and for differentiating capital costs. Additionally, our work can be extended to study abnormal types of market friction, such as global public health crises and climate - related shocks.

Does Market Manipulation Reduce the Information Efficiency of China's Stock Market? Empirical Evidence from the Shanghai A - share Market's High - Frequency Trading Data

SUN Guangyu   LI Zhihui   DU Yang   WANG Jin

(School of Finance, Zhejiang Gongshang University; School of Economics, Nankai University; Research Institute of Bank of China; CIB Fund Management Co., Ltd.)

Tremendous increases in scale have been achieved in the development of China's A - share market over the past 30 years. At the end of 2020, there were 4 154 listed companies in the A - share market, and the total value of the market was 80 trillion yuan. This equates to greater than 70% of China's 2020 GDP, meaning that the A - share market is the world's second largest stock market, after that of the United States. However, the frequent abnormal fluctuations that have occurred in the A - share market indicate that the quality of the market is not high.

In particular, there have been continual illegal transactions in the stock market in recent years: China Securities Regulatory Commission reports that the illegal profits from market manipulation in 2020 totaled 416 million yuan. Clearly, such occurrences severely damage the legitimate rights and interests of investors and the healthy development of the capital market. To explore this illegal behavior from the perspective of stock market quality, we monitor and attempt to identify suspicious tail - market manipulation in China's stock market. Based on the results of this monitoring, we empirically analyze how market manipulation affects the information efficiency of China's stock market and suggest ways for regulatory authorities to improve market quality.

Many studies explore the factors influencing information efficiency in the Chinese stock market. Recent studies explore these factors from the perspective of investors and find that institutional investors (Xin et al., 2018), foreign investors (Qinlin and Zhengfei, 2018), and investor sentiment (Yang et al., 2020; Xiong et al., 2020) are responsible for abnormal changes in information efficiency. However, scholars rarely analyze the relationship between market manipulation and information efficiency from the perspective of illegal traders. This is a crucial relationship to understand, as the capital advantage and shareholding advantage of market manipulators means that their manipulations have a profound effect on the formation of stock prices. In addition, market microstructure theory (O'Hara, 1995) holds that the process of formation of security prices is closely related to the type of traders involved. Thus, in the process of stock - price formation, market manipulators may either (i) play the role of informed traders, whereby they use information advantages to bring stock prices closer to their intrinsic values through value investment, which increases information efficiency, or (ii) play the role of uninformed traders, whereby they use capital advantages and shareholding advantages to speculate on stock prices to cause them to deviate from their intrinsic values, which decreases information efficiency. Therefore, it may be unclear how market manipulation affects information efficiency.

Accordingly, in this paper, we explore whether market manipulation is necessarily harmful and the mechanism by which market manipulation affects information efficiency. Specifically, we use the daily high - frequency trading data of the Shanghai A - share market from 2013 to 2018 as a research sample. Then, based on the abnormal characteristics of stock - trading indicators in this sample, we construct a model to identify tail - trading manipulation and empirically test the effect of market manipulation on the information efficiency of stock prices. From these investigations, we obtain the following findings.

(i) Market manipulation has an adverse effect on information efficiency, primarily via abnormal changes in stock liquidity and volatility after market manipulation. These findings remain stable after controlling endogeneity. (ii) Manipulation has less adverse effects on the information efficiency when the enterprise is state - owend or have a high quality of information disclosure.

Our findings on the adverse effects of market manipulation on information efficiency indicate that financial regulatory authorities should improve market - monitoring and early - warning systems, and increase penalties for violations.

Macroeconomic Information and Financial Market Connectedness: Evidence from A DCC - MIDAS Model

ZHOU Kaiguo   XING Ziyu   YANG Haisheng

(Lingnan College, Sun Yat - sen University; School of Economics and Trade, Guangzhou Xinhua University)

Understanding the correlation between financial markets is key for the effective implementation of coordinated supervision. The financial sector is the bloodline of the real economy, and enhancing the capacity of financial services for the real economy requires the coordination and alignment of financial markets with the macroeconomy. A well - informed and well - run financial market should be able to effectively reflect the characteristics of the macroeconomy. Making good use of macroeconomic information and accurately estimating dynamic correlations between financial markets are important for the accurate implementation of cross - market coordinated supervision and the efficient monitoring and early warning of risk resonance between markets.

This paper uses the DCC - MIDAS model to incorporate macro - level low - frequency variables into the analytical framework of high - frequency correlations among financial markets and uses the covariance matrix estimation accuracy comparison method proposed by Engle and Colacito (2006) and Laurent et al. (2013) to compare the macroeconomic information model and the long - term market volatility information model in terms of the estimation efficiency of dynamic conditional correlation coefficients. Additionally, it systematically investigates and discusses the cyclical characteristics of the impact of each macroeconomic variable on the correlation between financial markets. This paper presents direct evidence of the impact of macroeconomic information on financial market correlations and bridges a research gap regarding multi - market correlations. The study more accurately captures the causal factors causing financial market resonance, and the mechanism of macroeconomy influencing financial risk, provides feasible ideas for the implementation of coordinated cross - market regulation in the context of different shocks, and presents a basic framework for the construction of real - time monitoring indicators for financial risk mixing by combining macroeconomic information and financial market data.

This paper uses monthly data of China's industry value added, M_2, consumer price index, and economic policy uncertainty index from January 2006 to June 2018, totaling 150 sample points, and daily yield data of the stock market, money market, foreign exchange market, and bond market during the corresponding sample period, totaling 3 258 sample points. The following findings are obtained:

(i) Industry value added and M_2 negatively affect financial market correlations, and economic policy uncertainty and inflation levels conversely. The robustness of the results is not affected by the way macroeconomic information is introduced into the financial market correlation analysis framework. (ii) AS macroeconomic information is a long - run component of market correlations, the macroeconomic information model achieves an efficiency increase of at least 1.45% over other models based on market information. Real economic performance, economic policy uncertainty, and M_2 are the most important factors affecting financial market correlations, whereas inflation is less important. (iii) the impact of industry value added and inflation on financial market correlations is relatively robust, whereas economic policy uncertainty and M_2 show cyclical characteristics. During economic upturns, loose monetary policy is more likely to trigger financial market correlations, economic policy uncertainty inhibits financial market correlations, and the efficiency improvements brought by industry value added and monetary policy information are larger. Meanwhile, the efficiency gains from economic policy uncertainty and monetary policy information are higher during economic downturns.

Based on the main findings, the following policy recommendations are proposed: (i) cross - market coordination and supervision should be informed by the role of macroeconomic factors in the analysis of inter - market correlations and prevent the upside of financial market correlations in advance. Gradually form a systematic set of financial market risk resonance monitoring indicators. (ii) cross - market coordinated supervision should be informed by the dynamics of the economic cycle, flexibly apply policy tools according to the stage of the economic cycle, curb financial market risk resonance with macro policies, and dynamically adjust the proportional weights of each macro variable in the monitoring indicators. (iii) pay attention to the channel role of macroeconomic information in market connections, gradually release macroeconomic data, focus on its economic signal role, be wary of the market transmission of market panic, and guide investors to pay attention to the operation of China's macroeconomic fundamentals.

Do Purchase Restriction Policies Reduce the Corporate Value of Listed Real Estate Companies?

LIANG Ruobing ZHANG Dongrong FANG Xin LIN Xixi

(School of Economics, Xiamen University)

In the past 20 years, the rapid economic development and urbanization of major Chinese cities has led to rising house prices. According to the National Bureau of Statistics, the average cost of housing in 35 large and medium - size cities increased from 2 267 yuan per square meter in 2002 to 15 356 yuan per square meter in 2019. To curb excessive speculation in the property market and stabilize land prices, house prices, and price expectations, local governments began issuing a series of house purchase restriction policies in 2010. By the end of 2011, 46 cities had restriction policies on issues such as house quantity, household registration, and loan proportion. These policies were lifted in 2014 in most cities as the property markets stabilized.

However, the rapid increase in housing costs in 2015 and 2016 led to a new round of housing purchase restrictions in 60 cities by 2019. Although they differ in details, the prime goal of all of these policies is to curb rapidly rising house prices by restraining demand in the housing market. As a powerful tool for stabilizing and regulating the real estate market, these purchase restriction policies have had a great impact on real estate companies and even the real estate industry, which is a pillar of the Chinese economy. As a result, these housing market policies have attracted the attention of all parts of society.

Using a dataset of listed real estate companies from the 2008—2013 and 2015—2019 periods, this paper uses difference - in - differences (DID) models with an intensity index to empirically analyze the impact of the two rounds of housing purchase restriction policies on listed real estate companies and to identify the main channel of influence. As the real estate projects developed by listed real estate companies in different cities are different, the house purchase restrictions have different effects in different cities. To address the issue of intensity difference across real estate companies, this paper uses specific identification with accumulative intensity indexes.

First, this paper uses the proportion of listed real estate companies' sales in each city to construct an intensity index of house purchase restrictions, and then it uses an intensity DID model to determine whether either round of house purchase restrictions significantly reduces the market value of real estate companies. Then, this paper analyzes the heterogeneous effects of different house purchase restriction polices. It finds that in the first round, the most effective policies are those that control household registration, are applied to the whole city, and impose a two - house limit. In contrast, in the second round, policies applied to specific city districts and restrictions on resales are also effective.

Second, this paper analyzes the operating performance data of listed real estate companies and finds that purchase restrictions have no significant effect on most business performance indicators, with the exception of a negative impact on the solvency of enterprises in the first round. This suggests that purchase restrictions may increase the operating risk of real estate companies and have a negative impact on the development capability of enterprises in the second round. For the property market, this paper finds that the first round of purchase restrictions does not have a significant impact on urban property prices, but the second round significantly curbs the rise of house prices. Hence, the two rounds of policies have different impacts on the expectations of stock investors due to their different effects on the real estate market.

Third, this paper analyzes the daily performance of real estate companies listed on the Shenzhen and Shanghai stock markets. Both rounds of purchase restrictions have significant negative impacts on the daily return rates and the monthly search indices of the real estate companies, showing that the effect of purchase restrictions on the value of listed real estate companies is mainly caused by investor expectation. These findings are of great significance for understanding the development of China's real estate market, specifically the effects of the current adjustments. They suggest that the two rounds of house purchase restrictions changed the market value of listed real estate companies by changing investors' expectations, reflecting the role of housing policies in stabilizing expectations. The aim of the real estate policy is to have a long - term influence on housing markets and investors' expectations by strengthening the attitude that " a house is for dwelling rather than for speculating".

06 International Economy & Trade

How Anti - dumping Affects Cross - border Mergers and Acquisitions

YANG Lianxing

(School of Economics, East China Normal University)

In recent years, global economic growth has slowed, and anti - dumping trade barriers have become increasingly common measures for trade protection. Uncertainty in the external environment of global economic development has intensified. According to China's Ministry of Commerce, in 2020, Chinese exports were subject to 132 trade remedy investigations in 28 countries (regions), involving approximately 13.1 billion U. S. dollars. At the same time, Chinese companies' cross - border M&A have been undergoing a rapid development trend. According to the UNCTAD World Investment Report 2020, China's foreign direct investment flow in 2019 was 136.91 billion U. S. dollars, the second highest in the world. It has ranked in the top three in the world for 8 consecutive years. Cross - border M&A have become the main form of foreign direct investment by Chinese companies. Therefore, whether the trade barriers encountered by China have led to the rapid growth of corporate cross - border M&A, and how companies should rationally identify and respond to the opportunities and risks of cross - border M&A brought about by trade barriers are urgent questions with both theoretical and policy implications.

Trade barriers have multiple effects on enterprises' foreign direct investment. Current theories suggest that cross - border capital flows are complete substitutes for international trade, and capital flows mainly come from trade barriers. Early research on Japanese samples shows that anti - dumping regulations promote multinational investment by Japanese companies in Europe and the United States, and companies use cross - border M&A to replace product exports, thereby saving transportation costs and tariff costs (Belderbos, 1997; Barrell and Pain, 1999). However, other studies find that strong trade barriers strongly control the foreign investment of enterprises. Given the various forms of internationalization available to enterprises from countries that are the target of trade frictions, the host country often adopts the "full caution" principle, making it possible for enterprises to cross trade through investment more difficult to achieve. Only multinational companies in developed countries tend to use cross - border M&A to circumvent anti - dumping policies. From the perspective of industry, technology - intensive industries are more likely to adopt cross - border M&A in response to anti - dumping regulations than labor - intensive industries.

Based on the Thomson Financial Mergers and Acquisitions (SDC) database, this paper uses a sample of Chinese companies' cross - border M&A and the World Bank's anti - dumping database to comprehensively examine the impact of anti - dumping regulations on cross - border M&A. This paper makes three innovations. First, the literature focuses on the macro levels of country and industry, and from this view there are few studies of how anti - dumping regulations affect enterprises' cross - border M&A. By constructing multi - level anti - dumping and cross - border indicators of M&A, this paper comprehensively considers the effectiveness and internal influence mechanisms of micro - enterprises' use of cross - border M&A as a response to anti - dumping regulations, and it effectively enriches and expands related fields. Second, this paper finds that contrary to the literature, anti - dumping regulations do not directly induce corporate cross - border M&A but have a significant cross - industry and cross - "host country" inhibitory effect. Third, there are few studies of the relationships between the scale, effectiveness, and type of cross - border M&A and the relationship between anti - dumping and cross -

border M&A, and this paper shows that the dimensional indicators influence each other in complicated ways. As a result, this paper provides a foundation for further research on the incentive effects of trade barriers.

Import Tariff Shocks and Chinese Import Behavior

ZHANG Guofeng   LU Yi   JIANG Lingduo

(School of International Trade and Economics, University of International Business and Economics, School of Economics and Management, Tsinghua University)

The expansion of imports is one of the key determinants leading to changes in China's economic growth patterns and influencing China's development of macro - and micro - policies. Due to a series of import - promoting policies, the value of China's 2018 imports was USD 2.14 trillion, exceeding the value of 2001 imports by 8.77 times. However, China faces profound changes in the international environment. For example, U.S. trade protectionism affects the production and operation of Chinese enterprises. To safeguard the World Trade Organization (WTO) regime and China's legitimate rights and interests, China imposes retaliatory tariffs on U. S. products. It is still unknown whether U. S. exports to China are significantly decreased by the shock of retaliatory tariffs, and whether China's total imports and domestic production chains are affected by the tariff shock. Discussion of the above issues not only helps China deal with the complexities of U. S. protectionism, but it also provides important theoretical guidance for further relaxation of import restrictions.

In this paper, we use the multiple - period difference - in - differences method to investigate the effects of Chinese retaliatory tariffs on U. S. products. First, we discuss the effects on imports from the U. S. The identified effects satisfy statistical robustness conditions, including the parallel trend test and the placebo test. Second, we explore the effects of retaliatory tariffs on total imports from all over the world, including the diversion of import origins from the U. S. to other countries. Third, we explain the impacts of tariff shocks from the perspective of upstream and downstream connections. Furthermore, we include heterogeneity analyses regarding import demand elasticity, technology complexity, and enterprise ownership.

Our monthly trading data from January 2017 to June 2020 are provided by the China General Administration of Customs. As enterprise names and ID codes are not included in the dataset, we aggregate the transaction data into imports at the HS8 product level. The data regarding China's additional import tariffs on U. S. products come from the official website of the Ministry of Finance of China. These data include the list of HS8 products that are subject to additional tariffs, the list's date of publication, and the effective dates of the additional tariffs. The data regarding the U. S. additional import tariffs on Chinese products come from the website of the Office of the United States Trade Representative. We match the Chinese HS8 product codes with both the U. S. product codes and the Chinese industry codes of input - output table.

First, we find that China's retaliatory tariffs on U. S. products initially cause a significant decrease in the total value and quantity of imports from the U. S. However, the decline in imports becomes less rapid after implementation of the tariff exclusion list. Second, China's total imports and domestic production chains are not significantly affected, meaning that the negative effects of retaliatory tariffs are generally controllable. China's imports from the U. S. are replaced by imports from larger trade partners, with the support of Chinese most - favored - nation (MFN) tariff reductions. Third, although China imports of flexible products, non - fuel primary products, high - tech products, and private enterprises from U. S. are affected by the retaliatory tariffs against the U. S. , the total imports of these products and enterprises are not significantly affected. Therefore, China's overall trade environment remains stable and positive.

Our conclusions have important policy implications. First, China's retaliatory tariffs cause precise and powerful local impacts on U. S. exports, and thereby encourage the U. S. to abide by the applicable WTO rules. Second, it is necessary to mitigate the negative impacts of retaliatory tariffs through supporting government actions, such as accelerating the release of tariff exclusion lists and using tax incentives, subsidies, and financial supports to decrease the costs of intermediate inputs.

We contribute to the literature on three grounds. First, compared to the numerical simulation data used in most of the literature, we use actual data from China's imports and lists of products subject to retaliatory tariffs. Second, we discuss the effects of retaliatory tariffs on imports from the U. S. and the rest of the world, and our consideration of import diversion helps explain the local and overall effects of the tariffs. Third, we investigate the effects of upstream and downstream tariff shocks and include heterogeneity analyses across different industries and enterprises.

In the long term, trade frictions between China and the U. S. will impact the stability of China's industrial production chain, its industrial transformation, and the upgrading and innovation of Chinese enterprises. These topics will need to be further explored in future research.

The Effects of Labor Costs on the Scale and Scale and Upgrading of China's Processing Trade

MAO Qilin   SHENG Bin

(Center for Transnationals' Studies, Nankai University)

In 2004, China's Ministry of Labor and Social Security implemented minimum wage regulations that extended the minimum wage system to all parts of the country. This significantly has increased the labor costs of firms and gradually removed the low - cost dividends that processing trade firms have traditionally enjoyed. In recent years, the transformation and upgrading of processing trade has become a focus issue, and the report of the 17th National Congress of the Communist Party of China clearly states that the transformation of the growth mode of foreign trade must be accelerated based on quality, the import and export structure must be adjusted, and the transformation and upgrading of processing trade must be increased. Therefore, it is theoretically and practically valuable to study the scale change, transformation, and upgrading of China's processing trade from the perspective of increases in minimum wage and labor costs.

To this end, this paper performs a difference - in - differences analysis of the effects of labor cost or minimum wage increases on the scale and upgrading of processing trade based on the micro data of Chinese firms from 2000 to 2013 and by treating the promulgation of China's minimum wage regulation as a quasi - natural experiment. This leads to three main findings. First, although labor cost increases significantly reduce the scale of processing trade, they promote the transformation and upgrading of processing trade firms via a backpressure mechanism. Second, mechanism tests show that labor cost increases encourage processing firms to increase their fixed investments, increase on - the - job training and research and development expenditures, and improve production efficiency, which collectively promote the development of processing firms. Third, a study of the relationship between labor cost, resource allocation, and the upgrading of processing trade at the urban level reveals that improvements in the efficiency of export market - share allocation is a key channel via which labor cost increases stimulate increases in urban processing trade.

This study has important policy implications. For a long time, cheap labor costs have underpinned the rapid development of China's processing trade. However, China's processing trade is typically characterized by large quantity and low quality, and it often lacks its own brand and core technology. In addition, most companies involved in processing trade are original equipment manufacturers rather than finished item manufacturers, and export expansion is mainly supported by a large number of low value - added primary processing products. This paper finds that although labor cost increases do not contribute to the expansion of processing trade scale, the backward force mechanism significantly promotes the upgrading of firm processing trade and improves the efficiency of resource reallocation, which promotes the upgrading of urban processing trade. This shows that China may slightly increase the minimum wage standard and improve the wage security system to encourage processing trade firms to reduce or abandon their excessive dependence on low - cost labor strategies, and to strengthen research and development innovation and improve efficiency to avoid the low technology trap. These measures will promote the transformation and upgrading of processing trade firms and ultimately enhance their position in the global value chain and capture value - added export opportunities.

The main contributions of this paper are as follows. First, this paper may be the first to systematically and comprehensively examine the effect of the minimum wage system and labor cost increases on China's processing trade. The findings of this paper therefore enrich the literature on the economic effects of minimum wage law. Second, in the context of the open economy and the global value chain, this paper devises a comprehensive index and evaluation system for studying the transformation and upgrading of processing trade, and thoroughly probes the transmission mechanism underlying the transformation and upgrading of processing trade driven by labor - cost increases. Third, this paper investigates the micro - level effects of labor cost increases on the upgrading of firms' processing trade and the macro - level effects of these increases on the transformation and upgrading of urban processing trade. It thus enriches the literature on the reallocation of resources that occurs in response to increases in the minimum wage or labor costs.

Service Trade Liberalization, Marketization, and the Productivity of China's Manufacturing Firms

PENG Shuijun   SHU Zhongqiao

(School of Economics, Xiamen University)

The servitization of manufacturing has become a significant trend in the development of global manufacturing, and it is also an important part of the upgrading of China's manufacturing value chain. After the 2008 financial crisis, China's service imports grew rapidly, and net service imports have continued to expand. As the competitiveness of China's service industry is relatively low, it is critical to explore whether service trade openness promotes the development of the service industry, the production efficiency of Chinese manufacturing enterprises, and the upgrading of the value chain.

First, although China's economic growth has steadily progressed, most studies of the impact of service trade openness on manufacturing are based on data before 2007 and thus cannot address the current situation. Second, the definition of service sectors in the literature is relatively narrow. Third, few studies consider the regulatory role of marketization in the process of service trade openness.

Our main contributions are as follows. First, we build a theoretical framework and then empirically analyze the effects of service trade openness on the labor productivity of manufacturing enterprises under domestic product substitution. More importantly, we explore the regulatory effect of marketization on the openness of service trade. Second, we use the Chinese Industrial Enterprise Database for 2012 and the Service Trade Restriction Index (STRI) of the World Bank, which not only extends the research of Beverelli et al. (2017) to a firm-level study but also explains how the openness of service trade has both promoted the productivity of China's export-intensive manufacturing enterprises and inhibited the productivity of non-exporting enterprises. The productivity promotion effect of service trade openness on export enterprises is stronger in the non-eastern region, but the adverse impact of service trade openness on non-state-owned enterprises and non-export enterprises in the eastern region is even greater. Third, we discuss the regulatory effect of marketization on the openness up of China's service trade. The result shows that domestic marketization has a dual effect on the openness of service trade. Marketization has not only weakened the negative impact of the openness of service trade on non-export enterprises, but also strengthened the positive effect of service trade openness on export firms. Overall, our conclusions are different from those of other studies and provide meaningful policy insights for the establishment of China's dual-circulation development pattern: the international economic cycle should be kept open to promote development, and the domestic economic cycle should be used to expand domestic demand. Therefore, it is necessary to ensure that export firms benefit from trade liberalization, and also to prevent non-export firms from being exposed to excessive negative competition brought about by trade liberalization. Marketization has a vital role in both these functions. We also indirectly explain the improvements in the competitiveness of China's manufacturing products after its accession to the WTO, especially after the 2008 financial crisis. However, further research is needed to determine whether this improvement has been in quality or price.

We use firm-level theoretical and empirical analyses of Chinese data to explain the abnormal results in Beverelli et al. (2017). Unlike Zhang et al. (2013), Sun et al. (2018), Mao and Fang(2020), we use the STRI of the World Bank, which uses a broad definition of service sectors. Moreover, we consider more types of service trade approaches and more service trade sectors. As a result, the conclusions of this article are relatively novel. Although the empirical results show that the competitiveness of Chinese manufacturing products has improved to a certain extent, it is unclear whether this competitiveness comes from quality improvement, price advantage, or both. In addition, although the substitution effect of intermediate goods produced by manufacturing enterprises on imported intermediate goods cannot be observed directly, problems such as whether there is domestic service substitution for foreign services and how the liberalization of service trade affects the upgrading of China's service industry require further study.

Can Increasing the Export Tax Rebate Stabilize Employment and Foreign Trade?

WANG Junbin   LIU Hebei

(School of Public Finance and Taxation, Southwestern University of Finance and Economics; Maritime Silk Road and Guangxi Regional Development Institute, Guangxi University of Finance and Economics)

In recent years, trade protectionism has increased globally, exacerbating trade frictions between countries, such as those between China and the United States. To cope with these adverse effects, the Ministry of Finance and the State Taxation Administration of China have successively increased the export tax rebate for some products. Meanwhile, employment and foreign trade are major issues in China's economy. Therefore, exploring the effect of China's export tax rebate policy on employment and foreign trade is of great theoretical and practical significance. Taking Sino-US trade friction as an example, this paper examines the mechanism by which China's export tax rebate policy stabilizes employment and foreign trade and how it mitigates trade friction using dynamic stochastic general equilibrium (DSGE) model.

First, this paper studies the cyclical characteristics of China's employment and net exports. Quarterly data from 1994 to 2020 show that employment is relatively stable. However, net exports are highly volatile. China's employment and net exports have weak procyclical characteristics that are significantly different from other countries and the simulation results of other DSGE models in the literature. Second, to explain the cyclical characteristics of China's employment and net exports, this paper constructs a symmetrical two -

country open - economy DSGE model with an incomplete financial market and incomplete price pass - through. Using macro data from China and the United States to calibrate the model, the numerical simulation shows that the model better fits the cyclical characteristics of China's employment and net exports under the shock of domestic export tax rebates and other countries' technology shock. The wealth and expenditure transfer effects caused by the change in terms of trade are the main internal transmission mechanisms.

To clarify the mechanism of the export tax rebate effect, this paper uses Sino-US trade friction to conduct a counterfactual experiment to explore whether increasing the export tax rebate can stabilize employment and foreign trade. The simulation shows that when China unilaterally increases its export tax rebate by 1%, employment increases by 0.05%, and net exports increase by 0.28% and then decrease gradually, showing strong persistence. Increasing the export tax rebate can stabilize employment and foreign trade. A 1% increase in both China's export tax rebate and the United States' import tariff increases employment in China by 0.03% and net exports by 0.16%, and then employment and net exports decrease gradually and show strong persistence. Lerner neutrality is not established. Although the effect of the export tax rebate in stabilizing employment and foreign trade is currently weakened, it remains effective. Therefore, China's export tax rebate policy not only completely offsets the adverse impact of other countries' tariff increased on China's employment and net exports, but also produces a positive net effect. Although the net effect of increasing the export tax rebate is small, it indeed helps stabilize employment and foreign trade. Furthermore, the Bayesian estimation method proves that this conclusion is robust.

This paper makes two contributions to the literature. First, it expands the literature on the cyclical characteristics of China's employment and net exports. The two - country open - economy model in this paper not only explains these cyclical characteristics but also explores the internal mechanism of the effect of China's export tax rebate policy. Second, the two - country open - economy model can simulate and evaluate the effect of China's increasing export tax rebate on stabilizing employment and foreign trade in various circumstances.

07 Inclusive Finance & Social Development

The Win - Win Effect of Corporate Social Responsibility: Evidence from Targeted Poverty Alleviation Programs

PAN Jianping　　WENG Ruoyu　　PAN Yue

(School of Economics and Management, Southeast University;
Xiamen National Accounting Institute; School of Economics, Xiamen University)

Targeted poverty alleviation(hereafter: TPA) was proposed by Chinese central government in 2013. TPA requires firms to provide specific and effective assistance to poverty - stricken people throughout China. This assistance should seek to solve the problems that cause people to be trapped in poverty. Accordingly, a number of socially responsible firms have initiated TPA programs.

We summarize that there are three motivations for firms to perform corporate social responsibility (CSR) such as TPA. The first is altruistic motivation, which involves firms giving assistance to others in society without receiving a return. The second is managerial agency motivation, which involves managers using firms' resources to enhance their own social image. The third is strategic motivation, which involves firms performing CSR activities to acquire strategic resources, such as social reputation and political connections. Although there are many studies on CSR, most studies only consider philanthropic donations and do not consider non - cash assistance (e. g. , technical and educational assistance). Moreover, previous studies focus on whether and how much firms donate but do not examine whether donations achieve their desired effects. These studies conclude that the motivation of CSR is not altruistic and may be another form of managerial agency cost. We believe that this conclusion may misinterpret firms' motivation to perform CSR.

Thus, we explore firms' motivation to perform CSR by examining whether their motivations to engage in TPA and the effects of their doing so are different from those related to philanthropic donations. Our sample includes all of the non - financial A - share firms listed on the Shanghai Stock Exchange and Shenzhen Stock Exchange. We manually collect firms' implementations of TPA from annual reports and CSR reports. We find that engaging in TPA reduces firms' financial constraints and thus increases firms' performance and shareholder wealth. Furthermore, we find that TPA spurs local economic growth and enhances residents' income within targeted regions. Furthermore, TPA does not cause significant damage to the regional environment. We also find that firms do not participate in TPA to conceal misconduct or to divert investors' attention from stagnant stock prices, which allows us to exclude managerial agency as a motivation. Overall, our findings suggest that firms' participation in TPA is driven by altruistic and strategic motivations and ultimately creates a win - win situation for firms, society, and the environment.

Our findings provide important information for policymakers who devise methods to reduce poverty. Specifically, our findings suggest that the governments should encourage firms to deeply embed themselves in poor regions of the world, as by doing so, firms can use technology and talent to increase the efficiency of poverty alleviation. In addition, subsequent to the implementation of rural revitalization strategies in China, firms should establish long - term mechanisms to systematically achieve rural revitalization. For example, by allocating more advanced technology and talent to rural areas, firms could integrate themselves with local economies and thus obtain returns from resource complementarity.

Our study makes several contributions to the literature.

First, we clarify what motivates firms to perform CSR in terms of why they engage in TPA. Studies conclude that firms' motivations to perform CSR are not altruistic and may be used as a tool to achieve managerial goals. However, we evaluate the effects of CSR and find that firms' engagement in TPA is motivated by altruism, suggesting that firms genuinely wish to improve social welfare, rather than to simply pursue managerial self - interest. Our study thus provides a new theoretical perspective that gives a better understanding of what motivates firms to engage in CSR.

Second, our study clarifies whether engaging in CSR produces unilateral benefits or creates a win - win situation. Many papers find that CSR produces benefits for only one party. For example, Chen et al. (2018) find that engaging in CSR reduces a firm's profitability and shareholder wealth. Lu et al. (2020) find that these reductions in profitability and shareholder wealth occur in state - owned enterprises (SOEs) and in non - SOEs; thus, CSR improves social welfare at the expense of shareholder wealth. In contrast, we find that engaging in TPA increases shareholder wealth and promotes local economic growth without damaging the local environment; thus, engaging in TPA can create a win - win situation. This is a new perspective that broadens understanding of the effect of CSR on firms' profitabilities and social welfare.

" Living in the Moment" or " Saving for the Futuren? Long - Term Effects of Earthquake Experiences on Chinese Urban Household Savings Rates and Consumption Habits

ZHANG Yuan   LIU Qiannan

(China Center for Economic Studies, Fudan University)

Economic theory demonstrates that a household increases its precautionary savings rate over time to cope with natural disasters and smooth consumption. However natural disasters such as earthquakes, floods, droughts, hurricanes, and insect plagues have different effects on households, and thus the empirical testing of combinations of different kinds of natural disasters will generate biased estimates.

Approximately 2.7 billion people worldwide live in areas that are considered seismic zones, but the economic literature inadequately depicts their consumption and saving patterns. This paper holds that earthquakes, unlike other natural disasters, threaten the lives of people who dwell in seismic zones, and thus trigger fear and anxiety in these people. Consequently, those who live in seismic zones may have different consumption and savings habits than those who live in non - seismic zones. This paper hypothesizes that the long - term effect of earthquakes results in residents living in a seismic zone exhibiting a "living in the moment" attitude, which affects their consumption and saving habits. Specifically, although the experience of earthquakes has no significant long - term effects on levels of household income, the earthquake - associated risk of death and psychological shock has significantly positive effects on hedonic consumption, which reduces rates of household saving.

This paper uses nationally representative household survey data from the National Bureau of Statistics of China that covers 18 provinces from 2002 to 2009 and conducts empirical tests to obtain the following conclusions. First, each experience of an earthquake ($M_L \geq 4.5$) reduces the rate of household savings by 0.2 percent point. Second, the frequency of earthquakes experienced by household heads does not have significant long - term effects on levels of household disposable income, but does have significant positive effects on levels of household consumption. Third, an increase in the frequency of earthquakes experienced by household heads leads to an increase in household hedonic consumption (such as the consumption of cultural entertainment, non - essential health care, cosmetology, and luxury goods), but has no effect on non - hedonic consumption. Fourth, several robustness checks are carried out (e. g., controlling for the frequency of earthquakes when household heads were 7 years old and controlling for the experience of earthquakes with an $M_L > 6$) on subsamples that did not migrate from a seismic zone, and the above conclusions remain valid. Fifth, empirical evidence from migrant workers suggests that the endogeneity problem in the empirical models does not affect the conclusions.

This paper contributes to academic research and policymaking in China. In terms of academic research, this paper's first contribution is to the literature on the effect of earthquakes on household consumption and saving patterns, as it provides empirical evidence from urban China. It also provides evidence from economic research to the psychology literature, revealing the effect of the risk of earthquake - associated death on individual consumption behaviors; this has implications for the optimal location of companies that provide hedonic products or services. Second, this paper helps to explain the savings rates in China from the perspective of consumption behavior shaped by earthquakes.

In terms of policymaking, this paper's first contribution is to highlight a way to promote domestic consumption. China has a very high household savings rate compared with other developing and developed economies, and the Chinese government consistently endeavors to promote domestic consumption to boost economic growth. In recent years, the Chinese government has emphasized the need for reform on the demand side and on the supply side to better match both sides and thus improve economic growth. China has a huge domestic market, which serves as a substitute foreign market, and this suggests that improving domestic demand rather than export demand will be fruitful, especially as the China-US trade relationship is not healthy. Thus, this paper indicates that policies aimed at promoting domestic consumption should focus on reshaping consumption habits, i. e. , encouraging spending on cultural entertainment, non - essential health care, and other hedonic consumption. Second, the coronavirus disease 2019 (COVID - 19) pandemic is also a natural disaster, and it warrants more academic research. The conclusions from this paper suggest ways to determine the effects of the COVID - 19 pandemic on household consumption and savings rates. The findings of this paper also suggest that new COVID - 19 - associated habits, such as mask - wearing and the frequent use of hand disinfectants, will have long - term effects on consumption habits and household savings rates.

Financial Literacy and the Household Savings Rate: The Role of Financial Planning and Borrowing Constraints

WU Weixing   ZHANG Xuyang   WU Kun

(Research Center for Applied Finance in School of Banking and Finance, University of International Business and Economics; School of Economics, Beijing Technology and Business University; School of Economics, Beijing Wuzi University)

Savings and consumption are critical topics in household financial decision-making research. A suitable and reasonable balance of savings and consumption in a person's life, known as consumption smoothing, can enhance a person's utilities and happiness. Rapid developments in financial technology have decreased the costs of individual participation in financial markets, and thus increased the heterogeneity of participants. Financial literacy plays an increasingly important role in financial decision-making, as financial products are constantly being enriched.

There is no consensus on the impact of financial literacy on household savings rates. Lusardi (2008) and Jappelli and Padula (2013) argue that improvements in financial literacy may encourage families to engage in financial planning, avoid excessive consumption, and increase savings. In contrast, Jappelli and Padula (2017) and Song et al. (2019) argue that financial literacy promotes consumption. These contradictory results occur due to the researchers' focus on different aspects and characteristics of financial literacy, which play different roles in household savings.

We use data from the China Consumer Finance Status and Investor

Education Survey conducted by the China Financial Research Center of Tsinghua University in 2010 and 2011 to examine the relationship between financial literacy and the household savings rate. We use instrumental variables to mitigate endogeneity concerns and explore the mechanism that links financial literacy to household savings, especially the role of financial planning and borrowing constraints.

We find that financial literacy plays a significant role in household decisions about savings and consumption, and that the relationship between financial literacy and the household savings rate has an inverted U - shape. Financial literacy is positively correlated with financial planning, but negatively correlated with borrowing constraints. When financial sophistication improves, households that engage in financial planning try to make sure the accessible of affluent asset. When financial literacy surpasses a certain threshold, the role of financial planning in restraining consumption is weakened and its role in asset allocation is enhanced. Higher financing capacity helps households reduce future risks, thus the savings rate gradually declines. We further reveal that the inverted U - shaped relationship between financial literacy and savings rates does not mean that households with high levels of financial literacy are more likely to have insufficient savings or engage in excessive consumption. We demonstrate that families with higher financial literacy are more likely to maintain stable savings, and have a low probability of living hand - to - mouth. When the family's financial literacy improves , the increase in financial planning is less likely to have the effect of reducing consumption and is more likely to increase the optimal allocation of assets. That is, the focus of such families' financial planning shifts from increasing the savings rate to the preservation and appreciation of savings.

We make two main contributions. First, we clarify the relationship between financial literacy and the household savings rate and identify the mechanism that links them. Rising levels of financial literacy not only enhance financial planning but also reduce borrowing constraints. The influence of these two factors on the household savings rate varies with the level of financial literacy, which explains the inverted U - shaped relationship between financial literacy and the household savings rate. Second, we identify the causes of different household savings rates. Households with low savings rate can be divided into two types. The first type consists of families with low levels of financial literacy. Such families lack financial awareness and have higher borrowing constraints, making it difficult for them to accumulate savings. The second type consists of households with higher levels of financial literacy. High - level households have more stable savings, better liquidity, and more diversified asset allocation. Accordingly, low savings rate in the first type of families require close attention. Distinguishing the causes of differences in the household savings rate is of great significance for improving residents' welfare and enhancing the pertinence of financial education policies.

The Influence of the Peer Effect on Participation in China's New Rural Pension Scheme

ZHANG Chuanchuan   ZHU Hanyu

(School of Economics, Zhejiang University; National School of Development, Peking University)

China has developed one of the largest social security systems in the world. However, the proportion of the eligible population that participate in voluntary social programs is far below 100%, which limits the cost - sharing and welfare - protection functions of these programs.

Low rates of participation in voluntary social programs are not a China - specific phenomenon, as they are seen in many other countries (Currie, 2006; Matsaganis et al., 2008). Based on a thorough literature review, Currie (2006) concludes that information friction, stigma costs and transaction costs are the key factors that determine individuals' participation in such programs. However, as acknowledged by Currie (2006), rates of participation in these programs are usually well below 50%, and thus are not wholly attributable to these three factors. Alsan and Yang (2018) and Zhang (2019) show that migration policy and cultural norms, respectively, also affect participation in voluntary social programs. However, these factors only explain the low participation in voluntary social programs with specific policy or cultural backgrounds and are not a general explanation for the low participation in such programs worldwide.

Thus, this paper investigates the role of the peer effect on participation in voluntary social programs, as the peer effect plays an important role in individual decision - making and is an important factor in the uptake of social health insurance (Duflo and Saez, 2002; Liu et al., 2014). We use data from China Family Panel Studies to estimate whether the participation rate of people's neighbors (within the same village) affects people's participation decisions by examining participation in China's New Rural Pension Scheme (NRPS). Our conventional ordinary least squares (OLS) estimate shows that a 1% increase in people's neighbors' participation in the NRPS increases the likelihood of people's own participation by 0.76%, which is significant. We follow Case and Katz (1991) and Duflo and Saez (2002) by using an instrumental variable (IV) approach to detect causal inference. Specifically, we instrument neighbors' participation rates using their average age, which is known to be an important predictor of uptake of social pensions. That is, people's neighbors' age, as demonstrated by Duflo and Saez (2002), can be treated as exogenous when controlling for people's own age. The IV estimate is consistent with the conventional OLS estimate, as it shows that a 1% increase in people's neighbors' participation in the NRPS increases the likelihood of people's own participation by 0.42%, which is significant.

We then explore two mechanisms that may underlie this peer effect: an information transmission - based mechanism and a social norm - based mechanism. To determine if an information transmission - based mechanism exists, we test whether the peer effect decreases as the duration of the NRPS increases. Our OLS and IV estimation results suggest that such a decrease occurs, which supports the existence of an information transmission - based mechanism. We also find that the peer effect is larger if people primarily obtain information from their neighbors, rather than from media such as television and the internet. To determine whether a social norm - based mechanism exists, we measure local clan culture using common surnames and test whether the peer effect is larger in villages containing clans than in villages that do not contain clans. We find that a larger peer effect exists in villages with a stronger clan culture, and as clans are groups with strong cohesion and unified norms, these results support the existence of a social norm - based mechanism.

We also explore whether heterogeneous effects exist by separating the sample according to sex and educational attainment. We find that men have larger effects on their peers than women and therefore probably lead participation in voluntary social programs.

In summary, our findings suggest that the peer effect has a strong influence on people's participation in voluntary social programs, and that the peer effect is driven by information transmission - and social norm - based mechanisms. In addition, we find that the peer effect is asymmetrical: some groups have larger effects on other people's participation decisions than other groups. Our study contributes to the growing literature on the role of the peer effect in individual decision - making, and to the literature on the determinants of participation in voluntary social programs.

The policy implications of our findings are clear. First, enforcing policy advocacy and increasing policy publicity can effectively promote voluntary participation in social programs. Second, using policy interventions to increase the rate of participation of leaders in voluntary social programs effectively increases the overall rate of participation in such programs.

The Determinants of School District Housing Price Premiums from the Perspective of School Quality

ZHANG Xun   KOU Jinghan   ZHANG Xin   LYU Guangming

(School of Statistics, Beijing Normal University; Department of Economics, Fordham University)

Many studies confirm that high-quality educational resources have a capitalization effect that results in price premiums for housing in school districts. High-quality educational resources, as measured by physical capital investment in schools and human capital investment in teachers, may be determined by the quality of a district's school education or the quality of its students (the peer effect). Few studies consider the mechanisms contributing to the formation of high-quality educational resources, especially the extent to which school quality determines the quality of educational resources. However, these mechanisms can be examined by using pricing information from the real estate market.

Using records of second-hand housing transactions in Beijing and unique data regarding education quality at the school level, we are among the first to quantify the power of education quality in explaining school district housing premiums, and thus estimate the economic value of education quality. China's unique institutional background makes it possible to quantify the effect of school quality on school district housing premiums. Unlike most European and American countries, where education funding comes from property taxes, China's education investment depends mainly on general fiscal expenditures by local governments. Hence, in China, the causal influence of education quality on housing prices can be identified by relating school district housing price premiums to education quality data at the school level. This allows us to quantify the relationship between education quality and school district housing premiums and thus explore the mechanisms contributing to the formation of high-quality educational resources.

We use the hedonic model with boundary fixed effects. Specifically, we identify the housing transaction records on both sides of each elite school's attendance zone boundary to control for unobserved factors. We then use this information to calculate each school district's housing price premium. We further match the school education quality data with the second-hand housing transaction records to quantify the role of education quality in the calculated school district housing premiums.

Our results show that education quality, measured by the physical capital investment in schools and the human capital investment in teachers, explains 64.71% of the overall price premium on school district housing. Our results are robust to various confounding factors, including the potential effects of newly built primary schools, education reforms, and access to private schools. Furthermore, we quantify the power of education quality in explaining housing price premiums in three high-quality educational districts in Beijing (Xicheng District, Dongcheng District, and Haidian District). We find that high-quality educational resources come either from concentration of high-quality students within a district or from improvements in school quality due to long-term accumulation of education spending.

From a Chinese policy perspective, the education equalization reforms implemented in recent years promote high-quality equity in compulsory education, which will help curb inflation of school district housing prices and moderate price fluctuations in the real estate market. Our findings indicate that the main sources of school district housing price premiums are physical capital investment and the quality of human capital at the school level, and that recent education reforms can help stabilize housing prices. Therefore, the recent equalization reforms to compulsory education will significantly improve overall school quality by increasing both physical capital investment and human capital investment in weak schools. Furthermore, given the importance of student quality (the peer effect), increasing intergenerational mobility and continuing to advance equalization of opportunities may also be important ways to stabilize school district housing prices.

We contribute to the literature in three ways. First, we add to the literature by discussing the relationships between education quality and school district housing price premiums using a unique dataset that measures education quality at the school level. By matching the education quality data with housing transaction records in the real estate market, we quantify the power of education quality to explain school district housing premiums and explore the mechanisms that contribute to the formation of high - quality education resources. Second, in the context of China, we identify the causal relationship between school quality and housing premiums based on a hedonic model with boundary fixed effects. Third, We take advantage of various stock indicators to measure education quality, including fixed asset value, school building area, the teacher-student ratio, and average teacher salary. Based on the heterogeneous effects identified among three high - quality educational districts in Beijing, we also examine how policy can influence high housing prices in school districts.

Risk Diversification and the Reform of China's Mixed Basic Pension System

PENG Haoran   CHENG Chunli

(Lingnan College, Sun Yat - sen University)

China reformed its basic pension insurance system in the 1990s from a pure "pay - as - you - go" plan to a mixed system consisting of two accounts: a social pooling account operating as a pay - as - you - go plan and a personal account operating as a funded pension plan. The original intention of this reform was to achieve both fairness and efficiency in the provision of basic pensions in China. However, due to a failure to deal with the transition costs, the social pooling account accumulated large deficits. To guarantee pension payments, local governments misappropriated funds in the personal accounts, creating a large number of "empty" personal accounts. As the scale of the empty personal accounts grows, the design of the mixed basic pension system is starting to be questioned. Some scholars propose abolishing personal accounts and going back to the pure pay - as - you - go plan. Until now, the problem of empty personal pension accounts in China remains unresolved. To address this issue, we try to answer two important questions. First, what is the theoretical foundation for China's mixed basic pension insurance system? Second, what is the optimal mix of the social pooling and personal accounts in one pension system?

In the face of the population aging, many countries are considering reforms of their basic pension insurance systems. In the pension insurance literature, there are growing concerns regarding the sustainability of pay - as - you - go systems and their negative macro - economic impacts. There are also increasing worries regarding the high investment risk and redistribution restriction of funded pension systems. The two pension systems carry different risks, so there is no one clearly dominating the other. The internal return rate of the pay-as-you-go system depends on the growth rate of a country's total social wages, which depend on the quantity of labor supply and labor productivity. Although in some developed countries, the investment return rate of the funded system can be substantially higher than the internal return rate of the pay-as-you-go system, it does not necessarily indicate that the funded system is the optimal one for those countries. Doing so may overlook many other risk factors and the transition costs of pension system reform.

Since a pay-as-you-go pension can be regarded as a quasi-asset, some researchers have been working on designing public pension insurance systems from the perspective of risk diversification in pension investments. In this paper, we adopt the same perspective and construct a two-period consumption utility maximization model to study the optimal split of a representative employee's pension contribution between a social pooling account and a personal pension account in the Chinese mixed pension system. When making his or her pension investment decision, the representative employee faces three types of risks related to: the total labor supply, the wage growth rate, and the pension funds' investment return rate. Based on our theoretical results, we numerically estimate the optimal ratio of the two plans in China by collecting data on the growth rate of China's basic pension insurance contribution per capita, the trend of the working-age population, and the investment return rate of the National Social Security Funds. We then perform sensitivity analysis on our results. Finally, using our optimal design for the mixed pension system, we calculate the pension contribution required to achieve a goal set by the Chinese government for the pension replacement rate.

Acknowledging the significant differences in the demographic, labor productivity, and capital market in different countries, governments of all countries should carefully design their basic pension insurance system according to their specific environment and their ability to deal with risks. The optimal mix of the social pooling account and the personal account in China is determined by its own characteristics of the internal return rate of the pay - as - you - go plan and the investment return rate of the funded account. At the current stage, we find that the pay - as - you - go plan should play the dominant role in China's basic pension insurance system, but inclusion of a small - scale personal account can diversify the risks that the population aging brings to the pay - as - you - go plan. Given China's goal of achieving a pension replacement rate of between 40% to 45%, keeping its basic pension system financially sustainable will be challenging. We suggest that the Chinese government pay more attention to the long - term investment of its pension funds and adopt various family supporting policies to establish a child - friendly society and thereby increase the population's fertility rate. Furthermore, the Chinese government could consider some specific parametric adjustments to the pension insurance system, such as extending the retirement age, to better align the assets and liabilities in the pension insurance balance sheet.

Urban Service Diversity and Labor Mobility: An Analysis Based on Big Data of Meituan and a Micro Survey of a Floating Population

ZHANG Wenwu　YU Yongze

(School of International Economics and Trade, Nanjing University of Finance and Economics)

China's economy is entering a new stage of high - quality development, and with the decline of the global demographic dividend and the concurrent release of the regional demographic dividend, the competition between cities for talent and labor forces has gradually become a key focus of the new era. Thus, the study of labor force allocation now focuses on what features are used by cities to attract and retain talent. In China's new urbanization process, people - oriented features are becoming an important part of urban talent attraction and management policies, and urban features that meet consumers' various preferences and personalized needs are gradually becoming an important driver of labor mobility. The production capacity, types, and supply modes of urban services are crucial supports of urban convenience and comfort and provide many ways to improve the welfare of local workers. The increasing demand of cities for labor and the fierce competition between cities to attract talent leads to the following key questions. What role does the diversification and convenience of urban service supply play in labor migration? What kind of talents are attracted and retained by urban service diversity? The answers to these questions will have extensive practical significance and implications.

To this end, this study analyzes the effect of urban service diversity on labor mobility from the perspective of comfort and convenience. Thus, an analysis is performed on the data of Meituan, a food-delivery company, and the data from a dynamic monitoring survey of China's floating population in 2017. To deal with the endogeneity problem, the geographical distance between a city and its provincial capital is used as the instrumental variable, and the results confirm that urban service diversity has a significant effect on labor flows. Specifically, a 1% increase in the urban service diversity of a city leads to a 3.23% reduction in the probability that floating population-associated labor will leave that city. That is, if the endogenous problems caused by individual and urban characteristics and missing variables are controlled, a higher diversity of urban services decreases the probability of labor force selection and mobility.

The results of grouping regression based on age nodes and skill levels also reveal that various labor groups have different sensitivities to urban service diversity. For example, the younger population is less likely than the elderly to leave cities with a higher diversity of urban services. In addition, initial analyses show that the mobility and migration probability of the young and middle-aged labor forces decreases by 4.62% for every 1% increase in the urban service category. Furthermore, although the comfort welfare afforded by urban services is important for highly skilled workers and low-skilled workers, highly skilled workers have a greater sensitivity to such comfort welfare.

We also analyze the effect of adjustments in urban and regional environments, and find that the construction of urban informatization technology and the level of marketization have a positive effect on the attraction and retention of talent via their effects on urban service diversity. That is, the construction of information technology (such as urban mobile Internet services) and increased market sophistication attracts labor to live in a city to take advantage of modern products and services, and it therefore reduces the probability of labor mobility or migration. In addition, the results show that labor flow in the central and western regions is less affected by the diversity of urban services than labor flow in the eastern regions. Specifically, the coefficient of the cross terms of age and skill level reveal that labor forces with strong ability or younger age currently prefer to stay in eastern cities. Furthermore, we find that labor flows in big cities are more sensitive to the diversity of urban services than labor flows in small and medium - sized cities, which shows that the comfort welfare represented by the diversity of urban services is an important channel by which large cities draw a population dividend from small and medium - sized cities.

The results of this study have novel implications for the development of policies designed to attract and retain labor force talents, which are part of the urban competition for talent in China. In particular, as the urban economy of China is entering a new stage of high - quality development, the spatial reallocation of labor involves quantitative change in terms of scales of flow and cross - regional migration, as well as qualitative change in terms of the direction of labor structure optimization and efficiency improvements. Moreover, the advantages enjoyed by cities that stem from their ability to attract and retain a high - quality labor force depend on their offering workers a "livelihood channel" of employment and a channel of improved general comfort and welfare. Urban managers and policy designers should therefore make plans based on this reality to cultivate and develop market patterns that are more in line with individual's welfare preferences and thereby to gradually improve the quality of urban labor forces by increasing the diversity of urban service supply systems.

Factors Affecting Online Celebrities' Tips

LIAO Li   WANG Xincheng   WANG Zhengwei   ZHANG Jinyan

(PBC School of Finance, Tsinghua University; Business School, University of Hong Kong)

Rapid economic growth has led to an increase in residents' wealth, and how people dispose of their wealth has become an increasingly important research topic. In recent years, the online celebrity economy has developed rapidly, and tipping live stream performers, a new wealth disposal method, has attracted attention. What motivates audiences to tip online celebrities? What are the rules of audience tipping behavior? This research is quite important, because a better understanding of tipping behavior is necessary to guide the healthy development of this industry. On the one hand, tipping plays an important role in the online celebrity economy, so exploring the influencing factors behind tipping is conducive to the sustainable development of the online celebrity economy. On the other hand, the online celebrity economy also appears some chaos, so the study of tipping behavior can provide theoretical support for the formulation of regulatory rules. However, a lack of data has limited research on this topic.

This study uses a unique dataset from five multiple - channel network (MCN) agencies to examine this issue. The dataset from these five MCN agencies consists of panel data from 2019 on the income and duration of each live stream of 41 online celebrities who play the same game. Two main findings are made. First, the entertainment accompany of online celebrities increases both the speed of accrual and the amount of the celebrities' income. In other words, longer live streams generate higher incomes. The intensity of tipping also increases with the length of the live stream. Thus, the entertainment accompany of online celebrities satisfies the spiritual needs of the audience, making the audience more likely to tip. In the analysis, the influence of the "star - making" activities of MCN agencies is eliminated by deleting the most popular online celebrities to test the robustness of the conclusion. Second, there is a significant positive correlation between head - tippers and non - head - tippers. That is, there is a herding effect in audiences' tipping behavior. To eliminate the concern of a false regression, the live experience of online celebrities is used as a heterogeneity test.

The findings partially explain the rapid development of the online celebrity industry; the interactions between celebrities and audiences and between audience members jointly promote the rapid growth of the online celebrity economy. As companionship encourages audience members to tip, celebrities can increase their income by increasing the duration of their live streams. Furthermore, the tipping of head tippers influences that of non - head tippers and vice versa, allowing the celebrities' income to continue to grow. Therefore, the online celebrity economy demonstrates characteristics of the " Matthew Effect".

This study makes several contributions to the literature. First, it adopts a micro - research perspective on the factors that influence online tipping, which will contribute to future research on the online celebrity economy. Second, this study is one of the first to use the income data of online celebrities. The unique and rigorous dataset obtained from MCN agencies is not only the basis for credible conclusions, but it also provides a basic framework for future research on the online celebrity economy. Third, it separately examines the tipping behavior of head tippers and non - head tippers, verifying the existence of the herding effect. Finally, this study provides new empirical evidence for the Matthew Effect.

Due to the limited number and dimensions of cooperation samples, a detailed exploration of the online celebrity economy is not provided in this study, leaving some problems for future research. For example, the dataset does not include information on each audience member's tipping behavior, making it impossible to analyze audience members' motivations in detail. Furthermore, there are many types of online celebrities and this study does not consider the factors that affect the income of online celebrities in other fields. Finally, different platforms may have different share ratios and platform rules, creating strong heterogeneity in the relationships between viewers and streamers on different platforms. Although it does not address the above issues, this study begins the development of principles for understanding the new economic model represented by the online celebrity economy and provides a reference for institutions seeking to guide and regulate such economic activities, ensuring their healthy development.

08 Corporate Governance & Corporate Finance

Board Faultlines and the Firm Pay Gap

XU Canyu   LI Xuanbo   LIANG Shangkun

(School of Business, East China University of Science and Technology;

School of Accountancy, Singapore Management University;

School of Accountancy, Central University of Finance and Economics)

The pay gap between corporate executives and ordinary employees is related to both the company's performance and the fairness and stability of social distribution. Government departments have promulgated a series of policies and regulations to limit the pay gap. However, these salary - limiting policies have mainly been imposed by external regulatory forces, and their implementation has not been uniform; in addition, these policies have had a limited effect on non - state - owned enterprises. In this context, the internal governance perspective suggests that it is necessary to study the issue of executive salaries from the ground up, which is also instructive for understanding the pay gap in different companies.

The board of directors is the core of a company's internal governance. Exploring the factors influencing the board's supervisory function will clarify the causes and consequences of the pay gap. Unlike the literature focusing on individual characteristics, our study is based on faultline theory. With the extension of the company's operating time, the board of directors may form different small groups. Small groups have different profit - seeking motives, and differ in management concepts, methods, and awareness, which makes it difficult for the board of directors to perform its supervisory function effectively. The phenomenon of multiple small groups within the board of directors is called "board faultlines". Such faultlines are common and have a serious impact on its functioning. Accordingly, we explore whether the existence of small groups within the board of directors affects its supervisory function and the firm pay gap.

Based on data from a sample of Chinese A - share listed companies from 2005 to 2019, we examine how board faultlines affect the firm pay gap. Our findings suggest that (i) board faultlines significantly promote the pay gap; (ii) board faultlines based on deep - level attributes have stronger and more persistent effects on the pay gap; (iii) a high degree of industry competition alleviates this positive relationship; (iv) the impact of board faultlines on the pay gap leads to lower firm performance.

Our study makes three contributions to the literature.

First, we enrich research on pay gap governance from the perspective of board faultlines. We find that the harm to the board's supervisory function caused by board faultlines is a source of executive power. Therefore, attempts to address the pay gap should examine the formation of board faultlines. Our study thus provides a new direction for pay gap governance research and practice.

Second, we contribute to research on the measurement and economic consequences of board faultlines. We consider eight director characteristics and optimize the measure, overcoming the limitation of the number of subgroups and making the measure more accurate. In terms of economic consequences, studies typically focus on corporate performance, value, and cross - border mergers and acquisitions. Our study discusses the impact of board faultlines on the board's supervision and the firm pay gap, which constitutes a useful supplement to the literature.

Third, our findings have practical significance for improving the company's salary incentive mechanism and board supervision. We find that the pay gap does not have an incentive effect, and even has a negative impact on corporate performance. Therefore, the company should pay attention to the reasonable combination of director characteristics when choosing directors. It is important to prevent the formation of faultlines while achieving diversification of the board of directors, to emphasize the board's overall goal, and to alleviate the harm of identity with a subgroup. These measures will improve board supervision and compensation incentives.

Unemployment Insurance and Financial Leverage of Firms

PENG Zhang   SHI Xinzheng   LU Yao   WANG Hao

(School of Public Finance and Taxation, Central University of Finance and Economics; School of Economics and Management, Tsinghua University; Bain & Company)

The increasingly marketized labor market in China leads to more frequent job-hopping, imposing higher unemployment risk on employees. This trend makes unemployment insurance more and more important. Unemployment insurance is a crucial labor protection policy. It provides unemployed people with the means to meet their basic needs and keeps society fair and stable. Although unemployment insurance is a positive benefit for individual employees and society, how it affects employers is still unclear. We investigate the impact of unemployment insurance on firms' financial leverage.

Recent studies show that labor and leverage are closely related, but most of these studies focus on U.S. firms. The labor market in the U.S. is quite different from that in China. How labor factors affect firms' leverage in China is still unclear. In theory, unemployment insurance can have both positive and negative impacts on leverage. First, increases in unemployment insurance may lead to lower leverage. As higher unemployment insurance can compensate employees when they lose their jobs, the employees are less sensitive to unemployment risk, thus they require less risk premium and firms' labor costs are reduced. When firms have more free cash flows and revenue, they may use internal funding to replace debt financing and even repay debt, which leads to lower levels of leverage. We call this channel the "labor cost channel". Second, higher unemployment insurance lead to fewer labor costs. Most labor costs are fixed costs, so lower labor costs result in lower operating leverage. The managers can choose higher financial leverage when the operating leverage decreases, thus leading to a positive relationship between unemployment insurance and financial leverage. We call this channel the "operating leverage channel". Third, Agrawal and Matsa (2013) find that firms' conservative financial policies can partially eliminate employees' unemployment risk. When unemployment insurance increase, employees are more tolerant of unemployment risk, so firms can take higher leverage. We call this channel the "bargaining channel".

Using Chinese public firms' data from 2009 to 2019, we find that a 1% increase in unemployment insurance, on average, leads to a 0.021~0.38 percent point decrease in firms' financial leverage. Then, we test the labor cost channel. We find that unemployment insurance are negatively related to employees' wages, especially non - executive employees' wages. Lower employees' wages are associated with lower leverage, less debt financing, more internal financing, and a higher probability of repaying debt. These results are consistent with the labor cost channel. Further tests show that this effect is more pronounced in provinces with high unemployment rates because the employees in these areas are under larger unemployment risk; this effect is also more pronounced in SOEs because the overindebtedness problem is severe in SOEs. We also find that unemployment insurance have a significant negative impact on firms' long - term debt ratio but no impact on their short - term debt ratio.

We conduct several robustness checks. First, to address the potential endogeneity problem, we respectively use the Social Insurance Law enacted in 2011 and the Guidance on Adjusting Unemployment Insurance Standard enacted in 2017 as natural experiments and conduct both difference - in - differences estimations and instrumental variable regressions. All of the results are consistent with the main result. Second, we address the multicollinearity problem caused by the high correlation between unemploymentand minimum wages. Third, we try alternative specifications, address the potential impact of investment, and use alternative sample periods. The main result holds for all of these robustness tests.

We make the following contributions to the literature. First, we contribute to the understanding of Chinese labor and finance. The labor and finance literature has recently attracted scholarly attention, but few studies use Chinese data. We fill this gap. Second, we contribute to the research on Chinese unemployment insurance policies. Most current papers on unemployment insurance policies are from the perspectives of individuals, industries, or regions. In contrast, we investigate unemployment insurance from the firm's perspective. Third, our findings add to the literature on capital structure.

This paper has implications for policy makers. Our results suggest that higher unemployment insurancecan lower firms' leverage, indicating that more supportive unemployment insurance policies not only benefit employees but also firms and society.

Job Satisfaction and Firm Innovation: Evidence from " China's Best Employer Award 100" Winners

XU Hongmei   NI Xiaoran   LIU Yanan

(International Business College, South China Normal University;

School of Economics, Xiamen University)

This paper examines the relationship between employee job satisfaction and firm innovation. Theoretically, this relationship is ambiguous. On the one hand, according to stakeholder theory, improved job satisfaction can provide additional compensation and incentives to employees, enhancing their engagement in long - term business activities and reducing their expectation of immediate rewards from short - term activities. Given the high - risk, long - term nature of innovation projects, these effects would be beneficial to firms' innovation and long - term growth. On the other hand, improved job satisfaction may also have a negative impact on firm innovation. Due to agency problems, managers may try to increase employees' job satisfaction by promising high salaries and benefits in exchange for favors. If the increase in job satisfaction reflects the presence of these effects, it should be detrimental to firm innovation. Moreover, programs designed to improve job satisfaction have high costs, which can be deleterious to firm performance if firms consequently invest less in innovative projects. We conduct empirical analyses in this paper to explore tie ambiguous relationship between employees' job satisfaction and corporate innovation.

We measure job satisfaction using the "China's 100 Best Employers Award" list. Our full sample consists of 16 876 firm - year observations for firms listed on the Shanghai and Shenzhen stock exchanges between 2011 and 2017. Our baseline results show that the "Top 100" best employers apply for more patents than other listed companies. To eliminate self-selection bias, we use the propensity score matching strategy (PSM) to find a group of non-"Top 100" firms with characteristics similar to the "Top 100" firms. We find that in the PSM sample, the "Top 100" firms apply for about 47% more patents than the matched firms. In addition, we find that job satisfaction mainly improves "Top 100" firms' innovative patents and patents for utility models. Further tests show that job satisfaction mainly improves firm innovation by increasing firms' tolerance of failure. Last, we provide evidence that job satisfaction has a significantly positive effect on firms' innovation efficiency and total factor productivity.

Our paper contributes to several stands of the literature.

First, we contribute to research on the labor force and innovation. Most studies explore the impact of employees' stock ownership, the employee-manager pay gap, and employees' income tax on corporate innovation. In this paper, we examine how employees' job satisfaction affects firm innovation by using inclusion in the " China's 100 Best Employers" list as a measurement of job satisfaction.

Second, most studies mainly discuss the impact of labor protection on firm behavior from the perspective of stakeholder protection. Although policy changes can enhance labor protection through legislation, firms' willingness to treat employees well may not increase simultaneously. Consequently, employees' job satisfaction may not change significantly. Unlike studies that focus on the effects of labor protection, we examine how employees' perceptions of firms' incentive system, culture, training, and organization affect their human capital investment in innovation activities.

Third, our study has policy implications. At present, people tends to pursue better quality of life and greater job satisfaction. Therefore, the previous high-speed economic growth pattern based on sacrificing employees' welfare may no longer be sustainable. Our study provides empirical evidence for this view. These results indicate that modern enterprises should not only rely on employees' hard work but also pay attention to their multifaceted aspirations and job satisfaction. In this way, firms can better use their human resource potential and improve innovation.

The Effect of Managerial Ability on Capital Market Stability

ZHANG Lu   LI Jincai   YUAN Zhenchao   YUE Heng

(College of Economics and Management, China Agricultural University; Beijing Capital Airport Food Management Co. , Ltd.; College of Economics, Shenzhen University; School of Accountancy, Singapore Management University)

After nearly 30 years of development, China's A - share market has gradually become the second largest capital market in the world. However, the capital market is not stable. The sharp decline in stock price can lead to a major loss of investors' wealth and is not conducive to the healthy and stable development of capital markets. Therefore, reducing the risk of sharp decline in stock price has become a hot topic.

Existing literatures attribute the risk of sharp decline in stock price to managers' self - interested hoarding of bad news from the perspective of agency costs and information asymmetry. Managers' behaviors are mostly viewed within the framework of principal-agent theory and are regarded as homogeneous. However, managers are at the heart of business operations, and their personal characteristics, such as perceptiveness, cognitive ability, and values, significantly influence corporate decisions (Hambrick and Mason, 1984). In modern companies, managerial ability is reflected in managers' efficiency in transforming corporate resources into value, relative to their industry peers (Demerjian et al. , 2012) . Compared with low - ability managers, high - ability managers can accurately understand technology and industry trends, effectively predict product demand, improve project investment efficiency, organize employees, and reduce the moral hazard caused by information asymmetry. Therefore, managerial ability plays a decisive role in ensuring the realization of business objectives.

We explore how managerial ability affects capital market stability using a sample of China's A - share listed firms from 2007 to 2020. Our main proxy for managerial ability is derived from the DEA - Tobit model developed by Demerjian et al. (2012) . According to the literature, we use the negative coefficient of skewness of firm - specific weekly returns and the down - to - up volatility of crash likelihood to measure the risk of sharp decline in stock price. The results indicate that managerial ability is significantly and negatively related to both measures of the risk of sharp decline in stock price, suggesting that managerial ability effectively mitigates stock price crash risk. We find that the effect of managerial ability on the risk of sharp decline in stock price is more pronounced for non - state - owned enterprises, for firms with a lower holding ratio of major shareholders, and for firms with lower levels of marketization.

We also discuss the potential mechanisms by which managerial ability can reduce the risk of sharp decline in stock price. We find that managerial ability results in the reduction of a firm's risk, as measured by performance volatility and litigation. Similarly, we find that managerial ability improves corporate governance, as measured by the management expense ratio, discretionary accruals, and information transparency. These findings provide direct evidence that managerial ability reduces the risk of sharp decline in stock price by decreasing a firm's risk and improving corporate governance.

This study may have several theoretical and practical contributions. From the theoretical perspective, the current literature on the risk of sharp decline in stock price mostly uses the principal-agent framework to analyze the negative impact of managers' self - interested behaviors. We investigate the positive effects of managers from the perspective of managerial ability and find that managerial ability mitigates the risk of sharp decline in stock price. Thus, our results supplement the literature on the factors affecting the risk of sharp decline in stock price. In addition, analyzing corporate behavior from the perspective of managerial heterogeneity has become a hot topic. Compared with demographic factors, such as age, gender, and education, managerial ability is a more comprehensive manifestation of managerial heterogeneity. Our conclusions clarify the importance of managerial ability in business development and enrich the literature on the economic consequences of managerial ability. In terms of practical implications, our findings indicate that the relevant policy makers should take effective measures to stimulate and protect managerial ability.

Short Selling, Dual Governance, and Corporate Fraud: An Empirical Test Based on Market - oriented Governance

XU Xixiong　ZHAN Heng　LI Wanli

(School of Economics and Business Administration, Chongqing University;
College of Finance and Statistics, Hunan University)

The effective restraint of corporate fraud is crucial to protect investor interests and enhance the running efficiency of the capital market. The margin trading and short - selling system launched in 2010 is an important institutional innovation in China's capital market that broke the long - standing "one - sided market" pattern in which short selling was constrained. Compared with other investors, short sellers are more motivated to track and monitor management misconduct (Karpoff and Lou, 2010) and deter management through short selling, thus forming effective external supervision (Massa et al., 2015). China's short - selling system allows investors to short company stocks based on negative information and thus profit from this information. Short selling causes negative information that is illegally hidden by companies to send risk signals to the market, which may attract regulatory attention and increase downward pressure on stock prices, possibly leading to a serious decline in market value and reputation loss for companies (Karpoff et al., 2008). Therefore, management restrains its unethical behavior to maintain the company's market value (Li et al., 2017). However, studies on the relationship between short selling and corporate irregularities are insufficient.

Using data from Chinese A - share listed companies from 2008 to 2017 and combining the bivariable probit model and a difference - in - differences model, this paper explores the dual governance effect and transmission path of short selling on corporate fraud from the perspective of market - oriented governance. We find that short selling not only significantly reduces the fraud tendency of the target company but also significantly improves the probability of violation detection. Moreover, we show that short selling significantly reduces the time taken to detect violations. This indicates that the dual governance effect of short selling on corporate violations is mainly realized through two channels: ex - ante deterrence and ex - post punishment. Additionally, the results suggest that the volume of short selling by the target company increases significantly in the year when a violation occurs, which indicates that short sellers have information advantages and a high sensitivity to violations by the target company. Further tests reveal that short selling may have a dual governance effect on corporate irregularities through internal corporate governance efficiency and external market information efficiency. These tests show that short selling strengthens the supervision and intervention of internal governance bodies such as major shareholders and independent directors on corporate violations, thus restraining the trend of prior violations. Moreover, we show that short selling increases the attention paid to the company by analysts in the external capital market and the transmission efficiency of negative information, thus increasing the probability of post - violation detection. We also find that the governance effect of short selling is influenced by the regulatory environment (legal supervision, internal control, and industrial violations) and the characteristics of the target company (company growth, market size, and stock price volatility).

This paper makes the following contributions to the literature. First, it expands research on the economic consequences of short selling. Studies on short selling mainly concentrate on the price efficiency of the capital market. However, recently, scholars have begun to focus on the effects of short selling on corporate decisions, including the quality of information disclosure (Karpoff and Lou, 2010; Li et al. , 2017), earnings management (Massa et al. , 2015), investment and financing strategy choices (Jin et al. , 2015; Gu and Zhou, 2017) , and corporate innovation (Hao et al. , 2018; Tan and Qian, 2020) . This paper focuses on corporate violations and sheds light on the economic consequences of short selling. Second, it elucidates the effect and transmission mechanism of short selling on corporate irregularities. Unlike previous studies (Meng et al. , 2019) , this paper breaks through the single perspective of signal transmission theory and constructs an analytical framework from the dual perspectives of the information efficiency of the capital market and the efficiency of internal corporate governance. It empirically reveals the dual governance effect of short selling on corporate violations. Additionally, we find that short selling significantly shortens the time taken to investigate and punish violations, especially when the short selling volume of the target firm increases significantly in the year when the violation occurs. Third, this study has crucial practical implications. It empirically reveals that short selling plays a market - oriented governance role in restraining corporate violations, suggesting that short selling could become a supplementary means to enhance investor protection. The results indicate that it is of great practical value to introduce a market - oriented governance mechanism of short selling to restrain corporate irregularities and enhance investor protection.

Opportunistic Tendency of Capital Operation in Listed Companies with Pyramidal Ownership Structure

ZHENG Zhigang   HUAN Zhen   HUANG Jicheng   ZHAO Xijun

(School of Finance, Renmin University of China; Agricultural Development Bank of China Shandong Branch)

A pyramidal ownership structure is quite typical of enterprise group organization in many countries and regions. A typical feature of this structure is the separation of control rights and cash flow rights as a means for strengthening control. Control rights reflect the influence of the ultimate controller on major decisions by voting at listed companies' shareholders' meetings, while cash flow rights denote the responsibility characterized by investment in capital contributions. The separation of the two is indicative of the asymmetry between taking responsibility and enjoying rights in a pyramidal ownership structure, and is often the source of negative economic externalities.

The literature on the negative externalities of the pyramidal ownership structure focuses on "tunneling" by the ultimate controller of listed companies by means of capital occupation and other channels. Different from the negative externalities examined in other studies, this paper investigates the opportunistic tendencies of the ultimate controller's capital operations with the aim of revealing other negative externalities of the pyramidal ownership structure.

In China's capital market, the pyramidal ownership structure is very common in both state-owned and non-state-owned firms. However, capital operations of state-owned listed companies are more influenced by national macroeconomic policies such as state-owned enterprise restructuring, industrial policy, and supply - side structural reform. As an example of the negative externalities of the pyramidal ownership structure, capital operation is more typical in non - state - owned listed companies. Therefore, this paper selects non - state - owned listed companies as the object for empirical research, using a sample from 2007—2017. This paper demonstrates that for listed companies characterized by a pyramidal ownership structure, with an increase in the pyramidal structural complexity, the listed companies' shares become more like "lottery shares", non - financial enterprises' financial asset allocation becomes greater, and more related capital operations are implemented. These behaviors do not improve enterprise performance as expected; rather, they evolve into opportunistic capital operation behavior to realize the short - term rapid appreciation of the wealth of controlling shareholders and their ultimate controllers.

This paper makes a novel contribution to the corporate governance literature, especially the literature on the negative externalities of the pyramidal ownership structure. First, in addition to the tunneling concept examined by the previous literature, this paper illustrates other negative externalities arising from the opportunistic capital operations behavior of firms' ultimate controllers. This paper constitutes an important expansion of the literature on the pyramidal ownership structure. Second, from the new perspective of the pyramidal ownership structure, this paper reveals the institutional incentives underlying the financialization of non - financial enterprises and the phenomenon of allocating capital from the real economy to the virtual economy. Affected by the incentive distortion of unequal rights and responsibilities, the controlling shareholders under a pyramidal ownership structure prefer to allocate financial assets to realize the short - term appreciation of the ultimate controllers' wealth in the face of uncertain industrial investment returns. Third, this paper shows that the opportunistic tendencies of controlling shareholders' capital operations under a pyramidal ownership structure attracts more investors to speculate in stocks. Therefore, companies under a pyramidal ownership structure characterized by "lottery shares" of listed companies have become a new influencing factor. Thus, this paper constitutes an important expansion of the literature on the factors influencing lottery stocks.

This paper shows that the negative economic externalities of pyramidal ownership structure has become a potential institutional root of the trend whereby capital flows from the real economy to the virtual economy and the severe volatility of financial markets. Therefore, to promote the healthy future development of the capital market and real economy, restraining the disorderly expansion of the pyramidal ownership structure is an important issue that must be urgently confronted.

Controlling Shareholder Equity Pledge and Employee Stock Ownership Plan "Instrumentalization": Evidence from the A - Share Market in China

QIU Yangqian　　HUANG Juanjuan

(School of Economics, Xiamen University)

With the promulgation of Guidance on the Implementation of Employee Stock Ownership Plans (ESOP) in Listed Companies in 2014, ESOPs provide a new type of employee incentive. In the period following the introduction of ESOPs, equity pledges have been common as an easy way for controlling shareholders to secure loans. These pledges create strong motivations for controlling shareholders to mitigate their risk of control transfer by maintaining stock price stability.

According to the theory of "shareholder opportunism", controlling shareholders with equity pledges are motivated to find effective tools to manage the prices of their pledged stocks. Equity pledges by controlling shareholders intensify the separation of cash rights from control rights. The existence of pledge arrangements can indicate a company's lack of funds and high potential capital demands. These factors may encourage controlling shareholders to actively participate in the structure of a company's incentive system as a mechanism to align the interests of insiders, such as managers and key employees, with their own. For controlling shareholders, ESOPs provide an incentive method that has low cost, a short planning cycle, low supervision requirements, and almost no performance threshold. Hence, ESOPs offer a highly convenient mechanism to bind the interests of company employees with those of controlling shareholders with equity pledges.

To investigate the relationship between the pledges of controlling shareholders and the implementation of ESOPs, we analyze a 2013 to 2018 sample of A - share listed companies in China. We find that the probability of an ESOP increases significantly if a company's controlling shareholders have equity pledges and also increases with the shareholder pledge rate. Furthermore, the greater the risk of control transfer that controlling shareholders are exposed to is, the higher the probability of an ESOP being implemented is. We argue that ESOPs are useful to controlling shareholders as a mechanism to increase a stock's price in the short term, but they do not improve a company's long - term value and operating performance. Our further research on corporate governance shows that the power of controlling shareholders has a significant positive impact on the relationship between the pledges of controlling shareholders and the likelihood of ESOPs implementation. In contrast, variables relating to the board of directors and independent directors are found to have no significant effect.

Our findings have two main implications. First, because controlling shareholders face the risks of share price decline and threat of losing control, they will encourage ESOPs implementation to serve their self - interests, especially when their equity pledge rates are high. This relationship with the motivations and short - sighted behaviors of shareholders weakens the role of ESOPs as an employee incentive. Second, ESOPs are convenient for controlling shareholders because they offer flexible establishment, short lock - in periods, and low restriction and supervision requirements. Our further finding that internal corporate governance has no significant influence on ESOPs implementation should be important to regulators and investors. The restrictions on ESOPs can be improved by making changes, such as lengthening the lock - up period and increasing the information disclosure requirements. However, internal and external governance should also be improved to reduce the role of self - interested controlling shareholder behaviors in corporate decision - making.

Regarding our contributions to the literature, we expand on research into the economic consequences of equity pledges. First, by examining the significant impact of ESOPs on company incentive plans, we find empirical evidence that controlling shareholders with equity pledges have significant influence on the binding of stock price management to insider interests. In such a situation, an ESOP loses its power to improve a company's long - term market value and operating performance. Second, the extensive literature discussion of shareholder and executive incentive systems focuses mainly on the impacts of shareholder power (i. e. , the shareholding ratio); we contribute new empirical evidence that controlling shareholders are motivated to reduce their risk of transfer of control by influencing company incentive systems. Our results provide direct and powerful evidence regarding why and how controlling shareholders become involved in company incentive systems.

Can Relaxing Short Selling Constraints Inhibit M&A Goodwill Bubbles?

SUN Shilu ZHANG Feiyan ZHENG Jianming LIU Yanxia

(College of Economics and Management, Beijing University of Chemical Technology; Business School, University of International Business and Economics)

Goodwill bubbles generated by the M&A boom have recently become an important financial risk factor. The economic consequences of such a bubble for listed firms and the capital market as a whole have raised concerns among shareholders and regulatory authorities. Thus, preventing goodwill bubbles has attracted much attention from practitioners and academics. Managers are deeply involved in the entire M&A process, directly participating in the formulation and implementation of M&A plans and being the main decision makers in the selection and valuation of M&A targets. Therefore, managers' motivation directly impacts M&A, including the scale and amount of goodwill.

Principal-agent theory holds that agency conflicts in M&A activities cause executives to pay more attention to their private interests at the expense of shareholder wealth created by M&A activities. Furthermore, the existence of agency problems drives executives to rely on their information and decision - making advantages to increase the frequency and scale of M&A and even pay a higher premium to complete M&A, which leads to the overestimation of goodwill. This leads to the question of how to prevent goodwill bubbles. In addition to internal control quality and external auditing, the innovation of basic market mechanisms is required to restrain goodwill valuation bubbles.

The implementation of a margin trading mechanism is an innovation in China's stock market and opens the door to short selling. Research on short selling predominantly focuses on two areas. The first is the effect of short selling on the liquidity, stability, and efficiency of stock prices. The second is the effect of short selling on corporate financial decisions, such as earnings management, investment policy, and firm innovations. Studies generally indicate that short selling has the function of price discovery and can be an effective external corporate governance mechanism that reduces earnings management, improves the efficiency of corporate investment, and enhances innovation expenditure and output. However, few studies have investigated whether short selling can restrain the formation of goodwill bubbles caused by M&A decisions.

We explore the effect of short selling on M&A goodwill bubbles using a sample of Chinese A - share listed firms from 2007 to 2017. Our findings are as follows: (i) After lifting the short - selling constraint, excess goodwill significantly declines and goodwill assets also decline, which indicates that the short - selling transaction mechanism significantly inhibits goodwill bubbles; (ii) The restraining effect of short selling on the M&A goodwill bubble is stronger for private enterprises than for state - owned enterprises; (iii) Short selling can restrain goodwill bubbles through channels such as increased analyst coverage and increased managerial incentives; (iv) The effect of short selling on goodwill bubbles is more pronounced for firms in regions with more developed financial intermediaries or lower industry competition; (v) Short selling improves stock price efficiency by restraining goodwill bubbles; (vi) Short selling increases firm profitability.

Our study makes three main contributions to the literature. First, this article based on the deregulation of short selling in the capital market, provides new ideas for how to suppress the M&A goodwill bubble, and contributes to the literature by examining the effect of short selling on goodwill bubbles. Second, as an external governance mechanism, the short - selling transaction mechanism plays an effective governance role in M&A decisions. Studies examine the governance effect of the short - selling transaction mechanism based on the performance of M&A but ignore the impact of short selling on goodwill valuation bubbles, which are an important invisible economic consequence of M&A. Thus, we fill a research gap in this new field. Third, we find that short selling can restrain goodwill bubbles through channels such as increased analyst coverage and increased managerial incentives, which has implications for policymakers to improve the structure of China's capital market and protect the interests of investors.

Spillover Effects of Minority Shareholders' Activism on Bondholders' Wealth: An Empirical Study Based on Network Voting Data

ZENG Aimin WU Wei WU Yuhui

(School of Accounting, Zhejiang Gongshang University;
School of Management, Xiamen University)

In Recent years, China's bond market has achieved rapid development. However, since China's first default case of "11 Chiaori Bond" in 2014, the rigid bond repayment rule has been violated and bond default has occurred frequently. This has caused investors and regulatory authorities to worry about default risk in China's bond market because bond defaults not only harm the interests of investors but may also lead to systemic financial risk. At the corporate level, bond defaults are closely related to the financial performance, solvency, and information asymmetry of the issuers. Therefore, it is of great importance to seek innovative governance mechanisms that can help reduce information asymmetry, improve corporate performance, and strengthen financial stability to protect bondholders' wealth.

An important change that has occurred in China's corporate governance mechanisms in recent years is that minority shareholders have begun to actively participate in corporate decision-making through online voting. However, the consequences of minority shareholders' participation in corporate governance to safeguard their interests are unclear. Research generally suggests that minority shareholder activism positively affects the company and shareholder interests; however, few studies examine the impacts of such activism on external stakeholders.

Using online voting data from all listed companies in the Shenzhen Stock Exchange from 2008 to 2018, this paper explores spillover effects of minority shareholder activism on bondholders' wealth (who are among the most important external stakeholders of a company) and empirically examines the internal mechanism and moderating effect. The results show the following: (i) Although minority shareholders subjectively participate in corporate governance to protect their interests, their behavior can also significantly increase bondholders' wealth, and this positive spillover effect still exists after controlling for potential endogeneity; (ii) Exploring its internal mechanism, it is found that minority shareholder activism does not significantly affect the quality of corporate information disclosure and that the positive spillover effects of this activism on the wealth of bondholders is mainly achieved through improving the company's performance and enhancing its financial stability; (iii) Positive spillover effects are stronger when the internal governance environment of the company is poor, investors have learning effects, or external information channels work effectively.

The innovations and contributions of this paper are as follows. First, unlike previous studies focusing on the impact of minority shareholder activism on the company and shareholder interests, this paper examines the impact of such activism on bondholders' wealth, which may help regulatory authorities develop new ways to safeguard the interests of bondholders and promote the healthy development of the bond market. Second, based on corporate performance, financial stability, and information disclosure quality, this paper investigates the internal mechanism of the positive spillover effects of minority shareholders on bondholders' wealth, thus enriching research on the governance effect of minority shareholder activism. Third, by examining the potential factors affecting minority shareholder activism, this paper provides a means for minority shareholders to better participate in corporate governance through online voting.

Based on the above conclusions, we put forward the following policy suggestions: First, Regulatory authorities should strengthen the education and guidance of minority shareholders and effectively use the positive spillover effects of minority shareholder activism. Second, regulatory authorities should establish a better institutional environment to ensure the active participation of minority shareholders in corporate governance, and companies should provide convenient conditions to help minority shareholders make suggestions. In the practice, regulatory authorities should continue to promote the construction and effective use of online voting platforms and improve the relevant voting and trading rules; companies should adjust the traditional positioning of minority shareholders, optimize the corporate governance structure, improve the enthusiasm of minority shareholders to participate in corporate governance, and strengthen the education of minority shareholders so that they can participate in the company's decision-making more effectively and in more aspects.